Task Strategies

WILLIAM J. REID

Task Strategies

An Empirical Approach to
Clinical Social Work

with contributions by

Julie S. Abramson
Anne E. Fortune
Norma Wasko

Columbia University Press
New York   1992

Columbia University Press
New York   Oxford
Copyright © 1992 Columbia University Press
All rights reserved

Library of Congress Cataloging-in-Publication Data

Reid, William James, 1928–
     Task strategies : an empirical approach to clinical social
work / William J. Reid; with contributions by Julie S.
Abramson, Anne E. Fortune, Norma Wasko.
          p.   cm.
     Includes bibliographical references (p.   ) and indexes.
     ISBN 0–231–07550–2 (acid-free paper)
     1. Social case work—United States. 2. Problem solving.
I. Abramson, Julie S. II. Fortune, Anne E., 1945–
III. Wasko, Norma. IV. Title.
HV43.R383   1992
361.3′2′0973—dc20   91-40553
                                                                  CIP

⊗

Casebound editions of Columbia University Press books are
Smyth-sewn and printed on permanent and durable acid-free
paper.

Printed in the United States of America

c 10 9 8 7 6 5 4 3 2 1

Contents

Preface

Over the past two decades a considerable body of literature has accumulated on task-centered practice—nine books and scores of published papers. This volume attempts to add to this knowledge base in several ways. First, and most important, it develops applications of the model for a range of problems frequently encountered by clinical social workers: difficulties of families and children, anxiety, depression, alcohol abuse, inadequate resources, and psychosocial problems associated with mental and physical illness. The focus is on how problems in these areas can be specified and assessed and how strategies consisting of tasks by clients and practitioners can lead to the alleviation of these problems. Although the methods developed enhance the task-centered model, they are designed for use within any practice framework. Second, the book updates and extends previous formulations of the model, while incorporating recent advances in task-centered work with families. Third, it articulates a relationship between the model and empirical practice and demonstrates how the model can be used as an exemplar of that mode of practice.

It is hoped that the book will be of interest to practitioners, educators, and students in social work and related professions. Practitioners who use a task-centered approach will be able to draw on the new formulations and methods presented in the book. Practitioners with other orientations should still be able to make use of the task-centered interventions that are linked to specific problems. Social work educators may find the book of value as a text in undergraduate and graduate practice courses. Because it presents a form of empirical practice, including research techniques for assessing clients and for measuring practice processes and outcomes, the book may also be relevant to courses on clinical research.

In expressing my thanks to the many people who made this book possible, I turn first to my colleagues who took part in writing specific chapters: Julie Abramson, Anne E. Fortune, and Norma Wasko. Essential to this endeavor were the resources provided by three resourceful deans: Richard L. Edwards, Susan R. Sherman, and Lynn Videka-Sherman; I am deeply indebted to each of them. Consultations from experts in mental health—Larry Doyle and Henry Epstein—and in alcohol treatment—Barry Loneck and Linda Rotering—were most appreciated. I am grateful for the competent and patient services of Jean D'Alessandro, who typed the manuscript, and for the literature searches and editorial work so diligently performed by my graduate assistants—Janet Wheeler, Steven Press, and especially, Andree L. Heintz. Finally, I owe more than words can express to the many students and practitioners whose cases and ideas became a part of the book.

W. J. R.

Task Strategies

CHAPTER 1

The Task-centered Model and Empirical Practice

This book sets forth a task-centered model of clinical social work with individuals and families. It updates earlier presentations and adds a new dimension to the model: task-centered strategies for a range of common client problems encountered in social work. These strategies can be used either within the framework of the task-centered model or to supplement other approaches.

The book also attempts to strengthen the empirical practice movement in clinical social work. Its major contribution in this respect is to provide a well-developed example of such practice, one that integrates treatment and evaluation methodologies and that differentiates these methodologies according to problem. Although there is an extensive literature *about* empirical practice in social work, there are few comprehensive models of such practice.

In this chapter I will begin with an overview of the task-centered model as it now stands. I will then take up the empirical practice movement. The chapter will conclude with an analysis of the model as a type of empirical practice and a discussion of the need for problem-specific forms of that practice.

The Task-centered Model

The task-centered model is a short-term problem-solving approach to social work practice. (Reid and Epstein 1972, 1977; Reid 1978, 1985;

Goldberg, Sinclair, and Gibbons 1984; Epstein 1980, 1988; Fortune 1985.)
Its basic characteristics and principles are summarized in table 1.1.

The various dimensions of the task-centered model set forth in table
1.1 will be elaborated upon in subsequent chapters. At this point I would
like to take up certain aspects of particular relevance to the focus of
the present book, which, as noted, will concern itself with the use of
task-centered strategies to resolve particular types of problems faced
by clients.

The basic thrust of these strategies is to mobilize clients to take
problem-solving actions in their life situations. We refer to such actions
as the client's external tasks. The model is designed to help clients
clarify their problems, to identify actions (tasks) needed to resolve
them, and to implement these actions or tasks. Treatment sessions are
devoted largely to the planning and preparation of these tasks and to
resolving obstacles to their implementation. Other kinds of tasks, those
undertaken by clients in the session (session tasks) and those done by
the practitioner (practitioner tasks), are ancillary to the client's external
tasks. Although the model makes use of conventional techniques, including helping clients develop insight and express feelings, such techniques are generally directed toward facilitating task completion.

Explicit tasks, I believe, provide the most efficient means of achieving a resolution of target problems and desired contextual change. But
almost as important is the creation of a therapeutic climate in which
the client's actions, whether confined to explicit tasks or not, are viewed
as a major vehicle of change. The focus on action possibilities gives
the client a range of options to consider and stimulates him or her to
think of new ones. The completion of the task provides clients with
evidence that they can take action to solve their problems. Success
breeds confidence and motivation, helping clients to undertake new
and more difficult initiatives, some of which may occur apart from the
formal tasks worked out with their practitioners. Doel and Marsh (in
press) put it nicely: "The task-centered approach is based on the view
that we are more likely to act ourselves into a new way of thinking
than to think ourselves into a new way of acting."

What is more, the process of thinking about, engaging in, and suc-
ceeding at problem-solving action provides the client with solid ex-
periential training in tackling life's difficulties. Clients can learn to
express complaints and distress in the form of solvable problems and
to plan ways of dealing with them. In the process—and this is of greatest
importance—they learn that their own actions can make a difference.

TABLE 1.1
Task-centered Model: Basic Characteristics and Principles

Empirical orientation	Preference is given to methods and theories tested and supported by empirical research; hypotheses and concepts about the client's system need to be grounded in case data; speculative theorizing about the client's problems and behavior is avoided; assessment, processing, and outcome data are systematically collected in each case; a sustained program of developmental research is used to improve the model.
Integrative stance	The model draws selectively on empirically based theories and methods from compatible approaches—e.g., problem-solving, cognitive-behavioral, cognitive, and structural.
Focus on client-acknowledged problems	Focus of service is on specific problems clients explicitly acknowledge as being of concern to them.
Systems and contexts	Problems occur in a context of multiple systems; contextual change may be needed for problem resolution or to prevent problem recurrence; conversely, the resolution of a problem may have beneficial effects on its context.
Planned brevity	Service is generally designed to be short-term (six to twelve weekly sessions within a four-month period).
Collaborative relationship	Relationships with clients emphasize a caring but collaborative effort; the practitioner shares assessment information, avoids hidden goals and agendas; extensive use is made of client's input in developing treatment strategies, not only to devise more effective interventions but also to develop the client's problem-solving abilities.
Structure	The intervention program, including treatment sessions, is structured into well-defined sequences of activities.
Problem-solving actions (tasks)	Change is brought about primarily through problem-solving actions (tasks) undertaken by clients within and outside the session. Particular emphasis is placed on mobilizing clients' actions in their own environments. The primary function of the treatment session is to lay the groundwork for such actions. In addition, practitioner tasks provide a means of effecting environmental change in the client's interest.

In an action-oriented therapeutic climate, agreed-on tasks often function as "pump-primers." Once clients begin to do something about their problems and to experience success, they can begin to generate their own tasks, which are often more ingenious and substantial than those formally developed as a part of treatment.

The task-centered system has been cited as a major approach in clinical social work (Germain 1983; Meyer 1983; Garvin and Seabury 1984; Turner 1986; Hepworth and Larsen 1986; Orcutt 1990). Adaptations have been developed for most settings in which social workers practice, including child welfare (Salmon 1977; Rooney 1981; Rzepnicki 1985); public social services (Rooney and Wanless 1985; Rooney 1988); school social work (Epstein 1977; Reid et al. 1980); corrections (Hofstad 1977; Bass 1977; Goldberg and Stanley 1978; Larsen and Mitchell 1980); industrial (Taylor 1977; Weissman 1977); geriatric (Cormican 1977; Dierking, Brown, and Fortune 1980; Rathbone-McCuan 1985); medical (Wexler 1977); family service (Hari 1977; Reid 1977; Wise 1977); and mental health (Ewalt 1977; Brown 1977; Newcome 1985). Variations of the model have been developed for work with individuals (Reid and Epstein 1972; Reid 1978; Epstein 1980, 1988); families (Reid 1981, 1985; Benbenishty, 1988); groups (Garvin 1974; Fortune, 1985); for generalist practice (Tolson, Reid, and Garvin, in press); for nonvoluntary clients (Rooney, in press); and for managing human service agencies (Parihar 1983).

Although the focus of this book is on task strategies for particular types of problems rather than on the task-centered model in its entirety, an outline of the model for complete cases is given (table 1.2) and will be discussed briefly. The outline and discussion will serve as a guide to readers who wish to use the subsequent problem-specific task strategies within the framework of the model as a whole.

The content of this outline will not be presented here in detail but will be elaborated on in the remainder of the book, especially in the next four chapters, from the vantage point of dealing with a single problem. This first section provides a picture of the overall structure and process of a task-centered case.

When the model is used with a case as a whole, more than one problem is usually addressed (up to a limit of three in most cases). These problems are prioritized in order of importance by the client. Although the client's priorities become the practitioner's—that is, they agree on which problems are the most important to solve—the order in which problems are treated depends on tactical considerations. For example, in some cases it may make sense to start with an easier problem so that the client can experience initial success. In others, the priority problem as well as another one may be addressed simultaneously, and the focus may alternate between the two. Assessment begins prior to problem formulation, although problems may be tentatively formulated before their assessment is completed. In the model, problems are defined in relation to the client's expressed concerns rather than derived by practitioners from their own assessments. The assessment process normally covers the frequency and severity of each problem, a brief history of the problem, and identification of contextual factors—e.g., possible causes (chapter 2).

In addition to agreement on the problems to be addressed, the contract sets out the duration of service. The planned brevity of the model (six to twelve sessions) is based on a considerable amount of research that has suggested that brief, time-limited treatment has outcomes at least as good as open-ended treatment of longer duration and hence is more cost-effective (Reid and Shyne 1969; Gelso and Johnson 1983; Koss and Butcher 1986).

Moreover, a short-term structure tends to mobilize efforts of both the practitioner and the client, to force a focus on attainable goals, and to avoid the dysfunctional relationship complexities often found in long-term treatment. Finally, there is evidence that most change through interpersonal treatment is likely to occur rather early, within the limits of the present model (Howard, Kopta, Krause, and Orlinsky 1986). This is not to say, however, that time limits should be employed rigidly. In some cases, clients can profit from limited extensions of service. Recontracting for additional sessions is routinely done with clients who want more service and are making progress toward their goals. Other reasons for not adhering rigidly to time limits are inherent in the type of case and problem being worked on. Helping parents reunify with children in placement or working with the chronically mentally ill (chapter 9) are examples of types of clinical situations that may require longer periods of service, which, of course, may still be task-centered. An example of a "longer-term" task-centered case may be found in chapter 2.

Finally, an explanation of the treatment approach is given as a basis for involving the client as a collaborator. This explanation is often presented incrementally as the initial phase proceeds. That is, procedures may be explained as they are introduced rather than all at once.

The initial phase normally takes from one to two interviews although some cases may require more. It ends with setting up initial

TABLE 1.2

The Task-centered Model for Individuals and Families: Outline for Complete Cases

I. Initial Phase (Sessions 1–2)
1. Discussion of reasons for referral, especially with nonvoluntary client(s).
2. Exploration and assessment of client-acknowledged target problems and their contexts.
3. Formation of the service contract, including problems and goals to be addressed, explanation of treatment methods, agreement on durational limits.
4. Development and implementation of initial external tasks (see II-5 and 6 below).

II. Middle Phase
    (Each session follows the format below)
1. Problem and task review.
2. Identification and resolution of (actual) obstacles.
3. Problem focusing.
4. Session tasks (if two or more clients in session).
5. Planning external tasks.
    a. Generating task possibilities
    b. Establishing motivation
    c. Planning implementation of tasks(s)
    d. Identifying and resolving (anticipated) obstacles
    e. Guided practice, rehearsal
    f. Task agreement
    g. Summarizing task plan
6. Implementation of task(s) (between sessions)

III. Terminal Phase (final session)
1. Review of target problems and overall problem situation.
2. Identification of successful problem-solving strategies used by client(s).
3. Discussion of what can be done about remaining problems, making use of strategies identified in (2) above.

tasks, usually for the client (but sometimes for the practitioner) to do between sessions.

The middle phase starts with the next session. Changes in the problems and the outcome of the tasks are reviewed at the beginning of the interview. If tasks have been accomplished, new tasks are developed. Task development is usually preceded by an effort to pinpoint aspects of the problem (problem focusing) that will be addressed by the tasks. If tasks have not been attained, an effort is made to identify obstacles to task accomplishment.

Some obstacles, such as those concerning the client's beliefs, may be resolved in the session; others may require tasks in their own right. Still others might prove insurmountable, and in that case a different task strategy may be adopted (chapter 5.).

The typical session in the middle phase is largely devoted to the development of external tasks for the client, making use of the task planning procedures listed under II.5 in table 1.2 and discussed in detail in chapter 4. If two or more clients are present, as in family interviews, tasks in the session (session tasks) are customarily used. In these tasks, clients working together with the practitioners help plan out (or lay the ground work for) their own external tasks (chapter 3).

Although only one session is devoted to termination, the process of terminating is actually begun in the initial phase when the duration of treatment is set. Reminders of the number of sessions left as well as discussion of modifications of the original limits keep termination alive in the client's mind throughout the course of service. As the outline suggests, the final session is structured to accomplish specific objectives. It is designed to emphasize what clients have learned and accomplished.

Recent chapter-length overviews of the model as a whole may be found in Reid (1988, 1990). For book-length explications see Reid and Epstein (1972, 1977), Reid (1978, 1985), Fortune (1985), Epstein (1988), and Tolson, Reid, and Garvin (forthcoming).

Empirical Practice

During the past two decades a concept of empirical practice has taken shape in clinical social work (Briar 1990). Although empirical practice, like social work itself, is a fuzzy concept open to various interpretations, the following view is shared by many.

In general, empirical practice draws, as much as it can, on scientific attitudes, knowledge, and processes. In empirical practice one gives primacy to research-based theories and interventions but still maintains a skeptical attitude toward all theories and interventions. Due to the emphasis placed on research, empirical practitioners make an effort to become familiar with studies relating to populations, problems, and interventions they are working with. In treating individual clients, families, or groups, the targets of intervention are specifically stated, and devices such as direct observation and standardized tests are used to collect assessment data. Intervention methods are defined in terms of specific actions by the practitioner, and they are used as systematically as possible. Drawing from the methodology of single system designs, the practitioner monitors change and evaluates outcomes in relation to the interventions used (Bloom and Fischer 1982). Modes of scientific reasoning are used in the analysis of case data. For example, diagnostic inferences are backed up with evidence from the case, and alternative explanations are considered before a conclusion is reached.

Most clinical social workers use some of the elements just outlined, but only a minority use them to such an extent that their practice can be considered empirical. It is my belief that movement toward greater empiricism in practice will yield important dividends for clinical social work. It will result in greater use of methods that are demonstrably effective and in building repertoires of tested interventions. It will lead to more systematic treatment that is better supported by data. It will make practice more accountable, not only to agencies but also to clients.

Empirical practice is the current expression of a long-standing aspiration in social work to connect practice to a base of scientific knowledge and procedures. This goal can be seen in such early developments as the scientific philanthropy movement in the late nineteenth century and the survey movement at the beginning of the present century.

Pursuit of this goal has been much in evidence in the evolution of clinical social work. (For an excellent review of this history see Orcutt 1990). In *Social Diagnosis*, Mary Richmond (1917) set forth the first major formulation of the principles and methods of casework. This formulation was framed within a scientific paradigm. A social diagnosis was to be the product of fact gathering, forming hypotheses, and testing hypotheses with evidence from the case. By midcentury, a close relationship between casework and science was widely accepted. As Florence Hollis, a leading advocate of psychosocial casework, put it,

Casework is a scientific art. Certainly since the days of Mary Richmond we have been committed to objective examination of the facts of each case. We draw inferences from those facts, we diagnose, we view the individual against a frame of reference which is itself the product of informal research. We constantly alert ourselves to sources of error. (1963:13).

Although the ideal of scientifically based practice in clinical social work has been long accepted in principle, its impact on practice itself has been slow to develop. Only in the last few decades has there been a sufficient accumulation of practice-relevant research to warrant efforts to use scientific knowledge as a guide to practice, and there is still not a great amount of knowledge that is particularly useful. Moreover, the dominant modes of clinical social work and their related theories—e.g., psychodynamic treatment based on ego psychology—have proven to be difficult targets for scientific investigation.

However, during the past two decades, considerable progress has been made toward a scientifically based practice, perhaps more than has occurred since the beginning of the profession. Three developments appear to be responsible for this advance. Perhaps the most influential has been the behavioral movement, which began to influence clinical social work in the late sixties. This movement brought to social work not only an array of techniques based on research but also the technology for testing and evaluating interventions through single system designs.

The advance of behavioral methods in social work has been stimulated from within the profession as well as by other disciplines, notably psychology, psychiatry, and education, that are influential in many of the settings where social workers practice, such as mental health and child welfare agencies, schools, and the correction system. Even though only a small minority of clinical social workers would define their practice as primarily behavioral, many practitioners make use of well-tested behavioral methods, such as social skills training, token economies, stress management, and relaxation therapy. Although use of full-scale single system designs has been limited largely to the practice of students in field settings, there is evidence that some elements of these designs are employed by a significant number of practitioners who had received training in using them when they were students (Richey, Blythe, and Berlin 1987; Gingerich 1984).

The second development has been the increasing emphasis in social agencies on various types of operations research, including accountability systems, quality assurance programs, management information systems, program evaluation, and computer applications. Pressures on agencies for greater accountability, the introduction of scientific management methods, and advances in computer hardware have been among the factors behind this trend. Direct effects on practice have included requirements in many agencies that service goals be carefully specified and that outcome data on service cases be obtained routinely. A less direct effect has been the establishment of a climate encouraging greater systematization and scrutiny of practice.

The third development has been in social work education. Because of the steady growth in the number of faculty with doctorates and the increasing expectation that faculty do research, direct practice faculties have become more research-oriented than those of an earlier era. Direct practice faculties consequently are more likely to embrace and teach an empirical perspective toward human behavior and social treatment. Moreover, they increasingly draw on practice texts that espouse an empirical orientation (e.g., Fischer 1978, Gambrill 1983, Hepworth and Larsen 1986, Barth 1986). A recent survey of direct practice teaching in the first year of graduate education found that "action-oriented and task-centered methods are increasingly being used to teach social work practice" (LeCroy and Goodwin 1988:42). The authors attribute this trend to the increased emphasis on social work practice outcomes. More specifically, methods covered in one of the more widely used texts (Hepworth and Larsen 1986) include research-based approaches, such as relaxation training, cognitive restructuring, stress inoculation, and communication of empathy, with citations of relevant research. Teaching of single-system research methodology in both practice and research courses has been stimulated recently by an accreditation requirement of the Council on Social Work Education calling for students receiving training in evaluating their own cases.

These educational trends can be expected to have a gradual impact on practice in much the same way as the teaching of psychodynamic theories and methods did. Evidence that these trends have begun to make a difference can be found in Jayaratne's (1982) national survey of clinical social workers. Jayaratne found the great majority (84 percent) to be eclectic in their orientation to practice. Of these workers, almost 30 percent cited some use of a behavioral approach, and 17 percent indicated it was one of their two most-used orientations. Even more significant was the greater use of a behavioral approach at the expense of a more traditional and less empirical psychodynamic orientation among more recent graduates.

To evaluate the status and future of empirical practice, it is necessary to take a long view. Most social work practice today is not highly empirical by my definition; nor will it be tomorrow. My point is that it is more so now than yesterday and will be more so tomorrow than today. The trend is clear, but progress is slow.

To ensure that progress continues, and, it is to be hoped, at a faster pace, there is a need to continue the development of empirical practice models, especially those that fit well into the entangled realities clinical social workers face daily. Granted, structured, scientifically based practice approaches have been criticized for offering simplistic solutions to complex practice problems (Schön 1983; Wood 1990). Such criticisms are justified when models offer only oversimplified, mechanistic procedures for addressing the chaotic "messes" (Ackoff 1979) that practitioners must often contend with. In social work, at least, any empirical practice model should be viewed as providing the practitioner with *potentially* useful structures and methods. But the model should not serve as a blueprint. Rather, it should be used as a flexible tool in combination with whatever other resources the practitioner can bring to bear—in particular, the imagination and capacity to do what is needed whether or not it fits with the model. As they are developed through continuing research, empirical practice models may be able to offer more direction for practitioners; that is, they may help them gain better purchase on the complexities of practice situations. Yet, I cannot deny that empirical practice, as I have defined it, has a long way to go in this kind of systematization. Also, as Orcutt (1990) has suggested, new combinations of conventional and unconventional scientific models may be needed to provide an appropriate basis for clinical social work.

A path for development in empirical practice may then be to strive for an optimal balance between the requirements of scientifically based interventions and the demands of clinical situations in social work. The task-centered model, I believe, provides a useful framework for this development.

The Task-centered Model as Empirical Practice

From its inception the task-centered model has had a strong research orientation (Reid and Epstein 1972). Its evolution during the past two decades has been spurred by sustained programs of developmental research (Thomas 1984). In these programs, forms of the model have undergone repeated cycles of testing, evaluation, revision, and retesting (Reid and Epstein 1972, 1977; Tolson 1977; Reid 1975, 1978, 1985, 1987b; Reid et al. 1980; Rooney 1981; Fortune 1985; Rzepnicki 1985; Reid and Hanrahan 1988). In addition, experimental tests of its effectiveness were conducted apart from such programs (Gibbons et al. 1978; Larsen and Mitchell 1980; Wodarski, Saffir, and Frazier 1982; Jackson 1983; Goldberg, Gibbons, and Sinclair 1984).

In this body of research, consisting of more than thirty-five published studies and doctoral dissertations, the effectiveness of the model as a means of resolving specific problems of living has been repeatedly demonstrated. The demonstrations have included studies using control groups or equivalent devices to rule out extraneous factors (Reid 1975, 1978; Tolson 1977; Gibbons et al. 1978; Larsen and Mitchell 1980; Reid et al. 1980, Wodarski, Saffir, and Frazier 1982; Goldberg, Gibbons, and Sinclair 1984; Rzepnicki 1985; Newcome 1985) (see chapter 4).

This body of research as well as the summary in table 1 suggest that the task-centered model conforms to general criteria for empirical practice. However, it is reasonable to ask how it compares with behavioral approaches, the dominant form of empirical practice in social work today. The comparison is difficult given the many varieties of behavioral methods and the variations of the task-centered model.

Perhaps the comparison can best be approached from a historical point of view. Behavioral methods had their origins in experimental psychology and were then adapted to social work practice. These adaptations and the emergence of new technologies within the behavioral movement itself have led to an impressive array of successful forms of behavioral social work. Nevertheless, certain aspects of the behavioral paradigm have been difficult to adapt to many forms of social work practice. I can cite its focus on behavior as the unit of attention, its reliance on learning theory, and its use of rigorous, costly, single-case research procedures, such as direct observation and coding of specific behaviors over time, and delaying or interrupting intervention in order to obtain baseline data.

The task-centered model, on the other hand, had its origins in mainstream psychosocial and problem-solving casework of the late sixties (Perlman 1957; Hollis 1963). Also influential were other developments in social work, such as the emergence of planned, short-term service (Parad and Parad 1968a, 1968b) and the notion of task as a treatment construct (Studt 1968). From its inception, therefore, the task-centered model was oriented to the field of social work. Compared to behavioral approaches, it encompasses a wider range of problems, including especially distinctive social work concerns involving the clients' relationships to diverse environmental systems. For example, problems involving homelessness, inadequate financial resources, discharge planning, and conflicts between clients and organizations have always been among the targets of the task-centered intervention, whereas they fall outside the usual range of behavioral approaches.

The concept of a task as an action with its built-in notion of intent results in a different emphasis than the concept of behavior (White

1973). One can modify people's behavior without their knowledge or consent; to enable people to take action requires their cooperation. Action here can refer to complex configurations of behaviors as well as to discrete behaviors (acts). The concept of action is thus better suited for description of complex, undertakings—leaving home, entering an institution, developing rules for children's behavior, and so on.

Moreover, the task-centered model is designed to be eclectic and integrative. It draws not only quite heavily on behavioral methods but also on a range of other intervention approaches and related theories. In particular, the task-centered model does not accord the same primacy to learning theory as behavioral approaches do. While I see learning theory as useful in explaining the completion of some tasks, a broader theoretical perspective is needed, I think, to account for the many factors that motivate problem-solving actions.

Finally, the targets and intervention effects of behavioral approaches, as a rule, can be more precisely measured than those of the task-centered model. To put it in terms of a familiar expression, the task-centered model trades rigor for relevance. The trade-off, however, still preserves a strong empirical component for the model in regard to use of available research, commitment to research and development, and methodology for single case evaluation. The latter can, in fact, approximate the rigor of behavioral assessment when specific targets are addressed by specific tasks (Tolson 1977; Wodarski, Frazier, and Saffer 1982; Jackson 1983; Rzepnicki 1985). Techniques for single case evaluation of the task-centered model have been recently augmented by qualitative methodology (Reid and Davis 1987; Davis and Reid 1988; chapter 2). The introduction of qualitative methodology has been an additional attempt to investigate aspects of social work processes and outcomes that are not adequately captured by quantitative methods—another point of contrast with typical behavioral approaches, which generally do not use qualitative methods in single case evaluation.

Problem-specific Methods

There is a particular need for empirical practice approaches in social work that are problem specific—that show in detail how an approach can be varied according to the problem for which the client is being seen. Developments in this direction have been spurred by long-standing calls for devising effective methods for particular types of clients and problems (e.g., Fischer 1976; Kendall and Norton-Ford 1982). It is not enough to offer a general model with case illustrations to show how it might be adapted to particular clinical situations.

Most empirically oriented texts have not dealt systematically with adaptations for specific problems (Fischer 1978; Reid 1978; Gambrill 1983; Hepworth and Larsen 1986). Variations of such approaches for particular client or problem groups have been the province of journal articles and a few specialized books (e.g., Barth 1986). Indeed, there are few clinical social work practice texts of any kind that present in detail how a given model can be varied according to the type of problem.

The present volume is addressed to this need. It attempts to develop *task strategies* for a range of problems. At a minimum, these strategies provide menus of tasks from which practitioners and clients can jointly select as they work on given problems. When available knowledge warrants, combinations or sequences of tasks that may be effective for particular problems will be suggested. Needless to say, the task strategies presented can be combined with other methods in work on particular problems.

It is also hoped that this approach will contribute to the development of modular treatment not only in task-centered practice but in clinical social work as a whole. In modular treatment, modules consisting of interventions are matched to particular problems (Liberman, Mueser, and Glynn 1988). Different modules from different treatment approaches can be used in the same case depending on the problems dealt with and on the progress of the case. As Liberman, Mueser, and Glynn (1988) point out, modular strategies prevail in medical practice, where they have been successfully used for decades. Different remedies keyed to different problems are used in whatever combination appears to be the most effective for the patient. It should be noted that the modularization of medical practice was one consequence of its establishing a scientific footing. In prescientific medicine, certain therapeutic approaches, such as bloodletting, were used indiscriminately, regardless of the type of disorder. As clinical social work becomes more empirical, one can expect greater use of modular strategies. Eventually such questions as "what works best for this problem?" will replace such questions as "which treatment theory should I attach myself to?"

My contributors and I have attempted to fashion task strategies for problems that are both common and important in clinical social work practice, and the ensuing selection of problems and related task strategies organizes the bulk of the chapters of the book (chapters 6 through

11). Although some problem-specific, task-centered methods have been examined in earlier works (e.g., Reid and Epstein 1977), the current volume is the first systematic attempt to develop specific strategies for a comprehensive range of problems, including a number of problems not previously considered in detail. At the same time, relevant aspects of earlier problem-focused work are incorporated and updated.

In support of goals relating to both empirical practice and task strategies, I present a reformulation of the basic concepts and methods of the task-centered model (chapters 1 through 5). In part, I shall be reworking and updating familiar material in these initial chapters; but I shall also be adding new content in the form of contributions from empirically based practice and theory, including cognitive therapy, cognitive-behavioral approaches, and developments in cognitive and social psychology. I shall also attempt to integrate recent developments in task-centered family treatment (Reid 1985, 1987a, 1987b; Fortune 1985; Reid and Helmer 1987; Reid and Strother 1988; Reid and Donovan 1990). The reformulation will provide general concepts and methods basic to the specialized applications in the remaining chapters; it should be useful to readers familiar with the task-centered model and essential to those who are not. Case material has been drawn from a variety of sources including my own cases, those of my contributors, colleagues, and students. A principal source has been Task-Centered Family Treatment Project, consisting of over 120 single case evaluations (Reid 1987a).

In keeping with the tenets of an empirically based practice model, methods that have proven effective are emphasized. Relevant research is reviewed not only to identify evidence of effectiveness, but also to point out its limitations. Although extensive research reviews are beyond the scope of this volume, an attempt is made to provide as much connection as space permits to the empirical foundations of the methods presented.

CHAPTER 2

Problems and Their Contexts

The task-centered approach is addressed to the resolution of *psychosocial problems*. These are problems that arise in people's interactions with their environment. They are defined by people's internal discomforts in relation to events in their external world. A psychosocial problem, as Gordon Hamilton (1951) said many years ago, has *both* inner and outer aspects. To be sure, inner aspects may be in the forefront in some problems, such as anxiety or depression, but if the problem is psychosocial, the anxiety or depression is an outgrowth of interaction with the environment. In problems centered on environmental conditions, such as homelessness or unemployment, outer aspects may be salient but there is always an inner side of cognitive-emotional processes that causes the condition to be seen as undesirable.

In our theory, problems reflect wants that all people have—for peace of mind, satisfying relationships with others, adequate resources, and so on (Goldman 1970). When these wants are denied, problems arise. A father who reports that his child has a behavior problem wants his child to behave differently, a want he cannot realize. This view is similar to Kahney's (1986) notion of a problem as a "blocked goal." The term *unsatisfied want* better conveys the frustration characterizing psychosocial problems presented to social workers. Similarly, one can view problems as unmet needs. I prefer the term *want* to *need* because the latter is often used to state what professionals think clients should have, as in "Mrs. Moore needs to work through her grief over her husband's death." If we looked at what Mrs. Moore *wants*, we might find that she did her grief work during her husband's illness and now would like help in finding a job. Wants not only define problems, but provide the essential motivation for their resolution. If the client's wants have been misidentified or lose force, there will be little of his or her effort directed at a resolution of the problem.

Wants are informed by beliefs (Goldman 1970). In this formulation, beliefs provide the means by which people construe themselves and their worlds. Belief systems comprise, or at least determine, a person's knowledge, appraisals, perceptions, expectations, attitudes, attributions, and values. As I use the term, *belief system* corresponds closely to Frank's (1974) *assumptive world*. For example, Mr. and Mrs. DiLorenzo see their problem as their son Tony's poor performance at school. That they want him to do better defines the problem and motivates their actions, but their reason for wanting him to do better is based on their beliefs about the importance of education and the capabilities of their son. Other parents with sons performing at the same level might not be concerned.

The outer side of psychosocial problems consists of environmental conditions or events. Although these conditions or events sometimes occur only in the physical environment, they are likely to be social— that is, they involve interpersonal relations or human organization— so that the term *psychosocial problem* is appropriate. Environments precipitate problems through the creation of *stressors*—conditions or events that people find stressful. Stressors cover a wide range of phenomena from such major life events as divorce and illness, chronic strains related to an individual's major roles (spouse, parent, employee, and so forth) to microstressors, or the daily hassles of living (Pearlin and Schooler 1978). Accumulation of stressors over time can result in particular events becoming precipitants to problems for which help may be sought—the "last straw" phenomenon.

Although stressors are lodged in the environment, no event or condition is inherently stressful. Like beauty, stress is in the eye of the beholder. The process of defining something as stressful or not is referred to as appraisal (Lazarus 1989). In appraising an event, according to Lazarus and Folkman (1984), a person makes two evaluations. One is to decide whether the event is a threat to his or her well-being (primary appraisal), and the other is to consider what can be done about it (secondary appraisal). To translate this into our framework, a stressor occurs when one defines something as counter to what one wants. This primary appraisal, a form of transient belief, then triggers beliefs about what can be done. Whatever terms are used, stress is, as Lazarus and Folkman (1984:19) suggest, "a particular relationship between person and environment."

Target Problems

Target Problems are those concerns the practitioner and the client explicitly agree will become the focus of their work together. These problems are based on the client's wants as these are examined and expressed in the initial encounters with the practitioner. In this process, as will be shown, the client's initial conception may undergo change, or unexpressed difficulties may be brought to light. In any case, however the process unfolds, target problems are *acknowledged* problems; that is, the client must explicitly agree that a concern is his or her problem to be solved. "My kids are in foster care. I want them back." "I'm tired of feeling terrible about myself." "My mom bugs me." All these are examples of acknowledged, though not yet carefully specified, problems. As the last example in particular illustrates, clients do not have to accept personal responsibility for the problems they acknowledge. However, if what a client sees as a problem is the behavior of someone else, he or she may be limited in options for a solution.

Collaterals, practitioners, family members, and others may refer to a client as having problems the client does not acknowledge. "Mrs. Mandel is a neglectful mother," says a referring clergyman. (Mrs. Mandel stoutly denies the allegation). "Terry has a lot of repressed anger," concludes his social worker. (Terry insists he is not angry at anyone). These are examples of *attributed* problems. In task-centered practice, such problems do not provide a basis for collaborative work with clients to whom the problems have been attributed. Problem attributions may be useful in locating areas where target problems may be found, in identifying obstacles to solution, or in providing ideas for the practitioner's diagnostic thinking, but they would not constitute the principal targets of intervention. Thus, a wife may complain that her husband has a drinking problem, which he denies. The acknowledged problem thus far belongs to the wife, who, with the practitioner's help, may pursue different options, including trying to persuade her husband to acknowledge his drinking problem. The distinction between acknowledged and attributed problems clarifies who has the problem that will be the focus of work and sets the direction for this work.

There are two basic reasons for our restriction of service to acknowl-edged target problems. One reason is ethical: clients are entitled to service for difficulties that they understand and that truly bother them. Furthermore, clients have the right to know about and approve any change efforts the practitioner plans to implement. The other reason is pragmatic: clients who own their problems are more likely to work harder and more effectively at solving them than clients who have only a dim notion of difficulties and do not fully acknowledge them.

But doesn't this emphasis on client-perceived target problems simply reflect a generally accepted standard of practice? Although most prac-titioners would endorse the idea of coming to an agreement with the client on problems to be dealt with in treatment, there are many shad-ings of opinion that need to be considered. Some common practices that differ from our position include the following: (1) coming to an agreement with the client on the problem at a general level without specifying particulars, which may mask real disagreement at lower levels of abstraction; (2) agreeing with the client on a specific problem but not discussing "underlying" or contextual issues the practitioner hopes to change as a means of resolving the specific problem; (3) by-passing explicit agreement with the client on what the problems are but relating to difficulties as the client brings them up; (4) pursuit of a practitioner-defined problem based on his or her conception of what is normal, healthy, desirable, and so on. In the present model then, a target problem is a construction that emerges through the interaction between the client and the practitioner. It is this joint construction that will guide their collaborative, problem-solving efforts.

Context

Psychosocial problems (as well as tasks to solve them) are embedded in a context that influences and is influenced by the problem. Although the primary purpose of the model is to resolve the target problems, significant and enduring change in these problems is usually not pos-sible unless accompanied by some degree of contextual change. More-over, an important secondary purpose of the model is to bring about contextual change as a means of preventing the recurrence of problems and of strengthening the functioning of the client.

In the task-centered framework, this context consists of a hierarchy of multiple open systems (Tomm 1982; Reid 1985; Martin and O'Connor 1989). As Tomm (1982:76) put it, "within [hierarchical systems] each element or unit at a particular level of the hierarchy represents both a holistic system at that level and part of a larger system at the next higher level." To begin at the lower levels of the hierarchy, we can consider the various systems—circulatory, central nervous, cognitive, and so on—that make up the individual. The individual is a system at a higher level and in turn is usually part of one or more *microsystems* that may consist of a family or others with whom he or she lives, or a social network of which he or she is a part. These systems are a part of a larger *ecosystem* consisting of other systems, such as the neighborhood, social organizations, and the community.

The target problem generally involves some breakdown in one or more of these systems. Its context includes the remaining parts of the system in which the problem is located as well as other systems. However, only those systems that bear on the problem, or that are affected by it, form its context; not all of the multiple systems in which the client moves may be relevant. Context should be distinguished from a related concept—the environment. In our usage, *context* is what surrounds a problem; *environment* is what surrounds a system. Thus, Mr. Roper, as a system, has an environment. The context of his problem may consist only of part of that environment and those aspects of his person—e.g., his personality—which are related to the problem. Both context and environment shift in relation to the problem or system that occupies our attention. Should we focus on another of Mr. Roper's problems, we would have a different context. While his family is part of *his* environment, when we turn our attention to the Roper family, its environment consists of the neighborhood, community, and so forth.

Concepts useful in orienting the practitioner to the context of a problem are *causes, obstacles, and resources. Causes* are whatever brings the problem about. *Obstacles* block solutions of problems, including tasks designed to alleviate them. Causes and obstacles serve equivalent functions—to maintain the problem—and in practice the terms may be used almost interchangeably. *Resources* facilitate solutions. Whether a given factor is a cause or an obstacle on the one hand, or a resource on the other, depends on the problem. Thus, a father's intense involvement in the life of his son may be a cause or an obstacle if the problem involves the son's struggle for autonomy, but it may be a resource if the problem involves the son's need for financial help. In assessments of context, then, the two *most important* questions are: What obstacles are preventing *a* solution of the problem? What resources can be found to help solve it?

Procedures for Targeting and Assessing Problems

When the task-centered model is used as the main approach in a case, the client's problems are identified, explored, specified, formulated, and ranked in order of their importance to the client. Subsequently they are assessed, and progress toward their solution is reviewed. Revising and focusing of the problems are used as needed. Essential information is set down in structured recording forms. These procedures, which have been briefly covered in chapter 1 and are described in detail elsewhere (Reid 1978, 1985, 1988; Epstein 1980, 1988) will be discussed here in relation to work on a single problem area.

Problem Identification

Whether the problem is brought up in an initial interview or later in the case, practitioners attempt to determine how clients perceive their difficulties, to elicit relevant information about them, and to formulate problems in a way that clients find understandable and acceptable. There are basically three routes to identify the problem. The most common is through client initiation. Clients express complaints, which are then explored. Another route is interactive; problems emerge through a dialog between the practitioner and the client in which neither is a clear initiator. For example, Mrs. Cross, referred because of the academic problems of her eleven-year-old daughter, Sheila, mentions in passing a recent argument she had with her husband about Sheila. In response to the practitioner's inquiry about the argument, Mrs. Cross mentions other quarrels about their daughter. The ensuing dialogue reveals a problem in the marital relationship that Mrs. Cross agrees needs attention—now her acknowledged problem.

In the third route to problem identification, the practitioner is clearly the initiator. In work with voluntary (help-seeking) clients, the social worker may initiate the exploration of areas that appear to be unacknowledged sources of difficulty for the client, or he or she may explore problems that the client has acknowledged but has not asked for help with. In pursuing the inquiry, the practitioner may probe for possible areas of concern. In the first interview with Mrs. Walters, who has sought help for depression, the social worker comments "I have noticed you've said a couple of times how hard it is to care for your mother. There are services that might be of help to you. Is this something you would like to talk about?" In these situations the practitioner's purpose is to elicit and clarify possible concerns the client is in fact experiencing.

With nonvoluntary clients, the practitioner may be more assertive in initiating the identification of the problem. As Rooney (1988) has pointed out, clients may be involuntary in two senses: *social involuntary* clients do not seek help but are brought to the attention of social workers by schools, physicians, family members, or others in the client's social network. The client is seen for problems attributed by others. A very large segment of the clientele of social workers falls into this group—recalcitrant children and youth, substance abusing spouses, and elderly persons referred for protective care are among the examples. *Legal involuntaries* are clients whose service is "court-ordered." These clients, who include abusing and neglectful parents, battering spouses, and problem drinkers, are under court mandates to participate in counseling as a condition of probation, in lieu of sentences or fines, as a prerequisite to the return of their children, and so forth. In addition, the court decree may specify particular conditions (mandated problems) that must be corrected.

Both types of involuntary clients are under pressure from an external source, (e.g., school, family member, court) to change or face consequences (e.g., suspension, divorce, loss of parental rights). Regardless of the problems they may have in their life, such clients usually have little to ask of a social worker, except to leave them alone. Obviously, the identification of the problem must proceed on a different premise with them than with the client who actively seeks help for a problem. At the outset, the practitioner needs to take up the reason for the contact, explaining why he or she has become part of the client's life and making clear what mandated problems, if any, they need to be concerned about.

As Rooney (1988) argues, the client's response to this unwelcome intrusion can be fruitfully understood through reactance theory (J. Brehm 1972; S. Brehm 1976; S. Brehm and J. Brehm 1981), a social psychological theory that is concerned with people's responses to the loss of valued freedoms. In addition to providing empirically grounded formulations, reactance theory avoids the "client-blaming" connotations that have become attached to the concept of resistance.

Making use of reactance theory, practitioners should elicit from nonvoluntary clients their views of the imposed or mandated problem and respond empathically to the clients' expressions of these views (Rooney 1988; S. Brehm 1976). The client's right of choice, even in court-ordered contacts, should be emphasized. That is, the client can choose to accept the consequences of *not* accepting help for the imposed or mandated problem. Although these consequences may be grave (loss of parental rights or a jail term), the client should be free to consider and discuss them. Such an orientation is both ethical since it maximizes the client's choice and practical since clients are more likely to be cooperative if they are given the freedom to express their views and make their own decisions. This orientation articulates well the position of the task-centered approach.

In many cases clients will eventually be willing to acknowledge a mandated problem or one related to it. If not, the problem may be defined as the unwanted presence of the practitioner or others in the client's life. To solve this "problem," the client may be willing to do what is required to resolve the mandated problem.

Problem Exploration and Assessment

By the time the problem has been identified, the practitioner will usually have acquired some information about it. In some cases this information will be minimal; in others the problem will have been extensively explored by the time it is identified as the one to be worked on. Whether it is done within the context of problem identification or as a separate activity, the problem exploration needs to cover certain essentials: a factual description of typical occurrences of the problem (close examination of a recent occurrence is helpful here); frequency of occurrence; the seriousness with which the client views it; its apparent origins; what the client has done to alleviate it, and how well these efforts have worked. The relevant context of the problem needs to be examined to locate possible causative factors, potential obstacles to problem-solving action, and resources that might facilitate a solution. After some initial exploration, the problem may be formulated or defined with the client to determine if it is one the client wants to work on. The exploration may then be resumed. Indeed, the exploration of the problem continues during the life of the problem to gain in-depth information, to determine what changes have occurred, and to investigate new developments.

The problem exploration is the data gathering tool for assessment activities, which involve efforts to understand the dynamics of the problem and its contextual features as well as to delineate the frequency and severity of its occurrence. A largely cognitive process, the assessment is led by the practitioner but should also involve the client as collaborator. While the practitioner can contribute professional knowledge, the client has unique personal knowledge of the problem and its context.

Exploration of the problem and the assessment focus largely on the obstacles preventing a solution or on the resources that might facilitate it. For example, if Mr. Henry's problem is his inability to hold a job, what is preventing him from doing so (obstacles) and what would help him do so (resources)? This focus encourages solution-directed thinking and discourages focusing on causative factors that are remote and difficult to substantiate. This does not mean that less immediate considerations, such as historical or personality factors, are discounted. Mr. Henry's history of self-defeating behavior may help illuminate an important current obstacle that needs to be considered. We would then ask what aspect of the obstacle is open to change—perhaps his poor self-concept or lack of skill in self-presentation.

Role of Theory

Nor does this mean that relevant theory is eschewed. In exploring and assessing problems, practitioners may make use of a variety of diagnostic theories, depending on what best fits the problem at hand. In the task-centered model, problems are derived empirically from the clients' views of their difficulties as these are clarified in dialogs with the practitioner. Practitioners do not use theory to formulate problems, as in "Mr. Henry's difficulty lies in his unconscious, self-defeating tendencies." Rather they would start with a formulation, such as, "Mr. Henry has difficulty holding jobs," and then scan relevant knowledge, including theories, to locate possible explanations.

Certain guidelines are offered for this eclectic use of theory: (1) The hypotheses selected to explain the problem should be evaluated on the basis of data. This involves identifying empirical indicators for theoretical terms of the hypothesis and analyzing evidence to determine the likelihood of the hypothesis holding in the particular case. In other words, there are no problems that can be routinely explained by available theories since there is no theory sufficiently well-tested to produce reliable explanations. (2) Preference is given to theories supported by empirical research. (3) The practitioner does not limit himself or herself to a single explanation but rather considers alternative explanations.

(4) Any explanation arrived at is used tentatively; the practitioner is ready to revise it in the light of new evidence.

Problem Specification

An important goal of problem exploration and assessment is to delineate the problem as a basis for planning intervention and evaluating future change. A problem may be labeled by a word or phrase, such as "inadequate income" or "afraid to leave the house." Specification involves a more detailed description in which manifestations of the problem are spelled out in concrete terms. For example, a problem of quarreling might be specified as follows: Joyce and Louise quarrel daily about Tim, Louise's child. Joyce complains that Louise sets few limits for the boy. Louise resents Joyce's "interference." The quarrels are brief but bitter. Joyce frequently threatens to leave. They are likely to be followed by hours of hostile silence between them.

Some problems may involve several distinct manifestations. Thus Keith's problem of disruptive behavior in the classroom may be broken down into (1) talking out of turn, (2) not staying in his seat, and (3) bothering the children next to him.

Generally, data on the frequency and severity of occurrences of the problem (or for each manifestation) are obtained for a period preceding the initial interview. The data are normally elicited from the client (retrospective baseline) although collaterals and records may provide supplementary data. The period to be covered depends on the nature of the problem. For frequently occurring problems (e.g., daily occurrence) a baseline period of a week or ten days might suffice; with lower frequency problems (e.g., once a week), a baseline period of several months may be needed. In addition, or instead, prospective baseline information can be secured: the frequency of the problem can be recorded for a period of time (for example, two or three weeks) starting with the opening of the case but prior to intervention. Direct observation of the client's behavior can be used, especially in school and residential settings (For a presentation of observational procedures and instruments, see Bloom and Fischer 1982). The better the baseline data, the better one's evaluation of the effectiveness of one's intervention will be. However, obtaining prospective baseline data is time consuming and requires delaying the beginning of service. These are important costs in social work agencies. For most cases, simpler, retrospective data may be all that is possible (see Gingerich 1990).

RAIs

Additional assessment data for both understanding the problem and delineating it can be derived from instruments completed by clients. A wide variety of standardized instruments is available for the assessment of particular problems, such as anxiety, depression, poor self-esteem, and marital discord. One can also use a general instrument that may have subscales for the particular problem of interest. While any instrument can be used, practitioners prefer briefer ones, referred to as *Rapid Assessment Instruments* (RAIs). An RAI is brief (one or two pages) and quickly administered (usually in less than 10 minutes) (Levitt and Reid 1981). As a result, an RAI can be taken, and, if need be, scored in the session. A compilation of such instruments may be found in Corcoran and Fischer (1987). RAIs serve three functions in assessment (Reid and Smith 1989). First, they provide a comprehensive survey of a problem, tapping areas that might not have occurred to the practitioner or that clients, especially in family interviews, might be reluctant to get into. The client's answers to questions can often serve as the basis for probes in the interview. Second, in most tests the client's scores can be evaluated against norms indicating the possible severity of the problem. Finally, repeated administrations of RAIs can be used as a basis for the measurement of problem change (see Problem Review below).

Client Self-recording

Client self-recording can also provide useful data. I am referring to devices clients may use to record occurrences of their own behavior or cognitions or of the behavior of family members. These devices can take a variety of forms, including diaries, logs, and charts. Self-recording can be used not only to obtain baseline data, but also to monitor problem change on a continuous basis. It may also yield therapeutic benefits such as enhancing the clients' awareness of their own behavior (for examples see chapter 7). While such therapeutic effects need to be taken into account in interpreting client self-recording, the data can still be quite useful in assessing the problem behavior of the client and others. Getting clients to do the observations in the first place is more difficult. A good rule is to keep it simple; another is not to expect too much. A comprehensive review of self-monitoring procedures may be found in Bornstein, Hamilton, and Bornstein 1986.

Formulating the Problem and the Contract

Either during the targeting process or at its conclusion, the practitioner goes over the problem with the client to make sure they have a mutual understanding of the difficulty they will be focusing on. The step may be done in conjunction with problem specification. Usually practitioners initiate the process by restating the central concerns the clients have expressed. This formulation is not a simple summary, however. Practitioners attempt to frame the problem in a way that is most likely to foster constructive problem-solving actions on the client's part while still reflecting the client's own concerns. To set the stage for client tasks, the problem statement should reflect how clients might act differently to obtain what they want.

For example, Sarah Robbins has voiced many complaints about her aged mother, whom she takes care of (and who refuses to be seen). Mother still tries to run her life, doesn't show any appreciation of all she does for her, and loses her temper at the slightest provocation. At this general level, the problem might be formulated in terms of the mother's difficult behavior, in terms of the strain between them, or in terms of Sarah's difficulty in coping with her mother. Clearly, the last two formulations are preferable since they better prepare the way for the client to do something about the situation. This is not "blaming the victim" but rather putting the problem in the most solvable form. Sarah may be able and willing to initiate change in the way she copes with her mother; the mother is more likely to change in response to what her daughter does rather than on her own initiative. The problem should also be formulated at an appropriate level of specificity. If the client expresses the problem in the form of a host of specific complaints, the practitioner should identify a unifying theme, and the specific complaints can be used as examples. If the client's expression of the problem is general and vague, an attempt should be made to come up with concrete indicators of the difficulty. The practitioner's tentative formulation is given to the client with a request for feedback as to whether it accurately reflects the client's main concerns. The client then may agree with the formulation or offer suggestions for revision, which are usually incorporated.

Goals may be included as part of the problem formulation, depending on the nature of the problem and the client's readiness to engage in a goal-setting process. For some difficulties, a precise goal may be inappropriate. For example, a depressed person wants relief from his or her depression. To put this wish in the form of a specific goal would add little. Other problems lend themselves to the construction of goals. For an adolescent who is having academic difficulty, a goal might be to get Cs or better in four of his five courses.

In general, the purpose of the problem formulation is to capture the clients' major concerns in a way that sets the stage for them to begin to take remedial action. Formal considerations, e.g., the degree of specificity or the inclusion of goals, are secondary to this purpose.

The client's acceptance of the final problem statement leads to a contract that will guide the subsequent work. The practitioner and the client both agree to work toward the solution of the problem as formulated. The problem may—and often should be—revised as the case proceeds, or the client may simply decide it is no longer important enough to work on. Such changes should be deliberate, thoughtful, and worked out collaboratively by the practitioner and the client. In this way both can avoid aimlessly drifting into tangential issues or fruitlessly jousting with the "problem of the week," whatever that may turn out to be. Moreover, a contracted problem provides a fixed point of reference against which to measure progress and to assess the client's motivation for task work. If the client appears to lack interest in doing tasks, the practitioner can raise questions about the client's commitment to solving the problem as stated. Perhaps it should be revised or replaced? Such returning to a motivational source is difficult to do in the absence of an agreed problem.

Thus far in this chapter, we have seen how a problem becomes defined in the model. It is not solely the construction of the practitioner or the client; rather, it is formed through a structured process of collaboration, one that should assure both the appropriate input of an expert and the rights of clients to be helped with problems of their own choosing.

Problem Review

Changes in the problem since the client was last seen are reviewed in each session, preferably at the beginning. This is normally done in conjunction with a continued exploration and focusing of the problem. A recording format is presented below. A continuous record of change in the problem is useful not only for case planning, but also for evaluating the effectiveness of one's intervention. These session-to-session reviews culminate in a final review at the end of the case. If the task-centered approach is used as a module in a case that will continue after the module is completed, the review can occur whenever work on the problem is finished. Basically, the current status of the problem is explored, including its frequency and severity, as well as the clients' impressions of change and their perceptions of the role of the service in producing it. In addition, change can be rated in the final session(s) by the clients, the practitioner, and others on a scale measuring change. Or clients can complete a questionnaire following service.

Another means of evaluating problem change is to administer for a second time the standardized assessment instrument (RAI) that was used to assess the problem prior to intervention. "Before" and "after" scores are then compared to determine the direction and amount of change. One can extend this principle by administering the same instrument on repeated occasions during baseline and treatment periods. Repeated administrations strengthen the baseline measurement and can show how change over the course of treatment may have been affected by different methods of intervention. Administering, serving, and graphing the instruments can be greatly facilitated through the use of computer programs (Hudson 1990).

Finally, if observational measures were used to establish a baseline, they can be repeated when work on the problem is completed. As with RAIs, observational measures can be used repeatedly throughout work on the problem.

Problem Focusing

As noted, the exploration, assessment, and review of the problem continues throughout the case. Indeed, attention to the problem is a major theme in the middle phase (Reid 1978). For example, in mid-treatment interviews, the problem exploration is addressed to developments in the problem since the last session and adds depth and breadth to previous inquiry. At the same time, the focus has to be kept on specific issues for which tasks will be devised.

As one study suggested, well-focused attention on target problems in task-centered practice appears to contribute to a positive outcome (Blizinsky and Reid 1980). In *problem focusing* the practitioner attempts to make explicit connections between the issue on the table and the agreed target problems. If some reasonable link can be made, work may proceed, perhaps with a modified conception of the target problem. There may be need for further focusing, however, on what is to be dealt with in the session.

If a link between the immediate issues and the target problem is not possible, the practitioner has three options: (1) to deal with the unrelated issue as a temporary diversion, which may be the only course of action if the issue is an emergency (Rooney 1981); (2) to take the position with the client that the issue, while of legitimate concern, is tangential to the original target problem(s) and would be better left for the client to deal with; and (3) to formulate the issue as a new target problem, possibly replacing an original problem that is no longer of major interest. Which of these options is best pursued is largely a matter of judgment, but whatever choice is made, the client should be clear about what is being worked on and agree to any significant changes in the formulation of the problem.

Recording

Careful recording is essential for both case planning and evaluation. In the task-centered model, structured recording guides (Reid 1978, 1985; Videka-Sherman and Reid 1985) are used to record problems and tasks and to evaluate progress as well as for other purposes. They are supplemented by standardized instruments, records of observations, and client self-recordings. Illustrations are provided below.

Evaluating Problem Change

Evaluating change in the target problem consists of aggregating evidence on change from recording guides, RAIs, client questionnaires, and the like, and then interpreting this evidence. Interpretation is addressed to the following questions: How much change has occurred? Is it sufficient from the perspective of the client(s) and the practitioner? Are there indications that the change will be durable? What has caused the change? In particular, is there evidence that the efforts of the practitioner and the client(s) have been instrumental in bringing about the change? Does analysis of the change suggest a shift in treatment approach or that another kind of treatment may be indicated? Answers to these questions are needed for purposes of accountability to the client and the agency, of case planning, and of building the practitioner's knowledge of the effectiveness of his or her interventions.

To obtain definitive answers to these questions, one should ideally have systematic single case designs that would provide rigorous measurement and would rule out nonintervention factors as causes of change. Although they have important research functions, such designs are not sufficiently flexible to serve as the major media of evaluation in mainstream clinical practice (Blythe 1990). However, routine collection of data well-integrated into service operations—the approach described above—can provide useful answers to these questions. One can determine approximately the extent of problem change and whether clients viewed it as sufficient. Persistence of change over the course of treatment can be ascertained, and through telephone or in-person follow-ups one can learn if any change occurred after the termination of treatment.

Questions concerning the causes of change are more difficult to answer without controlled research designs, but informed inferences can be made. For example, if problems, goals, intervention processes, and so on, are carefully recorded and cast in empirical language, it becomes possible to use qualitative analysis to tackle the problem of the relation between intervention and change. This strategy is an extension of the well-established argument that experimental controls are not always necessary to make reasonable inferences that interventions are responsible for change (Kazdin 1981). This argument is most convincing when the effects are specific, detailed, predicted by the theory, and highly unlikely to be produced by anything but the intervention. Thus, no other viable explanations surface. Cook and Campbell (1979) refer to such explanations as *signed causes* because the effect bears the "signature" of the cause. Gilbert, Light, and Mosteller (1975) have identified *slam-bang effects* in which the intervention (the slam) is followed immediately by a large apparent effect (the bang). In signed cause or slam-bang situations, the case for the treatment being the cause of the change is fairly compelling because alternative explanations are not competitive.

In applications of signed cause analysis (Reid 1987, 1988; Reid and Hanrahan 1988) the following criteria have been used: (1) Use of the intervention must be followed by immediate change in the target problem. (2) The change must reflect the specific imprint of the intervention (the signed cause). For example, suppose a son is having academic difficulty with math and French. The father's task is to help him with his math homework. The father carries out the task and the son's performance in math (but not in French) improves. (3) There must be no plausible alternative explanations (maturation, history, instrumentation, and so on). In the example given, it would need to be determined that the son's difficulty in math was a stable or worsening problem and that the teacher did not change his or her instructional approach coincident with the father beginning to help with the homework.

Problem Assessment, Review, Recording, and Evaluation: A Case Example

The methods of assessing, reviewing and recording problems, and evaluating change used in the task-centered model will be illustrated through a case example. The example will also serve as a demonstration of the application of a task strategy to a specific problem. The illustration is drawn from work with the T. family (Reid and Donovan 1990) who had sought help at a mental health facility for problems with their three sons, who ranged in age from 13 to 17. Although the family presented a number of problems, I shall focus on its chief complaint—physical fighting, which usually started with the boys and then involved the parents. The task strategy devised by Timothy Donovan, the practitioner, consisted of two major components. The first involved work with the parents alone (ten sessions) to help them develop a collaborative approach to dealing with conflict among the boys. Tasks to lessen conflict and to foster cooperation and cohesion were used for this purpose. The second component involved work with the entire family (the next ten sessions). This phase of treatment made use of family problem-solving (session) tasks to develop ways of preventing conflict from leading to violence. It focused particularly on helping the boys create rules for handling tensions among themselves. For example, the boys were to ask permission to use each other's things, to avoid name-calling, and to "back off" before quarreling led to blows. Both components were carried out as planned and related tasks were eventually accomplished. The problem assessment and review are presented on the Target Problem Schedule below.

Target Problem Schedule

1. Case ID: *T. Family*
2. Problem #: 1

3. Describe problem as agreed with clients. Use reverse to record substantial changes in problem formulation, if any.

   The problem consists of fights that usually start with the boys but then involve whichever parent tries to intercede. The boys may strike each other with their fists, shove, wrestle, or throw things at one another. The involved parent (usually the father) may hit or slap the boys in an attempt to restore order.

4. Problem frequency
   Average of once a week for the past six months

5. Duration
   Approximately one year

6. Analysis
   The fighting among the boys is usually preceded by name-calling and quarrels. Arguments over using each other's possessions are a frequent precipitant. These episodes have caused the parents to feel increasingly helpless in their efforts to control the boys, and they seem to be a factor in Mrs. T.'s depression. Because of parental inconsistency in handling fighting among the boys (mother lenient and often wishy-washy; father strict and impulsively punitive), rules for handling disputes among the boys have not been developed. A further exacerbating factor is the father's drinking (most nights), which leads to greater violence on his part. However, all family members, especially the parents, seem motivated to work on the problem, and the parents seem willing to try to compromise their differences in handling conflict among the boys.

7. Measurement of Problem Change
   Type of measure used (check one):
   __x__ Frequency per week of problem occurrence
   _____ Change rating compared to baseline
   Session # When Problem Reviewed

1	2	3	4	5	6	7	8	9	10	11	12	13	14	15	16	17	18	19	20

   Frequency or rating for previous week

1	0	2	0	0	1	2	1	0	2	1	0	0	0	0	0	0	0	0	0

8. Comment on change
   Little change during parents-only sessions (1–10). The physical fighting ceased early in family treatment, which had focused on tasks for the boys to handle conflict before it led to violence. No instances of fighting were reported between the termination interview and a follow-up interview four months later.

Discussion

The problem is described briefly in the nontechnical language used in formulating it with the client. Frequency of occurrence, which might range from two or three times a week to several times a month, was estimated to average once a week.

The analysis lays out the basic scenario of the problem. Modifiable causes and obstacles are highlighted: the precursors to the fighting in the boys' quarreling, the parental inconsistency, and the father's drinking and involvement in the fights. Resources are noted—specifically, the family's motivation and the parents' willingness to work together. When the model is used with an entire case, one analysis is used for all problems combined since they may have causative elements in common.

The problem reviews in each session can be summarized either in terms of frequency, as in the example, or of change ratings. Change ratings are made on the following scale:

1 2	3 4	5 6	8 9	10
Considerably Worse	Somewhat Worse	No Change	Considerably Alleviated	Not Present

The scale is used when the frequency of the problem is difficult to estimate or when the severity is more important than the frequency. For example, a problem may consist of marital quarreling. It may be difficult to distinguish quarreling from bickering, which the couple does much of the time, and quarrels may range from minor spats to brawls. It may be impossible to determine the frequency of the problem, but an approximate rating of problem change may be possible. When frequency can be estimated, and severity is an important dimension, both scales can be used. When sessions are missed, the review covers the period since the clients were last seen with frequencies averaged by week.

The scale is based on the status of the problem prior to service. Thus, if a problem changes for the better from the baseline and remains that way, ratings would remain in the high range (e.g., considerably alleviated). When the model is used for an entire case, the scale is also applied at termination. Target problems together with the clients' overall problem situation are rated.

Use of RAIs

Several RAIs were used in assessment and evaluation of the T. case. One will be discussed for illustrative purposes.

A global measure of family change, the Index of Family Relations

(Hudson 1982) was given periodically during the treatment and at follow-up. The instrument measures attitudes and feelings about different aspects of family life. Initial scores of family members were in the range from forty to sixty, indicating significant problems (Hudson 1982), a picture consistent with other assessment information. Over the course of treatment, the parents' scores improved 26 percent over the initial assessment, but virtually all of this improvement occurred after the family phase of the treatment had begun. The two younger boys' scores remained stable while the oldest boy's scores worsened by 18 percent over the course of treatment. In general, scores did not change appreciably between termination and follow-up.

Client Questionnaire

Another method of evaluation consisted of a brief questionnaire completed independently by family members at the end of service. Family members consistently reported considerable or complete resolution of the main problem for which they had sought help; all reported to benefit from the treatment and evaluated the methods used positively.

Evaluation of Problem Change

It is clear from the data presented that the main target problem of physical fighting changed for the better. In fact, there had been no occurrence of it at all for five months following its abrupt cessation after the third family session. All family members concurred on this point and were satisfied with the change in the problem and considered it adequate. Why this change occurred is not so clear, however. Data from the problem review as well as from the Index of Family Relations suggests that the initial component of the strategy—work with the parents alone to strengthen their alliance—was not sufficient to bring about change in the problem. Quite possibly this component may have potentiated the family sessions that followed, but this surmise cannot be proven by the data. The sudden end to the fighting following the boys' successful completion of conflict-reducing tasks is evidence that the intervention may have been responsible (through the logic of a "signed-cause" or "slam-bang" effect). The lack of positive change in the IFR scores for the boys is puzzling. It may suggest a measure of independence between the functioning of the sibling subsystem, which changed dramatically in regard to fighting, and the siblings' feelings about their family (or parents).

CHAPTER 3

Tasks

In this chapter we consider the nature, functions, and varieties of tasks in helping clients. The chapter provides a synthesis of previous statements about tasks (Reid and Epstein 1972; Reid 1985; Fortune 1985; Reid 1987; Reid and Helmer 1987; Epstein 1988) and introduces new content.

Within the framework of the model, tasks are planned problem-solving actions. We shall first consider the most common and doubtless the most important class of tasks—those undertaken by clients outside the treatment session (client external tasks). We shall then extend the concept to include tasks done by clients in the session and tasks done by practitioners outside the session.

Client External Tasks

To make headway on their problems, most clients sooner or later must take constructive action outside the counseling session. Family members must learn how to talk to one another without provoking arguments. Problem drinkers must act to control or give up their destructive habits. Phobic people must deal with the objects they fear. Delinquent adolescents must begin to conform to community norms. Granted, some problems may be resolved in the social worker's office. Expressing feelings, developing self-understanding, and attaining new perspectives may suffice for certain difficulties. But for every client who leaves the social worker's presence with problems solved, there are many more who leave with work to do, but the work may have been made easier by the catharsis and insight of the counseling session.

In the helping professions this work is called by many names—tasks, homework, behavioral assignments, instigations, directives. It may be described as a process, such as generalization or putting insight into action. In the present model these various notions become translated into client external tasks. However, these account only for part of our notion of task, namely, for the tasks that are used to reinforce or extend the accomplishments of the treatment hour (hence the term *homework*) and the tasks that are generated by the practitioner (e.g., instigations, directives, behavioral assignments). What is not well accounted for are tasks that practitioners and clients design together and tasks that reflect major change efforts by clients and that are culminations, not supplements, of treatment sessions. When these two kinds of tasks are put together—an ideal in this model—the result is a collaborative effort involving the practitioner and the client(s) that leads to tasks that strike at the heart of the problem. The task in which the three teen-age siblings agreed to "back off" before fighting (chapter 2) is a quintessential example.

Levels of Generality

Tasks can be formulated at different levels of generality. General tasks set an overall direction for action, but they provide no procedural details (Mr. and Mrs. Dale will work out a plan for Mrs. Dale's mother). At this level, tasks translate goals into action terms and assign responsibility for the action to be taken. It is assumed that clients can begin to effect the task although it is left open when and how they do this. Not all goals can be put in the form of tasks. Thus, Mrs. Green's goal might be to obtain the return of her children from foster care, but her actions alone cannot achieve this goal.

Tasks at a concrete level are termed *operational*. These tasks spell out discrete, specific, problem-solving actions that are usually undertaken before the next session (Joanne will spend one hour each school night doing her homework). General tasks are broken down into operational tasks; the actual work of the model takes place at the operational level. General tasks may be used to provide an overall direction for the client's efforts (see chapter 8 for examples), but their use is optional. Operational tasks are essential for the implementation of the model. They may take many forms: for example, implementation of possible solutions arrived at in the session, home practice of skills learned in treatment, or assessment and monitoring of one's own or another's behavior. They may be structured largely by the practitioner or devised by the client. They may be carried out with a high degree of fidelity to an agreed plan, or they may be radically reshaped by the client. Throughout these variations, operational tasks are still discrete, specific, and problem-solving. By *discrete* and *specific* we mean that the tasks have beginning and end points, relate to concrete actions, and have a measurable outcome. For example, Henry will ask his group home supervisor about a pass during the coming week.

Tasks and Client Problem Solving

Tasks are problem-solving not only because they are directed at solving particular problems but also because they involve the client in self-directed, problem-solving activity. Even if tasks are structured by the practitioner, the clients should have some decision-making role in carrying them out, or the tasks should lead to progressively greater control by the client over their implementation. To prepare clients to carry out the tasks on their own, they should be made aware of the purpose of the task and how it will supposedly affect the problem. An ultimate goal in the use of tasks is empowerment of the client—to enable clients to design and carry out their own problem-solving actions.

Tasks as a Force for Change

Client tasks draw on a fundamental force in all therapeutic change—the clients' *effecting problem solutions through their own actions*. This idea, expressed in different terms, is a major theme in most theories of interpersonal treatment.

In behavior therapy, an obvious example, change is effected by the client trying new behaviors that are reinforced by outcomes he or she finds desirable. The form the reinforcement takes—a tangible reward, the attainment of a goal, etc.—may vary. The constant factor is that the client has enacted a solution behavior that has met with success. Behavior that successfully reduces problems tends to be repeated; hence, change occurs.

In the cognitive-behavioral and cognitive therapies (Dobson 1988), in which mental processes play a larger role in change, the role of client action is still central. Change may result from new actions that are guided and appraised by cognitive operations. When cognitive change is given greater prominence, as in Beck's (1976) cognitive therapy, cognitions need to be tested through action outside the session. Thus, clients may undertake actions to disprove existing cognitions or to confirm new ones.

In systems-oriented family therapies, change is seen as a function of new patterns of action and interaction by family members. In some approaches, such as structural family therapy (Minuchin and Fishman 1981), changes in family interaction occurring during the session are stressed, and tasks between sessions are used to solidify and extend these changes. In strategic therapies (Haley 1976), the major vehicles of change are directives (therapist-generated tasks) that instigate new behaviors by family members.

Psychodynamic therapies generally make less use of tasks than other treatment approaches. The primary change dynamics are thought to involve complex cognitive and emotional processes occurring within the session rather than actions outside it. Still, many psychodynamic practitioners make use of tasks as "homework" to enable clients to put into action insight gained during treatment sessions. It should also be noted that a central force for change in psychodynamic treatment occurs during the "transference" phase of the relationship when the client exhibits behavior toward the therapist dictated by earlier relationships. The therapist declines to play, in Strupp's (1989:718) words, a "complementary role in the patient's scenarios" but instead communicates to the client his or her understanding of what the client is doing. In this way, the client becomes aware of the inappropriateness of his or her reactions and begins to behave toward the therapist in a more realistic fashion. This new behavior is strongly reinforced by the therapist. In a sense, the client's actions lead to a successful resolution of the problem behavior. Although such resolution of the transference in psychodynamic therapy is not viewed in terms of client tasks, it relies on the same principles of change as tasks do.

Table 3.1 summarizes the various change-oriented functions of tasks as these are construed in the present model. The table incorporates the functions just reviewed in relation to different models of treatment and adds others. The first function—to take direct action—is the most common and important in the model. It is assumed that people can act successfully to solve a wide range of problems. The model attempts to stimulate and structure people's natural resourcefulness in problem solving; the remaining functions are auxiliary to the first. That is, attaining insight, correcting beliefs, becoming aware of limitations, highlighting self-efficacy, and learning by doing can be expected to enhance the client's efforts to deal with the target problems or with obstacles. At the same time, these remaining functions, especially the last, are important as a means of strengthening the client's general functioning and capacities for coping with problems. As illustrated in table 3.1, tasks may also be used to make the client more receptive to the development of insight (Saari 1986).

TABLE 3.1
Change Functions of Tasks

Function	Example
1. To take direct action to affect a problem or its context	Mr. Q. applies for and obtains employment.
2. To try out understanding gained in treatment session	Having achieved awareness of his tendency to be excessively critical, Mr. S. tries to emphasize positives in others.
3. To make clients more receptive to the development of insight	Ms. R.'s visit with her estranged mother arouses positive feelings which she was able to express in the session for the first time.
4. To change cognitions	Mr. L. records instances of good decisions at work to counter his belief that he always does the wrong thing.
5. To test one's abilities	Mr. Y.'s failure to limit his alcohol intake to five drinks a day convinces him that he needs help with his drinking problem.
6. To heighten sense of self-efficacy and mastery	By successfully completing her weight-control tasks, Joan feels generally more self-confident.
7. To learn through doing	Mrs. D.'s efforts to obtain services help her learn how to deal with community agencies.

Task Completion and Reinvention

Task completion refers to the client's carrying out the task as agreed to in the treatment session. In the literature, task completion (often referred to as compliance) is generally viewed as positive and non-completion (noncompliance) as a source of concern (Shelton and Levy 1981). The problem of noncompletion has been studied in a number of contexts including client follow-through on behavioral instigations (Levy and Carter 1976) and patient adherence to medical regimens (Meichenbaum and Turk 1987; Sackett and Haynes 1976). Noncompletion has been found to occur with sufficient frequency to be regarded as "one of the most serious problems facing health care professionals" (Shelton and Levy 1981:38). In two major studies of the task-centered approach, the completion rate (tasks substantially or completely carried out) ranged from 62 percent to 71 percent (Reid 1978, 1987). Although this completion rate is relatively high, perhaps reflecting attention to collaborative task planning and the clients' concurrence with the task, noncompletion is still a matter of concern.

Studies of task attainment within the model (Reid and Strother 1988) have suggested that noncompletion does not necessarily equal lack of progress. Clients may not do the task agreed upon, but they may do a modification of it, do something similar, or develop an alternative. What clients often do, then, is to engage in "reinvention," similar to people who adapt technology to their own purposes (Rogers and Shoemaker 1971). In some cases the client's reinvented tasks may accomplish more than the task originally agreed upon. In one case, for example (Reid and Strother 1988), a couple agreed to the task of monitoring their misreadings of body language and to record their observations on a chart. Instead, the couple used the blank chart, which they never completed, to remind themselves to control what they considered to be inappropriate expressions of body language. They accomplished this remade task quite ably, and thus moved more quickly to a solution of their problem than if they had stuck with the original task. In this case, the clients used the task in their own way as a stimulus to their own problem solving. In other cases, clients will make substantial modifications in the task to adapt it to the situation at hand. Such variations make it difficult to rate task progress or even to determine the connections, if any, between the original task and the client's problem solving. In any case, noncompletion need not be deplored; in fact, it should be encouraged if it results in a movement toward problem solutions. After all, the purpose of the task-centered approach, indeed, of most helping methods, is to help clients learn to make use of their own resources.

As deShazer (1982) has suggested, it may be possible to fit task designs to the client's response style. If a client tends to modify tasks while carrying them out, then tasks that are open to modification can be designed.

Multiple Consequences

Most tasks have consequences beyond the attainment of the immediate goals. Thus, the simple task for a child to clean his or her room requires that the child accepts parental authority and follows rules; moreover, it has implications for the child's relationship with the person supervising the task. Successful completion of the task may result in parental approval to which the child may respond positively, setting in motion a positive cycle of interaction. A task, then, simultaneously and sequentially affects multiple systems, and its possible outcomes must be viewed through multiple perspectives.

This principle can be used to therapeutic advantage in two ways. First, a task aimed at a target problem can be structured to simultaneously attain another objective, such as a contextual change. For example, Larry may agree to do his homework with parental help one hour each night as a means of improving his grades in school. Suppose he has an overly close (enmeshed) relationship with his mother but a distant relationship with his father, and suppose further that this relationship pattern is seen as an obstacle to Larry's success at school as well as a possible cause for other problems. The parent selected to provide the help might then well be the father, on the grounds that his helping Larry with his homework might bring them closer together. This aspect of the task could be reinforced by an agreement that the mother would not participate in the helping, and that Dad and Larry would reward themselves after a week of homework sessions with some mutually enjoyable activity. The second way is the reverse of the first: a task is aimed at a contextual change which, if attained, would affect a target problem. For example, in structural family therapy of anorexia it is assumed that excessive parental attention to the child's "sickness" is a means of avoiding parental conflict (Minuchin, Rosman, and Baker 1978). Thus, session and external tasks may be used to enable the parents to face these conflicts, thereby reducing dysfunctional preoccupation with their child's problem.

Practitioners also need to be alert to negative consequences (side effects) in their use of tasks. For example, providing children with tangible rewards for their compliance with tasks is a staple of task-centered and behavioral practice. Although tangible rewards can be effective in motivating children, one needs to be alert to possible negative aspects. Are the parents really comfortable with the idea, or do they resent giving Kevin money or treats for what he should be doing anyway? If their attitude is begrudging, how will this affect their relationship with him? What about siblings who may cry "unfair" if they are expected to comply without pay? Anticipation of possible side effects can lead to steps to avoid or minimize them.

In using tasks practitioners should be continually alert to multiple consequences, positive as well as negative ones, and be prepared to consider them in planning the tasks. In keeping with the principle of collaboration discussed earlier, practitioners involve clients in considering the possible outcomes of a task, including those that relate to contextual change. Thus, if the practitioner in the example just given thinks the father should be the one to help Larry with his homework, he or she gives reasons for the choice and elicits reactions from the clients. As collaborators, clients can act in ways that make it more likely that desirable outcomes will happen and that side effects will be avoided.

When to Use Tasks and When Not To

Use of external tasks in treatment has a broad range of application. Task-centered practice has been used successfully with most types of clients and problems treated by social workers (Reid 1990). However, in certain situations tasks may be particularly advantageous; in others they may be less productive.

Let us consider first the circumstances when tasks may be especially useful. First, many clients do better with an action-oriented mode of treatment than with one that relies on catharsis, insight, reflection, or other techniques that relate more to verbal, affective, and cognitive aspects. Less well educated or less articulate clients are likely to fall into this group, but there are many people, regardless of education or verbal facility, who prefer an action-oriented mode of treatment. They may find introspection, self-revelation, or affective expression difficult or unproductive but may do well with an approach that focuses on action inside and outside the session. Second, clients who prefer more introspective forms of treatment may find themselves unable to implement in their life situations what they have gained in their sessions. This impasse may be general or confined to a particular problem. Encouragement by the practitioner may not be sufficient. External tasks may be required to get the client moving. Finally, external tasks can often serve a dual diagnostic-treatment function early in treatment with clients who appear well-motivated and ready to change. Tasks at this point can give clients the opportunity to make substantial inroads on their problems; however, failures can be informative diagnostically, especially if attention is given to how the failure occurs.

Because tasks have a useful function in virtually any case, there are no contraindications to their use based on the type of clients. However, under certain circumstances one might wish to defer their use or change the circumstances before using them. If there is doubt about whether or not the problem has been correctly formulated, tasks, or at least those oriented toward change, may be premature. Tasks aimed at gathering data to help define the problem may be in order, however. These distinctions, among others, will be discussed in detail in the next section when different type of tasks are considered.

When the focus is on helping the individual client work through existential dilemmas (e.g., sorting out one's life goals) or on assuaging painful feelings (e.g., in reaction to loss), tasks assume a subordinate role to other methods of treatment, such as exploration, empathic listening, and interpretation (Reid 1978). However, tasks can serve an important ancillary function, especially cognitive tasks (Ewalt 1977), in which clients can systematically use reflection and recording of thoughts and feelings between sessions.

In some situations, clients are unwilling to take action on their own behalf. The most common example in social work is the purely protective case. In these cases, clients (or others seen) refuse to cooperate in altering conditions, such as child abuse, that the community finds intolerable. In such cases, however, the concept of the practitioner task may provide a useful means of organizing the practitioner's activity.

Finally, certain problems may not respond directly to client action. The course of action to resolve the problem may not be clear, as in some psychosomatic disorders, or client action may not be sufficient. For example, progressive alcoholics may not be able to complete tasks to stop or control their drinking. In such situations, client and practitioner tasks may serve a subordinate, but often critical role, for example, in enabling the client to secure needed help.

Types of External Tasks

Tasks done by clients between sessions can be classified according to a variety of dimensions. We shall consider several of the more important breakdowns in this section. Other approaches to classification of client tasks can be found in Brown-Standridge (1989) and Levy and Shelton (1990).

Goal

All tasks are ultimately aimed at the solution of a problem. They may vary, however, in terms of the specific goal they attempt to achieve. Four goals can be distinguished: (1) to assess the problem; (2) to bring about cognitive change in the client; (3) to promote change in the client's behavior; (4) to effect change in the client's situation.

Assessment tasks generally involve monitoring behavior, feelings, or thoughts through charts, checklists, or rating schemes. Clients may observe and record their own behavior, feelings, or thoughts, or they may monitor the behavior of family members. These tasks are used to establish baselines of problem frequency or severity as well as to investigate features that may be maintaining the problem. Assessment tasks are occasioned by the practitioner's interest in enhancing his or her assessment knowledge although the client may learn and benefit from the process of observing and recording—the well-known reactive effects of self-monitoring (Kopp 1988).

Closely related to assessment tasks is the second category, that of *cognitive tasks*, which aim primarily at increasing the client's understanding. In fact, tasks involving monitoring of behavior, thoughts, and feelings may be used for this purpose. What distinguishes assessment tasks from this type of cognitive task is their purpose—whether their instigation is related to the practitioner's or to the client's need for knowledge. Another subtype of cognitive tasks involves thinking through an issue or decision. For example, a person with a poor self-image may agree to think of his or her strong points, or a person may be asked to work out the pros and cons of different alternatives. A written product (e.g., a list) puts the task into concrete form and serves as a basis for review with the practitioner. Another subtype of cognitive tasks has a behavioral component, but the purpose of the task is cognitive rather than behavioral change (Beck 1976). For example, a wife seen in individual treatment maintains that her husband reacts with boredom and changes the subject whenever she talks about her job. She agrees to test out her belief by telling her husband about something that happened at work and noticing how he actually responds.

The purpose of *behavioral tasks* is to initiate a change in the client's behavior or a change in interactions between clients. The focus is usually on bringing about a modification of some enduring behavioral or interactive pattern. For instance, parents agree to try out a new way of disciplining their children, or a teenager's task is to be home before curfew. An isolated man will attempt to make one acquaintance during the week.

In *situational tasks* the clients attempt to alter their situations. For example, they may seek information, obtain resources, change living arrangements, or try to affect others. Derek agrees to ask his teacher for help. Harry will find a new apartment; Joan will explain to her boss why she has been late to work. Although situational tasks may involve (and cause) new behaviors, their immediate purpose is to alter a situation, not a behavior pattern. Thus, successful situational tasks tend to be unique, one-time actions, whereas successful behavioral tasks invite repetition until new behaviors are established.

Numbers and Interactions of Task Participants

A major division of external tasks concerns the number of task participants and the nature of their interaction. An *individual* task is undertaken by one client. The task may call for the client to interact with others (e.g., George will ask his supervisor about a transfer), but the task is still done by one client.

Shared tasks involve a single undertaking carried out cooperatively by two or more participants, at least one of whom is a client. That the participants are collaborators in the same undertaking is indicated by the form of the task statement. The subjects of the sentence are the participants and what they will do is set forth in a single verb. (Mrs. Dent and Karen will go shopping together; Mr. and Mrs. V. will discuss the possibility of joint custody of their children). The client's partner in a shared task may be a family member, teacher, homemaker, home health aide, a fellow resident, or the practitioner.

Reciprocal tasks involve two clients (or a client and another person) in an exchange of tasks. For example, Harry agrees to initiate at least one conversation a day; in return Susan will go bowling with Harry once a week. Unlike shared tasks, in which participants engage in a common activity, reciprocal tasks specify different activities for each participant and an agreement as to how those activities will be exchanged. There are two such types of reciprocal tasks: *symmetrical*, in which participants are of roughly equal status (e.g., spouses), and *complementary* tasks, in which one participant is subordinate to the other (e.g., parent and child, teacher and pupil). While symmetrical exchanges tend to be equal, complementary exchanges may reflect the hierarchical relation of the participants—a child's task may be to do an hour's homework each evening, whereas the parents' task may be to provide a small reward. Choosing between the three types of tasks (individual, shared, and reciprocal) becomes an issue only in multiple client situations (e.g., family treatment) or in collaboration between the client and others, such as teachers or caretakers. We shall focus on family treatment, the usual situation for tasks involving two or more participants.

In family treatment, individual tasks are used primarily in two ways. One category of tasks calls for individual behavior within the family situation—doing chores, ignoring rather than punishing the behavior of a young child, making requests of family members not involved in treatment, and so forth. The other category comprises a range of tasks external to the family but usually with consequences for the family, such as tasks undertaken by children to alleviate school-related problems, or a parent's agreement to attend an AA meeting. Such tasks are often distributed among family members or intimates with the understanding that each will do his or her part, but without an explicit reciprocal agreement. In addition to achieving specific goals, individual tasks can also be used to increase the autonomy of dependent or enmeshed clients, for example, teens in search of channels to express their need for independence or single mothers overinvolved with their children.

Shared tasks, too, have a variety of uses: to accomplish practical goals, such as getting homework done, to provide a structure for problem solving and practicing communication skills at home, and to build relationships, for example, in tasks involving mutually enjoyable ac-

48   Tasks

tivities. If they go well, shared tasks tend to promote cohesiveness
since they bring participants together in some joint activity. Tasks can
backfire, however, if they result in conflict or if one client feels pressured to participate. In working with enmeshed client systems, that is,
those that are already "too cohesive," preference might be given to
individual tasks (see chapter 6). Reciprocal tasks are used primarily to
promote positive interaction, to reduce conflict, and to help parents
control their children. These functions will be explored in greater detail
in chapter 6; suffice it to say here that they require a good deal of
planning in the session, preferably face-to-face planning by the participants themselves. In one study (Reid 1987a), the success rate for
reciprocal tasks without such face-to-face planning was 57 percent; with
such planning the success rate rose to 68 percent. As Rooney (1978) has
commented, reciprocal tasks tend to be "high risk, high gain." Because
two participants, usually with a strained relationship, must coordinate
an often intricate exchange, there are many opportunities for things to
go wrong. On the other hand, if successful, a reciprocal task can set
in motion a cycle of positive interaction leading to rapid progress.
Sometimes there is too much conflict (or too little cohesiveness) between participants for reciprocal tasks to be effective. In such situations
individual tasks may be indicated.

Straightforward Versus "Paradoxical" Tasks

Tasks can be classified as either straightforward or paradoxical.
Straightforward tasks are those in which the actions called for directly
reduce the problem if they are carried out. Most forms of treatment
use straightforward tasks. If Harry has a problem with school attendance, then a straightforward task might call for Harry to increase his
attendance. The definition of a *paradoxical* task is more controversial
because of difficulties with the meaning of paradox as it is used in an
interpersonal treatment context (Dell 1981; Fisch, Weakland, and Segal
1982; Ascher 1989). Although the term *paradoxical* may actually be a
misnomer, it has become so well established by usage that it is pointless
to invent another term. Actually a reasonable degree of consensus has
been achieved in what paradoxical as applied to tasks means at a
practical level. To use the words of Ascher and Efran (1978:547), "a
paradoxical task is one that requires clients to perform responses that
appear to be incompatible with the goal for which they are seeking
assistance." The paradoxical element arises from the apparent incom-

patibility between response and goal. Thus if the goal is for Harry to increase class attendance, a paradoxical task would instruct him to stay away from school.

Paradoxical tasks can be divided into those based on assumptions of *defiance* and those based on assumptions of *compliance* (Rohrbaugh et al. 1981). In defiance-based tasks, the assumption is that the task will achieve its goal because it will provoke the client into doing the opposite of what the task calls for. However, there is usually more than simple reverse psychology to defiance-based tasks. For example, by accepting a client's need to engage in dysfunctional behavior, a defiance-based task can free the client and perhaps family members from power struggles, may help the client achieve a new perspective on the problem, and may stimulate new efforts at solutions. For example, if Harry is advised that cutting classes is a childish phase he needs to go through before he can reach a mature decision about what he really wants to do, and that he should thus continue to cut classes until this phase is over, he is not only provoked to prove he is over the childish phase, but he may also be stimulated to have some fresh thoughts about the pros and cons of missing school. This example draws on an experiment by Kolko and Milan (1983) who found some empirical support for the use of such tasks with truant adolescents.

In compliance-based paradoxical tasks, the client attempts to comply with a task running counter to the goal, with the expectation that positive benefits will result from the effort to comply. Having an insomniac attempt to stay awake is a familiar example. Attempts to produce a problem can yield a variety of beneficial results. Spontaneous behavior is made deliberate, thus giving the client a chance to learn how to control it better. The client may see the behavior from a new perspective, perhaps gaining an awareness of its inappropriateness, or he or she may simply become tired of it. For some problems, such as difficulty falling asleep or achieving orgasm, trying too hard may make matters worse. By attempting to produce the problem, rather than directly solving it, the effect of trying too hard is removed and "paradoxically" a solution may appear. In terms of learning theory, negative practice (practicing the problem) may lead to better self-control, or extinction of the problem may occur because of satiation or lack of reinforcement, among other possibilities (Raskin and Klein 1976). Although learning theory provides useful (and demystifying) explanations, there is as yet no agreement about which learning principles best explain the phenomenon.

In the task-centered approach, straightforward tasks are definitely preferred. In fact, paradoxical tasks are used only when straightforward tasks appear to be getting nowhere. Evidence for the efficacy of paradoxical tasks is meager. Moreover, straightforward tasks provide a better fit with the collaborative, problem-solving orientation of the model. When a paradoxical task is used, it is likely to be one based on assumptions of compliance. One reason is that the rationale for the task can be shared with the client, and, in fact, there is evidence that being open with clients about how such tasks are supposed to work can actually increase their effectiveness (Ascher and Efran 1978). By contrast, the true rationale for defiance-based tasks must be withheld in order to mobilize the clients' oppositional tendencies.

Session Tasks

Thus far, certain characteristics of tasks have been delineated. They are planned problem-solving actions that are discrete and specific when put in operational form. It is easy to see how client tasks can also occur within the session. Perhaps the most widely used session tasks occur in interviews with two or more clients. The practitioner can have clients engage in face-to-face dialog and other activities that are planned, discrete, specific, and problem-solving in nature. Thus, clients together can make decisions, discuss feelings, practice communication skills, and so forth, in ways that actually solve problems or that closely resemble problem-solving actions in actual life situations.

In work with clients on a one-to-one basis, session tasks can be used to enable clients to take direct action on their problems in natural settings. In one case, for example, during a home visit, the practitioner set up a game-like room-cleaning task for nine-year-old Lisa whose messy room was a source of chronic tension between her and her mother. As the practitioner "kept score," Lisa energetically put in place over a hundred objects in the space of a few minutes. Session tasks involving clients gradually approaching feared objects are a basic method of behavioral treatment of phobias (Barlow 1988; see also chapter 7) A large variety of such tasks become possible when the session is not seen as confined to the usual office setting but as taking place wherever the client is having problems—at home, in school, in a group residence, and so on. However, even in traditional office settings, individual clients can undertake tasks involving role playing with the practitioner, or they can practice new behaviors or skills.

Varieties of Session Tasks

As noted, tasks done in the session normally involve two or more clients in face-to-face communication, but they may also consist of the practitioner and a single client if the client is engaged in a problem-solving action that mirrors actions in his or her life situation. The following classification of session tasks is organized according to treatment purpose. To simplify the presentation, the participants will be referred to as clients (the usual case) although note will be made of tasks that usually involve the practitioner and a single client.

1. Facilitating Assessment

These tasks are designed to provide the practitioner with assessment information. Any therapeutic benefits the clients achieve are incidental. (a) Enactments: clients are instructed to interact in accustomed ways in relation to a suggested issue (Aponte and Van Deusen 1981; Minuchin and Fishman 1981). (b) Standard tasks: a standard task, e.g., planning a picnic, is used to provide information on the participants' interactive patterns (Watzlawick, Beavin, and Jackson 1967)

2. Structured Problem Solving

These tasks involve rational give-and-take between two or more participants to solve a specific problem, negotiate a conflict, make a decision, etc. While any task is a form of problem solving, these tasks organize the process into a logical series of steps, which are briefly summarized below. (Not all steps are used in all tasks.) (a) Problem definition: clients identify and clarify issue(s) on which to work. (b) Clarifying positions: clients reveal to another (or to one another) their point of view, rationale, motivations, expectations, etc. concerning an issue (e.g., an elderly woman is asked to explain to her adult daughter why she wishes to continue to live in her own apartment; a husband and wife in turn tell each other what they expect in terms of their sexual relationship). (c) Generating alternative solutions: clients are asked to suggest potential solutions to their problem. Methods include brainstorming, i.e., emphasis on generating numerous alternatives without initially considering quality, followed by selecting the most promising (Osborn 1963), and free-flowing discussion, where solutions are developed by the clients through unstructured discussion. (d) Making concessions: clients are asked to offer concessions (usually behavior

changes) in order to resolve a problem. (e) Selecting a potential solution: clients select the solution to be implemented.

3. Planning Actions

Tasks in the session may be used to plan actions to be carried out
at home or in the family's environment (e.g., at school). These outside
activities may be implementations of solutions reached through problem solving, or they may be suggested or stimulated by the practitioner.
(a) General planning: an activity is planned "from scratch" in response
to an unspecified need or suggestion (e.g., a couple is asked to plan a
mutually enjoyable activity.) This category includes long-range planning (e.g., parents discuss goals for their retarded child.) (b) Planning
logistics: details of an activity already agreed upon are worked out.
For example, parents lay out the specifics of a chore system for their
children. (c) Identifying obstacles: clients attempt to identify potential
causes of failure in carrying out a task and to plan corrective measures
(Birchler and Spinks 1981).

4. Expressing Affect

These tasks focus on the expression of feelings. (a) Sharing feelings:
clients express their feelings about an emotional issue that has not been
adequately discussed (e.g., a mother and son discuss for the first time
their feelings about the father leaving home.) (b) Positive exchange:
clients are asked to reveal what they like or find attractive about one
another.

5. Enhancing Awareness

Tasks are set up to increase the clients' awareness or understanding
of their own or others' behavior, feelings, beliefs, etc. (without focus
on a specific problem or on problem solving). (a) Informative discussion: clients attempt to accomplish the above tasks through structured
or unstructured discussion (e.g., a husband and wife inform each other
what pleases them; a son tells his adoptive parents about his life with
his biological family.) (b) Reenactment: clients attempt to reproduce
an interaction that caused them difficulty in order to stimulate in each
other a greater awareness of motives or effects of behavior. The task
may become paradoxical if clients are instructed to repeat interactions
in ways that cannot be complied with. For example, clients may be
asked to restage a quarrel with its original intensity of feeling on the

assumption that an effort to do so will cause each to see the inappropriateness of their original reactions.

(c) Experiencing the role of others: clients take roles of others and act out scenes or discuss issues in order to gain a sense of the situations, perceptions, and feelings of others. Tasks may include role reversals as well as taking on the roles of persons not present in the session; these tasks may be done by a practitioner and an individual client. (See "Skills Training" below for another use of role play.)(d) Sculpting: clients use nonverbal means to express feelings, attitudes, etc. (Papp 1976) (e.g., a couple learns about differing needs for closeness by taking turns approaching each other and stopping at a comfortable distance.)

6. Skills Training

These tasks are designed to help clients acquire specific skills, which may be either cross-situational (e.g., communication, problem solving) or situation-specific (how to be appropriately assertive with a particular teacher). The emphasis is on improving performance rather than on solving particular problems. (a) Rehearsal and guided practice: clients or an individual client rehearse or practice specific skills with the practitioner playing the role of coach (Jacobson and Margolin 1979; Stuart 1980). (b) Parental modeling: through playing the role of his or her child, a parent demonstrates skill in handling a situation to the child (for example, a father plays his son and demonstrates how to reply to an antagonistic peer played by the son.) A more detailed discussion of session tasks used in communication skills training is provided in chapter 6.

7. Anxiety and Stress Reduction

Procedures to relieve anxiety and stress, which usually involve the practitioner working with an individual client, include relaxation training, systematic, and in-vivo desensitization. They qualify as session tasks if they are construed as problem-solving actions that the client can learn to do on his or her own.

Practitioner Tasks

Practitioner tasks or problem-solving actions done by the practitioner on the client's behalf outside the session are analogous to client external tasks. Like client tasks, practitioner tasks are set up and agreed to in the session and are subsequently reviewed. Most of the practitioner's environmental interventions can be structured as practitioner tasks. There are several reasons for extending the concept of task to the practitioner's environmental work. First, it provides an additional dimension to the social worker-client collaborative relationship that is so central to the model. Not only are practitioners, like clients, involved in task work, but the work of each is jointly planned and agreed on. This structure insures that the client has input into actions done by the practitioner on his or her behalf, consents to these actions, and has the opportunity to review them. Second, the idea of a practitioner task offers a basis for conceptualizing the practitioner's environmental interventions. One can consider types of different practitioner tasks, as is done below. Finally, practitioner tasks provide a record of the social worker's environmental activity and its outcome for case management and research purposes (Rooney 1978).

Practitioner tasks are classified according to whether their purpose is to facilitate client task work or whether they are done independently by the practitioner. In *facilitating practitioner tasks*, the practitioner intervenes in the environment to help clients do their own tasks, for example, a practitioner assists a client in making an appointment at a medical clinic by calling to find out about appointment procedures. In *independent practitioner tasks*, the practitioner does not enable the client to complete a specific task, but rather acts as the client's agent in the environment—e.g. obtaining general information about resources. Another method of classifying practitioner tasks is by the role of the practitioner. Here we adopt a familiar typology of practitioner roles in the environment: broker (connecting clients to external resources); mediator (resolving differences or enhancing the interaction between the client and others); and advocate (presenting the client's case to others) (Grinmel, Kyte, and Bostwick 1981; Germain and Gitterman 1981; Wood and Middleman 1989). Any of these roles can be filled with facilitating or independent practitioner tasks. That is, brokerage, mediation, and advocacy can be done either in support of, or in the absence of, client tasks. In general, we prefer that the practitioner's tasks be facilitating rather than independent since it is usually better to help clients do for themselves than to do things for them. However, independent tasks by the practitioner may be indicated when the risk of client failure to complete a task even with assistance is high, when the client is physically or cognitively disabled or is in a highly stressful situation. Under these circumstances, clients may learn less from their own tasks than from the practitioner's modeling of successful task performance. For further discussion of the practitioner's environmental activities, see chapter 11.

Task Structures in Case Coordination

Problems of coordination are inevitable when a case involves multiple service providers. Often the social worker is one of a half dozen or more practitioners serving the same client. For example, work with a troubled child and his or her family may involve a school social worker, one or more teachers, a school psychologist, a school nurse, a probation officer, and a case worker from a county child protection unit. In a mental health setting, the cast of characters in a given case might include a social worker, a psychiatrist, a clinical psychologist, a mental health aide, a sheltered workshop supervisor, an occupational therapist, and the director of a group home.

In such multiple-provider cases, a task structure provides a useful device for monitoring and facilitating coordination among different actors (Bailey-Dempsey 1991). Generally, one practitioner (the social worker for purposes of the present discussion) functions as a case manager or coordinator. Usually, a case conference or case management team meeting is used to bring the participants together, and the client is also present as a participant. In these sessions aspects of the client's problems that involve coordination among the participants are discussed and tasks for relevant participants, including the client, are developed. In addition to helping develop tasks, the social worker records the tasks on a sheet. If possible, copies of the sheet are made and distributed to all participants. The social worker may take the responsibility for monitoring and recording task progress and for serving as a facilitator and coordinator—e.g., giving reminders. He or she may also conduct a task review at a subsequent meeting of the participants. In teams or other groups of providers that work together frequently, responsibility for the role of case manager may be rotated. In any event, the practitioner who takes the role does so with the permission of the other participants and eschews an authoritarian approach.

CHAPTER 4

Planning and Implementing Tasks

The central strategy of the model consists of helping clients plan and implement external tasks. This function incorporates most session tasks since they are typically used to prepare for tasks to be done at home or elsewhere in the environment. Task planning and implementation are closely connected. The plan guides the implementation. How the task is carried out provides feedback for the next step in planning. This chapter presents the main components of this strategy, emphasizing sessions with individual clients. Adaptations for families and other multiple client situations will be taken up in detail in chapter 6.

Task Planning

The major components of task planning and implementation were set out in chapter 1 (table 1.2). These components of the Task Planning and Implementation Sequence (TPIS) are used in a rough stepwise progression. Variations in order may occur, however. For example, obstacles may be dealt with at any point and agreement may not be obtained until after the obstacles have been resolved or details of implementation have been planned. Often the session may shift back and forth among the components and the exploration of the problem. Not all components may be used for a given task. Upon completion of the task review, the process starts afresh with generation of possibilities for the next step although consideration of obstacles may intervene, as will be discussed.

Generating Task Possibilities

The first step in developing a plan is to generate ideas for possible tasks. These ideas come either from the practitioner or from the client. The practitioner generally starts the process either by inviting ideas from the client or by suggesting possible tasks. Sometimes a single idea will provide the basis for the plan. However the process unfolds, it is important to involve the client from the outset as an active participant.

The client can be asked to review what he or she has tried to do about the problem and to come up with ideas based on these past efforts, or the client can simply be asked to think of ideas. Ideas can be elicited and discussed one at a time, or brainstorming techniques can be used (chapter 3). Even when task ideas come primarily from the client, the practitioner asks clarifying questions, suggests modifications, and so on.

These methods can be applied to conjoint interviews. In addition, the practitioner can structure session tasks in which family members work out task ideas together in face-to-face dialog (chapter 6).

Giving clients the initiative works best with well-motivated, resourceful clients, or when tasks involve situations that are familiar to the client but may be difficult for the practitioner to grasp—for example, it may be difficult for the practitioner to think of appropriate tasks involving technical or even social aspects of the client's work situation. A common practice is for social workers to elicit task possibilities that both the practitioner and the client modify or add to. This is perhaps the ideal mode of task development since it involves the clients as collaborators in problem solving, yet enables the practitioners to make use of their own expert knowledge.

Sometimes, however, the client can generate only few ideas about possible tasks. In other situations, the practitioner knows about proven task strategies that are well fitted to the client's problem and circumstances. In still others, the practitioner may see an opportunity for critical action that may not be obvious to the client. In all these cases the practitioner becomes the primary source of task possibilities. Even if the practitioner offers a task as a suggestion, he or she makes sure to give its rationale and to elicit the client's reaction. Informed feedback from the client is a critical part of the development of practitioner-generated tasks. This does not prevent practitioners from presenting tasks in an authoritative manner when they are reasonably sure that these tasks are the best options for their clients, or when their clients need direction in order to make headway on agreed problems. Even in such situations, however, it is important that the social worker determines the client's willingness and perceived ability to do the task and, when possible, involves the client actively in planning the details of implementation.

Some mention should be made of plans for the initial task, which may be set up during the first interview. In fact, tasks set up during the first interview can often capitalize on whatever initial determination the clients might have to do something about their problems. At the same time, it is important that the initial task be successful as a means of building the client's sense of self-efficacy. At least, the first task should not end in a demoralizing failure. The initial task should be one that can make a dent in the problem and carries a low risk of precipitating a setback. Thus, clients might be asked to do something about the problem they have not been able to do. The step can be a small one, but it should allow them to take additional steps if they are able to. The task provides the opportunity for a larger gain; at the same time, it does not expose the client to a new kind of failure. For example, a husband and wife locked in a pattern of hostile avoidance might be asked to do one small thing during the week that the other would see as a "nice surprise."

Establishing Motivation

An essential resource for task accomplishment is an adequate degree of motivation. In the task-centered theory of motivation, a person's task behavior occurs in response to those unsatisfied wants that make up the problem (chapter 2). In order to undertake a task, the person must want something he or she does not have, in other words, he or she must have an incentive. The task by itself may not satisfy the want, but the person must see it as a step in that direction. That is, the client must be able to perceive how carrying out the task will obtain what he or she wants—the rationale for his or her task work. Such incentives and rationales provide the initial motivation for task performance.

If the task has a successful outcome and movement toward a desired goal occurs, the task actions are validated, or, to use the behavioral term, they are reinforced. The task participants mentally register their success. This feedback alters incentives and hence motivation for future actions. A similar action may be tried or the next logical (or a more difficult) step may be attempted.

Although goal attainment makes similar actions more likely in the future, failure may also be motivating. We learn from our mistakes and are willing to try again with greater effort, more skill, a new approach, and so on.

A key ingredient in one's willingness to do a task initially, or to persist, is one's belief that success is eventually possible. Bandura (1978, 1982, 1986) has developed this notion into a theory of "self-perceived efficacy." According to Bandura (1978:194), "efficacy expectations determine how much effort people will expend, and how long they will persist in the face of obstacles and aversive experiences. The stronger the perceived self-efficacy, the more active the efforts."

According to Bandura (1982), efficacy expectations depend on four sources of information: *enactive attainments*, or feedback from doing tasks oneself; *vicarious experience*, e.g., observing the performance of others; *verbal persuasion*, e.g., being given reasons why one can do a task; and *physiological status*, or one's sense of physical readiness to undertake a task. Research conducted by Bandura and his colleagues has suggested that enactive attainments exert the strongest influence on self-efficacy (Bandura 1986). Especially important as a motivator is the adoption of attainable subgoals. The attainment of subgoals strengthens self-efficacy and stimulates interest. Larger goals, whose attainment is more remote, have much less influence on self-efficacy and motivation.

The foregoing formulations have a number of practical implications. First, the practitioner should make sure that projected tasks will enable clients to obtain what they want. Further, clients should understand how the task at hand can help them achieve their goals. In this process, practitioners need to relate to the client's priorities and not to their own goals. This distinction can become easily blurred as practitioners nudge clients in the direction of working on problems the practitioners think are the most important. Cooperative clients may go along with this reprioritizing of their problem, but their motivation may be the weakest in just those areas where the practitioner is pressing the hardest.

In setting up tasks, exploration of the client's self-efficacy expectations may be indicated. How confident does the client feel about his or her ability to do the task? Attempts to heighten self-efficacy may include pointing out the client's abilities, reminding him or her of past successes in similar circumstances, use of role-played rehearsals, and refocusing the task on a more easily attainable subgoal.

Securing Agreement

The practitioner should always obtain the client's explicit agreement to undertake the task. Sometimes this step is overlooked in the give-and-take of discussion about the task, or the practitioner may propose a task and assume that it is accepted by the client if he or she does not express opinions to the contrary. Silence may not necessarily mean assent; it may indicate that clients have not heard or understood. Besides providing some assurance that the client is on board, an explicit agreement provides closure to a contract, in a sense committing the client to attempt the task.

Planning Details of Implementation

Most tasks require some detailed planning. Take a task seemingly as straightforward as "Bob will contact AAA Security to inquire about employment as a night watchman." Planning questions might include when and how Bob will make the inquiry. What information should he get? If the company is hiring, should he complete an application form? Planning not only helps prepare clients for the task, but it also teaches them how to plan, an important skill that many clients have not acquired. Finally, by giving attention to the particulars, task planning reinforces the importance of the task, increasing the likelihood that the client will remember it and attempt to do it.

In work with individual clients, the planning process is moved along largely by the practitioner's questions, which stimulate the clients to think about how the task is to be done. The questions may be supplemented by practical suggestions, usually phrased in tentative terms. In conjoint interviewing, the same approach can be used with clients who can do their own planning in face-to-face session tasks with the practitioner in the role of coach and facilitator.

In helping clients with task planning, a constant question is "How detailed should the plan be?" A good deal depends on the style and resourcefulness of the client and on the stage of treatment. Some clients react to planning as a constraint on their freedom of action and may be unable to relate to a plan that is too detailed. Others are sufficiently resourceful to do their own planning, especially in familiar areas.

In general, clients take on more of the planning responsibility as treatment progresses and as increasing emphasis is placed on strengthening their self-reliance. Despite these variations, certain guidelines can be offered. In general, planning should go far enough so that clients can get a clear sense of how the task can be done while allowing them sufficient flexibility to make modifications or to substitute a task that may be even more appropriate or effective. Unless readily apparent, the main "action verbs" of the task should be articulated. For example, if the task calls for clients to "back off" if they start to quarrel, some discussion of what "backing off" means, and how it can be done, would be indicated. Or if the task calls for a mother to show approval if her daughter cleans her room, ways of showing approval and what is meant by cleaning the room should be discussed.

Identifying and Resolving Obstacles

Dealing with obstacles to task attainment is a central component of the present model. It may occur at two points in task planning and implementation: either when the task is initially planned, or after a less than completely successful attempt at task implementation. In this section I shall review general procedures for dealing with obstacles at both points. (Additional techniques may be found in Hepworth 1979). In the next chapter, a range of common obstacles as well as strategies for their solution are presented.

Potential Obstacles

In the initial planning phase an effort is made to anticipate potential obstacles that may interfere with task attainment. Many tasks call for the exploration of "what if" questions, those dealing with important contingencies that may complicate task performance. For example, if a task calls for Janet to bring her boyfriend home so her parents can meet him, an obvious contingency is "What if he doesn't want to come?" Through exploration of contingencies, practitioners and clients can identify potential obstacles and perhaps develop ways of resolving them.

In addition to exploring contingencies as a means of identifying obstacles, practitioners can simply ask clients to indicate what they think might go wrong with their tasks. This antisabotage procedure, to use Birchler and Spinks' (1981) expression, can sometimes uncover obstacles that would otherwise go undetected since clients may be aware of potential pitfalls that may not be revealed in exploring contingencies.

The proposed task often relates to the client's previous efforts to solve the problem. Consideration of these efforts and why they may have fallen short can provide another means of identifying potential obstacles. For example, a task under consideration for Mrs. S. was to reward her son with praise and approval for coming directly home from school. Previous discussion of the mother-son relationship had revealed her difficulties in expressing positive sentiments toward the boy. Her difficulty in so doing might be identified as an obstacle.

Actual Obstacles

When a task has been attempted and attainment has been less than optimal, clients are asked to talk about what blocked successful implementation. If several tasks are on the table, the practitioner may delay inquiry about obstacles until all tasks have been reviewed to see if there are common threads or to determine which obstacle to focus on. Depending on circumstances, more detailed consideration of the obstacles may be delayed until additional exploration of recent developments in the target problems has been completed. In taking up obstacles, the practitioner takes care to give credit for effort, partial accomplishment, and reinventions of the task.

Options

In the framework of the model, the practitioner and the client have four options in dealing with potential or actual obstacles. First, they can attempt to resolve the obstacle. As noted, common obstacles encountered and general strategies for their resolution are taken up in the next chapter. Second, the task can be modified in light of the obstacle. For example, Mr. G.'s task was to work out a budget as a way of gaining control over his financial problems. He was unable to make much headway because his "financial mess" was "too overwhelming." Whenever he started to work on the budget, he would become "depressed." He was able, however, to complete the scaled-down task of figuring out what he spent for recreation and making a budget for these expenditures. As in the example, tasks are frequently made easier to accommodate obstacles, and normally the intention is to increase their "bite" the next time around. However, other possibilities occur. A task may need to be made more interesting, and perhaps more challenging if the obstacle is the client's boredom with doing it. In some cases a change of time or setting is needed.

Third, a different task may be substituted, one that circumvents the obstacle but still achieves progress toward the resolution of the problem. Because of their conviction that children should not be "bribed" to do what they are supposed to do, some parents are unable to complete tasks calling for tangible rewards contingent on their children's "good" behavior. However, they may be agreeable to using praise as a reward. They may also be willing to use more benign forms of punishment, such as withholding minor privileges, when behavior is not "good" rather than more severe forms such as spanking or grounding for prolonged periods. Frequently, more than one task is addressed to the problem. If an obstacle proves too formidable for one task, another may work.

The fourth and final option is used when all else fails. It consists of appraising the feasibility of continued work on the problem itself. Following the procedures discussed previously (chapter 2), the practitioner and the client consider whether the problem as formulated still makes sense to the client. Perhaps a reformulation may be in order. If the problem still has validity but remains intractable, they may decide to shift for the time being to another problem. The intractable problem may become more workable in response to progress made on another. But not all problems are amenable to change. It makes sense to concentrate on those that are.

Simulation and Practice

Plans of any type are more likely to be implemented successfully if they can be tried out beforehand. Thus, we have dress rehearsals, pilot projects, dry runs, pretests, and so on. Many task plans can be tried out in the session through rehearsals in which role plays are used to simulate the actions making up the task. In individual interviews, the practitioner can first take the role of the client and model appropriate task behavior with the client in the role the person (teacher, employer, coworker, family member, etc.) to whom the behavior will be addressed. The client can then try the task in his or her own role while the practitioner assumes the role of the other person. While taking the role of the other, the practitioner can present the client with different contingencies—enacting others as angry, provocative, uncooperative, and so on, depending on the likely challenges the client may face in carrying out the task.

Conjoint interviews open up numerous other possibilities for role play rehearsals. The practitioner can take the role of different clients to demonstrate task behavior. The clients playing themselves can rehearse a reciprocal or shared task they will be doing together. The clients or the practitioner can also take roles of people outside the session. For example, a father can take the role of his son whose task is to deal with an antagonistic teacher without getting into trouble. The son (or the practitioner) can assume the role of the teacher who proceeds to antagonize the son (played by the father). The father can then demonstrate how the son could respond to the teacher without getting himself into trouble. The son can then try out this behavior with the father (or the practitioner) in the role of the teacher. Although such varied involvements of clients in role plays may be difficult to pull off and may sometimes backfire, there are often gains beyond preparing clients for tasks. Thus, in the example given, the father may acquire some understanding of the difficulties faced by his son. The son, in turn, may appreciate his father's efforts to be helpful.

A rehearsal not only provides practice, but it may also reveal shortcomings in the client's performance as well as contingencies that have not been previously identified. This information provides feedback for additional planning, which may result in revisions of the task.

Up to this point, we have shown how simulations can be used in task preparation. By definition, simulations are not the real thing. While their portrayals may be intense and lifelike, the participants know they are acting. However, some tasks can be practiced in the session in pretty much the way they will be done elsewhere. Such tasks most commonly occur in conjoint family work. For example, tasks to improve communication and problem-solving skills can be done in the session using real problems as content (chapter 6).

In office sessions with individual clients, there are fewer opportunities for clients to do more than simulated tasks. However, when sessions or treatment encounters occur outside the office, for example, in the client's home, school, residential setting, or other environment in which the client is having difficulty, clients can often practice tasks by actually doing them. For example, during home visits parents can practice new ways of handling the demands of very young children, older children can practice home chores, or disabled clients can practice self-care routines. In other settings, clients can attempt a range of problem-solving tasks with their practitioners present. For example, an agoraphobic can enter a crowded place and stay for a brief period (chapter 7); a retarded person can attempt to make a purchase at a store; an isolated and timid resident in a home for the aged can try to initiate a conversation with another resident during the "social hour."

In such practice efforts, practitioners assume a coaching role. They provide initial instructions, encouragement, and praise as well as corrective feedback to improve the client's performance. As in simulations, the client's performance can provide the basis for additional task planning.

Summarizing

Before the session ends, practitioners should go over the essentials of the task plan with clients. This step is particularly important when a task plan is complex, when there are several tasks, or when task performers are children. With children, and with some adults, the practitioner is well advised to have the clients present their idea of what the plan is, giving the practitioner the opportunity to correct misperceptions or to add pieces that have been omitted. Writing tasks down with a copy for the client and another for the practitioner is another useful technique, especially when tasks are complex or when several task performers are involved.

Implementing

The next step is for the clients to implement the task prior to the next session. Normally, clients carry out their tasks on their own without the practitioner's involvement. There are some exceptions to this rule, however. As noted above, practitioners may help clients practice tasks in real life situations. In addition practitioners may sometimes assist clients in one-time-only tasks. These tasks are usually those that pose considerable difficulty for clients. A common example is when clients seek service under circumstances they may find confusing or frightening (chapter 11). In such instances, the social worker may provide support or coaching or may serve as a mediator or advocate. Sometimes practitioners may give clients telephone reminders about their tasks. Because of the intrusiveness of this procedure, clients need to endorse it fully before it is used.

Task Review

Tasks are generally reviewed toward the beginning of each session, a process that may be combined with a review of the target problems (chapter 2). Task accomplishment or constructive efforts are praised. The practitioner responds to task failure with empathy for the client's unsuccessful effort, or with an appropriate inquiry if the task was not attempted. Failed tasks lead to a consideration of obstacles and related options, as previously discussed. Task review and consideration of obstacles, if any, is generally followed by the generation of possibilities for the next task.

Assessing Task Progress

The task review provides the basis for assessing task progress. These assessments provide a way of measuring the implementation of the central means of effecting change provided in the model. They enable the empirically oriented practitioner to track the processes of change through the accomplishment of tasks. As discussed in chapter 2, this tracking provides the key to evaluating the effectiveness of task-centered interventions. The assessments are recorded on Task Schedules displayed and illustrated in figure 4.1.

This form can accommodate different ratings for different task participants, such as in shared or reciprocal tasks. In "tasks as planned," the person to carry out the task is put as the subject of the sentence. As noted, the task review covers the period *since* the preceding session, which may be more or less than a week. Specific explanations of reasons for failure or a short fall in attempting the task can provide clues for the revision of the tasks. Noting how tasks were reshaped can also lead to ideas about revisions of new tasks.

FIGURE 4.1
Task Schedule (with Illustration)

Case I.D. _____

_____ When planned (if ET) or tried (if ST). Sess. # _____ Date _____

Related Problem _____1_____

Client's initial commitment to task. (Use additional lines if different ratings for different clients and list clients on left.

       Low _____ Moderate __X__ High _____

       Low _____ Moderate _____ High _____

       Low _____ Moderate _____ High _____

Task as planned (use reverse to indicate revisions in task)

Jon will use an alarm to wake up each school morning in time to catch the school bus.

When task reviewed:

session #	3	4	5	6	7	8						
Progress since	1	2	4	no	2	4						
prev. sess. #												
Use additional												
lines if differ-												
ent rating for												
different												
clients and list												
clients on left												

Scale

    (1) minimally or not achieved;
    (2) partially achieved;
    (3) substantially achieved;
    (4) completely achieved;
(NO) no opportunity to carry out task.

Details of implementation (identified in review)—Include reasons for failure to do task if rating of 1. If ratings of 2 or 3, describe which aspects of the task were completed and which not. Note instances of task substitution or reshaping.

Session #3   Jon used alarm to wake up but then turned it off and went back to sleep. Mom had to wake him up.

Session #4   Jon got up on his own but dawdled and almost missed bus.

Session #6   Spring vacation

Session #7   Slept through alarm Weds. & Thurs.; he asked younger brother to wake him up if it happened on Friday.

Effectiveness

The core, or "middle-phase," methods of the model just presented are designed to alleviate problems in living. How well do they accomplish this objective? The key evidence bearing on this question is found in three group experiments and a number of single subject designs. In these studies, control groups or equivalent devices were used to rule out the effects of nontreatment factors, such as spontaneous improvement. The first of these group experiments was conducted primarily in two settings : a public school system and a psychiatric clinic, both located in an inner-city area on the south side of Chicago. Eighty-seven families, predominantly black and low-income, were seen by social work student practitioners who were trained and supervised in the use of the model (Reid 1978).

In accordance with the procedures set forth in the model (chapter 2), problems were specified with relevant family members who became the actual clients of the project. Problems relating to school adjustment of children and to interpersonal difficulties of adults were the most common. When the problem specification phase was completed, clients were randomly divided into two comparable groups. One group (the experimental group) received three weeks of intensive task-centered treatment, consisting of six interviews per case as well as related environmental work. The other group (the control group) was given three weeks of "placebo" treatment in which there was client-practitioner contact but no use of task-centered or other forms of systematic intervention. The amount of problem alleviation that occurred in each case was rated by "blind" judges who heard tape-recorded problem reviews that had been conducted with the clients and others, such as teachers who were familiar with the clients' progress. These judges did not know which cases had received the experimental treatment.

The control group then received the three-week, task-centered intervention package that had previously been used to treat the clients in the experimental group. A second comparison was then made: the amount of problem alleviation shown by the clients in the control group during the period of placebo treatment was compared with the amount of problem alleviation they experienced once they received task-centered treatment. Follow-up interviews were conducted with clients in both groups one to three months after termination of treatment.

Findings revealed that the amount of problem alleviation experienced by clients in the experimental group during the task-centered intervention was significantly greater than the amount experienced by clients in the control group while they were receiving the placebo treatment. Moreover, problem alleviation for clients in the control group showed a significant acceleration when they received task-centered service. Data obtained in follow-up interviews suggested that gains achieved by clients in both groups had been maintained following the termination of service. There was no evidence that these gains had been offset by the emergence of problems in other areas. An unexpected finding was that task-centered intervention seemed to be somewhat more effective with adults than with children.

The cases receiving task-centered treatment had outcomes that were statistically better than those in the control group, but what does this mean in terms of actual impact on the target problems? Were the findings significant clinically as well as statistically (Jayaratne 1990)? If the upper end of the scale used by the judges to rate problem change (problem considerably alleviated to no longer present) is used to define clinical significance, we find that in 42 percent of the cases receiving task-centered treatment, change in the main target problem met this criterion. However, it was met by only 26 percent of the cases receiving placebo treatment. The spread was even greater for the clients' overall problem situations—42 percent for the experimental and 19 percent of the control cases were rated as having achieved problem alleviation that was considerable or higher. When the placebo cases then received task-centered treatment, 54 percent of them experienced an acceleration of gains in their overall problem situations; only in 10 percent of the cases did the rate of progress slow. The pattern was similar for the main problem.

It seems reasonable to conclude from these various comparisons that the task-centered intervention achieved clinical as well as statistical significance. The impact was appreciable, especially considering that the amount of intervention was at the lower range of what the model provides and that the control condition quite likely provided some therapeutic ingredients in the form of problem specification and opportunity for client ventilation. On the other hand, the type of control design used provided a "relatively pure" test of the middle-phase methods since another important part of the model, problem exploration and formulation, was the same for both groups.

Because the impact of the model appeared to be less for children than for adults, an effort was made to improve the effectiveness of task-centered methods with children. The revised model was tested in a school setting with twenty-one children who were referred for academic and behavior problems and were treated by student practitioners (Reid et al. 1980). In each case, two problems were identified and formulated. The problems were then randomly assigned to treatment and control groups of three weeks duration. At the end of this period, the focus of intervention was shifted from the treated to the untreated problem. Ratings of change in the problems during treated and untreated periods were made by judges following the procedures used in the first experiment. Analysis indicated that problems showed the greatest gain during the periods when they were actively treated, thus providing clear evidence of the effectiveness of the model in direct treatment of children. Best results were obtained for academic problems and problems regarded as important by the children. The clinical significance of the gains was similar to the first experiment. For example, 48 percent of the problems receiving the experimental treatment were found to be considerably alleviated or no longer present at the end of the initial three-week period; only a quarter of the control problems showed this much change. As in the first experiment, the contribution of problem exploration and formulation was held constant in both the experimental and the control groups.

The most extensive controlled study of the model was a suicide prevention experiment conducted in England (Gibbons et al. 1978). Four hundred patients who had taken drug overdoses in apparent suicide attempts were randomly allocated to experimental (task-centered) and control (routine service) groups. Difficulties in continuing personal relationships, usually problems with a spouse, were reported in two-thirds of the cases. Independent research interviews were conducted with the patients four and eighteen months after the termination of service. Measures of change in personal relationships (a major target of intervention) favored the experimental group at both follow-ups, with statistically significant differences obtained at the second follow-up. At the second follow up, it was found that 36 percent of the experimental group, but only 26 percent of the control group, showed improvement in personal relationships. The difference suggests a moderate impact of treatment. There were no differences between experimental and control cases in respect to recurrence of suicide attempts, which happened infrequently in both groups. The study added to the empirical base of the model in several important ways. It provided a large sample, a different population, a long-term follow-up, and a test of the approach conducted by investigators other than the originators.

Finally, a series of controlled single subject designs have provided additional evidence that has bearing particularly on the efficacy of the middle-phase methods. In these studies, multiple baseline designs across a range of problems or clients (Bloom and Fisher 1982) were used to rule out the influence of nontreatment factors. In accordance with the principles of this design, the TPIS was introduced in a staggered fashion to treat different problems or clients *after* problems had been specified. Change in problems was then measured after the middle-phase methods were introduced. If positive problem change was most likely to occur after these methods were introduced, results were interpreted as evidence of effectiveness. All single subject tests that employed this design supported the efficacy of the task-centered methods. These tests involved application of the approach in treating the communication problems of a marital pair (Tolson 1977), in helping parents with children in placement (Rzepnicki 1985), in enabling a mother to improve her communication with her young child (Wodarski, Saffir, and Frazier 1983), and in avoiding self-destructive behavior in elderly ill clients (Thibault 1984).

The review of these studies has been cast in the language of outcome research replete with such terms as "effectiveness" and "clinical significance." In a collaborative intervention model, one also wants to make sure that the client's viewpoint is reflected. Actually, most outcome measures in evaluations of task-centered practice, including the measures used in the studies reviewed, are based on the clients' own accounts of change. Further, clients are asked to give their own opinions about change and the helpfulness of service on post-service "consumer" questionnaires. The overwhelming majority of clients in the numerous studies in which these questionnaires have been used report positive changes in the main problem for which they sought help as well as improvement in their situations in general. In addition, between 75 and 90 percent of clients report a high degree of benefit from service. (Ewalt 1977; Epstein 1977; Goldberg and Robinson 1977; Taylor 1977; Reid 1977, 1978, 1987b).

These studies suggest that the core methods of the model, stressing task planning and implementation, do have a positive effect on the clients' problems, an effect large enough to make a meaningful difference in the lives of many of them. Yet, many questions remain unanswered. What is the durability of these effects? How might they compare with results of other treatment models? Would similar effects be found with client populations and problems other than those evaluated? While evidence bearing on some of these questions will be introduced in subsequent chapters, much more research obviously needs to be done.

lationship-building activity. He wants to use the occasion to teach his son how to use tools; the boy is interested only in being with his dad and getting the treehouse built. He balks at being put in the role of a carpenter's apprentice, and the activity ends in conflict. In setting up such tasks, practitioners need to be alert to the possibility that the participants may have different agendas that may put them at cross purposes even though they may agree on the content of the tasks. Exploring what each participant hopes to gain from the task may be a useful step when there is reason to suppose that motives differ.

Low Motivation

Inadequate motivation to do the task satisfactorily is one of the most common obstacles encountered in task-centered practice. It becomes apparent when tasks are forgotten, put off, or given only half-hearted effort. In theory, this obstacle should arise less frequently than it does since tasks are presumably developed only from problems the client wishes to do something about. In practice, the process is often not so straightforward. The clients' motivation may fall prey to lowered self-efficacy, especially if previous tasks have failed, or the client's interest may abate if the problem appears to have changed for the better even though the change may be ephemeral.

Moreover, clients may verbally agree to problems they effectively deny. As noted in chapter 2, many, if not most, clients do not seek the social worker's help on their own initiative. They find their way to social workers' doors (or social workers find their way to their doors) through referrals from schools, physicians, courts, social agencies, and so on or because of their membership in families. Some of these clients do have problems they would like professional help with, but many do not. Under pressure from referring agencies, family members, and perhaps practitioners, these clients may agree to problems they really do not think they own. Still other clients, including those who are mandated to accept social work treatment, may be unwilling to acknowledge problems. Although resourceful practitioners may secure the client's agreement to work on specified problems, the client may still not be convinced that he or she really has a problem.

If poor motivation appears to result from task failure and lowered self-efficacy, tasks should be scaled back until an attainable subgoal is found. For example, Jon may not be able to achieve his task of passing a math quiz, but he may be able to increase his number of correct answers. If motivation slackens because of apparent temporary improvement, the practitioner can stress the need to continue task work as a means of keeping the problem from returning. When low motivation is caused by reactance (chapter 2), the practitioner can help the client express reservations about working on the problem. The option of not doing the tasks and its possible consequences should be discussed openly. It is important to relate to the client's point of view and to avoid trying to persuade the client of the perils of inaction.

It may be necessary for the practitioner and the client to reexamine the validity of the problem itself. Is the problem one the client really wishes to work on? Is it the client's problem or someone else's? Does it need to be discussed again or redefined? Is some other issue of greater interest? Through questions of this kind, practitioners can help clients focus on problems they really want to do something about—problems where their real motivation lies.

Motivation may also be adversely affected by dysfunctional beliefs, poor skills, and environmental stressors. These factors will be considered in the following sections.

Cognitive-Emotional Obstacles

In order to implement a task successfully, the client's cognitive functioning must be adequate to translate an abstract task plan into the actions necessary to carry it out. That is, the clients must possess adequate intelligence, judgment, and foresight; their beliefs about themselves and reality must be able to guide problem-solving action successfully and not obstruct it. In this section, we focus on obstacles to task implementation that relate to the clients' beliefs. Such obstacles, in our view, command center stage not only because they are critical to task performance but also because they are often more amenable to change than other cognitive factors.

Feelings as Obstacles

Many obstacles appear to occur at an emotional level. Clients may not be able to carry out tasks they agreed to because of anxiety, fear of loss, feelings of being overwhelmed, and so on. In the task-centered approach, it is assumed that such reactions are controlled by beliefs in accordance with cognitive theories of emotions (Barlow 1988). That is, it is assumed that feelings can be most effectively changed by identifying and modifying controlling beliefs. For example, Mrs. Hall, whose sight is failing, is unable to make an appointment with an ophthalmologist because of her dread of "going to an eye doctor." It is important to help her identify the beliefs underlying the anxiety. Perhaps Mrs. Hall has the belief that the doctor will find that she has an incurable disease leading to blindness, or that he will become angry with her for not taking medication he prescribed at an earlier visit. From a task-centered perspective, helping her locate and alter such beliefs provides the key to enabling her to control her anxiety and to take constructive action. However, this key will work only if she is allowed to express her fears to a caring and empathic practitioner. To put it another way, eliciting feelings and responding empathically to them sets the stage for helping the client do the necessary cognitive restructuring. This is a necessary, but usually not sufficient, condition for change.

Changing Beliefs

When a distorted belief appears to form an obstacle to progress on the problem or task, it is first necessary to help the client identify it in a way the client finds understandable and acceptable. The practitioner attempts to pursue this objective collaboratively with the client through questions and tentative comments. As Mahoney (1974:56) has observed, "When individuals are allowed to examine and evaluate the rationality or coherence of their own beliefs, resulting cognitive changes are often more effective and enduring than when a didactic strategy is employed."

For example, a mother tends to exaggerate her son's lack of obedience: "He never does anything he is told." The practitioner may suggest it would be good to get a more detailed picture of his disobedience and that they examine together how he responds to different things he is asked to do. Through this exploration the mother may gain a more realistic perception of her son. Thus, the process of identifying distortions may be sufficient to effect change.

When identification itself is not sufficient, the practitioner can direct the inquiry to areas likely to produce disconfirming evidence, or he or she may point out instances of such evidence revealed earlier. The practitioner may suggest tentative modifications of beliefs if clients have difficulty in making their own corrections.

The general principle is to help the clients obtain fresh input from their own reflections, from the practitioner, or from the environment. The goal is not to alter their belief systems radically, but rather to effect sufficient modification to enable them to proceed with their tasks.

External tasks provide a powerful means of modifying beliefs. Assessment tasks can be used by the clients to gather evidence on particular beliefs. Is Kevin always the one to start fights with his siblings, as his mother believes? Keeping a simple record of fights and how they got started might prove revealing. Additional examples are provided in table 7.1, chapter 7. Tasks can be directed at putting beliefs to experimental tests (Beck 1976) as in the example presented in the previous chapter of the wife who introduced her work into the conversation to see if, in fact, her husband would change the subject. In this kind of testing, it is assumed that the client's belief may be distorted and that the experimental task will produce disconfirming evidence. In some cases, the clients' belief may be substantially valid; if so, then tasks can be used to alter the reality on which the belief is based.

Types of Beliefs as Obstacles

Table 5.1 presents and illustrates a selection of types of beliefs that constitute common obstacles to task implementation. The table draws on several theoretical frames including attribution, cognitive, and psychodynamic theories. Specifically, the subcategories under beliefs about causes (attributions) were drawn from the work of Doherty (1981a and 1981b). The types of beliefs presented are neither exhaustive nor mutually exclusive. For example, beliefs from the past are contained in all other categories. The table is intended only to give a sense of the variety of beliefs that may interfere with task attainment. I shall comment on these beliefs in table 5.1 in greater detail. The commentary will provide some elaboration of these beliefs as well as suggestions for their modification.

As suggested, beliefs about one's world and self (table 5.1) may be open to modification through disconfirming evidence elicited in the interview or through disconfirming tasks done by the client in his or her life situation. With the practitioner's help, Mrs. J. in the example may be able to recall instances when her husband did not behave as she thought he would when liquor was served. A parallel task for the husband to control his drinking at the occasion would increase the chance of a favorable outcome.

The client's participation in a new social situation may also lead to

TABLE 5.1
Clients Beliefs as Sources of Obstacles

Type	Examples of Beliefs as Obstacles
A. *Beliefs about environment/ other people.*	Mrs. J. believes her husband will start drinking again if they attend any function where liquor is served; hence she won't agree to shared tasks of going to social events that Mr. J. wants to attend.
B. *Self-concept*	Mr. Z., who prides himself on being macho, has difficulty with a task asking for expression of empathic understanding of his wife's feelings.
C. *Self-efficacy expectations* Bandura (1986)	Jerry has trouble sticking to his math homework because he believes he is bound to fail the course.
D. *Attributions: beliefs about causation and responsibility* (Doherty 1981a, 1981b; Brehm and Smith 1986)	
1. Perceived responsibility for problem	Mrs. H. and her daughter are unable to carry out compromises to reduce their conflict because they both regard each other as responsible for the problem.
2. Perceived self-control	Because Mrs. G. sees herself as having little choice about what happens to her in the Golden Days Care Center, she finds it hard to undertake tasks to express her needs to the staff.
3. Perceived intent of actor	Mrs. N. reacts punitively rather than supportively to her son's difficulty with homework because she sees his school failure as an act of rebellion.
4. Perceived persistance of cause	Ms. H. believes that her boyfriend's excessive jealously about her will never change because it's a part of his personality.
E. *Beliefs with early origins*	Mr. W.'s belief that men in authority dislike him seems related to his belief as a child that his father rejected him.

TABLE 5.1 (*Continued*)

Type	Examples of Beliefs as Obstacles
F. *Automatic thoughts:* unarticulated beliefs that guide moment-to-moment behavior (Beck, 1976)	When her son caused her trouble, Mrs. N. often experienced half-conscious thoughts that he was like her divorced husband; when this happened her irritation increased.
G. *Beliefs based on faulty information processing** (Beck et al., 1979)	Mr. A., ill and elderly, believed his daughter was too involved with her own children to care for him properly. He saw any attention she paid to her children in this light (3). He also dwelt on her having left the house once without telling him (2,4), concluding that she was paying him back for being a burden (1,5). He complained she never responded to his requests promptly (6). Interviews with both and home observation suggested that the daughter was reasonable, attentive, and efficient in providing care.
1. *Jumping to conclusions* ("arbitrary inference") Drawing hasty conclusions from inadequate evidence	
2. *Fixing on one thing* ("selective abstraction") Focusing too much on particular details rather than on the larger picture	
3. *Seeing it everywhere* ("overgeneralization") Applying an idea to situations where it does not belong	
4. *Blowing things out of proportion and downplaying* ("magnification and minimization") Over- or underestimating the importance of an event	
5. *Taking things personally* ("personalization") Mistakenly interpreting a thing as reflecting on oneself	
6. *All or none thinking* ("absolutistic dichotomous, thinking") Putting things at one extreme or the other	

* Types of faulty information in processing are described in everyday language to facilitate communication with client, Beck et al.'s terms (1979:14) are in quotes.

a change in beliefs. In their discussion of ways of modifying the client's belief systems, Levine and Lightburn (1989) report the case of a client who had suffered a coronary and was unable to undertake needed exercises because of his belief that physical exertion would precipitate another heart attack. He was referred to a support group whose members were actively engaged in exercise on the assumption that participation in that social situation would change his belief. This case also illustrates how a traditional social work method—linking clients to resources—can be used strategically to help the client alter beliefs that constitute obstacles to task attainment.

When beliefs are too formidable to alter through such means, the practitioner may need to work with tasks that are consonant with those beliefs. Yet, with some ingenuity tasks can still be designed that will move matters forward. While Mr. Z., the macho husband in the example, may not be able to be very empathic with his wife, he may still be able to listen to her and respond "kindly" ("real" men can do at least that!).

Attributions (D) are of particular importance since the client's views of who or what is responsible for behavior and events are frequently at the heart of beliefs that form obstacles. For example, clients may have markedly different views of the causes of their problems than practitioners (C. 1). While practitioners may think in terms of interactional and "blame-free" formulations, clients are more likely to attribute causation to other persons, to bad luck, forces beyond their control, or (sometimes excessively) to their own defects. Practitioners need to elicit such attributions, to question them if they pose obstacles, and to suggest alternatives.

A frequent occasion for intervention arises when obstacles take the form of perceived low self-control, for example, when the client says, in effect, "I cannot control anything that happens to me." (D.) The principle of self-determination suggests that the maximization of the client's choice should not only be a perception but a reality. Moreover, there is research suggesting that the client's choice and participation generally result in better outcomes. Patient participation in decisions about care, discharge, and relocation have been found to be associated positively with such outcomes as patient satisfaction, levels of activity, and survival rates (Abramson 1988, 1990; see also chapter 10). There is also evidence that the clients' self-direction results in the persistence of learned behaviors after treatment—as if self-direction helped the clients integrate the behaviors into their own repertoires (Brehm and Smith 1986). However, emphasis on client control encounters risks if things turn out badly; the client is more likely to feel responsible for the poor outcome, and lowered self-esteem or depression may be possible concomitants (Brehm and Smith 1986). However, preparation of the client for negative outcomes may help prevent untoward distress should they occur. For example, the client can be helped to explore negative outcomes and to develop plans for coping with them—a process that Janis and Mann (1977) have described as "emotional inoculation."

Client tasks can provide an important means of increasing the clients' sense of self-control. Mrs. G. (table 5.1) may have a point when she says she has little choice about what happens to her at the Care Center. Staff do see her as a passive person and make choices for her. Helping Mrs. G. to develop, articulate, and obtain a simple request may give her grounds for believing that she may have some choice after all. This small heightening of her sense of perceived self-control (and efficacy expectations) may encourage her to become more assertive.

How one perceives the intention of another and the persistence of whatever caused his or her behavior becomes of particular significance in work with clients who interact with one another (D. 3). The practitioner is often confronted with the view that the intentions of another are malevolent ("She did it to hurt me.") and that causes of the behavior are persistent ("He has always been that way"). In dealing with such perceptions, the practitioner may suggest a reframing that may enable the client to construe the other's behavior in more positive terms. ("Perhaps she didn't realize it would hurt you. Maybe she thought her criticism would be helpful." "Do you think he may have reacted that way because of his problems at work?") As these examples suggest, the attempt is made to help clients think in terms of more benevolent intent and more transient causation.

When beliefs are residuals from earlier experience, their origins can be explored (E). In this process the client is helped to separate the past from the present. For example, Ms. Rogers, an incest survivor, may see men as sexually exploitative. During her childhood, that belief may have been quite functional, but now it is an impediment to developing heterosexual relationships.

Although these old beliefs may not fit new realities, they become "self-sustaining," as Segraves (1982) has pointed out. They persist in part because people tend to see what they already believe and may act on these beliefs in ways to call forth confirmatory reactions from others. Because he felt rejected by his father, Mr. W. (E) believes that men in authority dislike him. Given this belief, he may interpret incorrectly the behavior of such men as a sign of antipathy toward him. He may then respond with hostility, which may invite counterhostility in return. Now being treated with some genuine dislike by men in authority, he has received confirmation of his belief.

In conjoint interviews session tasks can be used in which clients can clarify and correct distorted beliefs about each other through face-to-face dialog. For example, Marcy, sixteen, had long resented her mother, Helen, for having left her father for Ted, her current stepfather, when Marcy was ten. Marcy blamed Helen not only for the breakup, but also for having deceived her father by having an affair with Ted. Mother and daughter discussed these events for the first time in an emotional session task structured by the social worker. Helen did not deny that she had taken the initiative to end the marriage nor did she deny the affair, but she calmly described her own struggles with Marcy's father, a problem drinker given to violent outbursts. Marcy had not heard this before, at least not in the way it was now presented. The task was a beginning step toward a change in Marcy's image of her mother—from seeing her as having betrayed her father to having some reasons for ending the marriage. The change seemed part of a decrease in the obstacles to an improved relationship between Marcy and Helen.

Automatic thoughts (F) are not necessarily dysfunctional. However, when they consist of beliefs that impede task performance, they become insidious obstacles since they occur with little awareness and hence with little chance for self-correction.

The presence of automatic thoughts can be elicited during the interview by asking the clients to focus on what goes on in their minds when certain events occur. Once their automatic thoughts have been identified, they can be treated like any other dysfunctional belief. Often simply making such thoughts explicit is enough to set change processes in motion.

Faulty information processing (G) is an inevitable part of human cognition but one that is often difficult to identify. Much of it occurs in the form of automatic thoughts with little awareness of the process. Also, it is often difficult to ascertain what is "faulty" and what is "correct" information processing since people usually have some basis for seeing things the way they do. Ultimately, what is "faulty" is best decided by the client, perhaps in response to the practitioner's questions and comments.

Skill

The clients' *skill* in performing a task becomes an issue if the task requires performance abilities that they do not possess. A retarded man may be unable to go to a sheltered workshop on his own because he lacks the skills necessary to take public transportation. In an assessment of skills, one needs to specify the actions required to complete a given task, then to determine if the client has the ability to perform these actions, and if not, to find out what is needed to help the client acquire the ability. Most skills of interest in social work are social in nature, and most clients already have these skills to some extent. However, careful delineation of skills provides clients with useful descriptions and sequences of actions that may well be more effective than their existing modes of response. Because they are likely to be familiar with the behavior required, most clients can achieve an intellectual grasp of these skills rather quickly and may be able to reproduce them quite well under the practitioner's guidance. Applying them in actual life situations is another matter. Often the skill requirements cannot be attained in the face of established response patterns and emotional needs. Table 5.2 presents a selection of social skills commonly used in work with individual clients. Skills more likely to be applied in work with families are taken up in chapter 6.

When deficits in social skills are viewed as obstacles to task performance, the strategy of choice is some form of social skills training. Such training fits well into the process of task planning and implementation presented in the previous chapter. The social skill to be learned is defined as the task. Given their expert knowledge of social skills, practitioners generally take more responsibility for shaping this task than is usually the case with other tasks. However, the process remains collaborative. Relating to the client's goals is perhaps the best way to establish motivation. Clients must see the proposed skill as helping them obtain what they want rather than as a therapeutic exercise.

The practitioner and the client explore together the situations in which a lack of skill poses obstacles for the client, and they determine how the client actually responds. The client's ideas about his or her goals in such situations are obtained and used as the basis for developing the skills to be learned. The client's ideas about how these goals can be met are elicited and incorporated into the task plan. As part of the task planning process, the client needs to have a cognitive grasp of what the skill entails, develop positive self-efficacy expectations, and address specific beliefs that may impede performance. For example, Mr. Renn believes that others will react with hostility if he becomes assertive. Ms. Borden believes that the job interviewer will react to her negatively because she is overweight. Once there is agreement on the skill (task) to be implemented, motivation is established, and obstacles are considered, then different forms of simulation become the focus of the session. In the initial role plays, the practitioner demonstrates the skill and the client acts as the "other."

Next the client, playing himself or herself, practices the skill, and the practitioner takes the role of the "other." The practitioner praises constructive aspects of the client's performance and provides corrective feedback. Role plays involving practitioner demonstrations or client rehearsals are repeated until both are satisfied with the client's performance. Details of implementation of the skill are planned as necessary. The actual implementation by the client is gone over in the task review in the next session.

The review may suggest ways of performing the skill more successfully; if so, the next task is to incorporate these modifications. Successful accomplishment of the skill may lead to a task calling for a more demanding level of the skill. When simple-to-difficult hierarchies are used, the ordering is tailored to the client's preexisting competence. The practitioner does not assume that clients are alike in what they will find easy or hard.

For some problems, skill training may be the dominant mode of intervention. For others, it may be used to work through a specific obstacle in a more broadly based strategy. Frequently, training is confined to interactions with one other person or to a particular social situation. For example, in work with wives of husbands with drinking problems (chapter 8), the wife may be helped to request that the husband come home after work rather than go to a bar or that he control his drinking at home. In addition, the wife may be taught how to enforce consequences if her husband continues to drink. Children in school settings may be taught how to respond to provocative or teasing behavior by peers in the classroom.

Communication skills, which may be regarded as a type of social

TABLE 5.2
*Components of Selected Social Skills**

Job Seeking	Problem Solving
○ Locating information about job openings	○ (Essentially clients apply the steps in the task-centered model (chapter 1) to everyday problems
○ Making initial contact	○ Problem identification
○ Completing job application forms	○ Generating alternative solutions and evaluating consequences
○ Job interviewing	○ Selecting the best solution
○ Dressing appropriately	○ Implementing the solution
○ Making positive statements about one's qualifications	
○ Answering interviewer's questions directly and concisely	
○ Asking questions related to job	
○ Showing interest in job	

TABLE 5.2 (*Continued*)

Assertiveness	Conversational	Heterosocial
○ Refusing requests	○ Asking and answering conversational questions	(Incorporates conversational skills)
○ Discriminating between reasonable and unreasonable requests	○ Making self-disclosing comments	○ Discriminating between "encouraging" and "discouraging" responses from others
○ Refusing firmly but politely	○ Making reinforcing or acknowledging comments	○ Use of informal invitations (e.g., having coffee, taking a walk)
○ Asserting positive feelings	○ Using appropriate conversational content—finding areas of common interest	○ Asking for date
○ Asserting requests	○ Conveying interest in other person's contributions	○ Handling refusals
	○ Displaying warmth	○ Arranging for date (e.g., where to go, who pays)
	○ Maintaining eye contact	

* The table uses several sources but principally Christoff and Kelley (1985).

skill, are taken up in the next chapter. Skills in problem solving (table 5.2) in social contexts are basically taught in any application of the task-centered model, which essentially follows a problem-solving format. Skill training aspects can be accentuated by making the steps of the model explicit before, during, and after its use and by having the client apply the format as a home task. The application of social skills training with the mentally ill, a population for which this kind of intervention may be particularly suitable, is taken up in chapter 9. General references in social skill training include Hollin and Trower (1986) and L'Abate and Milan (1985).

Uncontrolled Anger and Aggression

Obstacles as well as target problems may be related to the client's inability to control anger and its consequences. Inadequate control of anger is central to a wide range of difficulties addressed by social workers, including spouse battering, child abuse, and adjustment of children and adults in residential settings. Task-centered procedures for helping individuals to control anger and aggression have drawn on stress inoculation models (Novaco 1975, 1979; Meichenbaum 1985) as well as on training in social skills and problem solving (Bornstein, Bellack, and Hersen 1980; Small and Schinke 1983). These approaches, like those presented previously, fit into the basic framework of task planning and implementation of the model.

In developing tasks for anger control, it is useful to examine recent episodes of uncontrolled anger. On the basis of this examination, the client is helped to track processes leading to anger. What situations or behaviors provoke it? What cues does the client have that the anger may be getting out of control? In this process, misattributions can be identified (table 5.1). Thus, the client's anger may be triggered by the belief that another's actions are the result of malevolence or of not caring even though other explanations may make as much, if not more, sense. Other dysfunctional aspects of beliefs need to be considered. The client's anger may relate to past beliefs that are inappropriately applied to present situations ("When he does that—it's like my father all over again"). Automatic thoughts may help explain immediate angry responses to apparently neutral stimuli.

At the heart of planning tasks to control angry, aggressive responses is identifying alternative ways of coping with provocative situations.

At a cognitive-emotional level, the client can attempt to replace anger-arousing beliefs with those that may have a calming effect ("She is unresponsive because she has a lot on her mind, not because she doesn't care about me.") Self-talk that might increase one's sense of efficacy—"I can stay in control"—is often a helpful addition.

Uncontrolled anger or aggression often results from vicious cycles of interaction with another person. Making "smart moves" early in these cycles may often be the best way of keeping them from reaching the point of no return. Thus, in an example cited earlier (chapter 2), tasks, such as avoiding name-calling, asking before taking one another's things, and "backing off" when quarreling has started, were used to prevent conflict among three adolescent boys from erupting into violence.

As Stern and Fodor (1989:15) have observed, a task-orientation to provocative situations can facilitate adaptive responses. That is, the client should attempt to see the provocative situation "as a problem that calls for a solution rather than as a threat that calls for an attack." It is helpful for the client to have a repertoire of possible problem-solving responses to draw from—e.g., ignoring, responding verbally rather than physically, getting help. Such repertoires can be developed with clients to fit the kind of provocative situations they are apt to encounter. In this way, the client becomes better prepared to handle the range of unexpected contingencies that may develop in anger-arousing situations.

Rehearsal of external tasks through role plays follows formats previously discussed (chapter 4). In doing role plays, an attempt is made to expose the client to progressively greater provocation. The practitioner, taking the role of the client, may model appropriate responses, which the client then practices. Or the client may simply practice in response to the practitioner's feedback and coaching. As indicated (chapter 3), family members may serve as models or coaches.

External tasks may also be graded in difficulty, and initially clients may attempt to handle less provocative situations while trying to avoid those that might lead to uncontrolled responses. "Last resort" options, such as walking away before losing control, may be useful adjuncts to a plan. When the practitioner has some influence on the client's environment, as in a residential setting, caregivers may be brought into the plan. They may be able to help reduce the level of provocation in certain situations. With the client's awareness, they may also gradually attempt to increase the level of provocation to test the client's capacity to respond appropriately (Barth 1986).

The empirical basis of methods for helping people control anger is not yet a substantial one. Some studies have shown that these methods may be promising with a variety of client groups, including adults with anger problems (Novaco 1975), emotionally disturbed children (Small and Schinke 1983), violence-prone spouses (Deschner and McNeil 1986), abusing parents (Whiteman, Fanshel, and Grundy 1987), and conflicted parents and teens (Stern in press). Applications with abusing parents are taken up in chapter 6. Because effects have been generally modest, and because there is no evidence that any one method is more effective than any other, it makes sense to use a multicomponent approach, combining, where possible, skill training, problem-solving, cognitive, and environmental approaches.

Physical Functioning

In some psychosocial problems, illness and disability may be an intrinsic part of the difficulty, as in emotional reactions to being sick or disabled. In some cases, however, illness and disability may arise as obstacles to the solution of problems in other domains. Thus tasks to resolve problems of performance in work, marital, parental, and other roles may be blocked by obstacles in physical functioning. While health histories are not routinely obtained in the assessment of the problem, practitioners are alert to the possibility of such obstacles. For example, they may inquire if physical causes have been assessed for problems where such causation is commonly present, for example, reading difficulties. Practitioners will regularly press for medical evaluations of actual or suspected obstacles in the physical domain, and where feasible they will obtain firsthand data from the medical evaluation. It is important for practitioners who work with obstacles of this kind to know of medical and rehabilitation resources and to keep abreast of developments in these areas. More extended discussion of this topic can be found in chapter 10.

External Systems

The obstacles considered thus far have been located primarily in the client system. We now turn to obstacles in the client's external systems.

Where obstacles are located is somewhat arbitrary since any of the obstacles in the client's motivations, feelings, or beliefs are inevitably influenced by the larger systems of which he or she is a part. Perhaps the distinction makes sense largely in respect to the actions required; when obstacles are situated in the microsystems or ecosystems, some change in those systems is required for the obstacle to change. To simplify discussion, I shall assume that the client is an individual. When the family (microsystem) is the unit of attention (as it is in the next chapter), the concept of the client system is enlarged, and one's definition of external systems is modified accordingly. As noted, obstacles characteristic of family systems are taken up in that chapter.

Table 5.3 presents and illustrates types of obstacles found in external systems. Again, the categories are overlapping and nonexhaustive. They are intended to provide a range of useful concepts to identify and analyze possible obstacles. When clients are faced with obstacles in their external systems, there are basically three strategies that can be used, either singly or in combination: (1) expanding the intervention system, (2) empowering the client, and (3) doing independent practitioner tasks (see also chapter 11).

Expanding the Intervention System

In this strategy, an attempt is made to bring those responsible for the external obstacle into some form of participation in intervention sessions with the practitioner and the client. For example, the practitioner might suggest a joint session involving Mrs. L. and her ex-husband to discuss support payments and visitation rights (see table 5.3). Similarly, Rob, Tim's antagonist, might be seen along with Tim. Mr. T.'s presentation of his requests to a staff member in the presence of the social worker as a facilitator might help avoid the stigma of being "manipulative." Although it can be dramatically effective, this strategy entails the risks that the joint session may go awry and make matters worse. For this reason, the purpose and format of the session needs to be made clear to the person to be brought in, and some preliminary reading of his or her attitude should be obtained. This discussion, which might involve an individual session with the person, can be used as a basis for deciding whether or not to go ahead with the plan. In some cases, only one session may be involved; in others, the person(s) brought in may become clients in a continuing relationship. This option is, of course, limited to situations in which external obstacles can be

TABLE 5.3
Obstacles in External Systems

Source	Examples of Obstacles
Beliefs and behaviors of significant others including clients' interactions with them	Mrs. L. has tried to talk to her ex-husband about the child support payments he owes her, but he responds with complaints about not being able to keep the children for weekends. Rob tends to provoke Tim (the client) in class, leading to fights and making it difficult for Tim to stay out of trouble.
Organizations	
Labeling	The residential staff, who view Mr. T. as "manipulative," ignore his requests.
Service delivery	Mr. N. can't perform activities of daily living unaided and needs a home health aide to remain at home; the agency has denied his request but he's not clear why.
Involvement of multiple service providers	Mrs. B. is confused about what she needs to do to have her child returned from foster-care because she is getting conflicting messages from the different organizations involved in her case.
Neighborhood, community	Miss Q. is fearful about leaving her apartment because of recent street crime on her block.
Physical environment and resources	Mrs. O., who is elderly and recently blind, finds it hard to function in her home because of the many stairs.

identified with particular persons, who must also be willing to participate in at least one joint session with the client.

Client Empowerment

In this strategy, clients tackle external obstacles themselves and draw
on the help provided by the practitioner in the session. Essentially, the
means of change are tasks undertaken by the client. As usual, the tasks
are planned collaboratively with the practitioner, and the practitioner
may provide expert knowledge and coaching. For example, Mrs. L. and
the practitioner might consider different ways she could approach her
ex-husband about support payments. Mrs. L.'s informing him about

possible legal action and exploring ways of taking such action might be considered as tasks. The social worker might provide Mrs. L. with information about her rights and legal procedures. In the case of Mrs. B., it might be decided that she should inform the different practitioners about the conflicting messages and ask them to work out some resolution. The practitioner may offer suggestions about how she might go about this. To help clients deal with agencies in general, Hasenfield (1987) suggests specific empowerment techniques, such as "providing clients with information about their entitlements and how to claim them." One rationale for client empowerment is that the client is often in the best position to resolve the obstacle. Another is to enhance the client's own capacities and skills to deal with obstacles. The second rationale suggests that client empowerment may make sense even when the practitioners themselves might be able to resolve the obstacle more efficiently. However, when grappling with the obstacle may prove too difficult or demanding for the client (who may already be overwhelmed), client tasks alone may not be the best course of action. Mrs. N. may be a case in point. In such cases, the practitioner may use the third strategy, that of practitioner tasks, which may also foster client empowerment, as will be shown.

Practitioner Tasks

In this strategy, the practitioners themselves work directly on obstacles in external systems, either to pave the way for tasks by the client (facilitative practitioner tasks) or to attempt to resolve the obstacle without client action (independent practitioner tasks). Client empowerment can be enhanced by facilitative tasks. For example, Mrs. N.'s task might be to contact another agency about getting help at home after the practitioner has made a preliminary inquiry to determine if the agency can deliver the service. Most practitioner activity that takes the form of mediation or brokerage (chapter 3) can be structured to give the client meaningful tasks to do. In some cases, an independent task by the practitioner addressed to one obstacle can be combined with a client task addressed to another. Independent practitioner tasks are probably used most heavily when external obstacles are situated in organizations. The practitioner's knowledge of local agencies and his or her relationships with their staffs may provide a leverage clients cannot attain. This is especially true when obstacles involve multiple service providers and span several organizations. Usually these obstacles reflect uncoordinated or conflicted activity among the providers, with the client caught in the middle. As discussed in chapter 11, the practitioner may be able to take on a case coordinating or case management role—e.g., setting up a case conference attended by the service providers and, if at all feasible, by the client(s).

CHAPTER 6

Family Problems

In this chapter we shall consider problems and strategies in work with people who live together in intimate relationships: husbands and wives, parents and children of all ages, cohabiting couples of all gender combinations, and so on. To be simple, we shall refer to these intimate groups and couples as families.

My concern in this chapter is with family problems for which task strategies involving family members seen separately or together provide an apparently effective means of intervention. In later chapters I will consider problems affecting family members, such as depression, anxiety, and mental illness, for which more diversified approaches may be needed. For those problems, the role of family intervention will be considered within the context of broader approaches. Problems external to the family will be taken up in chapter 11.

The Nature, Formulation, and Assessment of Family Problems

As Wynne (1988) has pointed out, there is no generally accepted definition or typology of family problems; moreover, consensus has not yet been reached on a number of fundamental issues, such as whether to have a problem classification for the family's presenting problems or for its patterns of relationship. Even the desirability of such a classification is in dispute. I agree with Wynne (1988) that the question of the nature of the problem needs to be addressed within all treatment approaches.

Family Target Problems

In the task-centered approach, we begin with *target problems* that are essentially the family's felt difficulties as they emerge from a process of exploration and formulation collaboratively carried out by the practitioner and family members (chapter 2). The repetition of this process with large numbers of families produces a range of issues whose diversity defies simple classification. However, some groupings can be made. As Grunebaum (cited in Wynne 1988) has suggested, problems perceived by family members can be divided roughly into two groups: "relational problems" and "problem persons." In the first class fall most interactional difficulties between marital partners, between other adult dyads, between parents and children, and between siblings. Problems attributed to particular family members, either by professionals (e.g., anorexia, alcoholism, or mental illness) or by the family itself (e.g., Tommy doesn't do what he is told), belong in the second group. To these internal problems others can be added that the family views as external to its functioning or that of its members, e.g., lack of resources or conflicts with organizations.

Establishing a neat and useful categorization is complicated by the tendency of problems to overlap and shift. As suggested, practitioners may attempt to help family members redefine problems in directions that are more likely to facilitate solutions, for example, from person problems to relational problems. Also, families' perceptions of their problems may change in response to treatment. Still, problems do have objective manifestations that can be identified; changes in these problems can be tracked over time. In my view, working with slippery and shifting target problems is far better than working without them. Particularly in a collaborative model, both the clients and the practitioners need to have a shared conception of the difficulties they are addressing in order to work together effectively.

In understanding family problems a good deal of attention needs to be given to contextual factors, especially to those arising within the family system. Target problems influence one another and in turn are shaped by the structures and beliefs of the family. In task-centered work with families, practitioners focus both on the target problem and its context. Contextual change may be required before change in the target problem is possible, or contextual change may be desirable in its own right as a means of preventing a recurrence of the problem or of strengthening family life. However, the identification and pursuit of contextual change goals is done explicitly and collaboratively with the family, and tasks are used as the major means of accomplishing change. The goals become functionally similar to target problems. Thus, in order to bring about change in a boy's behavior problem (the target problem), the practitioner may need to help the parents create a more effective alliance or help the father to develop a better relationship with his son (contextual goals).

Any family problem needs to be understood not only within the context of family relations but also within that of the individual functioning of family members and the larger environment of which the family and its members are a part. A multisystems perspective is especially important in work with families. It is easy to become overabsorbed in family system dynamics and neglect other systems. Family treatment approaches have been rightly criticized for their neglect of the individual (Pinsof 1983; Nichols 1987) and the social environment (Johnson 1986). In agreement with Johnson (1986), the task-centered model starts with the target problem and then determines what combination of assessment data and treatment interventions (family, individual, and environmental) would lead to the most effective solutions of that problem.

Problem Formulation

Problem formulation with families is considerably more complex than with individuals. Among other things, the practitioner needs to cope with diverse perceptions of the difficulties, tendencies of family members to blame one another for problems, and elusive issues in family relationships. The distinctive principles of problem exploration and formulation with families are presented below.

- o Problems are usually explored and formulated in joint interviews with relevant family members;
- o Family members in turn present their views of the problems. If children are present, this "problem survey" is preceded by a short period of informal conversation involving the children to help them ease into the interview; the parent(s) speak(s) first, followed by the children.

○ Family members may use session tasks to explore facets of the problem in face-to-face-dialog, a device that is particularly useful when their individual presentations of the problem are vague and contradictory.

○ Whenever possible, the practitioner formulates the problems in interactional terms. For example, if Mom sees the problem as her daughter's coming home after her curfew, and the daughter sees the problem as her mom bugging her about coming home late, an interactional formulation would emphasize their disagreement about how to handle curfew issues.

○ The practitioner avoids "piling up" ownership of problems on any one family member.

○ In some cases the process of problem formulation may need to be extended over a sequence of individual and family interviews. For example, the case may begin with an interview with the one family member who seeks help, or family members may be reluctant to discuss certain problems openly with other family members present.

Methods of Assessment and Evaluation

In the treatment of families, as in work with individual clients, the interview provides the main means of assessing family problems and functioning and of evaluating change. Aside from its clinical value, seeing the family together makes it possible for members to correct and augment one another's perceptions and for the practitioner to get more than one opinion. As a result, distortions, while common, are less likely than in individual interviews. However, as noted, interviews with individual family members may provide important additional data, especially when there is reason to suppose that family members do not wish to reveal all they know in family sessions. Problems concerning marital infidelity, sexual abuse, and drinking, for example, may require individual interviews in order to obtain a complete picture.

Direct observation is particularly important in work with families. Observation of family interaction during the course of an interview, especially during session tasks, can provide the practitioner with clues about patterns of family communication, control, involvement, and alliance. In fact, session tasks can be structured for observational purposes. For example, having a parent and child engage in a play activity in which cooperative behavior is required, such as building a house with blocks, can be used to assess aspects of the parent-child interaction as well as parenting skills. Sessions in the home, where family members can interact more naturally than in the office, provide particularly good opportunities for direct observation.

A wide variety of published instruments can be used in family assessment; a selection can be found in Corcoran and Fischer (1987). Several that have proved useful in the Task-Centered Family Treatment Project will be described briefly.

The Hudson Clinical Assessment Package contains a number of self-reported family assessment tools, including the Index of Family Relations, Child's Attitude Toward Mother, Child's Attitude Toward Father, and the Index of Marital Satisfaction (Hudson 1982). These scales are brief, easy to administer and to score, and have a common clinical "cutting score"—that is, scores over 25 indicate, according to Hudson, a significant clinical problem. Because of their brevity, it is feasible to give them repeatedly in the course of treatment. Moreover, they can be used in conjunction with a computer program developed by Hudson (1990) that will calculate test statistics and print graphs of change over time.

The Family Assessment Device (FAD) is a sixty-item self-report measure that taps seven dimensions of family functioning (problem-solving, communication, roles, affective involvement, affective responsiveness, behavior control, and general functioning) (Epstein, Baldwin, and Bishop 1983; Miller, Epstein, Bishop, and Keitner 1985). General population and clinical norms are available for making comparative judgments about the functioning of particular families in general and in respect to specific dimensions. Somewhat too long for repeated administrations, the FAD provides good "before" and "after" measures by which to assess the outcome of a case. Given its variety of items, the FAD also provides helpful insight into specific disagreements among family members.

The Dyadic Adjustment Scale (DAS) is a thirty-two-item instrument to measure adjustment in marital partners and similar dyads (Spanier 1976). Like the FAD, it has subscales (satisfaction, cohesion, consensus, and affectional expression), and scores can be compared against samples of "normal" and "problem" dyads. The conceptual organization of the instrument and the quality of its items make it especially useful for clinical purposes.

Common Family Problems

In this section, I shall consider task strategies for a range of common family problems. Problems have been selected that capture those most likely to be dealt with by social workers as well as those for which a task-centered approach is most appropriate. Since considering the entire gamut of family problems that might fit these selection criteria would fill a volume, I have made use of themes that span different specific problems. Thus the category *parental coping and child behavior* incorporates parental maltreatment and the usual variety of behavior problems exhibited by children at home and in school. Under *conflict* and *communication* are subsumed most marital and parent-teen problems.

The task strategies presented will focus on direct work on the problem. Strategies involving contextual change, e.g., in the family's structural relations and belief systems, will be taken up in later sections.

Problems in Parental Coping and Child Behavior

Problems involving parental coping with a child's difficult behavior in the home (e.g., disobedience, tantrums) are generally so embedded in the parent-child interaction that it makes sense to see them as part of a single configuration. However, for expository purposes, I shall begin with the parents' side of the equation, i.e., with the focus on parental dysfunction.

Parental Coping

Problems in parental coping take a variety of forms. The most visible and troublesome breakdowns in parental performance occur in child abuse and neglect. But for every case of abuse or neglect, there are multitudes of others in which parents are simply not as effective as they could be. The result of less-than-adequate parenting is often, unfortunately, less-than-adequate children.

As noted, parents' difficulties in being parents almost always involve interactions with their children. However, emphasis on the parent is justified when the child is too young to be an active participant in counseling sessions or when deficits in parenting overshadow the child's role in the difficulty. The problems can be formulated to reflect the parent-child interaction and the child's contribution (e.g., Mrs. Brown has difficulty in handling Kevin's temper tantrums), or separate problems can be framed: one expressing the parents' trouble in coping, the other describing the child's misbehavior.

In helping parents, the practitioner stresses what parents can learn and do to become more effective in their day-to-day interactions with their children. The emphasis is on the positive: what the parent can do to become a better parent rather than on what the parent is doing wrong. A focus on parenting skills is a natural consequence (Polster and Dangel 1984; Schaefer and Briesmeister 1989). Skills are practiced in the session and then applied as home tasks.

The parent as observer. At a basic level, the parent can learn to be a more careful observer, noting especially the sequence of events in the child-parent interaction. Troubled parents have been found to interpret innocuous behavior as forecasting some negative consequence (Wahler and Dumas 1984). A child may be punished for such behavior, which may trigger a chain of mutually aversive interactions, or parents may unwittingly reward (reinforce) troublesome behavior in their children. If parents can be helped to gain an accurate picture of these sequences through observation and recording tasks, the stage is set for them to learn more effective ways of responding.

Commands. Parents often seek to control the behavior of their children, especially younger children, with some form of command. A useful distinction can be made between commands that are clear and direct and allow the child sufficient time to comply (alpha commands) and commands that are vague, contradictory, or otherwise do not enable the child to comply (beta commands) (McMahon and Forehand 1984). It is the difference between telling a child to "let go of your sister's arm" as opposed to "be good." Parents are taught to give alpha commands in clear language and to give appropriate reasons for commands.

Controlling anger toward children. When parental dysfunction takes the form of child abuse, a key component is "situationally tied anger, the fitful, child-directed anger that triggers specific abusive acts." (Whiteman, Fanshel, and Grundy 1987:469). For abusive and other parents who have difficulty managing anger of this kind, training in anger control may be an appropriate intervention (Novaco 1975; Barth et al. 1983; Whiteman, Fanshel, and Grundy 1987; Azar 1989).

The basic procedures for anger control outlined in chapter 5 can be applied in work with parents. At the cognitive level, particular attention needs to be paid to parental expectations and attributions. Abusive parents, for example, tend to have unrealistically high expectations of the children (Azar and Rohrbeck 1989) and to attribute negative intentions to children's behavior (Larrance and Twentyman 1983). Such expectations and misattributions combined with ignorance of developmental norms provide a fertile ground for aggressive responses. A two-year-old may be expected "to sit still and be quiet" for a lengthy period. When the child begins to behave "normally"—i.e., to move about—the parent may attribute the behavior to "being bad" and react with anger. Helping the client acquire more accurate beliefs about what can be expected of children at given stages and common reasons for their behavior may be necessary before the parent is able to accomplish child rearing tasks without excessive anger.

As Azar (1989) suggests, a fruitful area for parent tasks lies in anticipating and altering situations that might lead to difficult child behavior and parental anger, for example, giving the child a snack before the child becomes hungry and irritable. Tasks calling for on-the-spot problem solving (chapter 4) can be used to help the parent generate alternative ways of coping early with situations in danger of escalation. Such a problem-solving approach was found to be effective in controlling parental anger in a study by Whiteman, Fanshel, and Grundy (1987). It is worth noting that this same study also found the reattribution of causes of the child's behavior to be effective but not relaxation training, a commonly used component of stress-management and anger control methods.

Systematic use of rewards and punishment. Skills in this area consist of the parents learning how to reinforce or reward compliance or appropriate behavior, how to ignore minor misbehavior, and how to provide appropriately controlled responses to interrupt more serious forms of misbehavior. Parents are taught to note good or appropriate behavior and to reward it promptly with approval or praise. Harsh punishment, including corporal punishment, is discouraged. Rather, the parent is requested to substitute milder forms of punishment, such as time-outs, which involve isolating the child (on a chair, to a room, etc.) for brief periods. In deciding what to ignore and what to punish, parents can well be advised to use a principle nicely put by Pinkston (1984:217), "If you don't want to reinforce it or punish it, don't see it."

For less frequently occurring behaviors and for older children, point systems or token economies provide appropriate contingencies for the child's behavior. Reciprocal tasks are used. The parent gives the child a token in the form of stars or happy faces on charts, chips, etc., or records points earned (parental task) when the child completes his or her task, such as coming directly home after school or not hitting a sibling for a day. Tokens or points are accumulated and then exchanged for special rewards—e.g., food treats, toys, extra time watching TV. Points or tokens may be taken away for inappropriate behavior (response costs). Although they may strike some parents as unnatural or as a form of bribery, point systems are simply a version of the kind of contingency management that parents do all the time. As a means of controlling their children's behavior, parents commonly grant or withhold privileges. Point systems have the advantage of being more systematic and flexible and better in tune with known principles of behavior change. Thus the system can be designed to deliver the kind of positive reinforcement or response most needed to bring about the desired change for a particular child.

Another objection clients may raise is that they have tried similar techniques before without success. Parents can frequently point to instances of fruitlessly offering rewards contingent on good behavior or using some form of time-out that proved ineffective. Although it is true that both parents and practitioners draw from the same pool of methods for managing children, parent training provides parents with a systematic, well-tested set of skills that may have little resemblance to the haphazard and distorted versions that they may have used before. Parents might have set contingencies that were impossible for the child to attain, or they may have imposed a draconian withdrawal of privileges that could not be adhered to. As one parent acknowledged, "I practically used to say, 'You're grounded for the rest of your life!' " The parents' claim that "we have tried that stuff" should be explored for clues as to the kind of control methods they have been using. Differences between what the parents have attempted and what the practitioner is proposing need to be explained carefully and sympathetically.

The skills described can be taught to parents through a variety of methods ranging from programmed texts to individualized coaching of parents as they interact with their children. These skills can provide the basis for educative counseling with parents alone in office interviews. For example, a practitioner might instruct parents in the use of different forms of positive reinforcement or time-out techniques or help them devise and implement a point system for their children.

Controlling antecedents. As Blechman et al. (1989) point out, parent training that relies exclusively on manipulation of rewards and punishments requires considerable surveillance by the parents, which may be difficult for some parents (e.g., beleaguered single parents) to manage. Controlling antecedents whenever possible often provides a simple and less intrusive means of parental coping. For example, if the problem is that the child does not pick up his or her toys, the number of toys given to the child can be restricted or toys scattered about can be picked up by the parent and put away until the end of the week—Blechman's (1989) "Sunday Box" procedure. Controlling antecedents also has the advantage of stimulating problem solving in the child. Rather than learning to produce the one correct response, the child is challenged to come up with his or her own ways of dealing with the problem.

In my judgment, the most effective way to impart these methods is through sessions with the parent and the child together, preferably in the home, so that the parent has the opportunity to practice these skills with the child under the practitioner's guidance. This widely used approach has been called "performance-based" (Gordon and Davidson 1981). In describing these methods, I shall assume a single parent, which is usually the case (and usually the mother), and an only child. The approach can readily be extended to both parents, which is usually desirable if it is possible, and to sibling groups.

The general format is straightforward. The parent is first instructed in an individual session about the parenting skills to be learned. Instruction may consist of verbal explanation, written material (such as *Parents Are Teachers* [Becker 1971]), demonstrations of the target behaviors by the practitioner, and role plays. The role plays may involve the practitioner taking the role of the parent and the parent role-playing the child as a means of modeling skills. An exchange of roles then permits the parent to practice with the practitioner in the role of the child. When two practitioners are used, both can model skills through role play.

In the in-vivo training that then follows, the parent tries out the skills in interactions with the child. Toys or games may be used to facilitate the interactions. The practitioner provides on-the-spot coaching, including praise, corrective feedback, and additional instructions. The parent and practitioner then devise home tasks that involve specific practice of the skills for certain periods of time in addition to more spontaneous applications the parent may make. Skills are generally introduced and taught one at a time. After one skill is mastered, the next is introduced. Usually skills involving use of positive reinforcement and other nonpunitive procedures are taught first, a general principle in parent training and one that might be especially emphasized in work with parents who have histories of excessive use of punishment.

Mixed strategies. Although parent training can be used as the primary task strategy in a case, a more common practice in the task-centered model is to use parent training in combination with other strategies. A review of parent training in social work suggests this mixed approach is the norm (Polster, Dangel, and Rapp, 1987). Usually, only a part of the full gamut of skills is taught. Skills are selected to fit the needs of the problem and the parent. Finally, the attempt to help clients learn and apply parenting skills is often fraught with obstacles arising from their attitudes and feelings toward their children or stresses in their life situation (Wahler and Afton 1980). The following is an example of a partial and mixed parent training approach in which such obstacles were confronted.

Mrs. L. and her eight-year-old daughter, Julia, were seen in a Child Abuse Prevention Unit concerning problems involving the mother's parenting and the child's behavior. Mrs. L., a single mother, was referred because of intense, escalating conflicts with her daughter that had on occasion led to incidents of severe corporal punishment. The service was carried out largely in the home as part of the Task-Centered Family Treatment Project (chapter 1). Initially, only parent training methods were used. Mrs. L.'s difficulty in getting her daughter to pick up her room was selected as a representative problem. Mrs. L. was to reinforce Julia's room cleaning activities with approval and praise and to provide small tangible rewards contingent upon Julia's attaining specific goals. It was clear that this approach was not sufficient. The mother found it difficult to respond with approval or physical expressions of affection. Julia's school grades had been declining, and she was "forgetting" to bring assignments home, all of which was a growing source of frustration for Mrs. L. Her difficulties with her boyfriend were another source of aggravation. Interviews with Mrs. L. revealed her reservations about the "game plan" as she called it. She had doubts whether she really loved Julia. She was further inhibited by fears of being rejected by her daughter if she did reach out to her. In addition, she thought that a tangible reward was giving Julia too much. At several points she expressed resentment over being seen as "the problem" when the "real problem" was her daughter.

In addition to work with Mrs. L. on these issues, the practitioner had a joint interview with Mrs. L. and her boyfriend concerning their problems. She also developed a plan with Julia and the school to insure that Julia either completed her work at school or brought it home.

These interventions seemed to strengthen the parent training aspects of treatment. For example, Mrs. L. and Julia were able to negotiate and implement a point system concerning room cleaning and homework. The case terminated with significant gains in the mother-daughter relationship as well as in the daughter's behavior.

This case illustrates how parent training methods can be included with other interventions in a flexible approach. It also reveals some typical problems that might be expected to arise in "pure" parent training formats, e.g., the parents' inability to comply with requirements to positively reinforce the child's behavior and their unwillingness to accept major responsibility for initiating change. In addition, as might be expected, the relationship was fraught with complex emotional difficulties, not the least of which was the mother's ambivalence toward her daughter and her fear of being rejected by her child. In this case, and perhaps in most, such obstacles may need to be dealt with through counseling and other means of intervention in order for parent training to operate effectively.

Effectiveness. By the end of the seventies, considerable evidence had accumulated that parent training approaches worked well with well-educated, reasonably well-functioning parents coping with specific, well-defined behavior problems in their children (Gordon and Davidson 1981). As parent training was applied to less well-educated, more severely distressed parents struggling with more complex and pervasive problems in their children's behavior, the case for its effectiveness became less clear-cut (Blechman et al. 1989). Still, studies with encouraging findings have been reported for one important target of such training efforts—parents at risk for child abuse or neglect. For example, several studies have demonstrated that parent training, often including anger control procedures and other components, has produced better outcomes with such parents than alternative programs (Wolfe, Sandler, and Kaufman 1981; Lutzker and Rice 1984; Azar and Twentyman 1984; Szykula and Fleischman 1985; Whiteman, Fanshel, and Grundy 1987). Although these results may be sufficient to justify the use of parent training with maltreating or other types of poorly functioning parents, there remains a lack of knowledge about the specific contribution and long-term effects of such an application.

Focus on the Child

Although the principal task-centered strategy for the resolution of child behavior problems in the home is to bring about changes in parental functioning, children are normally very much involved in the intervention program. As suggested above, younger children (below the age of 7) may take part in session tasks in which the parent practices child management skills. In addition to participation in such tasks, older children are involved in problem solving and in task planning in the session.

Some of these tasks may be generated through interaction with the practitioner rather than with the parent. Moreover, a child may agree to do the task without a planned contingent response (e.g., a reward or restoration of privileges) from the parent. We have found that children can often be motivated to do individual tasks "for their own reward," out of a sense of obligation, a desire for mastery, or a wish to conform, among other reasons. This motivation should be utilized to full advantage since it enables the child to anchor behavior in natural incentives and does not require introduction or fading out of an artificial reward system. Parents should always be encouraged, however, to show explicit approval for task accomplishments.

School problems. A frequent family problem concerns school difficulties of children, such as nonattendance, poor academic performance, and disruptive behavior in school. Although such problems are not necessarily caused by the family, it must nevertheless cope with them and is usually a key resource in bringing them to a successful resolution. Once a school problem has been identified, the practitioner should make contact with relevant school personnel, such as the child's teacher(s), guidance counselor, or assistant principal, in order to secure assessment data, to elicit their opinions about what should be done, and to set the stage for cooperation. These practitioner tasks are of critical importance. Sometimes practitioners make the mistake of relying entirely on the child's and family's account of the difficulty and confine their helping efforts entirely to the family. We shall briefly consider three of the most common school problems presented by families: inadequate academic performance, disruptive behavior, and nonattendance. Fuller discussions of school problems may be found in Ginsburg (1990) and Barth (1986).

Inadequate academic performance can have many causes, including learning disability, attention deficit disorder, and a poor learning environment in the home. As the causes become clarified—and often many unknowns remain—realistic goals for improved performance can be set. With this and other school problems, a cooperative effort involving parents, child, practitioner, and school is called for. Tasks for parents usually involve one or more of the following: providing systematic rewards for improved school performance, setting up and enforcing a schedule for the child's homework, providing a conducive setting for doing homework, helping the child with homework, or having an older sibling provide the help, and conferring with teachers and other school personnel about the child's academic performance. Home notes systems, in which the teacher provides the parents with regular feedback on the child's progress, have been found to be especially effective as a means of increasing the child's academic performance (Drew et al. 1982). These systems not only provide a basis for parental reinforcement of improvement in the child's school performance, but they also enable the child to get systematic evaluations of his or her work and the teacher's approval if progress is made. Home notes can be augmented by parent-reinforced home study, a combination that proved to be effective in one study (Polster and Pinkston 1979). In some cases, session tasks may be needed in which the practitioner models ways of providing homework help for the parent, which the parent then tries out with the child.

Tasks for the child include bringing home assignments and doing homework according to an agreed schedule, requesting help from teachers when needed, and using good work habits at school. Practitioner tasks may involve classroom observation of the child, consultation with teachers about the child's learning needs, arranging for reinforcement from the teacher (approval, gold stars, etc.) of progress shown by the child, and, if needed, securing tutorial services. In addition, the practitioner may set up and participate in conferences involving the parent, child, teacher, and other school personnel.

In work with problems of *disruptive school behavior*, home notes, as previously mentioned, can be used by parents to reinforce improved behavior. Regular phone communication between school personnel and the practitioner or parents offers an alternative means of monitoring the child's behavior. In designing tasks for the child, attention is paid to coping with situations that may trigger disruptive behavior, such as provocation from peers or reprimands by teachers.

In interviews involving parents and child, use can be made of skills training session tasks (chapter 3) aimed at helping the child develop skills for coping with situations at school. The basic format consists of role plays involving the parent(s), child, and practitioner. In one variation, the parent takes the role of the child, and the child takes the role of a provoking teacher, peer, etc. The parent models how he or she would cope with the situation. In another, the practitioner takes the child's role, with the parent or the child in the provoking role. The practitioner can model coping responses. The parents' and the child's ideas about best the responses are also elicited. After appropriate coping responses for the child have been worked out, the parent (or the practitioner) can then role-play the provocateur, and the child can rehearse how he or she would respond.

Problem-solving tasks involving the parents and the child can also be used to suggest ways for the child to cope with difficult situations at school. In the process, the parents can be asked to share their own experience with similar situations when they were children to give the child ideas and also to enhance the identification between parents and child.

Problems of nonattendance often lead to referral of the family to the social worker; they also frequently arise in combination with other school problems. Some children do not attend school because of anxiety, a reaction referred to as *school phobia*. Usually the child fears something about the school situation itself—academic failure, being teased or bullied, and so on. Contributing (and sometimes primary) factors may be parental overprotectiveness, the child's anxiety over separating from the parent, attention received for being "sick," or other reinforcers available at home when the child does not attend school.

Task strategies are generally directed at (1) having the child return to school as soon as possible, (2) reducing anxiety-provoking elements in the school situation, and (3) eliminating reinforcements the child may be receiving at home while not attending school. The early return of the child to school has generally been found to be effective, especially in what Kennedy (1965) has called "class A school phobias" involving younger, anxious children with a fear of academic failure. Thus the child's task is to return to school, usually on a specific day, and the parents' task is to facilitate the return through providing emotional support, reassurance, and a reward for return. If a full return proves to be too much for the child or the parents, then the goal is approached step by step. Successive tasks are used to bring the child back to school gradually (Last 1985; Houlihan and Jones 1989). For a start, the child may wait for the school bus but not board it, or walk part of the way to school; later the child may be asked to spend a short time at school and then return home. Through this process, a full return to school is gradually accomplished. A parent or the practitioner may accompany the child as these progressive tasks are implemented (Thyer and Sowers-Hoag 1986). The purpose is to encourage the child to accomplish as much as possible without becoming excessively anxious.

In the second part of the strategy, the practitioner tasks are centered on work with the teacher and other personnel to identify and modify factors in the school situation that might be provoking the child's anxiety. For example, a child with test anxiety may be permitted to substitute a certain amount of homework for quizzes. The final part involves the parents' withdrawal of whatever "goodies" the child might associate with not attending, such as watching TV or having special snacks.

A somewhat different problem is posed by *truancy*, a far more common occurrence than school phobia. For children who are truant, school is not necessarily a source of anxiety but rather a source of boredom and aggravation. Truants, who are generally poor and unmotivated students, prefer to spend their time elsewhere rather than in school. Truancy also tends to be more sporadic than school phobia; tardiness and leaving school early in the day may also be a part of the pattern.

Reward systems monitored by the parents, home notes, and self-management methods have all been used as a means of increasing school attendance (Barth 1986). Since truancy is often peer-influenced, peers can sometimes be used to help truants return to school. The child selects a school-attending peer who lives nearby. The peer is asked to accompany the truanting child to school. I have found that even a "wake-up" call by a peer can be helpful. In one study, a peer approach accompanied by rewards for truants and peers was found to improve school attendance among Hispanic elementary school children (Morgan 1975).

Session tasks involving the parent(s) and the child can be used to identify reasons for the truancy and to work out a plan for increasing attendance. The plan may lead to tasks for parents, child, and practitioner. A reward system may be set up at home, or the practitioner may attempt to modify the child's situation at school—e.g., a change in classroom or in the teacher's approach. Sometimes the reasons for the truancy point toward the need for broader contextual changes. For example, a session task involving Karen T. and her mother revealed that Karen was cutting classes because of her unhappiness with her new school and community. Karen had attended school regularly in the community from which Mrs. T. and her two daughters had recently moved. Karen especially missed her friends and had been unable to make new ones. She felt alone and alienated, and this in turn fed her "hatred" of her new school. The task strategy was directed at helping Karen to get involved in two of her favorite activities as a way of making friends.

Conflict

Conflict is the common denominator for most difficulties in family relationships. Many problems are expressed directly in terms of conflict: between marital partners, parents and children, and siblings. Problems expressed in other terms, such as poor communication or lack of intimacy, often *become* problems because the family members are in disagreement about how these aspects of their relationship should play themselves out. Moreover, conflict may not necessarily be overt. One partner may suffer the other's behavior in silence. Conflict is present but covert. In most cases, the resolution of such hidden conflicts requires that they be brought to the surface.

Understanding Conflict

Conflict between family members involves intricacies of close interaction that have evolved over time. The interaction is entwined with cognitions, feelings, and behavior for which there are often no clear norms. For most intimates, the conflict that disrupts the interaction must be resolved or accommodated since it tears at the very fabric of what intimate relationships are about—affection, caring, trust, and support.

Of course, not all conflict is disruptive. Conflict is as much a part of intimacy as closeness, and most of it is taken in stride by most family members. Indeed, conflict serves positive functions by revealing differences whose resolution can enhance relationships and functioning. We focus here on conflict that cannot be satisfactorily resolved by the family members themselves.

In analyzing conflict, we are drawn first to its most obvious element: its substance or content. I have in mind here the "manifest content," that is, what participants themselves say the issue is. In some conflicts the content is the dominant feature. This is true particularly when the issue is a major one, such as geographic relocation or the decision to have a child. The substance of the conflict may appear minor to outsiders, including the practitioner, but it may be of major consequence to the participants because it threatens deeply held values or well-established rules or for some reason stirs up strong feelings. In one case, a disagreement over whether or not the wife should attend the wedding of her husband's disowned son (and her stepson) was the basic reason for seeking help and constituted the focus of service.

In other conflicts, the content is subordinate to the patterns of the participants' interaction. Thus, when a couple quarrels "about everything," the content of any particular quarrel becomes relatively less important. In most cases, however, there are typically several areas of conflict where content does seem to matter; various underlying factors may contribute to these conflicts. An integrated analysis, in which the content and the relationship aspects of the conflict are taken into account simultaneously, seems to be called for. Thus, in a marital conflict over how domestic responsibilities are to be shared, the practitioner must become immersed in the intricate way the content plays itself out and be prepared to make thoughtful contributions to such issues as caring for children and division of household chores. At the same time, the practitioner needs to be aware of the dynamics of the marital relationship with its patterns of communication and control, differing conceptions of marital roles, and so on. Despite the dependence of much conflict on personality, structural, and other contextual factors, focus on more immediate causes may yield knowledge that can help family members in the unending task of conflict resolution or management.

Regardless of what it is about, any conflict is expressed through some form of communication between its participants, and communication also provides the usual means of resolution. The communication styles of participants are of considerable importance in determining the outcome of a conflict. A volatile, name-calling interchange can turn a minor disagreement into a raging battle that may scar a relationship permanently. A tightly controlled interchange, in which interests and feelings are suppressed, may produce the appearance of a resolution while the conflict continues to fester. A reasoned but assertive interchange may bring the conflict to a mutually satisfactory solution. It is recognized, of course, that communication is the means by which feelings and thoughts are expressed. A person in a rage may use words like weapons. Moreover, a conflict can be so centered on differences in interests that it may matter very little how it is expressed.

Be that as it may, what is said and how it is said can be decisive for a range of conflicts in which participants are in some control of what they say and where some compromise is possible. Therefore, learning more effective ways of communicating can be one key to conflict resolution. Thus communication training, to be considered subsequently (see *Communication*), is an important tool in conflict reduction.

As we know, family conflicts frequently escalate, sometimes to the point of physical violence. After a certain point in an escalating conflict, participants often are unable to control their actions, and the conflict itself gets out of control. As a result, it is important to identify more readily controlled actions that typically occur early in the escalation. For example, in one case a wife would react with sullen silence when her husband was late without a good reason. The silence would provoke the husband into angry comments about her childish behavior and resulted in escalation. It was found that it was sometimes hard for the husband to be on time, but he could make an effort to let his wife know beforehand when he was going to be late. This effort did not entirely satisfy his wife, but it enabled her to avoid the kind of hostile withdrawal that in turn had provoked her husband.

Reducing Conflict through Session and External Tasks

In the present model, the preferred strategy for a problem of conflict is for the participants to work out a solution in face-to-face interaction, while the practitioner assumes the roles of mediator, facilitator, and coach. The structure used is one or more session tasks set up by the practitioner in which the participants make use of problem-solving methods to come to an agreement. A plan for implementing the agreement is devised, and the participants commit themselves to carry out the plan through an external task prior to the next session. This combination of session and external tasks is referred to as the Family Problem-Solving Sequence (FPSS) (Reid 1987a, b).

This strategy focuses on the manifest content of the conflict. It may suffice for cases in which target problems consist of specific manifest conflicts though there may also be latent or systemic components. That is, if clients focus on such a conflict and want help with it, it is appropriate to center intervention on resolving the content issue through problem solving. In so doing, latent and contextual factors may need to be dealt with, but only as far as is needed to resolve the focal issue. Even when a pervasive pattern of conflict rather than a particular conflict is of central concern, a problem-solving approach may still be useful as a means of settling disputes that may be especially troublesome, particularly when underlying factors prove intractable. In such cases, emphasis is usually placed on developing the participants' skills in conflict negotiation—or in problem-solving communication, as discussed below.

In using a problem-solving strategy, the practitioner does not follow a fixed format. Rather, the amount and kind of structure is adapted to what the clients can use most productively. For this customizing the practitioner draws on the procedures for problem-solving session tasks. These procedures, summarized in chapter 3, are adapted below to conflict situations.

Setting up the session task. The task starts when clients begin to discuss their problem in a face-to-face dialog while the practitioner observes them. Prior to this point, the practitioner indicates the general purpose of the task and what the clients may wish to focus on. Some clients find talking to one another difficult to do, perhaps because of a need to convince the social worker directly of the rightness of their views. Practitioners also find it hard to insist that clients talk to each other. In some instances, practitioners may be reluctant to impose a conversational structure on their clients; in others, practitioners find it impossible to let clients struggle on their own. In any event, in one study (Reid 1987a), premature communication between practitioners and clients was found to be the major reason for the failure of session tasks.

In setting up the task, it is therefore important to stress that clients should talk directly to one another, and having them face each other helps. Comments directed at the practitioner should be redirected at the appropriate participant while the task is in progress. Observations, suggestions, and other comments from the practitioner should be brief and end on a note that turns the conversation back to the clients. If these procedures are followed, clients usually have no difficulty conversing with each other. It is, after all, something they are used to.

Ground Rules. As part of the initial structuring of the task, the practitioner can suggest that certain ground rules be followed. The rules can be gone over orally, or clients can be given a written list. The following is a list of the more commonly used ones.

1. Participants should focus on the problem itself and on solutions for it rather than on each other's personal qualities.

2. In the case of disagreement, participants should attempt to make some concessions, that is, they should be prepared to accept something less than (or different from) their conception of the ideal solution to the problem.

3. Participants should try to see positive elements in each other's proposals, acknowledge the positives, and try to build on them.

4. Each participant should offer to take some constructive action to help resolve the problem.

5. Problem behaviors or possible problem-solving actions should be spelled out as specifically as possible.

Which of these guidelines are emphasized, how they are phrased, and whether they are presented at the beginning or introduced more gradually over several tasks will depend on a variety of factors, including the family's apparent problem-solving capacity and style, the amount of overt conflict among family members, and the nature of the problem being worked on.

Problem formulation. The conflict may be specified with the participants prior to the problem-solving task in accordance with the procedures presented earlier. Alternatively, it may be identified only in simple and rough terms, and the participants may be asked to begin the task by working out a definition of the problem themselves. In helping the participants specify the problem prior to the task, the practitioner can take a more active role in the process, perhaps resulting in a clearer and more expeditious statement of the conflict. On the other hand, letting the clients do the work provides a means of preserving their autonomy and developing their own skills. The latter option is preferable if clients are in fact able to formulate their problem on their own. However, the first option may be needed with clients who are too unfocused or conflicted to carry out this part of the task on their own.

Clarifying positions. A procedure often useful early in problem solving is to have clients reveal to one another their point of view, motivations, rationale, expectations, and so on concerning the issue. For example, an elderly woman prefers to return to her own apartment following her discharge from the hospital, but her daughter wants her to go to a residential care facility. The mother may be asked to explain what is important to her in her living arrangements following the discharge. The daughter, in turn, may be asked to explain to her mother her concerns about her mother's welfare following the discharge. The focus is on where the participants are coming from, rather than on the "solution" each participant would like the other to accept. It is hoped that through clarification of positions common ground may be found on the basis of which a solution acceptable to both may be developed.

Generation of alternatives. Generation of alternatives or possible solutions makes up the bulk of the problem-solving tasks in most approaches. Traditionally, the main procedure suggested is brainstorming (Osborn 1963), in which participants are asked to generate numerous alternatives, initially without considering their quality. Then the most promising alternative is selected. While having clients generate alternative solutions is usually central to the process, in our view brainstorming often is not. In many situations, there may be only two or three viable alternatives, which are quickly recognized. It may be more productive to pursue these often complex alternatives in depth than to have clients spawn a number of possibilities that make little sense. Moreover, clients in an appropriately serious mood struggling with emotionally charged conflicts may have difficulty getting into the swing of brainstorming with its inevitable trivial solutions. However, brainstorming can be quite effective with less serious problems for which a wide range of solutions are possible.

Practitioner-suggested alternatives. When clients are unable to generate alternative solutions acceptable to one another, the practitioner may suggest one or more possibilities. Practitioners may also draw on their own expert knowledge or clinical experience to offer possible solutions that may not have occurred to the clients. "Some couples in your situation have tried thus and so. Do you think that might work for you?" Practitioner-generated alternatives are best used conservatively, after assiduous attempts have been made to elicit possible solutions from the clients. Finally, the practitioner's suggestion should be presented as an *alternative* to be considered along with others rather than as *the* solution.

Offering concessions and exchanges. If the clients do not do so on their own, the practitioner may ask them to indicate concessions or exchanges they would be willing to make to reach a solution. A concession involves the client's giving up a previous demand. An exchange is an offer to do something for something in return. The something in return may be a concession or another behavior. If concessions or exchanges are offered but an impasse continues, the practitioner may use what has been offered to develop and propose a solution for the clients to consider.

Planning implementation. For some solutions reached in the session, implementation is fairly obvious, and little planning may be required. However, most solutions, including many that may appear to be relatively straightforward, require some planning, which can be done as part of the problem-solving task or in a subsequent separate task. In any case, the work in the session culminates in an external task, which may be referred to as a "home" task if it is to be done, as most are, in the context of family life (Reid 1985).

> For example, the conflict between Bob and Marie concerned Bob's wish to have Debbie, his daughter by a former marriage, visit every weekend instead of every other one. Marie, who found Debbie difficult to handle, had been opposed but agreed to Bob's proposal if, in exchange, Bob would finish in two weeks the work on a spare bedroom where Debbie could stay during her visits. The solution seemed simple enough, but planning the home tasks to implement it revealed some overlooked difficulties. It turned out that Bob's schedule really wouldn't permit him to finish the room in the allocated time; both of them remembered that they were planning a weekend trip the following month. Would Debbie come along on this or other trips? As is often the case, planning the implementation led to a modification of the original solution. The visiting on every weekend could not start until the room was finished; Debbie's coming along on weekend trips would be decided on a trip-by-trip basis.

The amount of detail to be spelled out will vary according to the participants' needs and preferences. Some clients are more comfortable with a detailed plan; others do better with less specificity. Such differences among clients generally become clearer after initial tasks have been tried (deShazer 1982; Brown-Standridge 1989).

Securing agreement. When the planning process is completed, it is important to obtain explicit agreement from the participants that they will in fact attempt to carry out the tasks. Some practitioners use written agreements that describe the tasks of each participant and that are signed by each. In my view, written agreements may be useful in some circumstances, for example, when there are several tasks to be undertaken by different participants. The written format then helps everyone to remember his or her tasks. However, for most situations "putting it in writing" does not add enough to an explicit oral agreement to warrant the paperwork. Besides, some clients, and some practitioners, have a negative reaction to the formality of a written agreement.

The practitioner's role. Various aspects of the practitioner's role during the problem-solving tasks have been referred to thus far. The principal interventions used by practitioners at different points in the process are summarized below.

o Reminding participants of ground rules or introducing rules as necessary
o Structuring discussion—e.g., keeping clients focused
o Clarifying and specifying client contributions
o Summarizing areas of agreement and apparent solutions
o Offering alternative solutions
o Helping clients plan external tasks to implement solutions

As can be seen, some interventions (e.g., offering alternative solutions) are more intrusive than others (e.g., structuring discussion). A general principle is to intervene sparingly and with less intrusive interventions if clients appear to be making progress.

Cognitive Methods in Conflict Reduction

Session tasks can be designed to identify and modify such dysfunctional cognitions as overattention, disturbed perceptions, automatic thoughts, malattributions, unrealistic expectations, and irrational beliefs. Such cognitions may be addressed because of their contribution to a focal conflict or to a pervasive pattern of conflict between the clients. Different task formats are used.

The face-to-face communication between the clients may, in itself, help correct some cognitive dysfunctions. For example, participants may be able to correct perceptions or expectations on the basis of new information obtained in the dialog. The practitioner can facilitate this process with questions and comments.

In one session task, Kim listened in silence while her husband, John, complained about her behavior. One of his complaints was her "flying off the handle" when criticized. The practitioner quickly commented that "Kim has just heard a lot of criticism without losing her temper," to which Kim added that she got upset only when the criticism was unfair. The practitioner's intervention highlighted disconfirming, in-vivo evidence concerning John's global perception of Kim's reaction to criticism, which led to a more focused, discriminating discussion of the issue.

In another case, the practitioner reinforced a wife's own awareness of her automatic thoughts in interpreting her husband's silence as anger directed toward her.

In addition, the practitioner can identify more explicitly possible instances of cognitive dysfunction that might become evident during the dialog. Thus, the practitioner might question the expectation of a husband who thinks it is his wife's responsibility to help his mother with the dishes after Sunday dinner at his parents' house while he and his father have a postprandial chat in the living room. As the example suggests, possible dysfunctions are identified in a questioning mode to stimulate the clients' thinking and further discussion rather than as assertions that might evoke oppositional responses from them.

Reenactments in the session of past interactions can also be used to identify cognitive dysfunctions and to provide a basis for their modification.

> Sue, a young adult, lives with her mother who, according to Sue's complaints, is always telling her what to do. Mom protests she is only trying to be helpful. A recent episode in which Sue accused her mother of interfering is reenacted in the session with Mom and Sue in their own roles. At the conclusion of the reenactment, the practitioner asks them to recall the thoughts each had about the other during the reenactment. In this way the practitioner and the participants can explain and modify occurrences of such cognitive events as automatic thoughts, attributions, expectations, and beliefs. Perhaps Sue had the thought that Mom's offer to mix the meatloaf was a message that she (Mom) could do it better, whereas Mom's thoughts were centered around Sue's touchiness and fears of her outbursts. What happened in the reenactment can then be used as a basis for examining cognitive reactions in the actual episode and in similar episodes at home.

In the type of task described thus far, the clients' communication about some behavioral aspect of their conflict is used as a means of bringing to light and correcting cognitive dysfunctions. Another strategy is to use awareness-enhancing and problem-solving tasks (chapter 3) to enable clients to clarify and negotiate differences in the cognitive elements of their conflict. Here it is assumed that the dysfunction is not so much in the cognitions of each client but rather in how their cognitions fit together. This approach applies particularly well to differences in expectations. The clients may be asked to reveal what they expect of one another in a given situation, and discrepant expectations are then identified. The clients then attempt to compromise on the differences. Although the latter task is similar in content to any problem-solving approach to conflict negotiation, the emphasis on expectations calls attention to the cognitive aspects of the conflict, including how the clients' positions relate to social norms. For example, are certain expectations reasonable in this particular situation?

Home tasks to change dysfunctional cognitions generally involve an extension of the work done in the session. The clients may agree to try out new ways of perceiving or thinking about events in their lives or to try changes in what they expect or believe. They may agree to continue discussions about expectations they had begun in the session or, more specifically, to work out together specific expectations for specific situations.

Finally, they may be asked to systematically collect data to test out problematic cognitions. For example, Rich has the perception that his wife Alice is unfair in disciplining his son from a former marriage. Alice doesn't think she is unfair but views Rich as favoring his son over her two children from her former marriage. Tasks for both might be to keep their own logs of their attempts to discipline the children, noting what was done and rating the fairness of the actions. The data can then be used to check their perceptions.

In our experience such tasks, while often not done too systematically or for the stipulated length of time, usually have some positive benefit, at least in making the clients more aware of the realities their cognitions supposedly describe. In addition, observing and recording tasks can affect the behavior in question. Thus, Alice and Rich might make a special effort to be "fair" in their disciplining during the task period. Such reactive behavior may be troublesome in a research context, but can be a useful way of stimulating change in a clinical situation. (See also the case reported by Reid and Strother (1988), which is discussed in chapter 3).

Special Types of Conflict Situations

The format just presented can be used with any type of family conflict. For certain situations, however, additional considerations apply. Two of these will be discussed: conflict between parents and children, and conflict between siblings.

We have already considered problems involving dysfunctional parental and child behavior. When problems involving parents and children are framed as conflict issues, attention is focused on clashes in their interactions. Methods reducing conflict—negotiation, compromise, and so on—are used to find solutions.

Although we have used these methods with parents and children as young as seven, a conflict-reduction approach usually makes more sense with preadolescents and adolescents, who are more likely to have adequate verbal skills. Moreover, parents are usually more willing to negotiate with older than with younger children. A well-developed negotiation model for parent-teen conflict may be found in Robin and Foster (1989).

Sometimes parents are reluctant to negotiate with children of any age on the grounds that children should do what they are told. The parents' position needs to be respected, but some persuasion may convince them to give negotiation a try. Perhaps the best argument is that the child is not doing what she or he has been told (hence the conflict) and that a discussion with the child may enable the parents to obtain the child's cooperation.

A useful goal for parent-child negotiation is the development of acceptable rules and consequences for the child's behavior. When framed in this way, the parents are placed in an authority position— one that parents reluctant to engage in such dialogs will find more comfortable—yet the child has an opportunity to provide input. In helping the parent(s) and child negotiate rules, the practitioner may ask each of the participants to state his or her conception of what a desirable rule should be and what the consequences should be if the child does not follow it. Reciprocal home tasks to implement the agreed rules are then developed. The child's task is to comply with the rules; the parents' task is to provide a consequence, e.g., a tangible reward or expression of approval for compliance or withdrawal of a privilege for noncompliance.

When parents themselves are in disagreement, a session task involving just the parents to work out their differences may be in order. When the parents are deeply divided, this task may be done without the child present. When one parent takes the child's side, tasks addressed to cross-generational coalitions (to be discussed below) may be employed.

Sibling conflict presents a common family problem and, according to some studies, is the most frequent form of domestic violence in the American family (Gelles and Cornell 1985). A task-centered approach to this problem is presented in detail in Reid and Donovan (1990) and illustrated by the T. case (chapter 2). The first step consists of work with the parents to enable them to develop a cooperative, consistent approach to handling disputes between their children. Parental inconsistency and disagreement is a typical cause of sibling conflict. Then the siblings negotiate their conflicts directly without parental interference, using the format presented earlier. Particular attention is given to their developing rules for preventing precursors (triggers), such as

name-calling or taking one another's things. The oldest sibling, especially if he or she is the aggressor, may be given special responsibility
for seeing that the rules are respected. The parents may be requested
to help the children follow the rules and to impose consequences for
failure to comply.

Effectiveness

The Family Problem-Solving Sequence (FPSS) just described was
tested in a study of forty-six task-centered family cases (Reid 1987a).
The combination of in-session problem solving and external tasks (that
is, the FPSS) proved more effective in bringing about immediate problem change than the use of external tasks only or of no tasks at all.
The FPSS as well as the alternate conditions did most poorly when
the conflict involved parents and adolescents who were in relatively
serious trouble in school or in the community. With the seriously troubled adolescents, too much emphasis may have been placed on developing reciprocal tasks in which appropriate behavior by the teen
was to be rewarded by the parents. Such tasks—e.g., contingency contracts—are frequently unsuccessful if one can judge from relevant research (see Stern 1989 for an excellent review). As Stern (1989) argues,
tasks of this kind may run counter to the adolescent's striving for
autonomy, and parents may not control the rewards that really matter
to the teens. Increasing the emphasis on parent-teen negotiation in
reaching mutually satisfactory solutions (the session task part of the
FPSS) may offer more promise (see *Communication* below).

Although studies comparing *cases* receiving the FPSS with those
receiving no treatment or alternative treatment have not yet been conducted, indirect evidence for the effectiveness of the FPSS can be obtained from controlled studies of problem-solving communication
training that are reviewed in the next section. Such training generally
involves in-session problem solving that leads to external tasks, as does
the FPSS. The main difference is that the FPSS emphasizes working
out solutions to problems rather than explicitly teaching problem solving. Nevertheless, the positive outcomes that, as we shall see, have
been found for problem-solving training provide a measure of support
for the efficacy of the FPSS.

Direct Development of Home Tasks

Up to now we have considered strategies in which clients negotiate
their conflicts in the session (session tasks), leading to home tasks that

implement the agreements that have been reached. An alternative strategy is to develop home tasks directly through discussions led by the practitioner in the kind of free-flowing give-and-take characteristic of family interviews. This approach is indicated when family members are unable, because of a high level of conflict or other reasons, to use the session task format, or when they have not used it successfully. This alternative strategy is also indicated when the practitioner wishes to pursue an idea for a home task that the clients are not likely to hit upon through their own dialog. The idea should be sufficiently "good" to override the disadvantages of not having the clients work out their own solutions. Often the better ideas are those sparked by prior discussions with the clients and further shaped by the clients' input after they have been suggested tentatively.

The practitioner may suggest reciprocal tasks addressed to altering factors leading up to the conflict situation, or he or she may recommend that the clients agree to back off or disengage in the early stages of quarreling. Tasks may be developed to alter structural or other contextual features of the conflict, including changes in patterns of involvement and alliance, as will be discussed further below.

Communication

Family problems, especially marital difficulties, are commonly presented as problems in communication. In many other cases as well, a problem in communication provides a constructive way of formulating issues originally presented in terms of the undesirable behaviors of individual family members.

Human communication is an interpersonal exchange of messages that contain implicit and explicit meanings. It takes place largely through three channels: language, paralanguage (in which meaning is conveyed through vocal behavior, such as tone of voice, rather than words), and kinesic communication (body language). Like conflict, a communication has both "content" and "relationship" aspects (Watzlawick, Beavin, and Jackson 1967:112). The content of a message describes its substantive meaning, but messages also make a statement about the relationship of those communicating. If a husband asks his wife to make him breakfast, and she responds by asking him what he wants, the content of the exchange concerns meal preparation. Its relationship or "process" aspect suggests the husband's dominance in this interaction. These distinctions are basic to understanding communication problems, which may occur in any channel or in incongruities between them.

Common Problems in Communication

The phrase "problems in communication" is often used loosely to refer to almost any kind of relationship problem between family members. More rigorous and useful definitions pinpoint specific aspects of communication processes. At this level, the term *communication problems* is most likely used to describe difficulties involving marital partners or parents and older children. What follows is an attempt to isolate a configuration of more common problems.

- ○ *Criticizing, accusing/blaming* The theme here is finding fault in the other or in one another. Problems of this type often grow out of interactive escalation. Common tendencies, especially in heated exchanges, are to attribute faults to global, stable characteristics ("You're an uncaring person"), to present catalogues of faults unrelated to the immediate issue ("gunny sacking"), and to blame the other for past wrongdoings (see chapter 5).

- ○ *Domineering/nagging* Persistently telling another to do things, behave differently, and so on, often in a bossy manner, characterizes this problem. This kind of communication often elicits hostile-defensive responses (especially with teenagers!). Escalations are common: the more A nags, the more defensive and uncooperative B acts, leading to increased nagging on A's part, and so on. A is likely to complain that there would be no need to nag if B did what he or she was supposed to. B is likely to counter that there is no need to do it, that it is none of A's business, or that he or she would do it if A would lay off.

- ○ *Problems in sharing* This problem usually involves one person wanting the other to be more expressive and open and to share thoughts and feelings more. Vicious cycles can develop when A presses B to be more responsive; in reaction B may become more withdrawn, which causes A to press more. Given the evolution of sex roles in our culture, it is not surprising that family members wanting greater responsiveness from others are likely to be wives (in regard to their husbands) and mothers (in regard to their teenage sons). Sometimes the problem takes the opposite form: one partner reveals more than the other wishes to hear. One unburdens while the other feels over-burdened. Vicious cycles also occur. The more A reveals, the more B avoids communication, which increases A's need to talk.

o *Not listening/cutting off* A person doesn't "hear" what the other is saying or interrupts the other's talk to present his or her own point of view. This includes "disqualification" (Watzlawick, Beavin, and Jackson 1967), in which a person's communications are not taken seriously by another.

Building communication skills

Communication problems can be addressed directly through tasks in the session and at home that are designed to enhance the participants' communication skills. In accordance with the problem orientation of the model, we emphasize skills in *problem-solving* communication.

The supervised portion of the training takes place in session tasks; external tasks are used to extend the practice of skills. Although the planning of follow-through on the solutions reached in the session tasks is an important feature of training, this aspect is given somewhat less stress than in the FPSS (discussed above), in which tasks are aimed primarily at resolving particular conflicts.

This strategy is indicated not only when deficits in communication performance are the difficulty, but also when these deficits make it difficult for clients to negotiate conflicts. Another indication is conflicts that are so diffuse and shifting that a one-at-a-time problem-solving approach would make little sense. Although communication training cannot be expected to resolve the conflicts of the clients, it may enable them to handle their conflicts more effectively.

As with parent training and problem solving, the practitioner attempts to develop a particularized training approach geared to the needs and abilities of his or her clients. Although the skills below can be used in sequence in a comprehensive training program, they are usually better employed selectively to deal with specific deficits in communication skills. Various session task structures can be used. Communication training can take place within the context of problem-solving tasks that emphasize communication skills rather than the particular problem under discussion. Tasks enhancing awareness or positive exchange tasks can be used as well as those focused specifically on the skill in question. With these types of tasks the following skills can be worked on.

Listening. As a skill, listening requires being attentive to what others are saying. A good listener takes in the full content of the message and not only what he or she wishes to hear. A session task for improving listening skills involves two participants paraphrasing what the other has just said before responding (Jacobson and Margolin 1979). For example, when Alice finishes her response, Mark summarizes without editorializing what Alice has just said before responding to her communication. Alice listens to his response and paraphrases it in return. Before each response, participants have the opportunity to correct the other's paraphrase for omissions, etc.

Paraphrasing gently forces each participant to listen and to show that he or she has understood the other. In the process, each becomes more aware of the other's point of view. Moreover, paraphrasing slows down the communication process, makes it more deliberate and orderly, and often adds a touch of humor. As a result, it lessens the likelihood of interruptions, angry responses triggered by certain expressions, and shifting of the topic. Because it tends to dampen quarrelsome tendencies, paraphrasing can provide a useful structure for problem-solving communication.

Expressing dissatisfactions. Listening and acknowledging are ways of comprehending and clarifying what others are saying. Expressing dissatisfactions involves stating what one sees as difficulties. The focus is on disclosing dissatisfaction seen in the behavior of another participant, perhaps the most common and difficult type of self-expression in families. The skill here is in stating something undesirable in another person in a manner that conveys one's feelings and perceptions while minimizing angry or defensive reactions on the part of the other person. Being specific about what is undesirable provides a way of both being clear and keeping angry reactions in check. The practitioner stresses the importance of limiting statements to particular behaviors while avoiding pejorative labels or sweeping accusations: "I don't like it when you shut me up if I want to talk about something on my mind," as opposed to, "You're only concerned about yourself," or "You never want to listen to me." In addition, the discloser should make reference to his or her own sources of discomfort, as in the example above. "I" statements (Gordon 1970) or "owning up to your feelings" (Liberman et al. 1980) help locate part of the dissatisfaction in the person making the disclosure and avoid focusing simply on what the other is doing wrong. Beginning statements in the first person, followed by a specific indication of what one is upset about and an illustrative example, is a good way of disclosing problems. "It makes me angry when you're going to be late and don't call, like last Tuesday when you came home at 7 o'clock." Direct statements of the dissatisfaction are preferable to indirect "hints" that leave the other person guessing. Finally, statements should be limited to a single concern rather than becoming a "gunny sack" of complaints.

Self-disclosure and self-expression. The ability to express one's thoughts and feelings serves to provide other family members with feedback about one's position, intentions, and so forth as well as with sufficient stimulation and support. Session tasks may involve participants' discussing an issue that might elicit such self-expression. Mr. Rose, for example, was depressed about his situation at work but rejected his wife's efforts to draw him out. His wife was upset by his irritable responses to her inquiries as well as by being "shut out" of an area of his life that he used to share with her. He agreed to participate in session tasks in which he was able to talk about his problems at work while she took the role of an attentive but not inquisitive listener. These tasks were followed up with similar discussions at home. By allowing Mr. Rose to share at his own pace and having Mrs. Rose restrain her inquiries, the couple was able to resume communication about his work.

When "overexpressiveness" is the problem, session tasks can be directed at having partners discuss an issue in such a way that both derive some feelings of satisfaction from the conversation. The "overexpressive" partner may be asked to pay attention to cues from the other about how much the other would like to know. The "avoiding partner" may be asked to provide these cues while at the same time showing understanding and support for what the other partner is sharing.

In addition to explaining what participants need to do to carry out a skill, the practitioner may model the skill in a role play with one of the participants or with each in turn. As Liberman et al. (1980:145) suggest, the participant with whom the role play is done can take on the role of another family member present, which has the advantage of allowing family members to see how they are being perceived by others, while avoiding "a too personal situation."

During session tasks the practitioner may make use of certain procedures to provide on-the-spot input. *Prompting,* which may take the form of whispered instructions to a participant, provides specific instructions to a participant about what to say or do next. In *doubling*, the practitioner speaks for a participant, a sort of mini role play; or a practitioner may take the role of a participant through a series of interchanges. *Encouragement* provides immediate approval for good problem solving. *Corrective feedback* calls the participant's attention to faulty performance and suggests how it could be improved.

In the present model the practitioner avoids "overtraining" by limiting his or her interventions during the session task. A crucial practitioner skill here is the tolerance of "mistakes" or deviations from the practitioner's conception of appropriate problem-solving communication. As Wells and Figurel (1979) suggest, the majority of the practitioner's interventions should be positive and reinforcing in tone. Whether complimentary or critical, the practitioner's interruptions should not be so frequent that the participants' interaction loses continuity and no longer retains the shape of a unit of work or task. Post-task discussions are used to provide feedback on performance, summarize accomplishments, structure subsequent tasks, and provide instructions for carrying them out.

Changes through problem solving. An alternative strategy is to use problem solving to help modify specific communication processes. A communication problem may be changed by first pinpointing what the problem is and then designing external tasks that clients can carry out to change it. The external tasks are generated through problem solving in the session, either through client-to-client dialogs or through discussions involving the clients and the practitioner. Any of the skills outlined above can be practiced in this manner. Thus, partners can agree to use "I" statements, be more self-revealing, and so on. For motivated clients who already possess but are not using the skills in question, or who can readily learn them in a discussion format, this more direct method may be more efficient than skill training. Moreover, a problem-solving approach may generate solutions that do not fit a skill training format. For example, a quarreling couple may agree to avoid certain topics, or a wife may agree to try to satisfy her conversational needs with her friends rather than with her taciturn husband.

Effectiveness. Controlled evaluations of communication training programs with distressed families have centered on either marital dyads (Jacobson 1977, 1970; O'Leary and Turkowitz 1982; Baucom 1982) or parents and adolescents (Robin 1981; Gant et al. 1981; Foster, Prinz, and O'Leary 1983; Robin and Foster 1989). This body of research has suggested that a communication training approach can help family members acquire communication skills and, further, that training can significantly reduce marital and parent-teen conflict. Although results have lacked consistency across studies and though maintenance of gains has been a problem in some of the programs tested, the approach appears to be a promising one, especially when target problems involve deficits in communication skills.

Concerning the alternative strategy—designing tasks in the session to change communication problems at home—evidence of effectiveness can be derived from studies of behavioral contracting (exchanges of reciprocal tasks) between family members. Several studies that compared communication and contracting approaches in marital couples found both to be superior to a condition of no treatment but neither to be clearly superior to the others (Jacobson 1970; O'Leary and Turkowitz 1982; Russell et al. 1984).

As previously discussed, for communication problems involving adolescents and parents contracting by itself may be of limited value. With such cases, a combination of communication training and contracting, with emphasis on the former, may be the intervention of choice, especially when the adolescents are older and the problems are severe.

Family Structure and Beliefs

I have thus far considered types of common target problems that constitute the focus of work in most cases. As noted earlier, such problems are often the products of contextual factors in family life. Family structure and beliefs are perhaps the most important of these dimensions. Sometimes these factors constitute the source of the target problems, but more often they arise as obstacles to be modified, or resources to be utilized, in the process of solving the more common problems that have been discussed.

In this section, I shall consider the role of these dimensions and how task strategies can be used to effect changes in them. In the final section, I shall suggest strategies for linking work on more common target problems to change in these dimensions.

Control

Control in family structure refers to such aspects as power, dominance and hierarchy. Like other structural dimensions, control refers to interactive patterns—who influences whom in family relationships. To use a common distinction in family theory, relationships can be defined as either *complementary* (with one person in a superior and the other in a subordinate position) or *symmetrical* (both persons interacting as equals) (Watzlawick, Beavin, and Jackson 1967). To determine patterns of control, one attends to the "process" or relationship-defining aspect of communication. For example, if a wife asks her husband "Have you taken your medicine," and the husband replies with "No, but thanks for reminding me," the wife takes the dominant or "one-up" position in a complementary interaction. But if the husband adds "Have you taken yours?" the interaction could be seen as symmetrical. Patterns of complementary and symmetrical relations become established through myriads of interactive episodes. Seldom does one pattern completely characterize a relationship. A husband may be dominant in certain areas, and a wife in others, and in still others the partners may relate as equals. Similar variations may occur between parents and older children. Thus, one should be cautious about such generalizations as "Mom runs this family" or "The kids control the parents."

There are many views on what is ideal in respect to patterns of control. Perhaps the dominant view in American society at present portrays an egalitarian relationship between spouses who exercise benign authority over their children who, in turn, are granted progressively greater freedom as they mature. Against the backdrop of this (and other) ideal types, we can consider several central issues that are frequently found in client families.

Power Struggles

A relationship is characterized by conflict over who is in control. Seldom is a relationship entirely consumed by such conflict. It is usually possible to identify the arenas in which power struggles are most likely to occur or are the most intense. For example, in most areas a husband and wife may relate on cooperative egalitarian terms or accept one another's dominance, but they may fight over control issues in regard to care of their child. The wife may feel that this is her domain and may resent the husband's claim to have an equal say. As the example suggests, what makes a conflict a power struggle is an explicit or implicit dispute over who has the right to make the final decision in given circumstances. Thus, an examination of power issues inevitably leads to consideration of the beliefs the participants have about who should prevail and why when disagreements occur.

Overcontrol

Problems of overcontrol arise in complementary relationships. Those in one-up positions exercise considerable control, which is accepted by those in a one-down position. If it were not accepted, a power struggle would ensue. The one-down partner may have negative feelings about the arrangement. He or she may feel put-upon, pushed around, and so on, but at the same time the individual may be unable or unwilling to become assertive and may in fact be relieved at not having to make decisions. A common result is for the one-down partner to become depressed or to develop somatic reactions. In a marriage the submissive partner may have been attracted to the dominant one because of the dominance, but he or she may now want less of it. In a parent-child relationship, problems are likely to arise as children become adolescents and want more freedom. In exploring these relationships, the practitioner needs to be aware of the ambivalence of the submissive partner and the possible gratifications he or she may derive from the subordinate role. This understanding must then be related to how the dominant partner exercises control and the gratification he or she receives from that role.

In some cases the one-down participant accepts the arrangement without voicing objections. Because the person in the one-up position is not likely to complain, the relationship usually is not presented as a target problem. It may, however, be a contributing factor to other problems. The syndromes of the overprotective parent and the compliant, dependent child both fall into this category. The child is typically seen for a behavioral or health problem and, in addition, may have some form of developmental disability that gives the parent(s) a rationale for the overprotectiveness.

Hierarchical Reversal

A generally accepted norm is that parents should be in control of their children. A breakdown of parental authority is most likely to occur with older children and adolescents in the form of power struggles, in which the parents' attempts at exercising control are rejected by their offspring. In some cases parents, especially single parents, lose (or give up) the battle for control with a reversal of the usual hierarchical structure. The child or children become one-up in the relationship, a position often maintained through such coercive behaviors as temper tantrums and threatened or actual violence.

In addition to being problems in their own right, issues concerning control can, as suggested, contribute to a number of target problems. Power struggles can be a major theme in conflicts between marital partners and between parents and teens. Overcontrol can foster withdrawn, dependent children prone to somatic reactions. Hierarchical reversal may be associated with acting out or aggressive behavior in children (Madden and Harbin 1983).

Task Strategies

The usual approach to helping family members resolve disputes over control is through conflict-negotiation tasks (see *Conflict* above) since a power struggle is essentially a form of overt conflict. However, when control is the issue, more attention is given to questions of the participants' claim to authority and to feelings about being put in a subordinate position. The subtask of clarifying positions can be used for this purpose. In other words, the conflict is examined at a level more general than the immediate issue, and an effort is made to help the participants clarify the more general question of who is in charge of what. Tasks involving clarification and modification of expectations may be useful here. Helping clients negotiate general rules (meta-rules) about their responsibilities can also help avoid power struggles. It is easier for family members to adhere to a rule they mutually agreed on than to accept what might be seen as an arbitrary decision of someone who claims to be in a position of authority. Thus, a young adult living at home may be able to accept an agreement to be responsible for a range of household chores but would resent his or her parents' attempts to tell him to do this or that.

In problems of overcontrol, the controlling family member needs to see the wisdom of allowing the controlled member to have greater independence of action. For the purposes of our discussion, we assume a dyad. Although the actual tasks may be undertaken by the person in the one-down position, the individual who is one-up has to have a rationale for "letting go." Possible frames include the burden on one-up of having to oversee one-down or that one-down will be more content or function better if he or she were more independent. Session tasks are structured so that the controlled member actively plans tasks to foster his or her independence while the controlling member takes a facilitating role. In some situations, the tasks can involve real life interaction. For example, in one case a mother and grandmother were helped to take "supportive observer" roles while their eight-year-old son (grandson) worked out homework problems that the two adults formerly used to do for him.

Modifying hierarchical reversal will be considered in relation to the single mother family, where it is a particularly frequent and troublesome problem. For the two-parent family, the techniques are similar to strengthening a weak parental alliance, which will be discussed below.

With the single mother family, hierarchical reversal typically occurs with older children who tend to win out over the mother in power struggles. A first step is to help both mother and children recognize the need for greater parental authority. A session task in which mother and children are asked to discuss "who should be in charge in our family" can be used as a point of departure. The next step is for the parent and children to negotiate in session tasks the rules for handling situations in which power struggles typically occur, e.g., curfews, household chores, homework. The rules should have clear consequences for the children for compliance (e.g., a reward) or noncompliance (e.g., withdrawal of privileges). The implementation of the rules and the consequences becomes a home task for the mother and children. When these tasks are successfully carried out, the practitioner praises the mother for enforcing the rules and the children for accepting the mother's leadership.

Involvement

Involvement (Epstein and Bishop 1981; Reid 1985) is used here as an umbrella term to refer to the variety of ways that "connectedness" among family members has been described in family theory: enmeshment/disengagement (Minuchin et al. 1967); differentiation (Bowen 1978); cohesion (Olson, McCubbin, and Associates 1983); and centripetal/centrifugal (Stierlin 1972; Lewis et al. 1976).

These terms reflect a variety of meanings derived from differing definitions and theoretical perspectives. The amount of overlap is considerable, however, and to a large extent indeterminate because of a lack of clear distinctions among the terms at an operational level. This collection of terms can be seen as one of the numerous "concept clusters" in family theory. Most writers view the involvement dimension (or its equivalent) as running from high to low degrees. Usually the optimum amount of involvement is thought to fall somewhere in the middle range. Problems reflecting extremes of overinvolvement and underinvolvement will be considered.

High Mutual Involvement (Enmeshment)

A high degree of mutual involvement among family members is most readily identified when it intensifies conflict. The large amount of interdependency among family members for meeting intimacy needs sets the stage for conflict. Perhaps because of the strength of these needs and the lack of other means of fulfilling them, family members place on one another demands that may be excessive and may invade one another's autonomy when these demands are not met. Patterns of escalating mutual frustration can ensue. The system becomes overreactive in that a frustrating response triggers chains of excessive reactions and counterreactions. High mutual involvement without conflict is more difficult to identify since the arrangement presents no immediate distress and may even be a source of gratification and protection for both parties involved. However, this type of overinvolvement may be part of the context of other difficulties. It may create a mutually reinforcing subsystem that is unable to adapt to the external world. Problem-solving actions and exploration of useful alternatives may be blocked.

Extremely high levels of involvement, while creating problems in many situations, may be highly functional under certain circumstances, for example, when the family is faced with an external threat and must make an immediate response. Moreover, in any consideration of involvement, a good deal depends on related family dynamics. Extreme involvement accompanied by a high degree of conflict among family members can create a pressure cooker of explosive forces. In the absence of conflict, the same level of involvement might result in a very stable family structure that may be quite functional for many purposes.

Low Mutual Involvement (Disengagement)

In this pattern, family members lack close connections with one another. Although they are not in conflict over the degree of involvement with one another, there may or may not be conflict around other issues. When conflict does occur, it is likely to be related to specific points of contention. For example, adult children who may have had little to do with one another for years may find themselves at odds over how to care for an aging parent. When conflict does occur in low-involvement relationships, it is likely to reactivate patterns established when the involvement was greater. These old patterns may produce general conflict if the distancing was the result of an "emotional cutoff" (Bowen 1978). As Kerr (1981) suggests, a cutoff is a way of dealing with unresolved involvements in a relationship by withdrawing emotionally from it. When family members who have resolved previous difficulties with a pattern of mutual withdrawal are brought together through a crisis event, their unfinished business may intrude.

Task Strategies

When relationships are characterized by mutual over-involvement (enmeshment), a basic strategy is to help clients develop separate interests, activities, friendships, and so on. These may be planned in joint sessions, but in keeping with the emphasis on individuation, face-to-face dialog between clients would not be used. In fact, individual interviews might be substituted for joint sessions to underscore the individuation theme.

Session tasks can be used to promote individuation when the enmeshed partners are present with other family members. For example, a mother overinvolved with her children can be asked to "take a well-deserved rest" while the father and children work out the solution to a problem in a session task.

It is useful to consider the lack of mutual involvement in relation to conflict. Although enmeshed relationships can be highly conflictual, prolonged conflict can drive people apart and lead to a lack of connectedness. In these situations, increasing involvement in nonconflicted areas may provide a strategy for conflict reduction.

The goal is usually to increase positive interactions between conflicted partners. One simple step toward this goal as well as toward reducing tension in the session is a session task in which clients are asked to say "something positive" or "something you appreciate" about each other. This task often produces gratifying results with teens and their parents. Many teens have never expressed directly to their parents what they appreciate or like about them; in fact, some teens react as if this was the first time they had ever thought about it. After some groping for words, clients are normally able to complete the task, sometimes surprising one another with what was considered positive. A follow-up task at home can request more frequent expression of appreciative and positive comments.

Instead of simply saying good things about each other, clients can be asked to act in ways that would please one another. This strategy has its origins in the "love days" (Weiss 1975) and "caring days" (Stuart 1980). In these approaches, clients agree to exchange pleasing behaviors. These behaviors can be identified from an instrument, such as the Spouse Observation Checklist (Patterson 1976). Clients can be asked to list as many things as they can think of their partner do that please them. Each client selects a number of these behaviors from the other's list and agrees, as a home task, to do them or more during the week. Although these requests may involve annoyances—e.g., "I am pleased when you pick up your clothes instead of draping them over the furniture"—serious conflicts are avoided. Originally developed for marital treatment and used largely in this context, this approach can be applied to any set of intimates, including parents and teens. As Ward and Jacobson (1985) suggest, the strategy is especially useful at the beginning of the treatment. It starts things off on an optimistic note and can give clients the kind of relationship boost that makes it easier for them to tackle specific areas of conflict. Even when intimates are at loggerheads over almost everything—as in the beleaguered parent/impossible teen syndrome—at least one or two positive behaviors on each side can usually be found and exchanged.

In some intimate relationships most interaction occurs around conflicted issues. The rest of the relationship has withered away into a pattern of mutual avoidance and pursuit of separate interests. Bled of good feelings and pleasant associations, the relationship becomes even more vulnerable to conflict, which in turn drives the intimates even further away from each other. To break such vicious cycles, the practitioner attempts to help clients identify activities they enjoy doing together and to develop ways of sharing these activities. The activities are usually identified and planned in session tasks and carried out through external tasks. Dinner out, attending movies or sporting events, shopping, and walks are common examples. For workaholic individuals, a home improvement project may be the ticket. Two or more activities may be planned, especially if it is hard for clients to agree on any particular one.

Used to moving on separate tracks, clients may not be willing to initiate such activities on their own but will do so at the practitioner's instigation. The practitioner emphasizes that the activity chosen is to be seen as a beginning and will, it is hoped, lead to others. It is also hoped that some meaningful though not quarrelsome conversation will occur, but this is usually not made a part of the task.

Client reinvention is common in doing such tasks. The clients may not carry out the activity they agreed on but may do another. Even if the activity is not carried out, its discussion and planning can sometimes stimulate awareness of the need to do more together, to talk more, and so on. For example, rather than going to a basketball game, a couple decided that they could spend more time together if they worked on the same household project rather than on different ones.

Enjoyable activity tasks are usually combined with more direct approaches, such as problem solving and communication training. In this way strains resulting from often tense direct work on the problem can be offset with the more pleasurable pursuits of the joint activities.

In some relationships lack of involvement is fomented by unresolved issues from the past, issues that often have never even been discussed. for example, an old extramarital affair casts a shadow over a marriage. For years a son has harbored unvoiced bitterness toward his mother because she left his father. Anger, mistrust, and resentment are among continuing reactions to such perceived wrongs. Although no longer an immediate cause of conflict, such feelings make conflict more likely and more severe.

Whether old wounds are currently fueling discord is not easily determined. Perhaps the best clues are references, often veiled or incidental, to the noxious event. The practitioner can then inquire about previous discussions and their outcomes. If feelings associated with the event are still present and have not been adequately discussed, the practitioner can then explore the clients' readiness to talk about them now. The practitioner's approach is tentative unless there should be good reason to suppose that feelings are present and that clients are willing to discuss them. If the signals are "go," then a session task is set up that is loosely structured to enable the clients to have the kind of dialog they feel comfortable with. As the dialog proceeds, the practitioner may attempt to draw out and clarify feelings, but he or she should also be prepared to terminate the task if the clients get bogged down in an accusatory-defensive pattern, or if the revelations appear to be too much for either client to handle. Following the task, the practitioner attempts to help the clients reframe the event to incorporate any new information revealed. This should be done in a way to help the clients achieve a more tolerant understanding of the reasons for each other's past behavior so that some forgiving and forgetting can take place. If necessary, additional discussions between the clients can be structured in the session, or home tasks can be set up to enable them to continue the dialog on their own.

> For example, Norma, age fifteen, had been in institutional placement for over a year. Trial visits home had been marred by acting out behavior and serious quarreling with her mother. Norma had blamed her mother for having divorced her father, following an affair with a man she subsequently married and who was Norma's current stepfather. In a joint session, Norma's criticism of her mother included her part in the marital break-up. The practitioner eased into a session task by encouraging Norma to tell her mom how she (Norma) saw things at that time. Norma attacked her mother's behavior, especially her infidelity. Her mother accepted her criticism without anger, explaining with surprising patience some of her reasons for turning away from Norma's father, a heavy drinker, to her current husband. Although still critical, Norma appeared to achieve some understanding of what her mother had gone through.

Alliance

Alliances are alignments or coalitions between family members to achieve a common purpose. Alliances reflect the cooperative actions essential to healthy family functioning, but certain kinds of dysfunctional alliances may bring about or maintain family problems.

Alliance Supporting Problem Behavior

Family members join together to justify, defend, or approve dysfunctional behavior of a member. Often the family is a nonvoluntary referral. For example, parents may blame the school for their child's behavior problems in the classroom.

Weak Parental Alliance

Parents do not form a consistent, united front in their interactions with their children. This may be due to a conflict between the parents over issues concerning their children or to one parent's withdrawal from child care responsibilities. In such cases, the boundaries of the parental subsystem often lack definition. That is, decision making about the children is more likely to involve a parent and a child rather than the two parents.

Cross-Generational Coalition

A special case of a weak parental alliance is the coalition of one parent and child(ren) against the other parent. The coalition, which may be implicit, disrupts cooperative parental behavior and compromises the authority of both parents. For example, Dad may consistently take the side of his teen-age daughter in her arguments with Mom.

Scapegoating Coalitions

Family members may form an alliance against another member, usually a child. The scapegoated member usually exhibits characteristics or behaviors that provoke the hostility of the scapegoaters. The distinguishing element of the process is an extra margin of hostility or blame heaped on the scapegoated member, which may result from conflict between the allied partners, a "detouring, attacking coalition" (Minuchin, Rosman, and Baker 1978). Or it may consist of blaming the scapegoated member for various frustrations that may or may not be related to his or her behavior.

Task Strategies

An alliance supporting problem behavior poses serious obstacles to both problem formulation and intervention. The practitioner is likely to proceed only when action on the problem has been mandated by the court or a protective agency. Considerations discussed previously for work with nonvoluntary clients apply here (chapter 2). When appropriate, the practitioner may undertake the task of obtaining information about the problem behavior from an outside source (e.g., the school) and of introducing the information in a nonthreatening manner. Assessment tasks for family members can be developed. Family members can be asked to get information from relevant outside sources themselves, or if the "problem" occurs at home, they can be requested to observe and record the frequency of problem behavior. The results of these data-gathering tasks can then be discussed in the session.

Whether weakened by distance, conflict, or cross-generational ties, an ineffective parental alliance can be a formidable obstacle in efforts to resolve child-related problems. Seeing parents alone for one or more sessions or parts of sessions may be necessary as a basis for concentrated work on the parental relationship (Reid and Donovan 1990). Session tasks provide the structure for face-to-face parental negotiation and planning concerning issues relating to the child's (children's) problems. In sessions involving parents and children, session tasks between the parents alone reinforce the parental alliance while deemphasizing any parent-child coalitions that may be present. External tasks, often planned by the parents together in the session, call for cooperative actions in respect to particular issues—e.g., the parents agree to support each other in disciplining the children. In this strategy, the focus is on the parents' cooperative behavior in regard to the children. Marital issues are addressed only if they relate to this focus unless the parents request help for marital problems not related to their roles as parents.

In helping family members to recognize scapegoating alliances, it is usually sufficient to obtain some acknowledgement that they may be too harsh in their judgment of the scapegoated child. They may not be able to recognize their tendencies to use the child as a vehicle for expressing surplus hostility. Part of the corrective strategy involves having the allied family members, who usually include the parents, state some positive things about the child, perhaps as part of a "positive exchange" session task. As an external task, the parents may be asked to record instances of the child's positive behavior during the week. At the same time, tasks are designed for the scapegoated child to behave appropriately in those areas where there may be negatively distorted perceptions of his or her behavior even if those areas are peripheral to the target problem. For example, if the parents exaggerate their son's teasing of his sister, the son's task may be to make a special effort to treat his sister well during the week. In this way, evidence to disconfirm the parents' excessively negative perceptions of the son may be produced.

Family Beliefs

I have considered beliefs of family members in various contexts, but up to this point the emphasis has been on problems resulting from discrepant beliefs between family members or from the dysfunctional beliefs of individual members. In this section, I shall examine beliefs that characterize the family as a unit, that is, beliefs that are shared by family members.

One type of family belief is the family myth, a belief that is idiosyncratic to a particular family. Family myths, as I use the term, contain some distortion of reality and serve a stabilizing or protective function. For example, parents may view the social agencies in a community as conspiring to take away their children, or a family may maintain the belief that a severe, irreversible disability of one of its members is a minor handicap that can be cured. Certain myths, such as that a particular child is inherently bad, can provide a rationale for scapegoating.

Family myths are rarely presented as problems by the family itself, but they may form difficult obstacles to the solution of the actual target problems. They are not easily modified because family members reinforce one another's perceptions and collectively interpret evidence to support these perceptions.

The practitioner may probe the family's beliefs to determine if the members are responsive to verbal approaches, e.g., pointing out facts that may contradict the beliefs. Although verbal approaches sometimes work, often more leverage can be gained through tasks that enable the family members to experience aspects of reality that they had previously not perceived. Having family members observe and record the behavior of a particular family member can be useful if the myth is being maintained by selectively ignoring the occurrence of disconfirming behavior. Session tasks that involve stating positives about a child seen as incorrigible can sometimes be helpful. Families can also acquire new information from experiences outside the family. Thus, a mother who shared her husband's belief that their three-year-old son's problem behavior was being exaggerated by his preschool teacher was asked to observe her son in action at the school. For parents suspicious about an agency's designs on their child, the practitioner arranged a conference with the agency executive who made clear the agency's intent to do what it could to help the family keep its children at home. It should be recognized, however, that not all family myths are dysfunctional. A family's unrealistic hope that a terminally ill member will somehow recover may help maintain the family's morale in a period of stress. Family myths that do not pose obstacles to the resolution of target problems are often best left alone.

A quite different kind of shared belief is derived from the family's cultural and ethnic identities. A Mexican immigrant family may, with good reason, view government agencies with suspicion. A middle-class black family may have a strong belief that its children should do extra well in school to prepare themselves for life in a discriminatory society. Such beliefs based on values and experiences of group members may be quite functional for many purposes. But they may not always fit the realities of the larger culture, a lack of fit that may become apparent in the family's coping with its external environment. When these beliefs no longer capture current realities in an adaptive manner, they become open to challenge and change. However, other beliefs related to the family's cultural and ethnic identity may be resources in its efforts to cope. For example, the belief found in some cultures that one has an overriding obligation to help members of one's kin may be a source of vital assistance to a family in need. Like any social work model, the task-centered approach needs to be applied with sensitivity to the beliefs and needs of ethnic minorities. But as always, it is important to relate to the client as a unique individual and to avoid applying cultural stereotypes. Often the practitioner must serve as "a culture broker" in helping the client and those in the mainstream culture to understand one another's actions. A case drawn from the Task-Centered Family Treatment Project illustrates some of these points.

> The Wus, a Chinese family that had recently immigrated from Hong Kong, were referred by a child protective agency because of possible neglect of their nine-year-old son, Eddie, whom they left alone at home while they worked in the family restaurant. Also, on one occasion the police caught him riding his bike at 10 p.m. The practitioner, also Chinese, helped the parents understand the expectation of closer parental supervision in the American culture. Among the Chinese, the availability of extended family members and neighbors to provide care makes it permissible to leave children of that age "alone." By formulating a task in terms the parents (given their culture) could understand (e.g., need to respect the law), the practitioner was able to get them to agree not to leave Eddie alone at night. Through other tasks, they also became able to do more with him. At the same time, the social worker was able to interpret to the agency staff some aspects of the parents' behavior, such as taking Eddie to the restaurant with them at night, that were normal in their culture.

CHAPTER 7

Emotional Distress

WILLIAM J. REID

NORMA WASKO

Although emotional distress may take a variety of forms, most encountered by clinical social workers can be grouped into two broad categories—depression and anxiety. In mental health settings and in private practice, depression and anxiety are major reasons for clients to seek help. In all settings depression and anxiety are frequent target problems or are often major components of other problems.

In this chapter we shall consider how a task-centered approach can be used to alleviate these two common forms of emotional distress. We shall first take up applications to problems of depression and then examine methods that can be employed with certain types of anxiety.

Understanding Depression

Problems in defining depression as a diagnostic entity are well recognized (Nezu, Nezu, and Perri 1989; Rush and Altshuler 1986). Perhaps the most widely used definition is that provided by the Diagnostic and Statistical Manual of Psychiatric Disorders (DSM-III-R, American Psychiatric Association 1987). The manual distinguishes between two types of depression: major depression and dysthymia. For diagnosis of major depression there must be present during the same two week period at least five of the following nine symptoms: (1) depressed mood; (2) markedly diminished interest or pleasure in activities; (3) significant weight loss or gain; (4) insomnia or hypersomnia; (5) psychomotor agitation or retardation; (6) fatigue, loss of energy, feelings of worth-lessness; (7) inappropriate guilt; (8) diminished ability to think or concentrate or indecisiveness; and (9) recurrent thoughts of death or suicidal ideation. Either depressed mood or diminished interest must be present. With the exception of (2) and (9), the symptoms must recur on a daily basis.

Dysthymia is a less severe form of depression that does not meet the criteria for a major depression. Its distinguishing characteristic is its chronicity; there must be a two-year history of depression. Moreover, dysthymia may occur simultaneously with a major depressive episode. Often, clients may recover from a major depression while continuing to experience dysthymia. The persistence of this condition appears to be related to the developmental experience of the individual, and it can therefore be characterized as an aspect of the personality. While it is important for clinical social workers to be familiar with these classifications, a somewhat broader definition has more utility. Social workers see large numbers of clients who may not meet formal psychiatric criteria for major depression or even dysthymia, but who nonetheless complain of being depressed and want help for these complaints. Their depression may arise as a consequence of their life situation, or it may be a reaction to specific environmental stressors. Usually the main symptom is a depressed mood, but other symptoms may also be present. There may not necessarily be a two-year history of depressed mood, and the depression may not necessarily be the client's primary complaint.

Depression is a recurring problem; most clients who report depression have had previous episodes. Most major depressive episodes run their course in a matter of several months, with five to eight months considered typical (Winokur 1978). It is a condition reported more frequently by women than by men. Less is known about the epidemiology of severe forms of depression.

The etiology of depressive episodes, whether severe or mild, is usually difficult to determine. A diathesis-stress model seems to fit best with the available evidence (Sacco and Beck 1985). In this framework, predisposing factors create a susceptibility to depression. These predisposing factors may originate in the person's genetic background and in his or her childhood development. Combined with these factors, subsequent life experiences may create additional predispositions.

Susceptibility to depression is perhaps most clearly seen in the cognitive sphere. As Beck and his associates have observed (Beck 1967;

Sacco and Beck 1985), a person prone to depression tends to have an unrealistically negative view of self, the external world, and the future, that is, the view is more negative than would be warranted by a reasonable assessment of one's limitations or even by a pessimistic outlook. Distortions toward the negative are maintained by the errors in processing information discussed in chapter 5. With a depression-prone individual, these errors overemphasize the negative. Thus, negative details about a situation are focused upon, the significant negative events are magnified and overgeneralized, events are given a negative twist and personalized, and black-or-white thinking usually favors the black side.

The depression-prone person may have a distinctive way of attributing events that supports the negative outlook. As suggested by the learned helplessness theory of depression (Abramson, Seligman, and Teasdale 1978), such persons tend to view themselves as responsible for negative events and to see the causes of the events as persistent and as having a broad impact. In more technical language, attributions are internal, stable, and global. For example, Lena may assume that her boyfriend broke a date because of her boring personality, that she will continue to bore him, and that as a result she may drive him off for good. Such attributions lead to a belief in one's helplessness to control future events, a belief that sets the stage for the development of depression.

Cognitive predispositions are usually intertwined with behavioral and environmental deficits. On the behavioral side, a lack of social skills has frequently been cited as a characteristic of depression-prone individuals (Hoberman and Lewisohn 1984; Billings and Moos 1982; Becker, Heimberg, and Bellack 1987). With a negative outlook and a tendency to perceive events to fit this viewpoint, the depression-prone person experiences particular difficulty in obtaining gratification from others and in resolving the social problems of everyday life. Thus, Lena might demand excessive reassurance from her boyfriend over the broken date, or she may be excessively accusative. By the same token, poor social skills are likely to lead to situations ready-made for negative interpretation, e.g., Lena's boyfriend becomes more standoffish in response to Lena's demands and criticisms.

Such dynamics can help form an environment in which the person receives few interpersonal rewards and little positive social reinforcement (Hoberman and Lewisohn 1984). In addition, environmental factors may operate on their own to create additional depressogenic stressors. Life strains associated with major social roles, such as spouse, parent, or employee, can make independent contributions to fostering depression in vulnerable persons (Billings and Moos 1982). Thus, in their review of the considerable evidence linking marital distress and depressive symptoms, Follette and Jacobson (1988:258) conclude that problem marriages at least for women "may be a major factor in the onset of depression." More generally, a family situation that is forever fraught with problems and offers few gratifications is likely to be depressogenic for family members. Mothers and wives are probably more vulnerable than other members given their traditionally high emotional stakes in family life and their disproportionate share of family responsibilities.

Role of Stress

The precipitants of many depressive episodes appear to be stressors that may consist of an accumulation of life strains and specific events. Stressors are typically defined as present or future losses of gratification, resources, relationships, and so on, which may take the form of such negative events as the death of a loved one, divorce or separation, or the diagnosis of a terminal illness or disability. While most studies have found associations between life events and depression (Clayton 1986), it has been difficult to demonstrate a strong empirical relationship. In summarizing available research, Clayton (1986:37) has commented, "Many people experience serious life events and don't develop depression, and many depressives report significant events before one episode but not another."

Research on antecedents of depression is complicated by difficulties in distinguishing between the factors that contribute to a depressive episode and those that may result from the depression itself. This dilemma has lead to the formulation of reciprocal models that assume that depressive episodes evolve in a spiral fashion from the interplay of "antecedent" factors and depressive reactions (Lewisohn, Hoberman, Terri, and Hautzinger 1985; Nezu, Nezu, and Perri 1989).

According to a reciprocal model, an initial depressive response to a stressful event can result in impaired functioning in important areas of the person's life, engendering additional stress. For example, a lack of emotional responsiveness, irritability, sensitivity to criticism, and a need for reassurance can contribute to marital problems. Such interpersonal factors, as well as poor concentration, can cause difficulties at work. It is not surprising that depressed persons are often rated low on social competence by observers (Nezu, Nezu, and Perri 1989) and elicit negative reactions from others interacting with them (Coyne 1976). In addition to specific stressors, life strains may over time gradually cause depressive reactions. Chronic strains in marital, parental, and work roles are the usual culprits. Again, the influence usually occurs through vicious cycles in which depressive reactions increase strain that in turn leads to heightened depression.

Assessment

When depression is one of the client's primary complaints, problem exploration and assessment are straightforward. A prior history of depressive episodes should be obtained, and the extent and severity of the current symptoms, following DSM-III-R criteria, should be determined. Particular attention should be given to the stressors that may have precipitated the depression or that may be maintaining it.

However, in some cases depression may not be presented as a complaint, but in the course of discussing other problems the client may reveal evidence of depression, moodiness, loss of interest in activities, poor appetite, and so on. Possible indicators should be explored to determine their frequency and severity, and the client should be asked about the presence of the other signs. If this exploration reveals that a significant problem of depression is present, the client may be asked if he or she wishes to work on it as a target problem. If not, the depression should be monitored as part of the context of the problems that become the focus of work. Whenever there are signs of significant depression, there should be an exploration for possible suicidal ideation and apparent suicide attempts.

Brief standardized self-report instruments can provide useful additions to the clinical interview in the assessment of depression. The most commonly used and perhaps the best validated one is the Beck Depression Inventory (BDI), a twenty-one item instrument that provides a particularly good measure of the severity of depression (Beck 1967). The Hudson Clinical Assessment Package (Hudson 1982) contains a measure of general contentment, which is well suited to the milder forms of depression often encountered in social work practice. Suicidal potential can be assessed through the use of a specialized instrument, The Scale for Suicidal Ideation (Beck, Kovacs, and Weissman 1979).

In addition to providing comparisons of the client with norms for clinical and nonclinical populations and allowing progress to be tracked over time, standardized instruments provide a comprehensive survey of possible depressive symptomatology. The survey feature is especially useful in cases of depression because it may detect more serious depressive symptoms, e.g., suicidal ideation, that may not emerge in a clinical interview.

Task Strategies

Task strategies for depression are shaped by the causative factors identified during the assessment phase. We shall move from the simple to the complex, starting with less complicated strategies in individual treatment and ending with more involved strategies used in couple and family treatment.

Coping with Stress

In most cases, stressors will pay a role in a depressive episode. In some cases, the depression may be triggered and maintained by identifiable stressors, such as a difficult work situation, financial problems, or an unsatisfying marital relationship. If the stressor is amenable to change through the actions of the client, then a reasonable first strategy is to help the client develop tasks to effect such a change. In the process, the client has a chance to modify directly whatever may be contributing to his or her depression. Moreover, he or she becomes involved in constructive action that in itself may have positive consequences even though it may not alter the situation. Thus, Miss T., a woman employed for many years in an insurance firm, became depressed over having been passed over for a promotion, which went to an employee with less seniority. As a treatment task, she had a much-dreaded session with the director of the unit who reaffirmed her value to the company in a way she found reassuring. Even though the work situation did not change, she felt better afterwards, in part because she had finally "done something" about it.

For depressed people, problem-solving action in itself can be therapeutic even though it may not succeed in solving the problem. However, in some situations there may be a risk that the action will only make matters, including the client's depression, worse. Risk assessment should be done collaboratively between the practitioner and the client as a part of the planning process in these situations.

When the stressors cannot be changed, or an effort to do so does not warrant the risk, clients can often be helped to develop better ways of coping. For example, an elderly man has become depressed in reaction to the stress of caring for his wife who has Alzheimer's disease. His method of coping is to get drunk, which not only exacerbates that problem but also leads to others. The practitioner tries to help him search for other coping mechanisms, which might lead to tasks—e.g., joining a caregivers group, obtaining more help from his adult children, developing interests outside the home that give him satisfaction. In some cases, action can be directed toward making a new start, hopefully one that will lead to obtaining new sources of gratification to replace those that have been lost. For example, clients depressed over a divorce can begin to plan new ways of obtaining companionship or whatever may have been valued in the marriage.

Increasing Life Satisfaction and Social Involvement

Whether or not specific stressors can be identified, depressed clients frequently lack pleasurable experiences, activities, and relationships. Although such a lack is one of the consequences of being depressed, it also serves to maintain the depression by keeping the client isolated and deprived of social and other pleasurable stimulation. Therefore, depressed clients can be helped by tasks that include the following:

1. developing and carrying out pleasant activities (Coyne 1986; Barth 1985; Burns, Adams, and Anastopoulos 1985; Hoberman and Lewisohn 1985);

2. developing new social relationships (Doerfler and Richards 1981);

3. becoming involved in a meaningful activity, e.g., attending church or joining a social organization (Staudemire and Blazer 1985; Rounsaville, Klerman, Weissman, and Chevron 1985);

4. identifying and using sources of social support (Billings and Moos 1982).

The extent to which tasks of this kind are used and when they are used will depend on the client's readiness. It is unwise to push a client prematurely into activities or relationships that he or she is not prepared to undertake. Simple tasks to increase pleasurable events may be enough for a start. As always, the practitioner needs to be guided by the client's interests, orientation, and patterns of activity prior to the onset of the depression. What were sources of satisfaction and social support? How can they be resumed at a pace the client is willing to accept? The possibilities outlined above should be explored with the client as possibilities and not be presented as prescriptions.

In some instances, individuals may require help from family and friends to overcome patterns of isolated dysfunctional behavior. The role of the practitioner in such circumstances is to engage the client's cooperation in efforts to involve these social supports. In these situations, the practitioner often walks a fine line between respecting the client's self-determination and insisting, based on experience and concern for the client, that some change needs to occur. The practitioner might explore with the client how significant others in his or her life might become involved to help provide more satisfying social involvement. For example, a woman suffering periodic blue moods who tends to isolate herself in her room might agree to accept her husband's help in carrying out a previously agreed upon outing to a dinner party. While the client might exhibit some initial resistance to planning the task, exploration may reveal this to be due to her sense of the task as overwhelming and impossible to do alone. Involvement of the spouse, with the client's agreement, in planning and carrying out the task may make it more manageable, and it may serve to alter both the client's appraisal of social expectations as well as marital communication.

Enhancing Social Skills

To obtain benefits from social interactions and activities, clients may need to improve their social skills. For this reason, social skills training has been widely used in the treatment of depressed people (Hoberman and Lewisohn 1985; Barth 1985; Nezu, Nezu, and Perri 1989). Emphasis has been placed on enabling clients to be more assertive in asking for help, expressing their needs, and in handling problematic situations. In the present model (as outlined in chapter 5), the needed skill is first identified and defined in collaboration with the client. For example, Mrs. George has been unable to speak up to her husband who refuses to be involved in treatment. Ways in which she can make her wishes known are explored in the session and certain options are selected. Through session tasks using role plays, the skill may be modeled by the practitioner and rehearsed by the client. In the example, the practitioner could take the role of Mrs. George and model how she might make her request. Playing herself, the client might rehearse the task with the practitioner in the role of her husband. A home task to implement the skill (e.g., Mrs. George will make a specific request of her husband) might be set up, planned, and reviewed in the subsequent session. Additional work in the session and further home tasks would follow. In some cases, a task might call for prescribed action to occur on multiple occasions (e.g., daily). If so, the client may be asked to keep a record of task trials and their results.

Almost any kind of social skill training may be indicated with a depressed client depending on factors contributing to the depression. One kind of training used by Barth (1985) with depressed teen-age mothers was designed to increase their ability to handle criticism. The skill is generally applicable to work with depressed clients who tend to be especially vulnerable to criticism. According to Barth, three skills are involved: paraphrasing, softening, and calming. Paraphrasing what the other has said enables the client to determine if the other's remark was, in fact, critical. Softening (acknowledging errors) and calming (giving the other credit for having a good point) gives the client a chance to enter into a rational discussion of the issue rather than responding without thinking. This skill can then be followed by assertive responses in which the client can make his or her own points about the issue. In lieu of paraphrasing, the client can simply ask what the other meant if criticism is suspected. Depressed persons often interpret neutral or ambiguous comments or gestures as criticism, and this can deepen depressed feelings and also lead to counterresponses (withdrawal or anger) and hence to further relational difficulties. Such "exacerbation cycles" (Storms and McCaul 1976) can often be interrupted by "checking out" what was intended before appraising the other's response as criticism or hostility (Reid and Strother 1988).

Self-Monitoring

Thus far we have examined tasks that were primarily intended to alter environmental contingencies. We now turn to tasks that are aimed more directly at internal changes. We begin with a set of tasks that use forms, worksheets, and other structural recording devices to enable the client to be an active participant in assessing and deciphering his or her own condition and in planning action to change it. Although many of these tasks are designed to obtain diagnostic information, they also can be expected to have an impact on the client—for example, to heighten self-awareness, stimulate motivation, and facilitate problem solving (chapter 3). Table 7.1 presents a selected listing.

As table 7.1 suggests, a wide variety of client self-recording tasks are available. The table gives enough information in most instances to suggest how these procedures can be carried out. Recording devices, which are usually simple, can be adapted to meet the special circumstances of the case, or new ones can be created.

Some clients have difficulty using any form of self-recording, which is usually expressed by not completing the forms. For others, forms are useful adjuncts; for still others, they become a vital part of the treatment experience.

A key to the successful use of these forms is the practitioner's attitude toward them as well as the skill with which they are integrated with the content of the session. The practitioner who communicates the belief that such recording devices are useful and demonstrates their practicality in assisting the client in understanding his or her depression is likely to be successful in using recording forms in treatment. When individual clients are reluctant to use the forms, the reluctance itself can be explored as a way of illustrating the negative cognitive habits and expectations that contribute to the depression.

TABLE 7.1
Self-Monitoring Procedures for Depressed Clients
Tasks Designed to Help Clients Learn and Implement a Problem-Solving Approach

Procedure	Description	Purpose
Problem orientation worksheet (Nezu, Nezu, and Perri 1989)	Client describes recent problem and reaction to it; compares to provided description of positive problem orientation (p. 146).	Comparison enables client to identify dysfunctional beliefs and approaches to dealing with problems.
Problem definition and formulation (Nezu, Nezu, and Perri 1989)	Client will list all facts and information regarding a problem situation, separate fact from fiction, and decide whether the information is useful for goal setting (p. 169).	Teaches how to recognize cognitive distortion, to understand nature of problem situation, and to identify salient factors.

(continued)

TABLE 7.1 (*Continued*)
Self-Monitoring Procedures for Depressed Clients
Tasks Designed to Help Clients Learn and Implement a Problem-Solving Approach

Procedure	Description	Purpose
Generation of alternatives worksheet (Nezu 1989)	Client will develop a set of alternative solutions to a problem situation and then gather information about each alternative (pp. 195–96).	Increases likelihood of identifying effective solution. By realizing range of options, client overcomes hopelessness, poor sense of control.
Identifying obstacles (Nezu, Nezu, and Perri 1989)	Client will describe "concrete obstacles that currently prevent attainment of desired goals" (p. 178).	Enables client to understand problem, begin to generate viable solutions.
Decision making worksheet (Nezu, Nezu, and Perri 1989)	Client will rate alternative solutions to problems, perform cost-benefit analysis of impact of each alternative on significant others and assess likelihood of implementation (pp. 198–212).	Teaches skills of realistic problem solving since client has to work through consequences of change. Deals with the anticipated value-differences and conflicts.
Solution verification worksheet (Nezu, Nezu, and Perri 1989)	Client will list predicted and actual consequences of solution plan (p. 222).	Enables clients to realistically assess their often perfectionist standards; reassess their goals.
Depression management skills (Barth 1985)	Client will identify feelings of depression commonly associated with particular situations (p. 326).	Teaches self-awareness of situation-normative moods of depression.
Pleasant and unpleasant events schedules (Hoberman and Lewisohn 1985)	Client will monitor pleasant and unpleasant events noting related affect (p. 56).	Teaches connection between situation and affect and behavior. Depression is defined as result of high rate of aversive experience, low rate of positive reinforcement, evidence from task reinforces framework and suggests ways to deal with depression.

(continued)

TABLE 7.1 (*Continued*)
Self-Monitoring Procedures for Depressed Clients
Tasks Designed to Help Clients Learn and Implement a Problem-Solving Approach

Procedure	Description	Purpose
Daily record of negative automatic thoughts (Sacco and Beck 1985)	Client will record and evaluate reasonableness of automatic thoughts (p. 14).	Introduces ideas of realistic thinking and dysfunctionality of habitual negative cognition. Teaches client to begin to question patterns.
Dysfunctional attitude scale (Sacco and Beck 1985)	Client will record habitual attitudes and advantages and disadvantages of silent assumptions.	Enables client to bring silent assumptions more fully to awareness and to question emotional underpinnings of automatic negative thoughts.
Weekly activity schedule (Sacco and Beck 1985)	Client will monitor his/her daily activities on an hour by hour basis and rate his/her sense of pleasure and mastery (p. 18).	Permits testing of assumption that he/she "never accomplishes anything." Useful in counteracting loss of motivation, tendency to ruminate and worry. Can serve as basis for planning activities to get client moving.
Worksheets to monitor self-appraisals (Barth 1985)	Client compares affect accompanying a negative and then a positive self-appraisal associated with contemplated action (p. 325).	Teaches awareness of emotional component of negative self-evaluation.
Cost-benefit analysis (Burns, Adams, and Anastopoulos 1985)	Client will evaluate benefits and costs of giving up habitual dysfunctional feelings, ideas and attitudes (pp. 198–212).	Allows client to prepare self for difficulties of change. Enhances sense of self-control, permits greater awareness and way of dealing with ambivalence about change.

(continued)

TABLE 7.1 (*Continued*)
Self-Monitoring Procedures for Depressed Clients
Tasks Designed to Help Clients Learn and Implement a Problem-Solving Approach

Procedure	Description	Purpose
Daily record of dysfunctional thoughts (Sacco and Beck 1985)	Client will substitute rational thoughts for negative automatic cognition and monitor accompanying affect (p. 15).	Enables client to grasp power of positive thinking.
Evaluation of planned pleasant events (Sacco and Beck 1985)	Client will monitor actual vs. anticipated pleasure from planned event (p. 17).	Enables clients to understand impact of negative expectations on their lives.

Modification of Beliefs Through Experience

Most self-recording tasks are designed to modify dysfunctional beliefs; they do so through a process of client self-monitoring and reaction to what has been monitored. As discussed in chapter 3, a more direct method requires the client to undertake tasks leading to experiences that will strengthen or disconfirm existing beliefs. Applications of this principle to both external and session tasks with depressed clients will be considered.

Depressed people are often convinced that they can do nothing right, that whatever action they undertake will wind up as a failure. To challenge this expectancy of failure, graded tasks likely to lead to a successful outcome can be used (Sacco and Beck 1985). A goal that the client regards as important is selected. A series of tasks, graded from easy to difficult, is set up to bring about step-by-step progress toward the goal. The goal itself may range from modification of a stressor to a relatively simple accomplishment, such as a home improvement project. However, attainment of the goal itself is secondary to the main purpose of providing the client with a successful experience. The grading of the task permits repeated successes as well as adjustments if difficulties are encountered.

As Perris (1989) has noted, depressed people frequently feel unable to do things and feel guilty about their inability. The belief is that "I have no control over my life, and that's terrible." Disconfirming tasks involve actions that let the client exercise choice. It is likely that the client is in fact more (or potentially more) self-directing than his or her feelings and beliefs would suggest, but the client may not listen when the practitioner points this out. An experience that counters the belief may be more convincing. Possible actions reflecting the client's choice and decision making are explored, and one or more are selected for tasks. The exploration may in itself be beneficial since it will clarify the client's critical range of choices. The task then involves making and implementing a decision (e.g., to take a course, make a purchase, take a trip) depending on the client's circumstances. When the client has a limited range of choices because of illness or disability, then the task may be more limited, perhaps as simple as a decision about what to read or what to wear. Yet its enactment may still be significant for the client.

Modifying Beliefs Through Cognitive Processes Alone

Although experience is often the best teacher, it is not the only way to change beliefs. Mental activity itself (or cognitive tasks, chapter 3) can be used to provide an additional means of controlling dysfunctional beliefs and of strengthening those that are functional. A frequently used task involves the client interrupting his or her own cognitions, such as self-critical thoughts likely to foster depression, and replacing them instead with positive self-statements, such as statements about assets and strengths the client may have (Sacco and Beck 1985; Hoberman and Lewisohn 1985). Although either part of this task (interrupting negative cognitions and using positive self-talk) can be used independently, emphasis is usually given to the positive self-talk side of the combination (Nezu, Nezu, and Perri 1989). A positive self-statement involves constructive action by the client and can be used at any time. It is often helpful for clients to write out and memorize a list of positive self-statements. Particular statements can be "called up" depending on the situation. For example, at work the client can use statements reflecting on areas of competence in that sector; other positive statements can be called up for the client's roles of parent, spouse, and so on.

More elaborate cognitive tasks involve an analysis of problematic situations likely to trigger depressive affect or ideation. In this process, the client essentially applies insights learned in treatment to arrive at a more accurate and constructive appraisal of the situation.

> For example, during her treatment sessions, Mrs. B. was helped to see that her boss's criticisms of her—which tended to precipitate depressed moods—were usually more the result of some frustration on his part than of her own performance. Her task was to take a break as soon as possible after being criticized and then to analyze the criticism in an effort to identify possible pressures on her boss that might be underlying them—in other words, to reach a more constructive attribution of their cause.
>
> Further work with Mrs. B. is indicated to keep her from applying negative thinking and affect to her new-found understanding of her boss's behavior. She needs to learn how to be assertive on her own behalf if she is to overcome her tendency to depression and her boss's tendency to criticize her.

This example shows how cognitive tasks may be integrated with tasks of social skills development. Further work with Mrs. B. might then include assisting her to develop skills of appropriate self-assertion in her dealings with her boss when he is criticizing her. In this way both can be clear on what performance expectations her job carries and can establish a process for fair evaluation of Mrs. B.'s work against which she *and* her boss must evaluate his complaints. By this means she will learn interpersonal competence in work relationships and develop a behavioral repertoire to augment the skills of constructive attribution.

Work with Families

All of the goals and procedures discussed for individual treatment—relieving stressors, increasing life satisfaction and social involvement, improving social skills, self-monitoring, and modification of beliefs—can be applied in the context of work with families. As with most individual problems, family involvement is desirable in treating depressed clients. Depressions are frequently reactions to family influences, and even when they are not, families can usually help speed the recovery of their depressed members. The degree of involvement depends, of course, on the circumstances of the case. Some clients do not want their families seen, or the family itself may want no part of treatment. When involvement is indicated and possible, it may range from a single session to full-scale family treatment. Conjoint sessions including family members as well as the depressed client may be used, or family members may be seen separately. Our emphasis here will be on conjoint treatment as the major modality in a case.

When depression of a family member is the primary identified problem and family treatment the method of choice, the practitioner must deal with issues that arise when one family member is cast in the role of the sick person. Although the tendency of families to identify one member as the sick one is a common occurrence, it is accentuated when the identified client is an adult with a condition like depression that is popularly regarded as an individual's mental health problem. In fact, the depressed clients themselves may readily accept the designation "sick." We agree with Follette and Jacobson (1988) that in such circumstances there is little point in trying to persuade the family to accept the perspective that the depression is a reflection of a family problem. However, most families will accept the idea that family stresses can *contribute* to the depression of the identified client, and they may be willing to consider ways of reducing the stress. In some cases, family members will be more comfortable in viewing themselves as helpers or resources in the treatment of the depressed member. This perspective may actually be preferred in cases involving depressions that do not appear to be a reaction to stressors in family life.

As treatment proceeds, the initial view of the identified client's role may become less of a factor as the family begins to work on day-to-day problems. By focusing on interactional and other family-related concerns, the practitioner can help deemphasize the "sick" designation of the depressed member. For this purpose it is useful to identify, if possible, target problems in addition to depression, for example, problems in family communication. The practitioner attempts to locate factors in family life that may be maintaining the depression as well as resources that may facilitate its resolution. Work then proceeds through sequences of session and home tasks following the general strategy of the task-centered family treatment model (chapter 2). Sequences especially useful in family-centered work on problems of depression are summarized below. The emphasis is on the session task component, which generally sets up the task to be done at home.

  o Structured Problem Solving

     The depressed client and spouse or other family member undertake problem-solving tasks in the session to resolve issues that may be maintaining or aggravating the depression. Solutions reached in the session are then implemented through external tasks following the session. For example, Mrs. A.'s depression appeared to be fueled by a family situation in which she felt "overworked, harassed, and neglected." Although she had a full-time job, her husband and teen-age son expected her to do the bulk of the housework and meal preparation. She struggled constantly to get her son to do household chores and school homework. Her husband was absorbed in community and recreational activities. They did little together as a couple. In-session problem solving with the parents and the son was used to work out a new division of labor, a homework schedule for the son, and activities involving the parents as a couple. In addition. Mrs. A. was seen individually concerning problems at work. Her depression responded favorably to this combination of family problem solving and individual treatment.

o   Enhancing Awareness

The structure of the session task enables the depressed client to express his or her needs and beliefs to other family members and to get feedback from them in return. Such tasks provide a good vehicle for helping the client improve skills in self-assertion and for correcting distorted beliefs.

Ned, a young man living at home with his parents, became seriously depressed and suicidal after breaking up with his girlfriend. Contributing to the depression was his conviction that his parents looked down upon him for being less successful than his older siblings. When he expressed this belief in a family session, his parents responded with immediate disconfirmation, which the practitioner underscored.

Tasks to enhance awareness can also be used to uncover patterns of interaction that maintain depression. Mrs. J., a young depressed wife, was asked to explain to her husband in a session task why she liked to pick fights with him, a behavior she had acknowledged. In the ensuing discussion she revealed that she tended to pick fights when she felt guilty, hoping that the predictably hostile, punitive reaction from her husband would make her feel less guilty. Further, she recognized that this was a carry-over from the way she had related to her father when she was a child.

o   Improving Communication Skills

Session tasks aimed at helping family members develop communication skills may be particularly useful for marital dyads in which one partner, often the wife, is depressed. An inability to accurately convey intentions and feelings as well as hostile, depreciating communication are common aggravants of depression. Communication training provides another medium for dealing with cognitive distortions (chapter 5). Attentive listening and paraphrasing exercises provide the opportunity for the depressed client to obtain accurate feedback about his or her beliefs (Follette and Jacobson 1988). As in session tasks to enhance awareness, the practitioner can structure communication to elicit such beliefs, or he or she can underscore disconfirming evidence when it appears. Communication skills training focuses on the sending and receiving of accurate messages and thereby also facilitates the correction of cognitive distortions. Home tasks can call for practicing specific communication skills or using them in ordinary conversation.

As noted, home tasks evolve from solutions, awareness, or skills arrived at or worked on in session tasks. Home tasks are used to implement solutions, translate awareness into action, and practice skills (chapter 3). The challenge in designing home tasks in family treatment of depressed clients is to achieve a balance in task allocations. One wishes to avoid having the other family members do all the task work or having the identified client be the only one with tasks. Such imbalances can reinforce the designation of the depressed client as sick and can foster a sense of inequity among family members. Thus, in one case a depressed mother expressed a need for compliments in a session task. A home task was developed in which Dad and the children would explicitly compliment Mom for her efforts. At the practitioner's suggestion, Mom agreed quite willingly to do one thing during the week that she especially thought should receive a compliment.

Effectiveness

The cognitive and behavioral methods that make up the bulk of the task strategies just presented have been tested in a number of experimental studies. A meta-analysis of thirty-one controlled studies found statistically as well as clinically significant effects for both cognitive and behavioral treatment packages (Nietzel et al. 1987). Although most of the programs in this analysis involved some form of group therapy, those that used individual treatment had better outcomes. Gains achieved by clients in experimental groups were maintained consistently during follow-up periods. The clinical significance of the effects were judged to be in the "moderate range"—a judgment based on the movement of treated clients toward the nonpathological range on measures of depression. To put it simply, most clients in the studies still showed signs of depression despite improvement. Yet, there is no substantial evidence that superior results are achieved by other forms of psychosocial treatment or by drug therapy (Beckham and Leber 1985; Billings and Moos 1985; Elkin et al. 1989). In fact, probably the most rigorous comparative study to date of psychotherapy and drug treatment for clinical depression revealed no significant differences between cognitive therapy, interpersonal psychotherapy, and drug treatment (Elkin et al. 1989).

Understanding Anxiety

Anxiety is a multifaceted form of emotional distress comprising a number of distinct diagnostic classes. We shall review the most common types of anxiety and related task strategies. Emphasis will be given to the problems of anxiety that are most likely to appear in the social worker's caseload and for which task strategies are appropriate.

There are innumerable ways of defining anxiety and related terms. One of the best-developed conceptions is found in recent work by Barlow (1988), and we adapt it for our purposes. According to Barlow (1988:235), anxiety is a "diffuse cognitive-affective structure." The cognitive aspect concerns a sense of apprehension about future events that are viewed as unpredictable, uncontrollable, and potentially dangerous. The affective aspect consists of an unpleasant, distressful mood subjectively experienced as feeling nervous, jittery, or on edge. Anxiety may contain elements of fear but can be conceptually distinguished from fear, which is "a primitive alarm in response to present danger" (Barlow 1988:20).

Fear, like anger, is a basic emotion. Although it is usually provoked by an appraisal of threat, it lacks the worrisome anticipation of the unpredictable and uncontrollable future events that is the hallmark of anxiety. Fear becomes a clinical problem when it occurs in the absence of a clear external danger; it is then referred to as "panic."

Etiology

Like depression, anxiety evolves through the interaction of vulnerabilities and stressors, perhaps beginning with a biological predisposition. Some problems of anxiety, such as phobias, may be traced to specific traumatic events, but for most problems the etiology is more complex and obscure. Being overprotected as a child, for example, may lead to a diminished sense of self-efficacy and hence predispose one to phobias and other forms of anxiety. Conversely, a history marred by repeated trauma, such as separation from parental figures, may likewise predispose a person to anxiety. Whatever its origins, anxiety is likely to be maintained by feedback cycles involving negative appraisals of life events. An event is interpreted as posing a threat to the person who sees it as unpredictable and uncontrollable. Attention becomes fixed on the event. Through automatic thoughts and processes of magnification and overgeneralization (Beck and Emery 1985; chapter 5), the possible threat posed by the event is enlarged and other possible events are interpreted as threatening and uncontrollable. Effective responses may be impaired, which causes the events to seem even more dangerous. The result is a vicious cycle in which anxiety feeds on itself. For example, a person predisposed to worry about contracting a fatal illness may interpret ordinary aches and pains as signs of the disease. In the process, he or she may become so preoccupied with the "symptoms" that they are sensed as "getting worse," thus pushing the anxiety to an even higher level. Similarly, individuals with performance anxiety (e.g., stage fright, test anxiety) will imagine themselves performing poorly, which will heighten this anxiety, which in turn will stimulate even more alarming thoughts. All of this is likely to impair performance, which will then add more fuel to the vicious cycle.

Types of Anxiety Disorder

The most widely used mode of classifying anxiety disorders is found in DSM-III-R (American Psychiatric Association 1987). We briefly describe and discuss selected types of anxiety problems suggested by this classification. The types to be presented were chosen on the basis of their frequency of occurrence in clinical social work and because of their fit with a task-centered approach.

Panic Disorder and Agoraphobia

These are the most common types of anxiety problems found in individuals requesting help. They are characterized by "panic attacks," in which the person usually experiences intense fear and related symptoms, such as dizziness, faintness, accelerated heart rate, chest pains, numbness, choking, hot flashes, chills, sweating, trembling, and fear of dying or going crazy. The attacks are generally brief and unexpected, although they may be associated with certain situations, such as crowded places. Most persons who suffer from panic attacks are likely to have agoraphobia as well. Agoraphobia literally means "fear of the market (*agora*)" and refers to fears of being in situations where help might be unavailable or from which it may be difficult to escape in the event of a panic attack. In severe cases, the person is afraid to leave his or her dwelling alone or will do so only when accompanied by another person and even then will travel only by one "safe" route to his or her destination.

Panic disorder may occur without agoraphobia and vice-versa. Usually the agoraphobic without history of panic attacks has experienced some of the symptoms of such attacks and is fearful of their recurrence. For reasons not clear, about 75 percent of agoraphobics are women (Barlow 1988).

In *social phobia* the person fears social situations in which he or she may behave in a way that may prove embarrassing. Stage fright is a classic example. Fears of acting inappropriately in such situations may impede performance and increase the motivation to avoid them.

In *simple phobias* the person's fears are confined to specific objects or situations, e.g., high or enclosed places, snakes, dogs. Although simple phobias are the most common anxiety disorders in the general population, they are usually not disabling enough to cause people to seek help. However, they may be presented as secondary problems.

Generalized Anxiety Disorder

The person with this disorder experiences unrealistic and excessive anxiety about various life circumstances—e.g., health, money, work, family. Most chronically anxious people apparently do not seek help from mental health professionals for their anxiety problems as such (Barlow 1988). Tranquilizers appear to suffice for many, and many simply accept their condition. However, dysfunctional worries over life circumstances frequently occur as obstacles to the resolution of target problems or as target problems secondary to the ones that occasioned the client's seeking help.

In regard to generalized anxiety as well as other disorders, our interest is not in making formal diagnoses but rather in understanding the problematic anxiety the client presents. The difficulty may consist of a mixture of types of anxiety, and it may frequently be combined with depression; further, as noted, some of the client's complaints may not satisfy DSM-III-R criteria for a disorder. For our purposes DSM-III-R provides a useful tool in understanding such problems, but in practice we focus on accurate specification of the problem as it emerges in the practitioner-client dialog. Its diagnostic classification is of secondary concern.

Assessment

In clinical social work, anxiety is often one of several problems and is usually explored, at least initially, together with other issues. It becomes a potential target problem when the client expresses concern about his or her anxiety as a source of distress, or when the anxiety interferes with efforts to deal with the problem at hand. Mrs. Smith's difficulty in accepting her daughter's departure for college, for example, is creating depression in her and friction in the relationship with her daughter, but neither of these issues can be addressed until her anxious, unrealistic fears (that her daughter will be raped, will mismanage her expense money, will become involved with the "wrong people," etc.) are examined.

Precipitants of anxiety reactions, especially cognitive processes, should be clarified, and the avoidance or other coping strategies the client uses when anxiety is experienced should be pointed out. An effort should be made to specify occurrences and contexts of anxiety episodes (e.g., number of symptoms, severity of panic attacks, and the situation in which they occur) for a period of several weeks prior to treatment. The clinician should also explore the life routines and patterns of the client in detail to obtain a clear understanding of the restrictive adaptations the individual and his or her family may have made to contain the client's anxieties. The social worker who probes may discover, for example, that Mrs. Jones never goes to the supermarket, but waits, sometimes days, until her son is available to shop for her.

A number of rapid assessment instruments to assess anxiety are available. These can provide empirical data to supplement the assessment interview. Several are summarized briefly.

The State-Trait Anxiety Inventory (STAI) (Spielberger, Gorsuch, and

Lushene 1970) is a forty-item instrument consisting of two scales, one for anxiety as currently felt, the other for proneness to anxiety. The scales can be administered together or separately. Substantial literature on the instrument is available. For a review, see Johnson and Sarason (1978).

The *Zung Self-Rating Scale (SRS)* (Zung 1971) is a twenty-item scale designed to assess anxiety as a clinical disorder. Although few validity and reliability studies have been done, the SRS can be used in conjunction with a comparable practitioner-administered scale, the ASI(see below).

Instead of, or in addition to rapid assessment instruments, practitioners can make use of structured interviews and scales that enable them to make judgments about the presence and severity of anxiety. Even if the interviews and the scales are not fully used, they can, like DSM-III-R, provide guidance as to what to look for.

The Anxiety Status Inventory (ASI) Zung (1971), as noted, has a parallel client self-administered instrument and consists of thirty items the practitioner can scale to measure the intensity, duration, and frequency of both "somatic" and "affective" anxiety.

The Hamilton Anxiety Scale (HAS) (1959) has fourteen items that, like the ASI, measure both somatic and affective aspects of anxiety. The scale can be scored in a manner comparable with DSM-III-R categories (Bech, Kastrup, and Rafaelsen 1986). A more extensive instrument is the Anxiety Disorders Interview Schedule—Revised (ADIS-R) (DiNardo et al. 1985). This structured interview schedule incorporates the Hamilton Anxiety Scale, contains measures of depression, and is fully compatible with the categories of DSM-III-R.

Task Strategies

We shall present task strategies for the disorders discussed. The fuller presentation will be for agoraphobia and panic disorders in light of their frequency and seriousness. As will be shown, key strategies applied to these disorders can be adapted to other problems of anxiety.

Agoraphobia and Panic Disorders

We will assume here that the client's problem is agoraphobia with panic, the typical configuration. The client's general tasks are to achieve control over his or her anxiety episodes and to achieve the desired independence and mobility when outside the home. These general tasks can be operationalized through a fourfold strategy consisting of (1) incremental exposure to anxiety-provoking situations, (2) inducement and control of panic attacks in the session, (3) cognitive restructuring, and (4) involvement of family members.

Incremental Exposure to Feared Stimuli

This consists of a series of tasks that enable the client to gradually become comfortable in situations that would previously have provoked anxiety or panic. Such tasks can either be practitioner-assisted or be completed by the client alone. When the client's phobias prevent any form of self-initiated action, the practitioner can accompany the client on initial forays into feared situations. For example, a first task might be for the client and the practitioner to spend a certain amount of time in a shopping mall. The next task would call for an increased amount of time in the mall, and so on. Even when the practitioner accompanies the client, the client is encouraged to practice between sessions. The treatment may begin with incremental tasks done by the client alone, or it may move to this format following one or more practitioner-assisted tasks. Exposure tasks initiated by the client have the advantage of enabling the client to develop a better sense of control; they avoid dependency on the practitioner and may result in a greater stability of gains (Barlow 1988; Jansson and Ost 1982). While it is important for the client to remain in the anxiety-provoking situation long enough to experience and master feelings of anxiety, it is not necessary, as was once thought, for clients to remain in the situation until "peak" anxiety is experienced (Rachman et al. 1986). In other words, the client needs to be challenged but not overwhelmed.

In some cases, exposure can be graded in terms of discrete steps. For example, in one case a woman fearful of going downtown to shop, was able to master a series of graded tasks involving waiting for the bus, boarding the bus, and going downtown on Sunday when the stores were closed, window-shopping (again on Sunday), until eventually she was able to complete a shopping trip when the stores were open. Such steps can be organized in the form of a hierarchy that can be worked out in advance with the client. Carrying out graded exposure activities can sometimes be facilitated through additional tasks, such as repeating coping self-statements ("I am getting through this; I am in control"), counting or some other mental exercise, or initiating a conversation with another person (Zane and Powell 1985).

Inducement of Controlled Panic Attacks

Inducing controlled panic attacks in the session may be indicated when panic is likely to prevent the client from completing graded exposure tasks. The panic may occur even in practitioner-assisted exposure (vivid examples can be found in Zane and Powell 1985). It may be preferable to induce better controlled "mini attacks" prior to the graded exposure procedure.

The purposes of this procedure are: (1) to enable both the client and the practitioner to learn more about the characteristics of the attacks, especially the physical and cognitive events that accompany them; (2) to enable the client to experience the attacks in such a way as to install the belief that he or she can survive and master them (Beck 1988). Hyperventilation (rapid breathing), focusing on sensations, and imagining oneself to be in a feared situation should be sufficient to initiate a mini attack with most clients. Once the client begins to experience anxiety, the attack can be brought under control by certain techniques, such as more regular breathing, rebreathing into a paper bag, using imagery to heighten and lower symptoms, reappraising automatic thoughts and bodily sensations, and using positive self-talk to interrupt fearful cognitions. Reassurance by the practitioner, before and during the attack, that the client is not going crazy and is not in the throes of a physical catastrophe can support the client's own coping efforts (Thyer 1987). Through these efforts, the client should come away not only with a sense of being able to control an attack, but also with specific techniques for doing so. Prior to using this procedure, the practitioner should ensure, if necessary through consultation with the client's physician, that the client's physical symptoms during a panic attack do not have a basis in physical pathology.

Cognitive Restructuring

This has already been touched on in the discussion of the preceding strategies. In general, the clients are helped to learn in the session, and to use in external tasks, new ways of thinking about their panic attacks and the situations that provoke them. The practitioner gives a non-technical explanation of agoraphobic and panic reactions based on available knowledge. Clients are then involved in a process of examining critically, with the help of the practitioner's questions, their beliefs about internal and external events that stimulate anxiety. The client is helped to reinterpret physical symptoms during panic attacks as symptoms of *anxiety* rather than of a physical disorder. The induced mini panic attack is useful in facilitating this process of reappraisal since the client should be able to demonstrate his or her control over the physical symptoms. The actual as opposed to the fantasized risks of being disabled by a panic attack in a public place are appraised. Distracting tasks, coping statements, and alternatives in case a panic attack gets out of control are considered. Automatic thoughts occurring during panic attacks or in phobic situations are identified and examined critically. The work in the session is used as a basis for external tasks designed to strengthen the client's cognitive response in anxiety-provoking situations. Clients are asked in their tasks to reinterpret symptoms, identify and examine automatic thoughts, and so on, in these situations as well as in their thinking about them.

Involvement of Family Members

This usually consists of eliciting the cooperation of the spouse or other adult living with the client. We shall confine our comments here to spouse involvement, which is the usual case. As Friedman (1987) has pointed out, agoraphobia usually becomes a dynamic in marital interactions. A common pattern is for the agoraphobic to draw from the spouse one or two kinds of polarized reactions: sympathy and support for the phobic and panic reactions, or an unsympathetic, tough-minded stance in which the agoraphobic is told in effect to get over his or her fears. Both responses are dysfunctional: the first tends to reinforce avoidance behavior; the second increases the client's anxiety and dependent behavior.

To alter these contextual obstacles, the spouse is invited to participate in the treatment of his or her partner's anxiety problems. An explanation of agoraphobia and panic is presented to the couple. The couple is asked to work collaboratively on resolving the agoraphobic's problem rather than on marital issues, but the latter may be taken up at a later point. The spouse may take on tasks that support his or her partner's efforts—for example, assisting in exposure tasks. Session tasks involving communication around anxiety issues may be used to help the partner avoid the polarities discussed above. Research evidence (Barlow, O'Brien, and Last 1984; Arnow et al. 1985) suggests that involving spouses in treatment adds to the benefit of treatment programs, especially when problems of marital adjustment are present.

Effectiveness

An impressive body of research attests to the effectiveness of the exposure-based treatment of agoraphobia. A meta-analysis of seventy-one controlled studies revealed that exposure-based treatment was effective in reducing symptoms of agoraphobia to a clinically significant degree. There was evidence that effects persisted throughout a follow-up period (Trull, Nietzel, and Main 1988). According to Barlow (1988: 408), who provides an excellent synthesis of relevant research, "60 to 70 percent of agoraphobics completing such treatment have shown some clinical benefit." However, there is still room for improvement. As Barlow (1988) notes, these data exclude dropouts (estimated at 12 percent). Moreover, only a small percentage of clients remains completely free of symptoms after treatment. Some of the newer methods reviewed in this section, including recent advances in the treatment of panic, use of cognitive restructuring, and family involvement, have shown promise (Barlow 1988; Beck 1988).

Social and Simple Phobias

As with agoraphobia, the key to the treatment of social and simple phobias is to enable the client to gradually master feared situations through progressive involvement with them. Family members, especially spouses, can participate in the treatment along the lines suggested for agoraphobia.

In treating social phobia, role-played session tasks can be used to enable the client to practice introductions, initiate conversations, or make speeches. These are followed by graded external tasks leading to incremental progress. For example, a man whose anxiety prevents him from initiating relationships with women may start out by saying "hello" at work to a woman he wants to become acquainted with. This may be followed in sequence by attempts to initiate a conversation and to ask her to have coffee with him. Cognitive restructuring may involve examination and reappraisal of the client's behavioral self-expectations, which are often excessive. He may think that any show of anxiety or anything less than a flawless self-presentation will make him an object of ridicule. It can be pointed out that people are more tolerant or more indifferent than the client supposes. It may also help to instruct the client to deliberately make mistakes in role-played self-presentations so he or she can become comfortable with being less than perfect. Clients can also practice recovery from "goofs" without losing composure. The approach outlined here can be used for a variety of problems involving social anxiety and avoidance that fall short of a diagnosis of social phobia.

In simple phobias, such as fear of animals or heights, session and external tasks involve incremental exposure. Session tasks may require "props," such as small animals, or may require the practitioner to accompany the client to the situation that is feared (Thyer 1987).

> For example, in one task-centered case, the client, Josie, age twenty-six, had a simple phobia about driving, especially on a busy expressway that she needed to take in order to get to work. Her anxiety was so intense that she was unable to complete the trip. The key treatment strategy involved a series of graded tasks in which Josie, accompanied by the practitioner, drove until she became too anxious to continue; then the practitioner took over. After some progress was made, a hierarchy was constructed that was modeled after the number of exits on the expressway. Josie would try to make exit 7 one day, exit 8 the next, until she arrived at work (exit 18). Eventually, she was able to drive the ten or so exits entirely by herself with the practitioner in the car. The practitioner's verbal support and reassurance were gradually replaced with coping statements (self-support and reassurance) that Josie spoke aloud to herself. In the last stage of treatment Josie drove by herself with the practitioner following her in her own car. Then she successfully took the last step of driving without being accompanied at all.

Generalized Anxiety Disorder

Task strategies for this disorder can generally be applied to any problem of persistent, dysfunctional anxiety. As noted, for many clients anxiety is an important secondary problem or stands in the way of resolving other difficulties. For example, a man's anxiety that he may be fired and unable to find another job may prevent him from being appropriately assertive with his boss. The goal is usually not to eliminate anxiety, but rather to help clients cope with it effectively so that it becomes more tolerable and less of an impediment to constructive action. The approach used is similar to, and draws upon, methods of anxiety management (Jannoun, Oppenheimer, and Gelder 1982; Butler et al. 1987).

In the interview procedures discussed earlier, identification of automatic thoughts and critical examination of the realistic basis of the anxiety are used to set the stage for more effective coping responses. Since the client's anxieties are likely to be more pervasive, more intertwined with life events, and apparently more realistic than phobic reactions, more attention may be given to this kind of cognitive restructuring. The practitioner does not try to talk clients out of their fears or to provide global reassurance. Rather, the practitioner tries to involve the client in a collaborative search for new ways of thinking about the threats the client finds troubling. "How likely is it you will fail the exam, given that failure on such exams is rare and that you have done well in your studies?" "Is it possible that some of your concern about Dave's leaving you is tied in some way to your fears of being abandoned when you were a child?" "You said a while back you tend to blow up anything minor into major diseases. How is this different?" Through such questions the social worker attempts to help clients engage in productive reflection (Hollis and Woods 1963) as opposed to rumination about their fears. However, the questions are only as good as the client's responses. The immediate goal is to bring about a dialog that will enlarge the client's perspective. As the questions suggest, a wide range of alternative viewpoints may be introduced, from more realistic ways of appraising threats to a recognition that past fears may be clouding current perceptions. Because the anxieties of these clients are so pervasive, the social worker cannot assume that a generalization of learning will readily transfer from one area of concern to another. Indeed, in most cases, a series of tasks built on cognitive reflection and designed to introduce rational thinking will need to be developed for each area of fear.

The focus on cognitive restructuring in the interview leads to different kinds of external tasks. One type calls for clients to continue fruitful lines of reflection on their own. These tasks should be related to a particular issue. For example, in one task-centered case, a young woman's anxiety was traced to her estrangement from her mother, who seemed to prefer the client's brother. One of the client's tasks was to identify why her mother's seeming greater attention to her brother was so upsetting to her (Ewalt 1977:32). As noted earlier (chapter 3), it is useful to have clients write out responses to such tasks that can then be brought in for discussion at the next session. It is hoped that cognitive tasks stimulate other kinds of constructive thinking about the problem.

A second kind of external task resulting from cognitive work in the session consists of statements that draw upon whatever understanding the client may have achieved. The client uses these statements in self-talk when anxiety mounts. For example, one client worried about forthcoming heart surgery found it useful to write the following statements, among others, on a card. "I have always had fears that any type of medical procedure would have catastrophic consequences, and these fears have always proved groundless." "The surgeon is very well qualified, and the mortality rate for this kind of surgery is very low." Repeating the statements, which he eventually memorized, proved helpful in controlling his anxiety.

A third kind of external task resulting from cognitive restructuring consists of action to test out, and hopefully cast doubt on, assumptions underlying the anxiety. A mother worried that her teen-aged son's friends would lead him into drug abuse and other evils agrees to invite them to a cookout so she can find out firsthand what they are like. A man afraid he will have a heart attack if he exerts himself agrees (with his physician's approval) to put his fears to the test by taking up jogging. Because such tasks involve exposure to anxiety-provoking stimuli, a graded approach may be indicated.

An evaluation of an approach emphasizing the components just described indicated that clients receiving treatment did significantly better on measures of anxiety reduction than a comparable group of wait-list controls (Butler et al. 1987). The wait-list group improved significantly after treatment began. Gains were maintained in both groups during a six-months follow-up period.

A related strategy involves attempts to modify the client's imagery. Anxiety is usually accompanied by negative images of the "worst" happenings, and these in turn create additional anxiety. A first step is to find out what the client's images are. Reliable, thoughtful repetitions of the image right through to whatever catastrophic consequence may be at the end can sometimes alter their content (Beck and Emery 1985). The very act of making reflexive "uncontrolled" processes of imagining deliberate can often result in more realistic thinking. If the images involve the client, or someone close to the client, behaving in a passive or helpless fashion, the client may be asked to imagine how he or she, or others, might get out of the situation. The client may then attempt to substitute the resulting coping images for the anxiety-producing ones outside the session. For example, although one man could not imagine himself acting differently, he could imagine being helped by "a fearless friend" who would come to his rescue, and he could make use of that image. Switching from anxiety-provoking to reassuring images has been found to be difficult for many clients (Jannoun, Oppenheimer, and Gelder 1982; Butler et al. 1987). The alternative imagery needs to be right for the client, and it may take some close collaborative work to develop it. Usually, the process works better if the positive imagery is substituted before the negative imagery becomes too intense. Techniques for altering imagery can also be applied to the phobic reaction discussed earlier.

As in the treatment of depression, client self-monitoring can often be beneficial. In fact, many of the instruments presented in table 7.1 can be used for both kinds of distress or can be modified for anxiety. The activities and reflections that are a part of these tasks are themselves useful for anxiety. Moreover, these tasks form a structure for cognitive work outside the session. The example below shows how an adaptation of the Daily Record of Dysfunctional Thoughts (Sacco and Beck 1985) was used by Mrs. Baker, who was being seen for anxiety and depression concerning her financial situation and her husband's health, among other problems. Hard pressed to pay bills resulting from her husband's cancer treatment, she was fearful of falling into extreme financial hardship, a condition she had experienced earlier in her life. An excerpt from the daily record she completed during treatment is given below:

Instructions	Mrs. Baker's Response
1. Describe actual event leading to emotion	Incoming bills threats to notify credit agency
2. Emotion	Fear
3. Rate degree (1–100)	90
4. Thoughts before or after emotion	I can't pay this—I'll have bad credit. I can't manage my finances
5. Describe realities	If I pay what I can—even $5.00 a week, I can keep them at bay. I am a responsible person
6. Rate Belief in realities described	75

Mrs. Baker found the record quite useful in controlling her anxiety.

Her own comments about it are instructive: "On paper my thoughts are organized. I can see other possibilities. I can put my situation in perspective, so I can feel differently about it."

Working with the family is also an important part of treating generalized anxiety, especially when the anxiety is focused on family issues. In fact, it often makes sense to suggest a definition of the problem in terms of family concerns rather than of a member's individual psychopathology (anxiety). In that way, spouses and other family members can be more effectively engaged in tasks to alter sources of anxiety. In one case, for example, a woman sought help for problems of depression and anxiety. A major source of her distress proved to be her marriage. One of her problems was the anxiety-provoking suspicion that her husband was being unfaithful. While she admitted that her husband had given her no cause to distrust him, her fears persisted. When the couple was seen together, it was apparent that the husband's lack of openness about his work and other activities outside the home as well as his curt responses to her questions were provoking her anxiety. The problem was reframed as one of marital communication. As he became more communicative about his activities and more explicitly reassuring, her anxiety about his unfaithfulness diminished.

CHAPTER 8

Problem Drinking

NORMA WASKO

WILLIAM J. REID

In this chapter we shall apply a task-centered perspective to the etiology and treatment of problem drinking. Our focus is on work with problem drinkers who appear in the caseloads of mainstream social work practice, rather than with those in specialized alcoholism treatment centers (although the two populations overlap considerably). In most cases, problem drinking will be one of several issues. In some cases, it may be a primary target problem; in others, it may be a secondary problem or an obstacle that impedes the solution of target problems.

This chapter focuses on problem drinking rather than on the broader topic of chemical dependency. Despite the seriousness of drug abuse and the attention it receives, alcohol dependency is a much more pervasive social problem and a more frequent clinical issue. There has been more experience with applying the task-centered model to alcohol problems than to drug problems (Reid 1986; Nofz 1988), and there is a greater variety of empirically based methods for alcohol treatment compatible with the model than there is for drug treatment. In view of these considerations, we decided to concentrate on problem drinking. However, since alcohol and drug dependency have a great deal in common and frequently occur together, much of what we say about the former can be applied to the latter, especially in regard to treatment methods.

Understanding Problem Drinking

As Goodyear (1989) has observed, problem drinking is the result of bio-psychosocial processes that include constitutional factors, cultural influences, environmental circumstances, developmental experiences, personality dynamics, the effects of conditioning and social learning, and psychological mechanisms. How all these processes interact to produce different degrees and kinds of abusive drinking is not clear at present.

When these processes produce alcohol dependency so severe that individuals can no longer control their drinking, it is appropriate to view them as being in the grips of a "disease." Indeed some of these individuals may have a genetic susceptibility to become alcoholics. But in accord with Vaillant (1983), we would agree that there is a continuum encompassing varying degrees of dependency, from drinking that is moderate-to-heavy, but controlled, to drinking that is chronically excessive and uncontrolled. In this view, it is possible for people to be mild alcoholics or a "little bit" alcoholic (Vaillant and Milofsky 1982). We shall use the terms "problem drinker," "alcohol abuser," and "alcohol dependent" in a generic sense to refer to individuals anywhere on this continuum; when the term "alcoholic" is used, it will refer to individuals close to the severely dependent end of the spectrum. As the foregoing suggests, we do not subscribe to the conventional "disease" conception of alcoholism that draws a sharp line between "true alcoholics" and other types of alcohol abusers. One reason for viewing problem drinking as a continuum is the lack of empirical evidence for clearly demarcated subtypes of alcohol abusers and for a clear line between alcoholics and heavy drinkers.

Perhaps the most accepted distinction is between problem drinkers found in clinic populations and those who exhibit problem drinking but have received little or no formal treatment. This latter group is distinguished from the former by lower levels of alcohol consumption, lack of withdrawal symptoms, and few or no hospitalizations for abusive drinking (Cahalan 1970; Heather and Robertson 1981). The differences between these two groupings are sometimes attributed to the fact that "prealcoholic" individuals in the nonclinic group have not yet attained the stage of full-blown alcohol dependence. The assumption is that ultimately the progression of the disease will lead to this end for most problem drinkers. There is, however, no strong evidence to support this assumption. It appears that there may be distinct groups of problem drinkers with quite different life outcomes from their abusive drinking behavior. It has been argued that less severe problem drinkers outnumber the seriously dependent clinic group by ratios varying from 3:1 to 7:1 and that so many of these individuals continue to experience problems with alcohol, in part, because few or no treatment programs have been designed to meet their different needs (Sobell and Sobell 1987). In our view, these less seriously dependent drinkers tend to dominate in mainstream social work practice.

Our knowledge of what happens to these groups over time is limited. Apparently many heavy drinkers climb on and fall off the wagon repeatedly throughout their lifetime and survive (Vaillant and Milofsky 1982). Others do not, but drink more or less continuously, until they die at a relatively early age from alcohol-engendered physical deterioration. With alcoholism, as with a variety of other maladaptations, social stability prior to onset is the strongest predictor of a positive outcome. Married, employed, well-educated individuals with higher levels of income tend to do better. As yet, there is no way to predict in advance, except for the most severely dependent and abusive drinkers, which individuals are likely to experience relapse or to have a poor long-term prognosis.

Research does show that negative, stressful situations are related to relapse. Depression, anxiety, social pressures that encourage drinking, interpersonal conflicts, and confrontations are all associated with resumption of drinking (Cocozzelli and Hudson 1989). Conversely, individuals who demonstrate natural recovery, or who maintain recovery after treatment, tend to possess good coping skills in dealing with stress and to have good social supports in terms of friendships, marriage, and work relationships. Positive life changes also appear related to an individual's ability to sustain recovery. Among these are marriage, birth of a child, and vocational satisfaction. Other significant factors include prior successful experience in coping that required efforts at self-control, such as dieting or cessation of smoking, and a worsening of one's health status (Cocozzelli and Hudson 1989).

Some authors reviewing recent studies suggest that the severity of dependence may not be as reliable a predictor of long-term outcome as the congruence between past experience, ideology about drinking (on the part of client and counselor), and present expectations the clients have about their ability to control drinking (Sobell and Sobell 1987). Moreover, since many severely alcohol-dependent individuals also have experienced numerous and severe associated life problems, it may well be that poor long-term outcomes are as much a consequence of these as of the dependence itself.

Does this then suggest that treatment should be focused largely on social intervention strategies? Not necessarily. In our view, the Gordian knot of the treatment of problem drinking lies at the boundary between the physiological and the psychosocial and is held fast by the experience of craving. The concept of craving has received considerable attention in the literature. The central question is the extent to which craving, which is believed to trigger drinking that is out of control, is activated by physical or psychological stimuli. One study (Hodgson, Rankin, and Stockwell 1979) found that severely alcohol-dependent persons who experienced craving were more influenced by blood levels of alcohol than by information about the amount of alcohol consumed. In contrast, moderately severe problem drinkers who experienced craving were more influenced by information alone than they were by alcohol blood levels. Here, it seems, was a difference suggesting that for the former group craving was triggered by physiological cues while for the latter external, psychosocial cues were more influential.

The physical basis for such differential responses is only gradually emerging. Recent research suggests that different levels of the neurotransmitter serotonin are associated with craving and that various medications such as Fluxotene may decrease the desire to drink (Paredes 1989). If this research is substantiated, it will tend to support the view of alcohol dependence as the consequence of a biochemical imbalance, at least in the case of some alcoholics, and to open the door to more advanced and less aversive chemical treatments than are currently available. The use of disulfiram (Antabuse) may go the way of the prefrontal lobotomy.

Finally, there is the issue of motivation. The conventional wisdom in the field is that the alcoholic is hard to treat because of severe resistance and denial and because he or she is poorly motivated and in the grip of "demon rum." The research literature, however, does not support this stereotype, but suggests that the empathy and skill of the practitioner and the willingness to negotiate treatment goals and strategies with the client are predictive of the client's engagement in treatment (Sanchez-Craig and Wilkinson 1987; Miller 1989). Further, it has been found that the empathy of the social worker is strongly associated with a positive treatment outcome (Miller 1989). Miller states that

The defense mechanism of denial has not been found to be more prevalent among alcoholics than among others. . . . Indeed, there is reason to believe that strong resistance to treatment is driven not by client personality but rather by characteristics of therapists and treatments themselves. (Miller 1989:263)

Practitioner and treatment characteristics aside, it may well be that there are alcoholics who are highly resistant and hard to motivate. It is necessary to define the subgroups that in fact fit this profile and the ones that do not. It seems likely that clarity in this area requires further research.

Problem Formulation

In task-centered practice, alcohol abuse is treated like any other problem. That is, it becomes a focus of treatment for the alcohol abuser when the person acknowledges the difficulty and agrees to work on it. As noted, problem drinking may also be worked on collaboratively if the client sees it as an obstacle to the solution of other issues. Excessive drinking is a common attributed problem, especially in work with families. "My husband is an alcoholic," says Mrs. B., "but he will do nothing about it!" If Mr. B. continues to do nothing, the *target problem* may concern what Mrs. B. herself is going to do. Subsequently, we shall indicate how spouses like Mrs. B. can deal with this kind of situation (see "Marital and Family Dysfunction"). At this point, we only wish to be clear about where the target problem lies.

A frequent issue concerns how confrontive the practitioner should be in getting the alcohol abuser to acknowledge that drinking is a problem. As with other issues, practitioners may point out behaviors that they think are self-defeating or that are hurting others, but they do not press when the clients reject these offerings. In some settings, however, there is a good deal of pressure on practitioners to be even more confrontive.

The pressure may come from supervisors and other agency staff who take the position that alcoholic clients need to be confronted with their drinking problem early in the contact and to be persuaded to do something about it. Unless this step occurs, they argue, other problems in the client's life or family cannot be satisfactorily dealt with. In fact, practitioners who do not vigorously pursue the client's drinking problem may be regarded as part of the "enabling system" that possibly encourages the problem by not taking action to change it. The underlying belief is that alcoholism is a disease with a downward course. Unless the worker engages the client system to deal with this disease, all other therapeutic efforts may be futile if not dysfunctional. Although this point of view is not new, it is being pressed more forcefully in many agencies as one outcropping, we suspect, of our most recent national movement against alcoholism.

The task-centered model does not call for singling out and attacking drinking problems that might be peripheral to the central issues of treatment. It is not automatically assumed that alcohol abuse will stand in the way of progress in other areas. Neither is the issue of abusive drinking ignored—certainly not in family cases in which the drinking of one family member could be one of a number of factors affecting the target problem. However, the task-centered practitioner is likely to be cautious about discussing the drinking issue in a confrontive way unless it appears to be an active obstacle to the resolution of the problem being addressed. In many cases it is not at all clear whether the alcohol abuse is contributing to the problem or whether it is necessary to modify it substantially in order to resolve the target problems. For example, Mrs. Grant's drinking appeared to be contributing to Kevin's poor school adjustment, but she was unwilling to give up alcohol. She was able, however, to alter when, where, and how much she drank so she could provide better care for the boy and help him with his homework. This change as well as work with Kevin to improve his academic performance resulted in tangible gains. Pressing Mrs. Grant prematurely about the drinking may have led not to constructive change but rather to a quick termination of treatment. Further, if the assessment suggests that Mrs. Grant's drinking is problematic to her well-being, the gains made in building a positive relationship with her by not immediately pressing the issue of her drinking may result in her willingness to make it a target problem later.

Assessment Procedures

The central questions for the practitioner whose client acknowledges a drinking problem as part of a constellation of other problems are: what to treat, in what order, how to treat, and, in some cases, whether to treat at all. Given our focus, alcohol abuse is likely to be one of several interrelated problems. The assessment guidelines below can be used selectively to direct the amount of attention to be devoted to it.

In the discussion that follows, we assume that the social worker will initially focus attention on whether or not alcohol dependence is a potential target problem or an obstacle.

Assessment of Problem Drinking

The assessment of alcohol dependence is central to decisions about how to treat clients with drinking problems. Currently a number of definitions of dependence are in use. As formulated by the DSM-III-R (American Psychiatric Association 1987), alcohol dependence is defined as a "cluster of cognitive, behavioral, and physiological symptoms that indicate an individual has impaired control of psychoactive substance use and continues use of the substance despite adverse consequences." The symptoms of dependence include, but are not limited to, the physiological symptoms of tolerance and withdrawal. To justify a diagnosis of alcohol dependence, an individual must manifest three of nine symptoms. Dependence is considered mild, moderate, or severe according to the number of symptoms demonstrated. Alcohol abuse is a residual category for maladaptive patterns of substance abuse that do not meet the criteria for dependence.

The difficulty with this formulation is that it mixes social, psychological, and physiological indicators together in an essentially qualitative grouping that leads to a yes/no diagnosis. One is either alcohol dependent or not. The description of the indicators leads one to suspect that they may have differing levels of impact and overlapping boundaries. A more satisfying formulation, and one gaining currency among researchers, is Skinner's division of alcohol dependence and the accompanying alcohol-related disabilities (Skinner and Allen 1982). His work characterizes the alcohol dependence syndrome as having seven dimensions: (1) a narrowing of the repertoire of drinking behavior to a stereotypic pattern to avoid withdrawal symptoms, (2) the salience of drink-seeking behavior over other life activities, (3) increased tolerance of alcohol, (4) repeated withdrawal symptoms, (5) repeated relief or avoidance of withdrawal symptoms by further drinking, (6) subjective awareness of the compulsion to drink and the accompanying inability to not drink, and (7) recurrence of the syndrome after a period of abstinence (Skinner and Allen 1982). A clear implication of this formulation is the probable existence of a strong physiological component of dependence. Using this framework for the assessment would require the clinician to obtain a careful description of current and past drinking behavior and to pay special attention to the narrowing and compulsivity of the drinking pattern.

The alcohol-related disabilities, which are the consequences of compulsive drinking, are patterns of maladaptive social and psychological functioning. They may be categorized in terms of (1) physical disabilities, such as liver disease, (2) psychological disabilities, e.g., affective disorders, intellectual impairment, etc., (3) social disabilities, e.g., family distress, job loss, etc. (Skinner 1984; World Health Organization 1982). The pervasiveness of distress in these areas suggests the severity of dysfunction and the level of difficulty the client will encounter in attempting to recover an adaptive life style. Assessment should proceed in all three areas, paying attention to strengths that may be called upon during and after the treatment.

Following Skinner's (1984) framework, data collected during the assessment phase should focus on current drinking history, alcohol dependence syndrome, and alcohol-related disabilities. We turn at this point to a more detailed discussion of ways to collect the necessary information.

Current Pattern of Drinking and Drug Use

Here the practitioner is concerned with obtaining as accurate a picture as possible of alcohol use and abuse over the past three months, because the literature indicates that in most instances abuse within this time frame will be reasonably representative of the past six to twelve months. Less detailed questions may be asked to verify this assumption and to obtain a perspective on the client's long-term drinking history. If the client's recall is fuzzy or inconsistent, corroborating information will have to be sought from family or friends. Information should be obtained about drinking patterns—(a) how frequent—whether daily, weekend, episodic, etc.; (b) number of abstinent days per week; (c) number of days of moderate consumption per week (defined as one to four standard drinks: 1.5 ounces of 80 proof liquor, a four-ounce glass of wine, or a twelve-ounce can of beer); (d) number of days of heavy drinking, including typical quantity, maximum quantity, and frequency of maximum quantity; (e) amount and kinds and consumption pattern of other psychoactive drugs (cannabis, cocaine and other street drugs, tobacco, caffeine, benzodiazepines) and psychotropic medications.

For clients who minimize the problem or are uncertain that they have in fact a drinking problem, a good assessment technique is the use of a self-monitoring task to determine the actual frequency and amount of consumption. The practitioner should provide the client with a week's supply of pocket-sized index cards upon which the date, time, place, kind of drink, amount of alcohol in each drink, and number of drinks is recorded. A space may also be left for recording antecedent events and consequences.

When individuals report serious functional problems, or withdrawal symptoms following cessation or reduction of intake of alcohol (anxiety, restlessness, irritability, insomnia, impaired attention and concentration, and in more acute reactions, delirium and hallucinations), alcohol dependence should be carefully assessed. The practitioner may elect to use the DSM-III-R or Skinner's criteria or decide to choose one of the standardized scales described below.

Standard Measures of Alcohol Dependence

Alcohol dependence may be assessed by using one of several brief assessment instruments, such as the Severity of Alcohol Dependence Questionnaire or the Alcohol Dependence Scale. Both of these scales are quick and easy to administer and are based on empirical studies of the alcohol dependence syndrome. In addition, individual client scores may be compared to population scores obtained for alcohol-dependent persons.

The Severity of Alcohol Dependence Questionnaire (SADQ) (Stockwell et al. 1979) is a twenty-item instrument with scores ranging from 0 to 60, designed to test the severity of alcohol dependence by measuring the "narrowing repertoire of behavior." Scores above 30 correspond to experts' clinical ratings of severe alcohol dependence. The authors state that scores below 30 predict the possibility of successfully controlled drinking in the long term (Lettieri, Nelson, and Sayers 1985). Results to date suggest this is a quick, reliable, and valid instrument (Stockwell, Murphy, and Hodgson 1983).

The Alcohol Dependence Scale consists of twenty-five items pertaining to excessive drinking, repetitive withdrawal symptoms, and loss of control over one's behavior while drinking (Skinner and Horn 1984). High scores are associated with missed treatment sessions, high rates of alcohol consumption, high levels of psychosocial problems, and high levels of physical symptoms with increased probability of liver disease. Studies indicate that individuals with low scores believe they can control their drinking while those with high scores believe that they require abstinence as a goal of treatment (Jacobson 1989a). The inclusion of items measuring the clients' confidence in their ability to control their drinking makes this an attractive instrument since recent studies in relapse prevention suggest that the client's belief in self-efficacy may be predictive of treatment outcomes (G. R. Jacobson 1989a).

Assessment of Alcohol-related Life Problems

Severely alcohol-dependent persons frequently report histories of abusive drinking of ten or more years, repeated involvement with treatment programs, loss of employment, marital and family breakup, as well as various legal and medical problems. In contrast, those who are less dependent report shorter histories of abusive drinking as well as fewer adverse medical and social consequences, and they have usually not received treatment for alcoholism (Sanchez-Craig and Wilkinson 1987). Aspects to be covered in this area of assessment include the impact of problem drinking on work, marital and family life (including adaptations of spouse and children), health, and cognitive functioning.

Use of a standardized instrument such as the Michigan Alcoholism Screening Test (MAST) (Selzer 1971) permits rating the severity of alcohol-related problems against standardized norms. The MAST is a twenty-five-item, structured questionnaire based on common signs and symptoms of alcoholism. Originally designed as a screening instrument to detect alcoholics in the general population, it is widely used in diagnostic interviews. One limitation is its tendency to produce high rates of false positive identifications (21 to 23 percent) when the recommended scoring levels are used. A score of 5 or above is believed to identify individuals prone to alcoholism (Jacobson 1989a). Jacobson suggests grouping the MAST scores along a continuum (0–4 = no problem, 5–9 = possible, 10–11 = probable problem, 12+ = likely alcoholism) and getting corroborating information, for example, by administering the MAST to the spouse or family using the third-person version (Jacobson 1989a). A brief, ten-item version of the MAST is also available (Pokorny et al. 1972).

Selection of Treatment Goal: Moderation or Abstinence

Once the diagnostic picture is drawn, the client and the practitioner together must tackle the issue of selecting a treatment goal. Although there is no way to predict in advance who will succeed and who will fail when moderation is the goal of treatment, there is some evidence that individuals with less severe alcohol-related problems may succeed with this goal while clients with more severe alcohol dependency problems tend to be more successful when abstinence is the goal (Miller and Baca 1983; Miller and Joyce 1979).

The goal is formulated collaboratively after the practitioner and the client have reviewed pertinent case data and after the practitioner has made recommendations. The basis for the recommendations—e.g., relevant research and literature—should be shared with the client to the extent feasible. The choice should clearly be the client's. Several studies of the treatment of problem drinkers have suggested that client responsibility for the goal selection promotes a positive outcome (Oxford and Hawker 1974; Sanchez-Craig and Lei 1986).

When the client's dependency on alcohol is severe, and its consequences disruptive, the practitioner welcomes the client's choice of abstinence as a goal. However, few severely dependent drinkers will initially opt for that choice. If they do not, the practitioner may present evidence and arguments for a goal of abstinence. However, many such clients will still prefer to try moderation in some form. If so, the practitioner helps the client give it his or her best shot. In deciding how strongly to recommend abstinence, the practitioner may be helped by research-based criteria developed by Sanchez-Craig and Wilkinson (1987:52) to predict which types of clients are likely to achieve the goal of moderation, "low to moderate levels of alcohol dependence, social relationships relatively intact, good health, and no history of treatment for problem drinking."

If abstinence is the goal, use can be made of Alcoholics Anonymous (AA) and other self-help groups, such as Al-Anon, for family members. Indeed, a client's main task can be to attend meetings of the group. Although there have been few studies of profiles of individuals who profit from AA, some characteristics identified have included—not surprisingly—(1) affiliative tendencies; (2) high levels of anxiety; (3) greater physical, psychological, and social decline; and (4) a tendency to be more influenced by feelings than by the intellect (McCrady and Irvine 1989). In any case, the possibility of AA attendance should be raised with all clients manifesting signs of severe alcohol dependence, and for those interested, attendance should be encouraged.

Although this chapter is based on the assumption that the practitioner will treat rather than refer problems of alcohol abuse, referral to specialized alcoholism clinics and programs may be considered for severe cases, especially if alcohol consumption is life-threatening or if detoxification is required. Often the referring practitioner can remain on the case and work on other problems, such as family issues, as needed.

Task Strategies for Treatment of Problem Drinking

Task strategies addressed to problem drinking will be developed in terms of the key dimensions of the impact of alcohol on the client: psychological dependence on alcohol, physiological and psychological craving, loss of control over drinking, marital and family dysfunction, and relapse prevention. The first three of these dimensions are not discrete; they overlap conceptually and in practice. The key phenomenon is psychological dependence. Craving appears to be the mechanism by which dependence is advanced until control over drinking is lost. Clinically, the process of treating problem drinking is dialectical. As the client's awareness of the effects of drinking deepens, defenses are gradually lowered. Task strategies reflect this process and may overlap. Not all dimensions and strategies presented here are used in all cases, nor are they necessarily used in the sequence given. What is done will depend on the needs and circumstances of the particular client. In addition, the strategies presented here will focus on individuals who can be categorized as seriously alcohol dependent on the spectrum of problem drinking. This will permit a demonstration of the task-centered approach with more difficult cases. Social workers dealing with less severe problem drinking may select those strategies most appropriate for their particular clients as determined by the assessment process. General tasks (chapter 3) are used as umbrellas for operational tasks not only to facilitate organization, but also to emphasize the client's role as the essential agent of change.

Psychological Dependence

Psychological dependence on alcohol is defined in terms of four elements: (1) the centrality of alcohol in the client's life, (2) self-doubt and anxiety, (3) the doubt that one can abstain from drinking, and (4) the sense of loss that is attached to the idea of giving up alcohol (Nace

1987). The recognition of these elements forms the general task to be undertaken by the client.

As the severe problem drinker's health, career, and family are increasingly in jeopardy, he or she becomes increasingly preoccupied with alcohol and now lives to drink. As the process continues, the individual is assailed by self-doubt about his or her competence in meeting the daily demands of family and work, a self-doubt that is eased through the uplifting effect of alcohol. Over time, the centrality of alcohol becomes so firmly entrenched that the individual begins to doubt his or her ability to change. This doubt, seldom expressed, becomes a fear, reinforced by failed efforts to control or stop drinking. Thus, the dynamic of psychological dependence is complete and protected by denial and minimization of the seriousness of the situation.

To Recognize the Priority of Alcohol in One's Life

To accomplish this general task a number of different operational tasks can be used. The monitoring task described elsewhere as a means of assessment is but one example. The client is asked to keep pocket-sized data cards (provided by the practitioner) to record date, time, circumstances, and amount of alcohol drunk, and to bring the cards to the treatment session (Steffen, Steffen, and Nathan 1986; Hester and Miller 1989). They are used in a variety of ways—initially to monitor alcohol intake, later to analyze situational factors that promote drinking, and still later as a source of data to evaluate the effectiveness of treatment. Criddle (1986) has clients record data on drinking behavior and graph it for presentation in the next session. In this way, resistant clients must grapple with the visually displayed facts of the quantity and pattern of their alcohol consumption.

In the initial stage of treatment, the client's skepticism over the seriousness and centrality of alcohol in his or her life presents a major barrier to work. The task-centered approach generally favors tactics of information sharing and Socratic questioning to develop the client's awareness of this obstacle. As we shall see, involvement of the spouse and family in carefully rehearsed tasks of confrontation are also within the scope of this approach.

When the client acknowledges that he or she does indeed have a problem, the social worker may suggest the task of reading educational material on the addictive process of alcoholism (Criddle 1986). This task sets the stage for future treatment and prepares the client by defining the physical, psychological, and social issues to be addressed.

To Recognize and Cope with Self-doubt and Anxiety

In the initial phase of work, self-doubt and anxieties are interpreted as normal. Operational tasks include: (1) identification of situations in which tension or self-doubt arise (Criddle 1986), (2) development of coping behaviors other than drinking (Steffen, Steffen, and Nathan 1986), and (3) definition of pleasurable nondrinking activities to replace those involving alcohol (Hester and Miller 1989). For those individuals for whom the goal of moderation is appropriate, additional tasks are set up to identify the internal cues and contexts of excessive drinking and to recognize situations in which controlled drinking may occur (Steffen, Steffen, and Nathan 1986). Strategies are then devised to limit the amount of alcohol consumed in a given time frame, for example, having fewer or weaker drinks, taking less frequent sips, or smaller sips, spacing and limiting drinks, and drinking only in specific situations (Hester and Miller 1989). Pocket cards are used to keep track of the situations and the number of drinks.

The client can develop a list of specific situations that elicit tension and anxiety in him or her and arrange the list in order of priority (Steffen, Steffen, and Nathan 1986). The client may begin the process in the session and complete it as an external task. The list is then used to explore what aspects of these situations are problematic and what the client's cognitive, affective, and behavioral responses are in each situation. In this way, social skill deficits and tasks building related skills may be defined. For example, the client may focus on lack of assertive behaviors that result in tension and increased drinking. The client may then role-play assertive behavior for similar situations in the session and practice these behaviors as external tasks (chapter 5). Specific behaviors will vary from refusing a drink to confronting a spouse or an employer. The particular issue depends on the characteristics and skills of the specific client. In the process, the client develops a repertoire of replacement behaviors he or she may substitute for abusive drinking when ready to do so.

To Face the Doubt that One Can Abstain From or Limit Drinking and To Recognize One's Sense of Loss Over Giving Up Alcohol

Work on these general tasks continues throughout treatment. The tasks of monitoring consumption and analyzing the patterns of problem drinking situations often result in a growing recognition by the client of his or her difficulty in controlling consumption.

The symbolic importance of drinking tends to become entwined with the individual's self-identification because of its centrality in key social roles and activities and because, for many drinkers, it is the route to emotional release. Giving up or reducing drinking causes drinkers to feel that they are required to give up a significant part of themselves with no prospect of replacement. Here clients are asked in the session to list all their life situations, both pleasurable and problematic, in which alcohol plays a prominent role. They are then asked to prioritize them and, beginning with the least important situation, to undertake a process of imagining each scene as it would occur if they were not drinking. In this way, they can anticipate their emotions in each case and discover the extent to which they rely on alcohol to experience emotion. The clients can become aware of the need to develop other means of releasing feelings. In any case, the feeling of loss that will accompany abstinence or marked reduction in drinking can be identified in advance and ways of dealing with it can be worked out so that the individual is prepared to encounter the actual experience.

To Test One's Ability To Limit or Stop Drinking

It is always hoped that tasks to limit or to avoid drinking will be completed successfully, and they should be conceived and formulated as potentially successful. However, task failure can be used to provide cumulative evidence over time of the client's inability to limit drinking. Thus it can serve to raise the client's awareness of his or her problems. Because this goal leads directly to the well-defended and very frightening idea of loss of control, clients who drink heavily may deny the reality they experience.

While many clients will not falsify their reports of how much alcohol they have actually consumed, others will. The client's agreement to the involvement of significant others in the treatment process is a good general rule of procedure to establish at the beginning of work with all problem drinkers. When dealing with individuals the practitioner suspects of lying about drinking, he or she may seek corroborating evidence from others, such as employers or family members. In this way, the reality of the situation can be maintained while the client's fear is acknowledged. Often the client's recognition of his or her inability to control drinking is the turning point in therapeutic work and signals movement into the middle phase of treatment. The sensitive practitioner will understand the client's need for denial and minimization while objectively pointing to the self-monitoring data (and corroborating information) as evidence the client needs to consider in evaluating his or her situation. At this point we turn to a case example illustrating psychological dependence and the way task strategies may be used to define the reality of the situation for the client.

Alma A. was a fifty-eight-year old aging beauty, long locked in a dead marriage with her sixty-three-year old husband, Arnold A., described by those who knew him as a verbally abusive, highly controlling individual. Shortly after recovering from coronary surgery, Arnold announced to Alma that he was going to get rid of her so he could enjoy the few years he had left. He promptly filed for divorce, citing Alma's alcoholism as the reason for the dissolution of the marriage. Alma appeared shortly afterward for counseling for anxiety and depression. After several sessions, it became apparent to the practitioner that Alma, in addition to being depressed, anxious, and furious over the divorce action, also appeared to have a personality disorder and a habit of alcohol abuse. The diagnostic issue of what preceded what was unclear. What did seem clear was Alma's drinking pattern of three to four cocktails several times a week when she went out with her friends as well as her long-standing habit of consuming five to ten doubles of gin every other Friday and Saturday at the local social club, with the result that she was usually quite drunk by the end of the evening.

Alma's drinking had long been a source of comfort to her in the ongoing war with Arnold. Her evenings with her friends had sustained her through thirty-seven years of a loveless marriage. The social worker soon realized that Alma's denial of her drinking problem was pervasive and had now, through legal action, become yet another battleground in the war with Arnold. The goal for work was pragmatic: to help Alma reduce her drinking to less abusive proportions, and then to help her cope with the issues of divorce. To this end a task was devised that required Alma to monitor the amount of alcohol, the number of drinks, and the occasions of consumption so that a base line could be established. Since she was quite clear that she did not intend to become abstinent, moderation was adopted as the goal with a sustained overall reduction in consumption justified, initially, on the basis of undercutting Arnold's divorce allegations, and, second, for reasons of health. Over a six-month period, Alma was able to maintain a drinking limit of two one-ounce shots of gin for a maximum of three drinking periods per week. At the end of the year, she reported she liked the effects of lost weight and enhanced sense of self-control and that she intended to sustain the pattern of moderate drinking.

Craving

This dimension refers to the subjective experience of wanting to experience the anxiety-reducing and pleasurable effects of alcohol. The phenomenon is believed to have two roots. One is physiological and represents the complex physical reactions to decreasing blood levels of alcohol. Individuals who are clearly alcohol dependent manifest these physical reactions as withdrawal symptoms. Other individuals, who may not be dependent, regularly appear to experience subtle physiological cues that contribute to the sense of craving for a drink.

The second root of craving is psychological, a learned response that occurs when the individual is exposed to stimuli, both actual and symbolic, and to environments associated with drinking. This combination of physiological and psychological cues defines the dimension of craving. Nace (1987) identifies the various manifestations of dependent craving as physical (the individual can taste the beverage and feels thirsty), compulsive (he or she cannot think of anything else), cognitive (the content of thought centers around alcohol), and affective (the individual experiences dysphoric moods, such as irritability, depression, anxiety, and resentment) (Nace 1987:74–5). Studies indicate that craving can be elicited by emotional states (either positive or negative) or by states of physical discomfort that lead to physiological arousal similar to withdrawal reactions—for example, accelerated heart rate, hyperventilation, tremors, and insomnia, may all trigger craving.

Often alcohol-dependent individuals believe that craving represents a character flaw in themselves. This negative self-evaluation in turn leads to guilt, shame, and hopelessness, which are counterproductive to positive efforts to limit or abstain from drinking. Work with individuals who evaluate themselves in this way requires education about the processes of alcohol abuse in order that they may define the phenomenon as part of the process of alcoholism.

There are therefore two general tasks for work within the dimension of craving: (1) to recognize internal and external cues and contexts that trigger physiological and psychological craving, and (2) to recognize and interrupt negative self-judgments that follow the experience of craving. Operational tasks focus first on monitoring one's urges to drink, paying attention to situational factors and to cognitive, affective, and physical cues that precede the act of drinking (Wallace 1985; Steffen, Steffen, and Nathan 1986; O'Farrell and Cowles 1989). These are followed by tasks that involve interrupting self-condemnatory thoughts, similar to cognitive tasks described elsewhere in this book (chapter 3).

A case example serves to illustrate how craving may present in a client seen by a social worker in a mental health or family service agency.

> Gerald L., forty-three, was referred to a local mental health agency by an Employee Assistance Worker in the company where he was employed as a program supervisor. At the time of referral, Gerald was experiencing an acute crisis over his pending divorce. He had a long counseling history that included treatment for moderate alcoholism, anxiety, depression, and marital problems. Several years earlier, Gerald had sharply limited his alcohol intake on his own initiative, and for the past two years he had contented himself with two drinks per night, averaging two drinking nights a week, until he was hospitalized six months ago for major depression. The current crisis arose when Gerald's wife had filed for divorce after his apparently successful recovery from the depression. Although Gerald was currently taking Nardil for his depression and was aware of the dangerous drug-alcohol interaction that would follow resumption of drinking, he nonetheless found himself craving alcohol.

> Work with Gerald consisted of support in dealing with the various practical issues he found so overwhelming. Since he was clearly experiencing craving and did not want to begin drinking again, a task was defined for him to monitor the cues and situations associated with craving. The results of the first week's self-monitoring were used to develop a series of alternative coping strategies, since it had now become clear that craving for Gerald was associated with the fear of loneliness he experienced when he returned to an empty apartment after work. Accordingly, a second task was to define a list of alternative activities and people that he might see after work. A third task addressed his punitive self-evaluations by first monitoring their content and then devising a series of positive self-messages and distractions that he could use to disrupt the negative cognitions. Gerald found that telling himself that he had "done the best he could and not to be so hard on himself" helped when combined with distracting activities, such as household chores or shopping. One month after initiation of positive self-talk, Gerald reported a significant decrease in his craving for alcohol.

Loss of Control

Most problem drinkers are unable to regulate how much they will drink. Loss of control is an essential feature of severe alcohol dependence. It is characterized by the experienced need to drink, which leads to the act of drinking, then the craving of more, leading to more drinking, and, finally, to intoxication. It is unclear how this progression is initiated and sustained. The various treatment models emphasize different aspects of the bio-psychosocial process. Research suggests that the *expectancy* of the amount of alcohol imbibed, rather than the actual level of alcohol content, governs the amount drunk; there is also some evidence that the physiological feedback processes differ in individuals who are alcohol dependent (Nace 1987). That is, such individuals do not have physical feedback cues that tell them they are drunk. It appears likely that loss of control is the outcome of a complex series of interacting cues and responses, both internally and between the individual and the environmental situation. Resolution of the debate about the mechanisms of the process awaits the development of an adequate explanatory model of alcoholism.

Clinically, however, the fear, guilt, and shame associated with loss of control are the central features of alcohol dependence, and result in a wide range of defensive maneuvers on the part of the problem drinker to avoid facing the destructive impact of his or her behavior. The prominent defenses of the alcoholic—denial, minimization, and rationalization—serve this dynamic. Until the reality of the loss of control is accepted, genuine change efforts are restrained. Therapeutic work around loss of control is central to all phases of the treatment, since relapse, or slips from sobriety, can occur at any time. Accordingly, general tasks in this area include (1) to evaluate and control over drinking, (2) to develop awareness of the cues and contexts of overdrinking that lead to intoxication, (3) to evaluate (reaffirm or change) the treatment goal of abstinence or moderation, and (4) to develop specific supports and strategies to limit or abstain from drinking.

To Evaluate Control Over Drinking

For the severely alcohol-dependent person who cannot control his or her drinking the recognition of loss of control constitutes major therapeutic progress while persistence of denial signals trouble for individuals in treatment. Tasks designed to directly further the recognition of loss of control are relatively few since awareness in this area seems to evolve slowly as a by-product of other work, or, on occasion, it may be precipitated by a traumatic event that sharply focuses the client's awareness. The monitoring of consumption and of the pattern of drinking appears to further awareness, as does the task requiring the individual to attend Alcoholics Anonymous and to discuss the meetings in the treatment session. One may speculate that the openness and acceptance without shame or guilt that fellow alcoholics provide is especially helpful. Wallace's (1985) task of having the individual construct his or her drinking history can also further the client's consciousness of the extent to which he or she has lost control of his or her life.

Acceptance of the reality of slips and anticipating situations in which they may occur is the central focus of relapse prevention as we shall see. At this final stage of therapeutic work, however, the goal of the recognition of loss of control has been accepted, and it becomes a cornerstone of the client's understanding of his or her vulnerability and of the necessary coping strategies he or she requires to protect healthy functioning.

To Develop Awareness of the Cues and Contexts of Overdrinking

Any of the self-monitoring devices may be used to attain this general task. Hester and Miller (1989) ask their clients to monitor their drinking behavior for several weeks and then analyze patterns in the data. Clients are instructed to look for different situational factors associated with overdrinking, including day of the week, time of day, place, people with whom they drink, whether they are hungry or thirsty, and activities associated with drinking (such as watching TV), amount of time or money at the individual's disposal, presence of various emotional states, habitual thoughts, and bodily tension. This analysis of cues and contextual factors is then used to develop specific strategies to limit or abstain from drinking.

To Reevaluate the Goal of Abstinence or Moderation

When the original objective is moderation, the standard task of monitoring consumption is used to establish a base line level of drinking against which efforts to limit drinking may be compared. Tasks to limit drinking (previously discussed) are used to obtain this objective. The purpose is to move toward a defined rate of alcohol consumption within a given time frame that is agreed upon in advance. If this goal is attained, tasks are continued to reinforce patterns of controlled drinking.

When review of the problem suggests that the goal of moderation is not working, the client may elect to pursue abstinence. Situations that may precipitate drinking are identified as a prelude to developing strategies to support abstinence. The client is asked to develop lists of activities that do not involve drinking and of support persons and people who do not drink or do not drink heavily (Wallace 1985). As Wallace notes, most alcoholic clients find that trying to remain abstinent in the presence of former companions who are still drinking does not work. The objective here is to develop a network that positively reinforces abstinence. This often requires developing new social relationships.

To Use Specific Supports and Strategies to Limit
or Abstain From Drinking

Whether the goal is moderation or abstinence, the general tasks of identifying at-risk drinking situations and devising coping strategies are the same. Each individual must define specific supports and strategies to limit consumption. Any of the tasks described earlier may be used. In addition, session tasks may be used in which clients role-play refusing drinks with clear, congruent verbal and nonverbal behaviors. Then they practice refusals between sessions as home tasks (Wallace 1985; Monti et al. 1989). Another kind of session task is to have clients imagine their drinking behavior accompanied by aversive consequences. The crucial factor common to these tasks is the specificity of the reenactment of cues, craving, and risk situations individualized to the particular client (Steffen, Steffen, and Nathan 1986).

Marital and Family Dysfunction

In general, family members, particularly nondrinking spouses, should be viewed as potential agents of positive change. When the alcoholic is actively denying that a problem exists, the family may, in many instances, be the only positively motivating force available to the practitioner. To view the spouse-family constellation in this way is not to rule out work with the family as client. The role shifts and behavioral adaptations that families make in response to alcoholism can set severely dysfunctional processes in motion that require therapeutic intervention with the entire family to set things right. In positing the spouse and family as both client and agent of change, we are following the work of Thomas, Santa, Bronson, and Oyserman (1987) whose Unilateral Family Therapy views the spouse as a client, requiring support and therapy to change maladaptive coping and communication, and as an agent of change to confront the alcoholic behavior of the drinking spouse. Although much of what follows assumes that the problem drinker is a spouse, many of the interventions can be applied, with some modifications, to family efforts to deal with an alcoholic adolescent.

The marital relationship of an alcoholic is usually quite strained. Over time, the frustration and unhappiness of the nondrinking spouse over the drinker's behavior result in frozen, highly negative patterns of communication that in turn become aversive and anxiety-inducing for the drinker. In this way, the nondrinking spouse's efforts to control and change the drinker's problematic behavior may have the perverse result of perpetuating it. Before the spouse can become an agent of positive change, work must be done to alter these habits of negative communication. In addition, since the nondrinking spouse may have developed maladaptive coping patterns, such as withdrawal and depression, in response to the alcoholic's behavior, therapeutic efforts will need to be directed toward assisting him or her to develop new ways of dealing with his or her own difficulties. Finally, because prolonged efforts to cope with the behavior of the alcoholic member can result in emotional stress, skewed relationships, and inappropriate role assignment to children, therapeutic efforts need to be directed toward promoting improved functioning of the family as a whole. These considerations lead to the following general and operational tasks.

The Nondrinking Spouse Will Attempt to Facilitate Constructive Change in His or Her Partner's Drinking Problem

Since many problem drinkers resist and deny the efforts of others to express concern about their drinking, the nondrinking spouse is often the first member of the family requesting help. However, both the level of the drinker's resistance and the spouse's determination are highly variable. Thomas et al. (1987) suggest alternative tasks for the spouse who wishes to do something about the drinker's behavior. The selection of the particular task depends upon the assessment of the drinker's readiness and the spouse's willingness to follow through with agreed upon consequences if the drinking spouse does not agree to treatment. In each case the nondrinking spouse practices in a session task role play confronting the drinker with the facts of his or her alcohol abuse. The purpose is to obtain agreement from the drinking spouse to enter treatment and to stop or decrease his or her drinking. The spouse or other family members carefully rehearse the intervention and explore the consequences they are willing to undertake. This approach is used only when alternatives are not feasible.

In order to avoid divisive alliances and to observe ethical considerations of confidentiality, the drinking spouse is invited to participate in the initial session with the spouse and family. At the first contact with the nondrinking spouse, the wording and timing of this invitation is carefully worked out. If the problem drinker refuses to participate, he or she is informed that the spouse/family plans to meet with the social worker to discuss how they can deal with their reactions to the drinking problems, and the drinker's permission is sought to reveal information about family events. In this way, all members of the family are informed about what is going on, and the social worker avoids the appearance of conspiring against the drinking member. In most instances, the effect of these interventions is to motivate the alcoholic to begin some form of treatment. When this does not result, the act of carrying out the task may be sufficient in and of itself to destabilize family dynamics and to move the rest of the family toward more constructive coping.

Other tasks that utilize nondrinking spouses as agents of change include having them monitor their own negative reactions to their partner's drinking behavior and develop and carry out a set of alternative reactions (Thomas et al. 1987). This task may be used either to prepare the nondrinking spouse for change efforts directed toward the drinker or to cope more effectively if such efforts fail. Another task requires nondrinking spouses to develop lists of behaviors they use to try to control their partner's drinking behavior (e.g., nagging, complaining, threatening). This task, in combination with others monitoring the effects of one's behavior on the drinker, sets the stage for developing the spouse's awareness of what behaviors reinforce problem drinking. At this point, the concept of enabling is introduced as the practitioner informs the spouse that he or she is not to blame for the abuser's drinking, and educates the spouse to think about which behaviors serve to reinforce or enable drinking. A task may be established here for the spouse to develop a list of his or her enabling activities along with a set of nonreinforcing substitute behaviors. An additional task that employs the nondrinking spouse as an agent for change and that may be used in the later phase of treatment requires the spouse to develop a list of high-risk drinking situations the drinker may encounter and a set of strategies for the spouse to follow in assisting the drinker in preventing relapse. This task requires that the counselor educate the spouse and the drinker about relapse prevention and explain that slips are defined as realistic events that are to be expected.

The Family Will Engage in Specific Activities to Modify the Drinking Problem

From the work of O'Farrell and Cowles (1989) we have derived a number of session and home tasks involving the marital dyad or the family as a whole and designed to facilitate change in the drinking habits of the alcoholic member when the latter is willing to participate in treatment. One of these tasks is well suited to helping the alcoholic client become engaged in treatment. In this task, the drinker defines the spouse's behaviors (and those of other family members as well) that can trigger drinking behavior. The list is presented in marital and family sessions and serves as the basis for negotiating different, nontriggering responses that are then implemented through home tasks.

Other tasks aimed at changing drinking habits include: (1) having both partners develop together a list of positively reinforcing behaviors for the nondrinking spouse to use when the alcoholic refrains from drinking; and (2) having the alcoholic client and spouse (or the entire family) develop a list of anticipated high risk situations in which relapse is likely to occur and discuss and rehearse coping strategies to prevent it. For example, the drinker may agree to allow a delay after the first drink. The spouse pair may agree to call the counselor; the spouse pair and other family members may agree to engage in a rational and realistic discussion of the slip. The important point here is that slips are defined as events to be expected and to be immediately dealt with rather than hidden or ignored.

Loss of control over drinking is often the core issue of marital conflict. Negative communication about this issue further divides the pair and reinforces the drinking behavior of the alcohol abuser. Two tasks can be used to deal with this dynamic. The first one limits and structures anxiety around drinking by having the marital pair agree that each day at a specified time the problem drinker will initiate a brief discussion with the nondrinking spouse to reiterate his or her desire not to drink that day. The nondrinking spouse is invited to voice any questions or fears that he or she may have about possible drinking. The drinking spouse answers these questions and attempts to offer reassurance. This "Sobriety Trust Contract" is practiced in the session before it is performed as a home task (O'Farrell and Cowles 1989). The couple agrees to refrain from discussing drinking at any other time and to keep the discussion brief and ending it with a positive statement to each other.

The second task, to be used when moderation is a treatment goal, has both spouses agree that the alcohol abuser will limit drinking to one to two drinks per day—in the presence of the nondrinking spouse and possibly before the evening meal. The nondrinking spouse will refrain from negative verbal and nonverbal responses to the other's drinking. Each agrees to pay the other a sum of money if he or she breaks the contract. As with the first task, careful preparation of the couple before undertaking this task is essential to its success. The goal of moderation must be supported by the assessment, and coaching about neutral and or positive verbal and nonverbal communication will be required. To the extent that humor can be introduced in regard to paying up, the risk of negative communication will be reduced.

The Family Will Attempt To Develop and Maintain New Family Patterns in the Recovery Period

There are a variety of tasks that may be applied to helping the family restructure roles and relationships during recovery. We will discuss only a few here. One is a variation of the enjoyable activities task (chapter 6). The recovering abuser develops and carries out a list of new, pleasant activities with other family members (Dulfano 1985), or both spouses together plan and carry out a series of pleasurable, nondrinking family activities (O'Farrell and Cowles 1989).

Dulfano (1985) outlines a task for the parental pair to define parenting responsibilities and tasks and the ways they can support each other in their parental roles. The purpose of this task is twofold. It brings the recovering problem drinker back into the family as a functional parent, and it will have the effect of removing children from inappropriate executive roles they may have acquired during the parents' struggle with alcohol. In a related task, Dulfano (1985) has the children who have assumed executive roles develop and carry out a list of age-appropriate pleasant activities.

Finally, O'Farrell and Cowles (1989) bring the entire family together in a task to plan for ways to continue and maintain the new family behaviors and relationship patterns after therapy. The key here is anticipating situations that might interfere with the new family behaviors and devising strategies for coping, for example, how to deal with slips. The task provides an opportunity to review family change and to contrast past and present ways of dealing with such issues. The idea of returning for a checkup session may be used by the family as part of their planned new way of dealing with problem situations that might undermine the family's hard-won change.

Relapse Prevention

Many individuals with a drinking problem either never developed adequate competence in dealing with stressful situations, or, although initially possessing such skills, have found that the destructive effects of their alcohol abuse have led to an erosion of their sense of confidence. In either case, tensions produced by social pressures around drinking, or in work and other relationships, can place the recovering drinker at risk for relapse (Marlatt 1985). Interventions framed in terms of this dimension focus on helping the individual develop competence in coping. A central therapeutic tenet to be communicated to the client in this phase is that slips *will* happen. They should be expected and planned for in ways that minimize negative self-evaluations. General tasks include: (1) to identify high risks for drinking situations, (2) to develop specific strategies and skills for dealing with high risk situations, and (3) to enhance one's sense of self-efficacy in relation to drinking, that is, one's confidence that one can cope and can abstain or limit alcohol consumption. As with earlier interventions, these general task strategies overlap. The same task may be used with a differing focus according to the particular therapeutic purpose.

To Identify High-risk Situations

As we have seen in earlier sections, a number of authors have devised tasks requiring the client to develop a list of stressful activities and situations that would have resulted in abusive drinking in the past (Wallace 1985; Criddle 1986; Steffen, Steffen, and Nathan 1986). In each case, the client is asked to establish a hierarchy of stressful situations and to devise a nondrinking strategy for coping with each situation.

To Develop Specific Strategies and Skills

The usual procedure of task implementation is to carry out strategies of exposure, moving from low to higher risk situations. One of the most completely elaborated strategies for this task is that of Annis and Davis (1989) who have their clients complete a one-hundred-item self-report Inventory of Drinking Situations. The IDS is designed to identify situations in which the client drank heavily over the past year. Client vulnerability to relapse is assessed in terms of unpleasant and pleasant emotions, physical discomfort, testing personal control, urges and temptations, conflicts with others, social pressure to drink, and pleasant times with others. Each of the hundred items is rated on a 4-point scale. This inventory becomes the basis for developing a hierarchy of least to most risky situations for the individual. Strategies are then defined for coping with each risk situation. For individuals who have a uniformly high risk profile (and who appear to benefit less from relapse prevention training than those with more clearly defined areas of risk) a second task has the client keep an hourly log in which both emotional states and interpersonal risk situations are carefully monitored and recorded. This task serves to stimulate the client's awareness of those situations that are, in fact, more risky than others and thus defines stages for relapse prevention training.

In order to develop the clients' skills, Annis and Davis (1989) have their clients develop an inventory of strengths and resources for use in confronting high risk situations. Such supports are conceptualized as (a) environmental supports—friends, family, others who can be contacted; (b) behavioral coping—previous problem-solving efforts used successfully in the past to avoid drinking, development of rewards, and alternative activities; (c) cognitive coping—rational thinking, planning self-talk and distractions, keeping the focus on desirable outcomes of not drinking; (d) affective coping—ability to face emotions, skills in dealing with anger and frustration, acceptance of what cannot be changed, spiritual beliefs, etc.

In addition to this systematic approach, a variety of other tasks for coping with stress are offered by various authors, and are similar to those presented here. Among these are tasks to practice assertiveness, to use fantasized desensitization procedures in imagined anxiety-producing situations, and to use problem-solving skills. Hester and Miller (1989) in a complex but novel task have clients develop (1) a list of positive and desired effects derived from drinking (such as courage, mood change, increased sociability, numbing of emotions, etc.), (2) a list of situations in which these effects are desirable, (3) an enumeration of the feelings the individual associates with the particular situations, and (4) a list of alternative skills by which to cope with the negative emotions in lieu of overdrinking, e.g., relaxation techniques, assertiveness, and mood management skills.

To Enhance One's Sense of Self-efficacy

Two task strategies can be used to help enhance the client's self-confidence. The first requires the client to define at each treatment session at least three external tasks designed to develop confidence in his or her ability to cope in high risk situations. The intention here is for clients to draw upon as many strengths and resources in relatively low risk situations as quickly as possible, consolidate their successes, and move to areas of higher risk. The task requires that the client monitor specific situations, cognitions, rise in tension levels, urges to drink, and attempted coping as a means of verifying progress and providing data for devising new skills and strategies.

The second strategy builds on the first. It requires the client to develop a set of anticipated problem situations in which drinking is likely to occur. For each situation, the client will develop, rehearse, carry out, and monitor the outcome of the coping strategy. The confidence-building component is strengthened by the criteria the client is asked to use in devising these tasks: (1) the task should be challenging; (2) only a moderate degree of effort should be needed to carry out the task; (3) the client reports coping by himself or herself with relatively little help from others; (4) the success of the particular task is part of an overall pattern of improved coping; (5) the client attributes success to growth in personal control; and (6) success at this task is highly relevant to the drinking problem.

A third strategy has the client use a detailed analysis of each situation posing a high risk of relapse to specify the conditions that make drinking likely to occur and then evaluate his or her confidence in coping successfully in a similar situation now (Annis and Davis 1989). This task, which is based on Bandura's (1982) concept of self-efficacy (chapter 4), pushes clients to assume active responsibility for managing their relapse training. A progression from the least to the most stressful situations is established.

Effectiveness

The effectiveness of any particular approach to problem drinking must be seen in the context of the general efficacy of the treatment of alcohol dependency. General statements about outcome must, of course, be made with caution given the complexities of measuring results (e.g., length of follow-up period and the criteria used, differences in populations treated, and variations in treatment programs). However, the findings of reviews of research studies are instructive. In one review (sixty-eight studies published 1978 through 1983 and covering 14,546 subjects with a minimum follow-up period of six months), Riley et al. (1987) found that 34 percent had successfully moderated or terminated their drinking and 40 percent were still drinking with associated problems. Subjects receiving behavioral treatment had a slight edge in recovery rates compared to those receiving other forms of treatment. Overall, the results of treatment were similar to those reported by a review of studies published in an earlier period (Costello 1975). Studies with shorter follow-up periods may show greater improvement, but as follow-up periods lengthen, recovery rates tend to decline, in some studies to less than 15 percent (Polich, Armor, and Braiker 1981; Helzer et al. 1985). Moreover, most outcome studies are based on the clients' self-report. When more objective measures, such as collateral data and blood and urine tests are used, results appear to be less favorable (Fuller, Lee, and Gordis 1988). Finally, it has been difficult to establish that the outcomes for alcoholism treatment programs are substantially better than no formal treatment (Vaillant 1983) at all, or that any given form of alcoholism treatment is superior to any other (Nathan and Skinstad 1987).

Such outcome research clearly suggests that no one has the final answers to treating alcohol dependency. As Riley et al. (1987:108) have put it, "The state of the art for the alcohol field is that no current treatment works very well, and our energies can be best spent on developing alternative treatments with demonstrated effectiveness." In this light, the kind of task strategies we have suggested have shown promising results across a range of studies including those evaluating self-control training (Sanchez-Craig et al. 1984), social skills training

(Chaney 1989), relapse prevention (Annis and Davis 1989) and marital/ family treatment (Thomas et al. 1987; McGrady 1989).

In general, most alcohol-dependent clients must struggle long and hard in their attempt to gain mastery over their drinking problems, either through abstinence or moderation. Help that enables the client to control or forego drinking for periods of time is not necessarily in vain even though it may not suffice to produce a permanent solution. Each day free of excessive drinking is important in its own right and may enable the client to deal more effectively with other life problems.

CHAPTER 9

Problems of Clients with Chronic Mental Illness

This chapter is concerned with the psychosocial problems of persons whose functioning has been severely limited by chronic mental illness. The main focus will be on the assessment and treatment of schizophrenic individuals, a prototypical and challenging group of clients that looms large in the caseloads of clinical social workers in mental health and other settings. Strategies for this group are generally applicable to other types of clients with chronic mental illness.

Understanding the Schizophrenic Client

Schizophrenia can best be thought of as a "multiply handicapping, life-long disorder" (Bellack and Mueser 1986:178). Its etiology, despite decades of scientific investigation, remains obscure. Although it is generally believed that its origins lie in a combination of genetic and environmental factors, the ingredients of this combination are still unknown. As with depression and anxiety, a stress-diathesis model can be assumed: constitutional vulnerability interacts with stressors to produce the disorder.

To clinical social workers, knowledge of its characteristics, its course, and factors influencing its course is of more immediate concern than the etiology of the illness. Fortunately, more is known about these subjects.

The onset of schizophrenia is usually in late adolescence or early adulthood. According to DSM-III-R (American Psychiatric Association 1987:184), the active phase is usually preceded by a prodromal phase characterized by "social withdrawal, impairment in role functioning, peculiar behavior, impairment in personal hygiene and grooming, blunted or inappropriate affect, disturbances in communication, bizarre ideation, and unusual perceptual experience." The length of this phase is variable, and its beginnings may be difficult to determine. The *active phase*, often triggered by stressors, is marked by such psychotic symptoms as delusions, hallucinations, loosening of associations (incoherent topic shifts), illogical thinking, and disorganized behavior. In the *residual phase*, which usually follows, the symptomatology resembles the prodromal phase, although blunted affect and role impairment may occur more frequently. Complete remission is rare. The usual course of the illness consists of repetitions of the acute phase followed by progressively more severe impairment during the residual phases.

Since the deinstitutionalization movement of the 1950s and 1960s, most persons with schizophrenic disorders have been cared for primarily in the community, although large numbers still lead quasi-institutionalized lives in community care residences, shelters, and other such facilities. Hospitalizations in psychiatric and, increasingly, in general medical facilities usually occur during the active phases.

In the majority of cases, the more florid symptoms of schizophrenia that appear during the active phase respond to antipsychotic medication. Continuance of medication is standard practice during the residual phases as a means of controlling the symptoms and preventing a relapse. Medication has its limitations, however. While it may be effective with "positive" symptoms, such as delusions and hallucinations, it has little effect on "negative" symptoms, such as apathy and withdrawal. Side effects such as akinesia, akathisia, and tardive dyskinesia are common. Many patients do not take the medication as prescribed. Finally, a significant percentage of patients apparently do not receive much benefit at all from any form of medication (Bellack and Mueser 1986).

It is now generally accepted that the interaction between the schizophrenic and his or her social environment plays a critical role in the course of the illness. Whether living in a group home, with family, in a single room, or on the street, the schizophrenic typically leads a marginal, problem-ridden existence. Alcohol and drug abuse are common. The schizophrenic's lack of social skills reinforces withdrawal and isolation. Apathy combined with poor vocational skills leads to irregular, low-paying, and often stressful jobs, or, in most cases, to chronic unemployment and dependence on public funds or family for support. Inadequate self-care routines join with other deficits to cause health problems. Within the context of such degraded and precarious environments, specific stressors have been identified. Perhaps the best documented of these stressors has been "expressed emotion" (EE) (Vaughn and Leff 1976; Miklowitz et al. 1984; Goldstein and Strachan 1987). Although EE, strictly speaking, is a measure of the family members' attitudes, presumably these attitudes are indicative of behavior. If so, families high on EE tend to relate to the schizophrenic member (SM) in a critical, intrusive, and often hostile manner. In low EE families, these relational tendencies are not present. Although it is not certain that EE contributes to the development of schizophrenia, schizophrenics living with high EE relatives have a much higher relapse rate (estimated at from four to six times greater) than those living with low EE relatives (Bellack and Mueser 1986). Further, there is evidence from experimental studies that EE is not simply a reaction to the behavior of the schizophrenic family member; rather, it exerts an independent influence on that behavior (Goldstein and Strachan 1987).

There is also evidence from brain research and behavioral laboratory studies that the reactions of schizophrenics to EE may be an expression of a more general deficit in their capacity to process complex stimuli (Anderson, Reiss, and Hogarty 1986) and to regulate emotional arousal. Thus, any environment where the schizophrenic is exposed to complex, emotionally arousing messages may be especially stressful and could prompt a relapse. This notion is in keeping with long-standing practice wisdom about risks in using intensive, insight-oriented treatment with such clients (Hollis 1958).

Assessment

Although social workers may not have the responsibility for making a formal diagnosis, they nevertheless need to be knowledgeable about diagnostic criteria for schizophrenia, and they have to be able to apply them. In some cases, social workers will see schizophrenic persons who have not been diagnosed, and the practitioners themselves will need to make a provisional assessment in order to determine if psychiatric consultation or referral is necessary or to develop a preliminary case plan. With previously diagnosed schizophrenics, social workers need to pin down the kind of schizophrenic symptoms the clients are exhibiting in order to work with them effectively and to interpret their behavior to others. It is particularly important that the practitioner is able to detect prodromal signs that may foreshadow a possible relapse.

Assessment of the psychiatric symptomatology, however, is only a part of a broad-based assessment of the client's adaptation in a number of areas. Although what will be investigated in depth depends on the problem, areas to be considered include sources and amount of income, current work adjustment and work history, health, housing, social and family relationships, transportation, and activities of independent living, e.g., the client's ability to care for himself or herself (Moxley 1989). In addition to interviewing the schizophrenic client, the practitioner may need to obtain data from case records, employers, family members, and other collaterals.

When schizophrenic clients are living (or involved) with their families, family interviews are usually indicated. Patterns of interaction among the schizophrenic client and the family members should be the center of attention, especially when there is evidence of expressed emotion. Aspects of family interaction to be considered will be taken up in greater detail in the discussion of task strategies below.

A variety of structured instruments can be used in the assessment of schizophrenic clients; a selective listing may be found in Kuehnel and Liberman 1989. One of the more comprehensive is the 120-item Independent Living Skills Survey (Wallace 1985), which covers self-care skills, eating and grooming, domestic activities, health care, money management, transportation, leisure activities, and work. The instrument is designed to be administered to care providers. Specific subscales relating to particular areas can be used or selected items can serve as checklists in collecting data from either collaterals or from the clients themselves. Schedules for structured interviews with mentally ill persons can also be adapted for purposes of clinical assessment; see Kuehnel and Liberman (1989) for examples. Finally, use can be made of RAIs (chapter 2) relating to specific problems the client may have.

Task Strategies

My presentation of task strategies will be based on the assumption that the major target problems involve the client's adjustment in the community where most work with schizophrenics takes place. Hospitalizations have become increasingly brief and have come to resemble the short stays of patients hospitalized for physical illness. In fact, some of the basic methods used in hospital work with schizophrenics, such as discharge planning, will be taken up in the next chapter on problems relating to health.

Although I will assume that the practitioner is based in a mental health setting, the ideas and methods presented can be applied in all settings (including most social work agencies) where clients with schizophrenia are part of the caseload. Finally, I will assume that the practitioner has both therapeutic and case management responsibilities for the client, that is, he or she provides the counselling services the client needs and also performs the linking, monitoring, advocacy, and other activities associated with case management (Moxley 1989; Vandiver and Kirk in press; chapter 3, this volume). This position reflects the historical role of social work, which has attempted to combine these functions (Moore 1990). At the same time, I will draw on the conceptual and technical advances that have emerged from the case management movement. An excellent review of the effectiveness of case management programs may be found in Rubin (1990).

Work with Schizophrenics and Their Families

From a task-centered perspective, involvement of the family at the earliest opportunity and continuing it with some form of family-oriented service generally makes sense when it can be done. Schizophrenic clients are often young adults still living with their families or dependent on them. Surveys report that between 30 and 50 percent of chronically mentally ill persons live with their families and that the great majority have social contact with family members (Lamb and Goertzel 1977; Love 1985). As the studies of expressed emotion referred to earlier have demonstrated, family dynamics have a critical influence on the course of the schizophrenic's recovery. Moreover, families can provide important emotional and tangible resources to facilitate this recovery. Family involvement is not always possible or indicated, and in some cases it must be approached with caution. Some families are not available or have given up on trying to relate to the client, and intense conflict between the client and the family may preclude conjoint work. Still, some contact with family members is usually advisable, especially when they can serve as resources for the client. When involvement of the whole family seems contraindicated, the clients themselves can be asked to suggest which family member(s) might be most helpful to them, and thus which one(s) might most profitably be seen.

Our approach has been influenced by two interrelated developments in work with schizophrenics and their families during the past decade: psychoeducational models (Anderson et al. 1980; Anderson, Reiss, and Hogarty 1986; Bernheim and Lehman 1985; Leff 1989) and applications of family behavioral treatment (Falloon 1988; Liberman 1988). Basic to these approaches and to our own is the education of family members, including the schizophrenic member (SM), about the nature and the course of schizophrenia and helping them develop the skills and resources to cope with it.

Relevant research on the disease, such as studies of EE, is introduced early in the treatment. The SM is identified as having a serious illness for which the family is not to blame. The family's difficulties in coping with the illness are recognized, but emphasis is placed on what the family can do to facilitate recovery. The need to maintain a "low-key" environment is stressed. In this environment, ideally, family members support the SM while avoiding either positive or negative overinvolvement. The SM is given the necessary psychological space to recover at his or her own pace. The family is expected to set limits on his or her behavior while keeping expectations and related criticism to a minimum.

Educating the family is done in family interviews. The multifamily workshops described by Leff et al. (1982) and Anderson (1983) offer a promising alternative when a sufficient number of families is available. The SM is seen together with the family, but he or she may also be seen individually depending on his or her preferences, degree of recovery, and the potential for conflict if included. As soon as possible, however, interviews of the whole family are used.

Deliberately designating the SM as "sick" runs counter to family therapy traditions in which such labels are generally avoided. However, as Anderson, Reiss, and Hogarty (1986) point out, more is gained than lost in identifying the SM as ill. Major gains are a stronger alliance with the family, increasing the family's tolerance for the SM's disturbing behavior, and recognition on everyone's part of the realities of schizophrenia as far as they are known. However, possible drawbacks, such as scapegoating the SM, need to be guarded against.

The use of tasks in work with schizophrenics and their families is a central feature of contemporary practice. As Anderson, Reiss, and

Hogarty have noted, "The creation of tasks helps to prolong the impact of the sessions and gives the patient and the family a focus and a sense of progress over time. . . . The use of tasks also allows clinicians to establish concrete structure and control with overly enthusiastic patients or overly critical families" (1986:144–146). What follows is a grouping of tasks related to different aspects of functioning of the SM and his or her family's involvement in treatment, but it is not necessarily assumed that the SM and the family are sharing the same household.

Participation in Family Life

The withdrawal, inertia, and apathy typically exhibited by the SM are difficult for families to accept—in fact, they appear to be the object of most of the negative criticism expressed by high EE families (Leff 1989). At the same time, the SM needs to learn how to function in the small society of the family as a preparation for functioning independently in society at large. Accordingly, tasks are aimed at helping the SM make as much of a positive contribution to family life as is possible given the stage of his or her illness. At a simple level, tasks may involve the SM's doing household chores as a way of contributing to family life or engaging in social and recreational activities with family members (e.g., games, outings). Ideally such home tasks are planned by the family, including the SM, in session tasks while the practitioner provides structure and guidance for the communication among the family members. The practitioner may intervene to question expectations of the SM that seem excessive or to reduce tension among the participants. In general, the practitioner attempts to have the session be a model for the kind of low-key interactions that it is hoped the family can achieve at home. If a session task format appears to be unproductive or too risky, the practitioner and the family members plan the task through practitioner-led discussion (chapter 6).

Regardless of the format used, the practitioner attempts to involve the other family members in the task activity. The purpose of this involvement is not only to provide support for the SM, but also to create a climate for the family to try to do things differently. Tasks may shared—e.g., house repair projects or outings—or other family members may undertake reciprocal or related individual tasks. For example, John (the SM) agrees to vacuum the house; his parents agree to make his two favorite meals during the week. Or John and his sister agree to go skating, an activity both like. In involving the SM and other family members in shared and reciprocal tasks, it is important that the family member(s) selected will be supportive and not antagonistic.

Disturbing Behavior

Practitioners are frequently presented with behavior that is disturbing to family members as well as to SMs themselves, behavior such as bizarre rituals, incoherent and delusional talk, and destructive or assaultive behavior. Disturbing behavior that occurs regularly can often be controlled by tasks for the SM that call for restraint or modification of the behavior (Bernheim and Lehman 1985). In one case, for example, a son was able to refrain from expressing delusional ideas to his father, who found them particularly upsetting, though he could still express them to his mother who was able to accept them. Usually such tasks are not set up as a part of reciprocal task plans (quid pro quo's) since family members may resent "making concessions" to curb behavior they consider inappropriate. However, an attempt is made to achieve a balance by having other family members do individual tasks relating to other problems.

Episodes of destructive or assaultive behavior may be particularly threatening to the family. As Bernheim and Lehman (1985) suggest, family members can sometimes anticipate these episodes by observing signs, such as agitation, irritability, and argumentativeness, and they can take steps to prevent them or to protect themselves. In one case, a daughter would cut up her mother's clothing with scissors during periods of agitation. The mother would then lock up her wardrobe (or what was left of it) when she thought her daughter was losing control. In another case, a single mother, who had been assaulted several times in the past, would call the crisis team at the mental health clinic at the first signs of aggressive behavior.

Family Conflict

Issues concerning the SM's behavior, including those just discussed, can lead to different forms of family conflict. The conflict may arise between the SM and other members, or other members may come into conflict over the SM. In either case, the practitioner makes use of the conflict reduction methods described in chapter 6, although some special considerations are applied. Areas of conflict are identified and the participants work out solutions in session tasks under the practitioner's guidance. Home tasks are then devised to implement the solutions. In applying this methodology to families of schizophrenics, the practitioner first of all makes sure that expressions of conflict in the session do not endanger whatever psychological balance the SM has achieved. In some cases, this may lead to separate sessions or split sessions so that intense conflicts between family members about the SM can be thrashed out in his or her absence.

When the conflict involves the SM, the practitioner must weigh the potential benefits of direct negotiation of the conflict against possible risks of putting strain on the SM's coping capacities. A certain amount of trial and error within acceptable risk limits is involved here. Some SMs can tolerate a good deal of conflict of certain kinds but may be quite reactive to other kinds. It is usually best to start with minor disputes as a low risk test of the family's and the schizophrenic's capacity for dealing with conflict. Session tasks focused on discussing expectations and limits and clarifying misunderstandings may bring about desired changes in themselves without requiring specific home tasks.

> For example, in one of our cases, Kevin, a twenty-year-old, who had been hospitalized for an acute schizophrenic episode, remained resentful at his parents for "railroading" him into the hospital. The resentment appeared to contribute to his conflicted relationship with them. In a session task, his parents explained to him why they had decided hospitalization was necessary. The precipitant, which Kevin apparently no longer remembered, was his partially acted out threat to jump out of an upper-story window. The parents were successful in conveying to him that their decision was based on their concern for him, rather than on their wish to punish him for causing them trouble. This new perception in itself, reinforced by the practitioner, seemed to ease tensions between Kevin and his parents.

Developing External Interests

It is important for the SM as well as for the other family members to develop interests outside the family. The lack of such interests tends to reinforce the apathy and withdrawal of the SM and leads to over-involvement on the part of the family. Absorbed in coping with the SM, the family members may forego external activity. As a result, enmeshment with the SM is likely to be accentuated. While initial forays into the outside world may involve the SM and other family members in shared tasks, the goal should be a balance of independent and shared activities. Direct work with schizophrenic clients to increase social involvement will be considered below.

Association with Self-help Groups

Some families find that membership in self-help groups, such as the National Alliance for the Mentally Ill, can be a source of external involvement and can also provide a way to connect with other families with schizophrenic members. Such groups can also furnish the family with practical information about local resources, and they can enable family members to channel their concerns for the SM into advocacy for the mentally ill. Further, affiliation with a self-help group fosters active use of social networks and communities, which is in keeping with the philosophy of the model. A task for the family can be to contact a self-help group. Or, as Bernheim and Lehman (1985) suggest, the practitioner can request permission for a group member to get in touch with the family (see chapter 11).

Modifying Family Structure

As discussed in chapter 6, a task-centered approach can be used to modify aspects of the family structure that are a part of the target problems or of the obstacles to their resolution. For the most part, these changes are accomplished through selection and organization of session and home tasks. With families of schizophrenics, this strategy is adapted to the overriding need to facilitate the SM's recovery. As a result, structural features that might otherwise be seen as targets for change may be accepted, at least initially, if they appear to be helpful to recovery. Thus, in one of our cases, a cross-generational alliance between Mrs. Caro and her nineteen-year-old schizophrenic son, Rob, served to "protect" the son against an impatient, critical father. Shared "enjoyable activity" tasks involving Mrs. Caro and Rob were used initially as a means of drawing Rob out of his room. After Rob had become more active, and his father's attitude toward him more positive, the father and Rob engaged in similar shared tasks.

Parental overinvolvement with the SM and cross-generational coalitions, in which one parent "protects" the SM from the other (as in the case above), are common in families of schizophrenics. Decreasing involvement and strengthening parental coalitions become general strategies in the long run; however, their implementation may be delayed to achieve immediate clinical goals. As they unfold, these strategies make use of a variety of devices, such as seeing parents separately, parents-only session tasks for purposes of planning and information sharing, tasks at home requiring cooperative, mutually supportive parental behavior in handling issues relating to the SM, and the development of all-around interests external to the family (as discussed above).

Effectiveness

The kind of psychoeducational family centered approach just described was found to be effective in a major controlled study conducted at the Western Psychiatric Institute (Hogarty et al. 1986) The relapse rate for patients receiving family treatment and drugs at one year follow-up was less than half of the rate for patients who received drugs only. The combination of family treatment, drugs, *and* social skills training proved even more effective. There were *no* relapses in this group at one year follow-up. It should be emphasized that patients in all groups received medication, without which neither the family treatment nor the social skills training would have been likely to be successful. Moreover, when family treatment was used, levels of expressed emotion (EE) declined between admission and follow-up, which suggests that the effectiveness of family treatment in reducing EE may have been a factor in preventing relapse. Earlier controlled evaluation research (Leff et al. 1982, 1985; Falloon et al. 1982) has likewise found large effects on relapse rates resulting from psychoeducational family approaches.

Working with the Individual Client

Although a family-centered approach may be the treatment of choice when feasible, much work with the schizophrenic client must proceed on a one-to-one basis. Families may not be in the picture, or may not want to be involved, or clients may not want to involve them. Nevertheless, as we shall see, the family can often contribute to the resolution of target problems in the context of individual treatment. Conversely, most of the individual intervention methods to be described can also be used within the context of family treatment.

General Considerations

Individual treatment of schizophrenic clients is typically concentrated on helping them with the self-management of their disorders and, as with anyone, with their problems of living (Lamb 1982; Coursey 1989).

In the task-centered model, as in most others, no attempt is made to affect the underlying psychopathology, that is, the schizophrenic processes. The orientation is similar to that used in social work with the physically ill. The practitioner does not "treat the illness" but rather helps the clients make the most of their lives despite the handicap of being ill. As Coursey (1989:351) observes, "having a schizophrenic disorder does not exempt one from the usual therapeutic problems or from help. Solving these problems does *not* remove the schizophrenia but may affect its course by reducing the stresses surrounding it." Positive symptoms of schizophrenia—e.g., hallucinations and delusions—are dealt with as one would with any target problem or obstacle. What immediate, modifiable factors may be causing the symptoms, and what can be done about them? Meanwhile, what difficulties are the symptoms themselves causing, and what can be done about these difficulties? Some clients can recognize symptoms for what they are and address them collaboratively with the practitioner. Thus, for one client, a task of telling her "voices" to "buzz off" seemed to be an effective way of controlling them. With other clients, symptoms have the appearance of undeniable reality. Although practitioners may cautiously probe the client's delusions or hallucinations to see how firmly they are held, they avoid either challenging or validating them. Rather, the practitioner responds empathetically to the upset the symptoms cause and tries to help clients deal with them. In one case, for example, a young woman was convinced that the residents who sat around the lobby of her apartment building started to talk about her when she walked through, which caused her to become quite agitated. Accepting her feeling of being upset, the practitioner involved her in brainstorming how she could cope with this troublesome situation. This discussion lead to the idea that she could enter the building unobserved through a back entrance.

With every client, a general goal of the task-centered approach is to increase the client's capacity for independent problem solving (Reid 1978). This goal receives special emphasis in the treatment of schizophrenic clients because of the difficulties such clients have in coping with the many kinds of problems they typically face. Similarly, Vandiver and Kirk (in press) stress the importance of enhancing the client's sense of self-efficacy.

Regardless of the problem being worked on, an attempt is made to involve the client in structured problem solving. In fact, in one test of the task-centered model, explicit teaching of problem-solving skills with schizophrenic and other psychiatric out-patients appeared to increase the clients' problem-solving abilities and enhanced the effectiveness of the model itself (Brown 1980).

By involving the client in problem solving, the practitioner assumes that the client is able to participate collaboratively in all phases. While always supportive, the practitioner avoids being overly "helpful." This caution applies particularly to goal setting, where practitioners may be tempted to take an overly directive role. As Anthony et al. (1988:221) observe ". . . when given the opportunity and some assistance, most persons with severe psychiatric disabilities can set reasonable goals" (see chapter 11).

Normally, a good deal of attention is paid to practical concerns, such as medication, employment, housing, and finances. Plans for handling these concerns should be worked out collaboratively. Although the practitioner may take an active role in the environment to help the client secure services and other resources, this activity is structured through practitioner tasks (chapter 3), which are discussed in advance and then reviewed with the client. Or, as suggested in chapter 3, tasks for the practitioner and other service providers may be worked out in case management meetings in which the client is an active participant. These structures offer the clients the opportunity to become aware of the practitioner's (and others') proposed environmental interventions and encourage them to add their own input to this planning in a way that strengthens their problem-solving abilities.

With these general considerations in mind, we turn to specific types of issues that commonly arise in work with schizophrenic clients. These include medication, social relationships, employment, and housing.

Medication

Failure to take antipsychotic medication as prescribed has been cited as the single most common reason for hospital readmission (Caton 1984). A large percentage of schizophrenic clients, perhaps between 24 and 50 percent, either do not take their prescribed medication or take less than the amount prescribed (Meichenbaum and Turk 1987). Thus, with many clients, facilitating adherence to a drug schedule is a key element of treatment.

A straightforward way of facilitating adherence is to build it into the task structure of the treatment. Thus, taking medication as prescribed and attending clinic appointments become ongoing tasks. This method has the advantage of making an assessment of medication compliance possible as part of regular task reviews that may also cover other client tasks as well as practitioner tasks. As a part of a "good" task review, which should be matter-of-fact and nonthreatening, such an assessment is more likely to elicit honest responses from the client and less likely to create defensive reactions.

As always in task-centered practice, it is important to understand the problems from the client's perspective. Side effects are often obstacles from the client's point of view.

For example, two of the more common side effects, tardive dyskinesia (abnormal involuntary movements) and extrapyramidal symptoms (e.g., hand tremors, listlessness, jumpiness), affect a substantial number of clients. Tardive dyskinesia may affect from 15 to 20 percent of those taking antipsychotics (Wittlin 1987); extrapyramidal symptoms may affect 40 percent (Johnson 1984). Many clients deny that they are still "mentally ill" while in remission, and by the same token they may reject the idea of taking medication, which, of course, is a constant reminder of their illness. Moreover, there may be no immediate adverse consequences of not taking the medication. A relapse may not occur for weeks or months following discontinuance, and when a relapse does happen, the client may not attribute it to a lack of medication (Wittlin 1986). Thus, it is easy to see how a client could develop a rationale for not taking medication. In addition, apathy, confusion, and memory deficits resulting from the illness or from the medication itself may make it difficult for the client to adhere to a routine of taking medication.

In exploring the client's attitude toward medication, the practitioner can emphasize the role of antipsychotics in preventing a relapse, while acknowledging the unpleasantness of side effects. In addition to tasks to take medication, tasks for the client might include meeting clinic appointments, discussing side effects with the prescribing physician, and asking a family member or significant other to provide reminders. Modeling and rehearsing those tasks that involve communication with others through role plays may be indicated. Client self-rewards for taking medication may also be useful. Through tasks of their own, practitioners (with the client's consent) may consult with physicians about possible changes in medication, arrange for clinic appointments, and instruct caregivers to remind the client. The practitioner or case aide can also provide telephone reminders. Skill-oriented approaches to helping clients comply with medication programs may be found in Meichenbaum and Turk (1987).

Social and Independent Living Skills

In recent years, a good deal of emphasis has been given to training schizophrenic clients in social skills (e.g., assertiveness, conversing, dating) as well as in skills of independent living (e.g., personal hygiene, shopping). Deficits in these skill areas and evidence (reviewed below) that training can make a difference in the client's life have spurred interest in this form of intervention.

In one-to-one work with schizophrenic clients, social skills training can make use of the formats outlined in chapter 5. With schizophrenic clients, it is especially important to keep in mind the considerable range of capacities one may find and to tailor the training accordingly. With more severely impaired clients, the pace of training may need to be slowed considerably. Skill components may need to be broken down into discrete segments and taught sequentially. For example, in his "attention focusing" model of skill training with severely impaired clients, Liberman (1988) breaks conversational skills down into three components; asking questions, giving compliments, and making requests for engaging in activities. The first component needs to be learned before the second is taught.

Schizophrenic clients may have difficulty in generalizing skills learned in the session to the myriad of situations they may encounter in real life. For this reason, a larger variety of responses may be practiced in role plays. In addition, the family members and others in the client's microsystem may be asked to facilitate the client's practice of skills and to respond to good performance with approval or other positive reinforcement.

More severely impaired clients may also profit from training in independent living skills, such as personal hygiene, housekeeping, doing laundry, shopping, and handling personal financing. Probably the most effective way to teach these skills is through in-vivo methods. For example, shopping skills are best taught while the client is actually shopping. Skills in personal hygiene, housekeeping, and laundry can be often taught by care providers in residences.

Research on the outcomes of social skills training with chronically mentally ill clients has suggested that such training does facilitate better adjustment to the demands of community living (Anthony, Cohen, and Cohen 1984; Bellack et al. 1984; Liberman, DeRisi, and Mueser 1989). One limiting factor identified by this research has been the difficulty many clients have in generalizing skills beyond the specific situations in which training has occurred. It will be recalled that a combination of family treatment and social skills training was particularly effective in one study cited earlier (Hogarty et al. 1986). In that same study, social skills training *alone* approximated the outcomes achieved by the family treatment program—20 percent relapse rate after one year versus a relapse rate of 49 percent for controls. In another controlled follow-up study, Wallace and Liberman (1985) found that at a follow-up after nine months in-patients receiving skills training had a lower relapse rate than a comparison group, and there was evidence that the learned skills were maintained in family and peer relationships. However, the 50 percent relapse rate after two years suggested that these gains had attenuated.

Although the effectiveness of social skills training with the chronically mentally ill has been demonstrated, it has not been determined how well such training generalizes to new situations and how long its effects persist. Its contribution as an adjunctive intervention, e.g., to family treatment, has been better established.

Residential Care

Finding an appropriate residential care facility is an important goal for many schizophrenic clients in their adjustment to community living. In table 9.1 some of the more common types are described. Group homes, halfway houses, and board-and-care homes account for the great majority. Lack of trained staff, inadequate programming, and poor living conditions are frequent problems, especially in board-and-care homes.

In regard to locating and entering a residence, client tasks might involve deciding on the kind of facility he or she prefers or on the timing of a transfer from one kind to another. The client may initiate contact or make an initial visit. How much responsibility clients take for these actions depends on their level of functioning, but they should be encouraged to assume as much as possible. For example, clients should be active participants in discharge planning meetings of therapeutic teams. In addition to facilitating client actions through providing information about resources, practitioners can locate and explore possible residences on the client's behalf or visit them with the client.

While in care facilities, clients need to cope with the usual problems of residential living. Difficulties may include conflict with other residents or staff or dissatisfactions with living conditions. When problems

TABLE 9.1

Types of Residential Care Facilities

Facility	Description	Population Typically Served
Locked, Skilled Nursing	Structured, restrictive setting with intensive programming, rehabilitation goals; high staff/patient ratio.	Severely impaired, symptomatic; unable to function in open setting
Group Homes	Structured, restrictive setting, small numbers of patients; close supervision; day structured with in-house activities and attendance at day-treatment programs.	Severely impaired, symptomatic; stays may exceed one year
Halfway Houses	Compared to group home, less structured and restrictive setting, less intensive supervision; otherwise similar in programming.	Less severely impaired; stays relatively short; good potential for independent living.
Board-and-Care Homes (Adult Homes)	Open settings with minimal supervision; patients share rooms; often large numbers of patients per facility; low staff/patient ratio; programming often rudimentary.	Able to function in community but often chronically impaired.
Foster Care	Family setting; small number of patients (less than five) who participate in family life.	Able to function in socially acceptable manner; in need of long-term care.
Supervised Apartments	Patients reside in an apartment complex, usually two to an apartment; supervision by staff who live in same complex.	Better functioning patients.
Satellite Apartments	Patients live in community apartments; minimal monitoring; emphasis on preparation for independent living.	Patients almost ready for independent living.

are seen as originating in the client, modification in the client's beliefs or actions may be attempted. When problems are seen as originating in an external system or in the client's interaction with it, the practitioner makes use of strategies such as expansion of the intervention system, client empowerment, and practitioner tasks (chapter 5). For example, the social worker may have a joint session with the client and a staff member to work out a conflict, may help the client develop skills in dealing with a difficult roommate, or, in an advocacy role, he or she may try to persuade the director of a residence to provide a needed service for the client.

Social Relations

Schizophrenic clients often need help in developing satisfying social lives. As always in using a task-centered approach, the practitioners are sensitive to what their clients want in the way of social relations, and they are careful not to impose their own norms. This position does not preclude asking clients about their wants in respect to social relations or suggesting possibilities to consider.

As indicated previously, training in conversational, dating, and other human relation skills may be necessary first steps. Helping clients to develop and implement tasks to increase their social involvements should be a logical result of skill training, or such tasks may be set up first, and training may be used as needed in the process of implementation. In addition to affiliative tasks (e.g., starting a conversation, engaging in an activity with someone), the client may take on tasks that involve exploring or joining social organizations. Day treatment programs and psychosocial clubs provide opportunities for social interaction with other clients and staff (see the section "Psychosocial rehabilitation" below).

Vocational Rehabilitation

For schizophrenic clients work is not only a means of earning income and achieving independence, but it is also a means of helping them organize their lives around a meaningful activity. While only a minority of clients can be expected to find and hold full-time jobs (Jacobs et al. 1984), some form of participation in the world of work is a reasonable goal for most.

The assessment begins with a work history, which is perhaps the best single predictor of employment potential (Strauss and Carpenter

1977). An assessment of prevocational skills, such as the ability to be punctual, to maintain concentration on tasks, and to relate to others, may be made from observing, or obtaining reports about, the client's participation in residential or day programs, including performance of "house-cleaning" chores. Such assessment data can be used as a basis for the kind of vocational assistance best suited for the client.

Clients with poor employment histories or severe impairments may need training in prevocational skills or basic job skills. Although such training can be given individually by the practitioner or in classes, one of the most effective vehicles is sheltered employment, in which clients have the opportunity to learn vocational skills at their own pace and with the help of specialized staff. Problems in adjusting to the workplace can be identified and worked through. In some cases, training may be needed to prepare the client for a sheltered employment experience. The training is then continued during this experience.

> In one task-centered case, Terri, a young woman with a diagnosis of schizophrenia and mild mental retardation, needed training in self-control prior to entering a sheltered employment program. Training provided by a social work intern attached to Terri's group home focused on helping her avoid outbursts of loud swearing, which would be unacceptable in the sheltered workshop. Terri's tasks included ways of controlling stress at work, such as going to her supervisor for help when she began to feel frustrated. Terri was able to keep the swearing under control after starting at the workshop with continued assistance from the intern and the workshop staff.

Sheltered workshops vary in the amount of training and staff support they provide. Some offer little more than low-level, low-wage employment, and for some clients this may be better than no employment. In any case, the kind of orientation and program of the workshop should be carefully explored prior to referral.

A step up from the sheltered workshop is transitional employment. The client works in a regular place of employment, but receives supervision and on-the-job training from mental health or rehabilitation staff. The client is paid normal wages for the job and is expected to meet the usual work standards. Recent developments include instruments that screen clients for employability and intensive job-related counseling (Bond and Dincin 1986).

As the name suggests, transitional employment should lead to regular employment. For clients with good work histories and with less severe impairments, neither training nor special employment settings may be needed. Some may be helped to find jobs or to acquire specialized training through state vocational rehabilitation agencies. Others may benefit from training in job finding skills, especially in job interviewing (chapter 5).

Job Clubs, following the original program by Azrin and associates (Azrin et al. 1975) have proven successful in helping clients find jobs on their own. Job Clubs offer job search training and provide a structure and resources to enable clients to locate jobs. By facilitating the client's independent job seeking, Job Clubs foster the kind of autonomy and self-efficacy in the client that are often missing in conventional programs. Many psychosocial clubs and psychosocial rehabilitation services to be discussed in the next section provide similar programs.

Social workers do much more than refer to vocational programs. They may provide training in prevocational and job seeking skills, explore and evaluate vocational programs, assist with job searches, and resolve job related difficulties through work with clients and employers.

Psychosocial Rehabilitation

A comprehensive approach to facilitating the adjustment of the chronic mentally ill to the community is provided by psychosocial rehabilitation centers. These centers are often out-growths of the psychosocial clubs and may still be designated as such. Originally, psychosocial clubs, such as Fountain House in New York City, were developed to meet the social and recreational needs of the mentally ill in the community. They are organized on a "club house" model in which members and staff interact informally in a range of programs and activities. Members are expected to take an active role in the club's operations from program planning to housekeeping chores. Clubs offer a milieu that fosters a sense of belonging, of being accepted and needed, and of optimism about the future. Many clubs, following the model of Fountain House (Beard, Propst, and Malamud 1982), have developed a range of programs and services that may include skills training, vocational rehabilitation, financial education, and case management. The opportunity for interaction with members enables the staff to make use of guided practice and other in-vivo tasks to teach prevocational and social skills (Peterson, Patrick, and Rissmeyer 1990).

CHAPTER 10

Health-related Problems

JULIE S. ABRAMSON

Social workers in health care settings assist clients and their families in dealing with psychosocial problems contributing to or caused by illness and disability. Although this chapter focuses on work with clients in such settings, its content applies to social work practice with sick clients in nonmedical settings as well. I shall begin with an overview of common problem areas and the contribution of the social worker to the resolution of problems in each. The relevance of the task-centered approach for social work in health care will then be reviewed and assessment issues for the various problem areas will be identified. The remainder of the chapter will set out task strategies for each problem area.

Common Problem Areas

The experience of being ill creates certain problems for clients and their families that are specifically related to the impact of illness and to efforts to cope with the ensuing changes. Most problems relating to illness that are dealt with by social workers fall into one of the following categories: (1) problems with adjustment to illness, (2) problems in decision making, (3) problems with the health care system, (4) problems with inadequate resources, and (5) problems unique to caregivers.

Adjustment to Illness

Serious illness, whether acute or chronic, has a physical, emotional, and social impact on individuals of a magnitude rarely encountered in dealing with other life events. Client responses to illness vary with the degree of threat to former roles and with the prognosis for recovery. They also vary with the phase of the illness. Mailick (1979) divides the experiences of the individual and family with illness into three phases: the diagnostic phase, characterized by uncertainty and a need for information; the adaptive phase in which individuals and families face the realities of changes in functioning; and the terminal phase, involving the resolution of the illness, its remission, or death. Additionally, illness in all phases increases feelings of loss of control over life circumstances for clients as well as for family members. Struggles to maintain or regain control can be a source of conflict between clients and families or between them and health care providers. Disagreements during the course of illness can also arise concerning adjustments in roles and responsibilities necessitated by changes in the client's situation. Social workers assist sick individuals and their families with many of the painful issues involved in making a successful adaptation to illness.

Decision Making

When a sudden onset of illness or exacerbation of a chronic condition results in hospitalization, the client and close family members invariably face critical decisions regarding treatment and posthospital care (Ell and Northen 1990). Similar decisions may be faced by clients remaining at home who have experienced a change in their ability to function in that environment.

It is the social worker's responsibility to engage the client and the family members in considering various options to address the physical, social, and emotional needs of the client and his or her family members. In order to do so, the social worker collects information from a variety of sources about the client's physical condition and functional limitations, social situation, and emotional status. Based on this assessment, information about appropriate resources to meet the client's needs is then provided to the client and the family as well as to other professionals. The options can include a return to the prior arrangement, increased assistance from family or friends, initiation of or continuation of formal services in the home, or a variety of institutional options such as boarding home, rehabilitation hospital, terminal care facility, or nursing home. Depending on its nature, the plan can require minimal or extensive help from professional staff and community resources. For some people, the need to have the assistance of others in the home presents an uncomfortable shift in their autonomy and well-being. If the decision is to institutionalize the client, it becomes a major turning point in the individual's life, requiring extensive adaptation and readjustment.

Social workers working with hospitalized clients are constrained in their planning with clients and families by recent changes in reimbursement to a prospective payment system based on diagnosis-related groups (DRGs). The penalty aspect of this policy has resulted in increased emphasis on timely discharges, thus significantly shortening hospital stays. The current regulatory climate creates pressures on social work discharge planners to compromise the traditional social work commitment to the client's self-determination in decision making (Berkman 1984; Caputi and Heiss 1984; Bendor 1987; Nason 1990). Yet, the client's control over decision making has been shown repeatedly to affect health status, utilization of medical care, activity levels, feelings of well-being, and mortality rates (Ferrari 1963; Pohl and Fuller 1980; Ferraro 1982; Lieberman and Tobin 1983; Rodin 1986; Coulton et al. 1988), especially for elderly individuals facing relocation. Clients in hospitals and long-term care settings have experienced improved health status, better psychosocial functioning, and even reduced mortality rates as a result of simple interventions to enhance their perceptions of control (Langer, Janis, and Wolfer 1975; Langer and Rodin 1976; Schulz 1976; Mercer and Kane 1979; Hunt and Hunt 1983; Slivinske and Fitch 1987).

Social workers can insure that clients participate actively in determining appropriate outcomes through the development of practice patterns that enhance the clients' control (Abramson 1990). However, such an approach to practice can be difficult to carry out when conflicts exist between those involved in making a particular decision. The illness of a family member affects the entire family unit; yet, different members may have varying needs and different preferences regarding a specific outcome. Social workers are trained to balance the needs of the various parties in a decision. However, evidence regarding sick or elderly clients indicates that often priority is given to family concerns, thus compromising the client's interests and influence over decision making (York and Caslyn 1977; Gambel, Heilbronn, and Reamer 1980; Coulton et al. 1982; Townsend 1986; Abramson 1988). Given the vulnerable status of the sick individual and the well-documented impact of loss of control over decision making, efforts to redress any circumventing of the client's concerns are essential.

The Health Care System

Problems with the health care system will be addressed in two ways here. The most critical issues are those that directly affect clients and families as they interact with professional and nonprofessional caregivers. However, problems are also encountered if difficulties in interprofessional or team functioning develop. The latter problems may have a negative impact on the appropriateness of decisions made about the client's care and may affect communication between clients, families, and professionals as well.

Numerous problems arise for clients and their families in their contacts with health care providers. Individuals have difficulty influencing medical decision making as a result of the depleting impact of the illness itself, compounded by prescriptive and paternalistic attitudes on the part of physicians that minimize involvement of the patient (Strauss 1972; Breslau 1981; Coe 1986). Opinions of older patients are discounted even more frequently (Marshall 1981; Rosow 1981). The focus on specialization inherent in the medical model contributes to fragmentation of care. Often, various medical problems of clients and family members are addressed by a network of health care providers who rarely coordinate their interventions. Social services are usually furnished by an additional array of providers. The complexity of such a delivery system can be overwhelming and difficult to negotiate. When someone is hospitalized, many of the issues identified above are further exaggerated by the increased dependence of the patient on providers and by the loss of individuality and control that occurs when institutional and staff needs are given priority over the concerns of the patient (Strauss 1972; Tagliacozzo and Mauksch 1979; Taylor 1979).

Social workers often serve as mediators and coordinators for clients and families in dealing with the health care system. Social work intervention may involve helping clients obtain or understand information necessary to make decisions about treatment or posthospital care. On occasion, social workers will organize joint meetings between clients, family members, and relevant providers to facilitate such decision making. They may intervene in conflicts about appropriate care regimens for hospitalized clients or consult with physicians or nursing staff about the most effective strategies to deal with a particular client's response to illness and hospitalization. They may also function as advocates for clients and families with those aspects of the hospital system identified as posing obstacles to good care.

In many situations, social workers carry out their role as mediators and coordinators through participation in interdisciplinary teams. Effective team functioning is a critical ingredient in good services to clients; yet there are many obstacles to good team decision making (Kane 1975; Sands 1990). In particular, conflicts arise from the views held by team members on patient care and from treatment models and values that vary by profession due to the socialization processes unique to each (Mizrahi and Abramson 1985; Sands 1989). The successful negotiation of such disagreements depends on the acknowledgement of the patterned responses of different professionals and on the development of collaborative strategies that take these differences into account (Abramson 1989). Understanding variations in professional socialization can also help social workers in dealing with collaborative problems outside of the team.

In their capacity as team members, social workers need to utilize skills to improve team processes, such as facilitating resolution of conflict, maintaining an overview of the team process, providing support for others, and clarifying the team contract (Abramson 1989). In this way, they expedite effective service provision to clients and their families. However, social workers on teams run the risk of overidentification with team objectives, which might reduce their motivation for client advocacy within the team (Mailick and Ashley 1981; Abramson, 1984).

Inadequate Resources

Individuals with chronic illnesses may be functioning marginally in their present living arrangements; changes in medical status or further deterioration may cause a crisis and require a modification of the previous living situation. Acute onset of illness or disability may mandate a shift in roles for the individual and for family members. Clients and families may find that new resources are required to respond adequately to the changed circumstances. Social workers in many settings serve as the link between the client and family members, other professionals, and the community resources necessary to respond to the client's needs (Wolock et al. 1987). Because approaches to obtaining resources for clients will be taken up in chapter 11, the discussion in this chapter will be limited to aspects specific to problems of illness. It must be noted that social workers in health care settings have at times relegated service provision to secondary status, preferring to stress the counseling components of their role (Caroff 1988). This unfortunate dichotomy between concrete and counseling services undermines the uniqueness of a comprehensive social work contribution to the lives of sick individuals and their families (Bailis 1985; Abramson and Mizrahi 1986).

Issues for Family Members/Caregivers

All of the problems identified above have significant implications for the client's family members or significant others. Adjustments must be made to the client's illness and to the changes it brings about in the family's life, in the sick individual, and in the family's relationship to that person. Family members are central participants in decision making about treatment, caregiving at home, or the need for institutional care. Each of these decisions brings a special burden of doubt, uncertainty, and sometimes guilt or anger (Solomon 1983). When the decisions made create additional demands on family caregiving, the lives of certain family members may change drastically. The illness of one family member often mandates that other members become expert in dealing with sometimes intimidating or unresponsive professional caregivers. Obtaining information about the illness and its prognosis or the implications of various treatment options may require an unaccustomed assertiveness. Similar attributes are required to obtain needed resources from unwieldy bureaucracies.

Despite the difficulties involved, families meet most of the needs of sick members for care; 80 percent of the elderly who need assistance are provided for by family members rather than by the formal care system (Horowitz 1985; Shanas and Van Nostrand 1988). In fact, individuals at risk for institutionalization are significantly less likely to be admitted to a nursing home if there are involved family members (Barney 1977; Prohaska and McCauley 1983). However, serious costs for caregivers have been documented and "attest to the fact that illness is a family experience" (Ell and Northen 1990:41). Caregivers show evidence of increased physical, psychological, and social difficulties that can be attributed to stresses associated with caregiving (Poulshock and Deimling 1984; Horowitz 1985; Bass, Tausig, and Noelker 1989; Raveis, Siegel, and Sudit 1989). The burden on the caregiver does seem to vary with the type of the client's impairment (Poulshock and Deimling 1984), with the relationship to the client (Cantor 1983), with the phase of the illness (Mailick 1979), and with the degree of support available from the social environment (Quinn, Fontana, and Reznikoff 1985; Stone, Cafferta, and Stangl 1987; Silliman, Earp, and Wagner 1988). Conflicted caregiver-client relationships are a source of particular strain (Brody 1985; Sheehan and Nuttall 1988; Norris, Parris Stephens, and Kinney 1990).

Social work interventions can modify the caregivers' burden in relation to a number of the issues identified as causing stress. Careful assessment of the typical patterns of relating in families can provide the basis for working out the balance of responsibilities for care among different family members. Identification of historical areas for conflict can allow the social worker to discriminate between a plan for care that will avoid conflict and one that is likely to evoke it. Tailoring formal care services to the particular needs of caregivers as well to those of the client can assure a more successful outcome.

Overriding Themes

Certain themes run through most of the problem areas confronting sick clients and their social workers. First of all, illness is experienced differently depending on whether it is acute or chronic. The needs of individuals and families will vary in relation to the type and phase of the illness, and therefore social work interventions need to vary accordingly. Secondly, social workers often encounter sick individuals at critical life junctures when decisions made about treatment, services, or relocation will have far-reaching consequences both for the client and for the family members. The assumption is made here that the social worker has a major role in the decision-making process. Finally, disagreements in the process of making decisions can be expected to arise given the constraints of the current regulatory climate and the potentially conflicting interests of those involved. Therefore, interventions to resolve conflicts constitute a major responsibility of social workers in health care settings.

The Relevance of the Task-centered Approach for Social Work in Health Care Settings

Task-centered social work practice affords social workers in health care settings a logical model for intervention with sick clients and their families. Clients with health problems usually require short-term, focused assistance with particular issues related to the impact of the illness on their physical and social functioning. Their target concerns are often specific and therefore amenable to the development of related tasks to be carried out by clients, family members, and social workers. The time frame for many such activities is defined by built-in parameters, such as the length of hospital stay, or by the phase of illness. Even clients with long-term, chronic illnesses, such as those receiving kidney dialysis, can benefit from working on problems in a structured, time-limited way. When working with sick individuals, the medical problem itself provides an organizing framework for focused social work intervention.

Task-centered social work also emphasizes the client's active determination of the problems to be worked on and of the tasks necessary to resolve them. This approach can assist social workers working with those who are ill in countering the feelings of impotence and loss of control frequently engendered by the impact of the sick role on the patient. As noted above, such feelings have negative consequences for clients. Therefore, in work with sick clients, it is critical to use practice strategies that enhance their control over decision making.

Illness and the need to make decisions to cope with its impact constitute a crisis for the clients and their families. Despite the emotional pain and stress associated with illness, the crisis provides an opportunity for changes in traditional individual and family patterns of coping and problem solving (Ell and Northen 1990). Engaging clients and family members in defining and carrying out tasks for the purpose of problem solving can teach them new skills and problem-solving approaches that can potentially be applied in the future.

Finally, the empirical perspective of the task-centered model integrates well with the research orientation of many health care settings.

Where social work is accountable to other professionals, such as hospital administrators or physicians, an empirically based practice model can be used to support claims of efficiency or better outcomes as a result of social work intervention. The model has a built-in capability to evaluate practice, thus providing feedback for practice and the modification of interventions. Such information is critical in the short-term work typical in health care settings. In hospitals, where social work practice is highly visible to other professionals and where there are pressures for certain outcomes, the capacity to document the effectiveness of specific interventions is invaluable.

Assessment

Assessment has been defined as "a differential, individualized, and accurate identification and evaluation of problems, people, and situations, and of their interrelations, to serve as a sound basis for differential helping intervention" (Siporin 1975:234). The assessment of problems related to illness is a complex task due to the interaction among physical, psychological, social, and environmental factors. Additional complications arise from the often only brief time available to assess hospitalized patients. Rarely does assessment in such cases extend over more than one or two direct contacts with the clients and family members; the assessment phase may be limited to a portion of one brief session. Sharp social work assessment skills are necessary to understand the key issues for clients and families in such a telescoped time frame. In interdisciplinary health care settings, the unique role of social work in the assessment involves the integration of data from a variety of sources in order to guide clients and their families in decision making, the development of a plan, and of the tasks to carry it out.

Areas for Assessment

The goal of the assessment process is to gather base-line information about the problems and needs of the clients and their families and to identify available resources in the physical, personal, and social environment to address these problems. Use of an eco-map (Hartman 1978) that visually depicts clients in interaction with their environments can assist social workers in developing a comprehensive overview of the client's situation, as can the Developmental Assessment Wheel that integrates psychological and social information (Vigilante and Mailick 1988). When time permits, participation in using these tools can engage the client and the family members in defining the problems, and it may provide a new perspective on the issues. Assessment of someone who is ill involves information about the following: (1) the individual's physical, psychological, and social functioning; (2) his or her interpersonal network; and (3) the formal resource network.

Assessment of Individual Functioning

First of all, it is necessary to establish the impact of the illness(es) on the physical functioning of the client (Fillenbaum 1986). There is a variety of sources for obtaining knowledge of the nature of a particular disease, its typical course and prognosis, and its psychosocial impact (Merck 1984; Moos 1984; Kerson and Kerson 1985). Such knowledge is an essential foundation for the assessment and can be sought from primary and consulting physicians as well as from the literature. Other professional caretakers who assess and try to improve the client's functional status can be most helpful; these include physical, occupational and speech therapists, dietitians, and home care or hospital nurses and aides. The client as well as caregivers in the family and the community can add significantly to the picture of the client's physical capabilities, in particular those related to activities of daily living (ADL). In addition, there are reliable multidimensional assessment instruments that assess ADL and social aspects of functioning; these include the Duke OARS (Duke OARS 1978) and the Comprehensive Assessment and Referral Evaluation (CARE) scale (Gurland and Wilder 1984).

Evaluating psychosocial adjustment to illness is a key element of the assessment. Reactions to the illness need to be examined in relation to appropriateness for the particular phase of the illness and in light of cultural patterns and past responses to illness and loss (Germain 1984). Information about past styles of problem solving and coping can reveal areas of strength as well as difficulty in confronting the current situation.

There are a number of assessment frameworks that can help in conceptually organizing the information collected, but only a few of them have been directly used in clinical work. Rolland (1987, 1988a, 1988b) has developed typologies of chronic illness and has tied these to phases of the illness and to the life cycle stages of the family. One scale of psychosocial adjustment to illness (PAIS) has been extensively tested (Derogatis 1986), and in its self-report form could be used with long-term chronic problems such as dialysis, lupus, rheumatoid arthritis, or chronic obstructive pulmonary disease. There are other approaches to assessment that are disease-specific and include cancer (Christ 1983), sickle cell disease (Nishirua, Whitten, and Jenkins 1980), hemophilia (Reiss, Linhart, and Lazerson 1982), and pediatric cancer (Adams-Greenly 1986).

It is also crucial to assess the extent to which psychological factors are interacting with the physical status and with decision-making capabilities. Depression and dementia are the most common mental health problems encountered with sick individuals, especially with the elderly. Substance abuse also is a major contributor to disease processes and can complicate recovery.

Depression is associated with illness at a prevalence rate of 5 to 20 percent. Debate continues about the proportion of symptoms that are a reaction to the illness and those that indicate long-standing problems (Wool 1990). Wool (1990) discusses the difficulties in making the diagnosis of depression because many of the vegetative signs of the disease are also present in the physically ill; Wool also points out that it is important to distinguish depression from normal grief. In addition, she notes that there may be organic or pharmacological sources of depression (Wool 1990). See chapter 7 on depression for further information on assessment and intervention. Information is provided there as well about assessment instruments such as the short form of the Beck's Depression Inventory (Beck 1978), which can easily be adapted to evaluating those who are ill.

Much has been written about the need for careful assessment of dementia and about differentiating one form of dementia from another and from depression (Hoyer and Clancy 1988). Social workers can document the existence of dementia by gathering systematic data from professional or family caregivers or by having caregivers complete a checklist, such as the Memory and Behavior Problems Checklist (Zarit and Zarit 1983), that records the frequency of certain behaviors as well as the reactions of caregivers. Referral to a geriatric evaluation team or other source for medical workup of the dementia is often necessary for a more definitive assessment.

Consultation also is useful when assessing the extent of a substance abuse problem. Specialists in alcoholism and other forms of addiction have expertise in obtaining accurate information about usage and also about appropriate treatment resources. Given the importance of alcohol as a causative or interactive factor in many diseases, management of medical care or planning for psychosocial needs cannot proceed without thorough assessment of intake patterns and of the ways in which the abuse has influenced aspects of the client's life. See chapter 8 for further information about assessment of substance abuse.

Assessment of the Interpersonal Network

The illness of a family member is a shared experience for the members of that family. A family typically deals with illness using the problem-solving approaches common to its culture. The availability of family resources for problem solving and for provision of care influences the decisions about the care of the sick member. Stressful family interaction has been implicated as a factor in the etiology and course of many illnesses (Turk and Kerns 1985; Grassi and Molinari 1987; Norris, Parris Stephens, and Kinney 1990), while family support is a positive factor contributing to recovery (Funch and Marshall 1983; Ell 1984; Ell and Haywood 1984; Goodwin, Hunt, Key, and Samet 1987). Finally, the illness of a family member creates special burdens for caregivers (Bass 1990).

Family relationships influence the client's recovery and the decision making about care for the client. Identification of key individuals in the family system is the first and most critical step in the assessment process. Unfortunately, social workers often work only with those family members who are most accessible or assertive about being included in the planning. Such an approach, although expedient at times, can backfire because it does not address issues of family structure or decision-making patterns. A simple questionnaire, filled out by clients, can help social workers involve appropriate family members or others in the client's social network. The questionnaire could request names (and addresses and phone numbers, if available) of those with whom the client has had contact in the last two months; a checklist could provide information about the frequency and purpose of contact as well as about the degree of closeness and the person's importance to decision making. Such information can provide a comprehensive picture of the family system and of potential supports.

Other tools can assist family assessment, either through direct use or by providing a conceptual framework for assessment. Arbogast,

Scratton, and Krick (1978) offer a family assessment schema that collects information about phases of the family life cycle, the psychosocial interior of the family (roles, coping and communication patterns, cohesiveness, and values), and social milieu factors such as socioeconomic status and social network information. Rolland (1987, 1988a, 1988b) ties such information to phases and types of illnesses, particularly in relation to life cycle stages of the family.

The Family APGAR, a brief questionnaire, tests five areas of family support (Smilkstein 1978), while the Memory and Behavior Problems Checklist (Zarit and Zarit 1983) both assesses the extent of dementia in clients and provides data about the burden on the caregiver. Bass (1990) offers a series of eight questions that can be used to assess a family's strengths in coping with a crisis. A shortened form of the Coping Health Inventory for Parents (CHIP) reveals parental coping patterns in relation to the serious illness of a child (McCubbin and Comeau 1987).

Assessment of typical family problem-solving approaches can facilitate the social worker's efforts to engage family members in addressing current problems. Data on family communication patterns and the family's cultural style can be used in helping families communicate effectively in family meetings where critical decisions need to be made. If disagreements arise about treatment or discharge decisions, information should be gathered about past patterns of family conflict so as to distinguish between historical difficulties and specific reactions to the current situation.

Assessment of the Formal Resource Network

The central element in the assessment of the resource network is the degree of match possible between the client's needs and preference for services, the needs and preferences of family caregivers, and the availability of relevant services from the formal community service network. Therefore, a successful outcome in this area is largely dependent on the adequate assessment of the client's and the family caregivers' needs. For example, a referral for Meals on Wheels will not work, even if the community resource is available in a timely fashion, unless it takes the client's food preferences and cultural attitudes toward food into account. Such a referral will also encounter difficulties if the family caregivers see Meals on Wheels as a public announcement of their failure to meet the needs of the client.

Knowledge of available resources in a community involves more than using resource books or lists. Information about the regulatory parameters of government services can assist social workers in advocating for clients when obstacles are encountered. Visits to the community agencies most frequently used can give social workers a qualitative sense of the way services are offered, and this can facilitate an effective matching process with clients. Such contacts also create bonds with the referral source that can smooth the client's path with that agency (Abramson 1983). For further discussion of resources, see chapter 11.

Engagement

Clients in health care settings often see social workers only after referral by other health care providers. They are more likely to be semivoluntary clients rather than clients who actively seek assistance. This is particularly true for hospitalized clients who are identified by professional staff as needing discharge planning services. Strategies for engaging nonvoluntary clients are discussed in chapter 2; engaging sick clients can be different in several respects. The crisis of illness can provide a handle for work with a client who might otherwise be unlikely to seek services. On the other hand, the powerful impact of acute illness may be so preoccupying for clients and family members that necessary decision making is obstructed. In such situations, social workers may have difficulty engaging clients and families in the decision-making process. These difficulties can be compounded by social work interventions with hospitalized clients that emphasize administrative agendas for early discharges rather than the concerns of the client. For example, a client who has had a stroke is often medically ready for discharge to a rehabilitation facility within a few days of the onset of the stroke. Yet, the client may be experiencing a grief reaction in response to loss of speech or mobility and therefore may feel initially that a discussion of discharge is premature and insensitive. Social workers hoping to engage such clients need to acknowledge the client's response to the illness as primary. Additionally, care must be taken to avoid identification with administrative agendas that are not in the best interests of the client. Hospital regulations can be presented as a painful reality, albeit one that clients and families need to confront.

Task Strategies

Problems faced by sick clients and their families are far-reaching and require a variety of task strategies. However, earlier in this chapter, I presented five categories of problems that lend themselves to a discussion of task strategies. These are: (1) problems with adjustment to illness, (2) problems in decision making, (3) problems with the health care system, (4) problems with inadequate resources, and (5) problems unique to caregivers.

Adjustment to Illness

Specific tasks emerge from the crisis of illness for clients and their family members in order to cope with their changed circumstances. Some of these involve dealing with the physical impact of the illness itself and with being a patient while others relate to confronting the assault of illness on the individual's sense of self and the resulting feelings of loss and grief. Additional tasks focus on the management of role shifts, both within the family and professionally. Tasks involving behavioral and lifestyle changes are often a part of complying with treatment regimens.

Heart disease, diabetes, and kidney disease typify illnesses that require significant lifestyle changes in diet, exercise patterns, and self-monitoring skills for many clients. Such changes often affect the spouse as well; in those situations, task strategies that couples can work on together are most effective.

> For example, Jim Conroy, a forty-eight-year-old black advertising executive had a serious heart attack. His wife worked in retailing; both jobs involved long hours and meals on the run. After he was medically stable, the Conroys met with the social worker for the Coronary Care Unit and agreed to reconstruct food intake patterns for a recent week, using their engagement calendars and collaboratively recalling the meals they had eaten together. This assessment task provided information about food preferences and intake, particularly as influenced by job demands. This information then served as the basis for determining changes that needed to be made. Further tasks were developed to modify eating behavior on the job and to work out shared responsibilities for food preparation at home. A joint exercise schedule was also arranged.

Family and interpersonal relationships often shift in the process of adjusting to illness, as exemplified in the following case.

Art Rickert, a thirty-two-year-old homosexual man with AIDS, was hospitalized for pneumonia. Art had had one previous hospitalization for an infection but did well on AZT, continuing to work at his job as a computer programmer. Art's lover, Bob, was able to care for him when necessary. Art had never told his parents about his homosexuality and so was hesitant to tell them about his illness. Therefore, he did not notify them when he was first hospitalized but cut back on his already limited contacts with them. After his second hospitalization, however, he began to feel that his parents should know about his situation. He was also motivated by his wish to insure that his family not challenge his plan to leave his money and resources to Bob in the event of his death. Due to increasing preoccupation with these issues, he approached the social worker in the AIDS clinic for assistance.

After a process of assessment and problem identification, the social worker and Art agreed that Art would contact his mother and ask her to come over for lunch. This choice was made because Art felt that neither he nor his father could handle a direct confrontation about his homosexuality. In one session task, Art and the social worker rehearsed the phone conversation; in another, they rehearsed what he would tell his mother when they met. Art's external tasks included making the call and cleaning and organizing his apartment so that his mother would feel comfortable there.

In addition, he took responsibility for reaching out to several friends who he felt would be understanding. Finally, Art agreed to attend a weekly support group for gay AIDS clients that the social worker led. The group had a buddy system through which new members were contacted individually by on-going members with similar backgrounds. Art felt that speaking with someone who had told his parents about the illness would be most helpful; this was arranged by the social worker.

Tasks in Decision Making

Those who are ill are confronted with the need to make decisions that will heavily influence their futures. Typical decisions faced by sick clients include the choice of treatment options, discontinuance of treatment, instructions regarding the use of life-sustaining interventions (Do Not Resuscitate orders or DNR), and the selection of the appropriate long-term or posthospital care options. A variety of task strategies can be used in helping clients and families make these decisions.

First of all, good decisions are based on adequate information about options; yet, clients and their families often find it difficult to obtain or understand the information necessary to make informed choices about treatment, DNR orders, or posthospital care. Health care professionals may be reluctant or have inadequate time to provide the needed information; they may also lack skill in communicating technical information about different interventions, about their consequences, or their impact on quality of life. Therefore, task strategies often need to be directed to obtaining appropriate information. These tasks can be defined as the responsibility of the client, family members or, if necessary, the social worker. Initial tasks usually focus on clarification of the information needed. As an external task, the client and family members can develop and bring lists of questions to a session; review and refinement of these and the development of a joint list then can be a session task. When families appear able to work collaboratively, their external task could involve creating a joint list of questions.

Once agreement on the issues is obtained, different sources of information such as specialized support groups, advocacy organizations, and potential resources for referral can be contacted so as to obtain a variety of opinions. Clients can also be directed to relevant literature. Where sources are evaluated as potentially difficult to deal with, session tasks, including writing out questions and rehearsal, can be developed that prepare the client and family members to request the information.

Other obstacles to effective decision making arise from the complexities involved in certain decisions. Families may have historic conflicts that impede decision-making efforts. Anxiety about death or about losses due to illness or treatment can affect the client's ability to consider options; denial can have a similar impact. Fears about loss of control or of dignity also occur in relation to options proposed for treatment or posthospital care. Unstated feelings about such issues or dysfunctional beliefs can be at the root of obstructive responses to decision-making efforts. Task strategies to address these feelings and beliefs are often required to move decision-making processes forward.

When families are reenacting prior relationship conflicts, accurate assessment of the contribution of past issues to the current situation is the first step. All parties to the decision making can contribute to the assessment by carrying out assessment tasks such as preparing a genogram or making a list of the most important occurrences in the family's history. The social worker can then use the available data to ask family members to separate feelings about past conflicts from their current disagreements. Task strategies that relate to working out family communication problems also can facilitate the process of conflict resolution. Session tasks that focus on mutual clarification of points of view, feelings, and preferred options can be effective. Further information about relevant task strategies for conflict resolution can be found in chapter 6.

When underlying fears or dysfunctional beliefs hamper decision making, task strategies should focus on getting the feelings and beliefs out in the open. A client can be asked to identify or record thoughts and feelings about negative consequences anticipated from choosing a particular option for treatment or a particular postdischarge plan. When fears relate more to anticipated rejection by others such as family caregivers or an employer, tasks that involve the client and the significant others in clarifying mutual feelings and expectations can be helpful. Distorted thought processes, such as seeing problems and solutions in black-or-white terms, can seriously undermine decision making as well. Task strategies that address changes in beliefs and ways of thinking are discussed in chapter 5.

For those weighing the consequences of additional treatment in the face of a probable terminal outcome, the choice may be between a more immediate death and an undefined extension of life, complicated by invasive or debilitating medical interventions (Coulton 1990). As in the following case, the social worker often is involved with clients and families struggling to make such decisions and can help them identify tasks targeted to the removal of the obstacles to effective decision making:

> The physician of a fifty-five-year-old woman with breast cancer and metastasis to the bones, told the patient and her two daughters that the client faced a painful death within a few months without further chemotherapy treatments. Previous chemotherapy had caused the client, Sue Fascelli, to lose her hair and to have frequent nausea and vomiting; she also became weak and debilitated. The doctor indicated that the proposed chemotherapy would not cure Mrs. Fascelli but could delay her death and would reduce the pain from the cancer in her bones. Mrs. Fascelli responded that she did not want to go through that procedure again, while her daughters, weeping, implored her to consider further treatment. They then contacted the social worker to ask her to convince their mother to have the treatment.
>
> The social worker suggested that they all return to see Mrs. Fascelli to discuss the issues involved in making this decision. During this session, in subsequent phone calls from each daughter, and in one additional visit with the client, the social worker assessed the relationship between

the daughters and the mother, the attitudes of all involved toward the illness and toward death. She evaluated the extent of their information about treatment options, the consequences of treatment, and probable outcomes, particularly in relation to the client's quality of life. She also contacted the physician to increase her understanding about the consequences of each outcome and to assess his position.

The social worker then met again with the whole family to decide on what tasks each needed to do to facilitate making a decision. Despite her reluctance to accept further treatment, Mrs. Fascelli agreed in response to the strong feelings of her daughters that her task was to attend a family meeting with the doctor and the social worker, in which the likely outcomes of each approach to her care could be spelled out in relation to its impact on the quality and length of her life. She agreed to take the lead in asking questions in such a meeting although her daughters were somewhat hesitant about this. To deal with her uncertainty about being assertive with the physician, she and the daughters agreed to an external task of jointly preparing a list of questions to be covered. She and the social worker met subsequently to go over the list and to rehearse in a session task how she might respond if the doctor brushed off a question. One daughter took on the task of getting additional information from outside sources. She was responsible for contacting the American Cancer Society and a friend who worked for a local hospice organization as a nurse and for sharing the information obtained with her mother and sister. Both daughters, at the request of their mother, promised not to pressure her with emotionally volatile outbursts. However, they did agree to meet with the social worker to talk about their difficulty in facing the loss of their mother. The social worker agreed to set up the family meeting with the physician and to let him know how they wanted to proceed.

Decisions about posthospital care can also be painful and difficult to work out, especially when major changes in living arrangements are necessary. As loss of control over decision making has serious consequences for the client, it is important to design task strategies that enhance the client's control. The task strategies discussed previously that focus on obtaining information relevant for decision making can be used strategically to help clients feel in control. For example, if the physical or mental status of clients impedes autonomous efforts to obtain information, they can still have the task of deciding what information should be sought and by whom. At times, it is helpful to arrange a formal designation process such as power of attorney or a written statement of delegation of responsibility to a particular relative.

When family members obtain information about a particular nursing home or other resource, their task can involve sharing this with the client, including photos taken, brochures, daily schedules, and personal impressions. These and other tasks can be designed to provide choices to clients, even when the alternatives appear limited.

Issues of autonomy also arise when young adults become chronically ill or disabled. Decisions made at this time need to acknowledge the adjustment to the illness as well as family issues. A basic task strategy in such situations is aimed at enabling the young adult to function with maximum autonomy while allowing parents to provide assistance without becoming intrusive.

Tasks in Dealing with the Health Care System

Some tasks in dealing with the health care system are related to getting the information necessary to make decisions about treatment or discharge and have been discussed above. Others involve efforts to obtain better, more individualized, or more coordinated care.

Due to a perceived lack of expertise, clients and their family members are at a disadvantage in trying to influence physicians or other health care providers regarding treatment decisions. Yet, clients frequently have critical information about their responses to treatment regimens as well as effective ideas about the management of the illness. Therefore, task strategies need to address the development of credibility in putting across a point of view to providers. The first step in doing so is often to help clients feel that they have the right to raise questions and to be taken seriously. Clients can provide documentation of their responses to medication or of symptom frequency by keeping a log. The same approach can be used to substantiate complaints about patterns of nursing care during a hospitalization. Learning techniques of assertiveness (see chapter 5) is useful in dealing with health care providers as is the development of question lists on which priority concerns are identified.

At times, the specialized orientation of medical practice will result in clients receiving overlapping medications from a variety of different physicians for several different conditions; on occasion, these medications will counteract each other or interact poorly. When clients have questions about the coordination of medications, they can carry out tasks of collecting all prescriptions and making lists of drug names, dosages, prescribing physician, and the condition for which the medication is prescribed in order to present this list to each physician. When such a task is too complex, the client can gather medication bottles together to bring directly to the physicians for review. Other tasks can focus on helping clients or family members to provide one physician with the name of another and with written permission to contact the other physician.

Clients with chronic conditions frequently gain a great deal of knowledge about the management of their condition. Those seen in teaching hospitals who do not have a private physician are treated by a series of physicians in training who may not provide a consistent or optimum treatment regimen. The client may recognize the inadequacy of the care provided but have difficulty persuading the physician of needed changes. Task strategies in such situations need to address tactful approaches with the physician and, in some cases, active advocacy tasks for the social worker as well. For example:

> Mike Alvarez, a twenty-eight-year-old paraplegic, had recurring decubitus ulcers on the buttocks that required plastic surgery followed by extended periods of healing. When he was discharged to the community during recovery, Mike regularly required readmission due to breakdown of the skin grafts as a result of inadequate care at home. He was treated by plastic surgeons in training who had little experience with paraplegics; they often labeled him as manipulative and demanding. Mike, who was bright and articulate but not well educated, used a tape recorder to record the history of the management or mismanagement of these ulcers over the previous year. The social worker arranged for the transcription of his statement; then she and the client edited it together for presentation at a special conference on Mr. Alvarez that she had persuaded the chief plastic surgery resident to call. She also encouraged the client to request to attend the conference and supported his request in her contact with the chief resident. More appropriate approaches to the medical management of Mr. Alvarez were developed at the conference with the input of the client.

Tasks in Dealing with Inadequate Resources

For many clients, illness affects functional capacities in relation to self-care and professional activities. Needs for services arise to compensate for changes in functional status or to help clients and families deal with the impact of illness. These needs can be met by informal caregivers or by formal services obtained from for-profit or nonprofit resources, depending on available finances. Typical service needs include transportation services to jobs, retraining or medical appointments; home-based provision of housekeeping and personal care services, medical monitoring, and occupational, physical, and speech therapy; institutional long-term care, rehabilitation or terminal care services; substance abuse programs; vocational rehabilitation services; legal services; housing and financial resources; entitlements; special educational services; medical equipment resources; and counseling or mental health services. Due to the complex, often overlapping or uncoordinated service network in most communities, clients may need assistance to access resources. In some circumstances, crucial services may not exist at all. Task strategies in obtaining resources are discussed fully in the last chapter and can be applied to most situations encountered by sick clients and their families.

Tasks with Caregivers

The management of daily activities can be a significant challenge for caregivers of physically or cognitively impaired clients. Caring for those with cognitive impairments is the most stressful (Poulschock and Deimling 1984) although caregivers of alert clients sometimes confront expectations of caregiving that vary from their own. Similar issues can arise among different caregivers. Task strategies for caregivers can be developed effectively in the following areas: (1) managing caregiving activities to minimize conflict; (2) helping caregivers meet personal needs within the constraints of caregiving; (3) addressing educational deficits in relation to the client's illness and its implications for physical, cognitive, and emotional functioning; and (4) improving caregiving skills.

In developing tasks to reduce conflicts among caregivers or between them and the client, it is important to distinguish between areas of disagreement that can be modified by changes in caregiving patterns and those that represent long-standing issues. Bass (1990:21) has developed a checklist to assess differing perceptions of care needs by recipients and caregivers that can be used to identify the source(s) of the conflict; the comparison then provides a basis for renegotiation of responsibilities and the way they are carried out. She uses a similar checklist to collect information from different family members about the time spent by caregivers on different activities and compares these to the family members' preferences (Bass 1990:25). Such task strategies clarify varying expectations and open up communication, thus facilitating caregiver-client interactions.

Individuals with primary caregiving responsibilities often struggle to meet their own personal and social needs; yet, the costs of inadequate attention to caregiver needs are well established. Task strategies that assist caregivers to arrange respite care for the client or that help them modify self-expectations to allow for more personal time can be critical to the caregiver's well-being. Bass (1990:27) again provides checklists that help identifying potential support available from others in the client's informal support system. Due to difficulties in asking for help or to historic family dynamics, many caregivers feel alone with their responsibilities. Feelings of isolation can make caregiving tasks more overwhelming and can also reinforce angry feelings about the lack of help from others. Tasks can focus on engaging a wider circle of family and friends in caregiving or on identifying community resources, such as day care settings or caregiver support groups, that can provide comfort and periods of relief.

Caregivers may have difficulty managing the care of those who are ill if they do not understand the functional limitations caused by the illness. Confusion can arise about the capacity of the client for self-care activities, the importance of particular treatment regimens, or about the meaning of certain behavior. Tasks can address these gaps in knowledge in a variety of ways. Advocacy groups organized around specific illnesses can be an excellent source of information both through relevant publications and through providing supportive services. Caregivers can take responsibility for locating such organizations, obtaining relevant materials from them, and attending educational or supportive programs. Other caregivers' tasks can focus on getting needed information about the current and future capacities of the client from physicians or various therapists (see also chapter 8).

Finally, such information can be used to work out different approaches to caregiving. Caregivers can identify those areas where their expectations of those cared for seem to be at odds with what they have learned from the educational programs and materials; they can then develop and try out more appropriate intervention strategies in consultation with the social worker. Additional improvements in caregiving skills can be worked out with assistance from other professionals who have expertise in dealing with certain problems. For example, specialists in geriatric psychiatry can assist with handling certain types of behavior. Others, such as occupational or physical therapists, can help in working out more effective ways of delivering "hands-on care." Occupational therapists, in particular, can help to modify the home environment for greater ease in caregiving. Nurses can train caregivers in medical monitoring or administration of medications. Learning new skills can ease specific burdens of caregiving while simultaneously increasing the caregiver's sense of competence and confidence; this often results also in a lessening of guilt and anxiety.

Many of the above-described task strategies to help caregivers were used in the following example.

> Mrs. Hanson, an eighty-two-year-old woman with moderate dementia due to Alzheimer's disease, lived with her daughter Janice and Janice's family. The daughter had worked as a secretary prior to her mother's illness; now, her husband Bud's salary as an auto worker was their primary income although her mother's social security and Medicaid benefits were helpful. Janice and Bud had two teenage sons. Janice's brother, Owen, and his family lived in the same community, and so did Margie, a younger single sister. Another sister, Edith, who had been closest to the mother, lived in another state.
>
> Mrs. Hanson had been hospitalized six months ago for congestive heart failure; at that time, a consultation from a geriatric evaluation team had been requested by the primary physician because of concern about her rapidly deteriorating mental status and erratic behavior. The diagnosis of Alzheimer's disease had been made by team members who then assisted the client and the family to plan for her care after discharge. The family decided at that point to move the client from her own apartment to Janice's home. Mrs. Hanson had agreed although her lucidity varied widely from one time to another. All of her children and their spouses participated in varying degrees in the decision making, in consultation with the team's social worker who continued to work with Janice after her mother's discharge.
>
> Although Janice was the primary caregiver, other family members accepted various responsibilities for care as well. Owen's wife went grocery shopping weekly, and Margie did some of the family's laundry. Both Owen and Margie came once a week to see their mother and would sometimes take her out for a drive or to dinner. Edith, who lived out of town, came for a few days every few months and tried to help out; however, her presence at times seemed like an additional burden since she was another mouth to feed. Margie, although living locally, had been alienated from her mother for most of her adult life and showed little interest in providing any personal care to her mother now.
>
> The social worker initially worked with Janice on her frustrations with

her mother's behavior. Mrs. Hanson had unpredictable sleep patterns and would sometimes get up during the night and go to the kitchen where she would rearrange items on kitchen shelves. She would also take articles of clothing from her daughter's or grandsons' closets when she was left unsupervised. To better understand this behavior and other aspects of her mother's disease, Janice carried out the task of attending a six-session educational series on Alzheimer's disease at the local hospital, which was followed by the formation of a caregivers' support group for those who had attended the series. She also took responsibility for inviting her two local siblings to attend with her. Following through on this latter task required some rehearsal with the social worker regarding how she would communicate her reasons for wanting them to share this experience with her.

Once other family members had a better understanding of the difficulties of caring for someone with Alzheimer's disease, Janice felt more comfortable asking everyone to help her work out a new caregiving plan that acknowledged her needs for respite and support. The social worker then began to work with the whole family, including the out-of-town sister, on this new plan. Each member was asked to list all necessary caregiving tasks, and the time they were likely to take. Comparisons revealed varying expectations that were then reviewed. Both her sisters felt that Janice spent too much time cooking special things for their mother and for other family members. It was agreed that Janice's two sons would prepare anything they wanted that was not on the family menu for the day. Everyone, including in-laws and grandchildren but with the exception of Margie, agreed to take on at least one personal care task each week; Margie agreed to take responsibility for all contacts with service providers to compensate for her inability to deal directly with her mother. Edith agreed to come and stay with her mother two weeks a year so that Janice and Bud could go on vacation with their family or just spend time doing other things. Owen and his family agreed to provide respite one full day each week.

In summary, a variety of task strategies can be developed in working with ill clients and their families. Illness provides a focus for organizing these strategies in that it requires role readjustment and affects physical functioning. The process of adjustment to illness also involves tasks that deal with the health care system and address gaps in resources. No tasks are more difficult, however, than those connected with the decision-making process, whether the decisions relate to treatment or to postdischarge options. Finally, caregivers have a special role with sick individuals, and task strategies are needed that support them in carrying out frequently difficult and burdensome responsibilities.

CHAPTER 11

Inadequate Resources

ANNE E. FORTUNE

The lack of tangible resources, such as adequate food, housing, or health care, is a component of the problem constellation in most applications for social work service. Inadequate resources may be the primary reason for service, for example, in applications for Aid to Families with Dependent Children (AFDC), for admission to a homeless shelter, or for use of a food pantry. But often it is a complicating and sometimes unrecognized aspect of other target problems, for example, a single working mother without employee insurance to cover her children's medical expenses, or a couple whose quarrels are worsened by misinterpretation due to gradual hearing loss. Whether a target problem or obstacle, the needed resources must be secured. In many cases additional strategies are needed to ensure that the client can avoid similar situations in the future. This chapter focuses on strategies to deal with inadequate resources and the conditions that maintain them.

Problems of Inadequate Resources

Basic Resources

Four basic resources are addressed in this chapter: employment, income, health, and housing. They were selected because they are critical to an individual's well-being in a developed society with a market economy, yet their lack is widespread in the United States and poses problems for the individuals affected as well as for society as a whole. The four resources are also connected with many other resources. For example, lack of income limits access to convenient transportation, to multiple wardrobes, to quality education, and to varied and healthy recreational activities. Consequently, discussion of these basic resources easily extends to other tangible resources, and the intervention principles are applicable to less severe instances of inadequate resources.

Employment

Employment is a source of income, social identity, and individual self-esteem, and it often defines family, generational, and gender roles (Aldous and Tuttle 1988; Briar and Knighton 1988). Consequences of unemployment include isolation from social networks, change in the family power structure, and parental difficulty in providing emotional support and cognitive stimulation for children. Unemployment is also related to child abuse, children's psychiatric and behavioral disorders, and child and parental health problems (Aldous and Tuttle 1988; Jones 1990; Rayman 1988).

In the United States, families headed by women are especially susceptible to unemployment, economic disruption, and poverty even when employed (Aldous and Tuttle 1988; Gordus and Yamakawa 1988). Minorities, especially blacks, are even more at risk for unemployment and its consequences; the unemployment rate for blacks is more than twice that for whites. Nearly half of the young black males are unemployed; their inability to contribute to their family's economic stability is considered important in the high rates of single motherhood, separation and divorce, poverty, drugs, and crime in American cities (Bowman 1988; Zimmerman and Chilman 1988). The employment and prosperity prospects for women and minorities will not improve as the U.S. labor market continues to shift from high-paying low- or specialized-skill industrial employment to low-paying service jobs (often without benefits) and to technical jobs requiring higher education.

Income

Adequate income is a necessity in any society that relies on the purchase of goods and services for individual survival. For most families, the primary source of income is employment. However, employment is no guarantee of adequate income. The low minimum wage, inflation, and the sporadic nature of much low-level service employment, as well as the lack of benefits associated with it, mean that some families with employed wage earners are below poverty level. Welfare income transfers such as unemployment insurance and means-tested programs like Aid to Families with Dependent Children (AFDC), food stamps, and Social Security Disability Insurance (SSDI) are not enough to get a family out of poverty (Aldous and Tuttle 1988; Zimmerman and Chilman 1988). The long-term consequences of poverty, like those of unemployment, include poor physical and mental health and malnutrition (Kruzich 1988; Zimmerman and Chilman 1988); in the United States, poverty disproportionately affects minorities (especially black and Hispanic), female-headed households, and children (Winnick 1988).

Health Care

Health affects most aspects of daily living: poor health is associated with a decrease in one's ability to work and therefore with an increase in poverty, with depression and other mental health problems (Kruzich 1988). In the United States, chronic health problems are associated with poverty and race (Manton, Patrick, and Johnson 1989; Syme and Berkman 1981; U.S. Department of Health, 1986). For example, the life expectancy of a black newborn is about 6 years shorter than that of a white child; the infant mortality rate is about 2½ times that of whites, and blacks have a dramatically higher incidence of nearly every major disease, homicides, drug overdoses, accidents, and alcoholism (Manton, Patrick, and Johnson 1989; Myers 1989; Redd 1989). Much of the difference is due to the greater rates of poverty and lifestyle factors associated with poor health. In addition to minorities and poor, elderly and unmarried persons also suffer greater ill health than the general population.

The poor, minorities, and the elderly—those who need it the most—are also least likely to have access to or to use health care (Davis et al. 1989; Manton, Patrick, and Johnson 1989). One of the reasons is that fewer of them have private medical insurance while more rely on government insurance (Medicaid and Medicare) with limited benefits or have no insurance at all. In addition, there is a shortage of public health facilities and private physicians in areas where the poor and minorities live, and the care offered is often inferior (Davis et al. 1989; Long 1989; Staggers 1989).

Housing

Homeless persons in the United States include several groups with different precipitating factors and needs. All are predominantly white (but minorities are overrepresented), male, poorly educated, and in poor health. Two groups, the chronically mentally ill (20 to 50 percent of the homeless) and chronic alcoholics (33 percent of the homeless), are more likely to be male, nonminority, single, without homes or jobs for a longer time, in poor health, with poor diets, and in need of health care (Cohen and Burt 1990; Hagen 1987, 1989). A third group, the "situationally homeless," includes one- and two-parent families evicted from housing, female victims of domestic violence (often with children), runaway or "throwaway" youths, and persons recently released from prison. In general, homeless persons need immediate services, such as emergency housing, food, crisis counseling, and public assistance; transitional services including detoxification, health and mental health services, job training, and counseling; and long-term options including housing, employment, and independent-living skills (Hagen 1989; Hutchinson, Searight, and Stretch 1986).

In addition to the homeless, there are those living in inadequate or substandard housing, at risk for health and mental health problems due to overcrowding, unhygienic conditions, exposure to disease-spreading rodents and insects, and dangerous physical conditions, such as exposed wiring or broken boards. Such conditions disproportionately affect the poor, blacks, and children (Winnick 1988).

The Context of Inadequate Resources

Clearly, a lack in one of these primary resources—employment, income, health care, and housing—is often related to lack in another. Unemployment often means loss of health insurance; the working poor may have neither employment-related insurance nor eligibility for Medicaid; the homeless are usually poor, unemployed, and without adequate health care. Such constellations of problems require complex interventions on many fronts. For example, a woman on AFDC who wishes to work needs stable child care, reliable transportation, marketable vocational skills, ability to prevent unwanted pregnancy, and job offers (Feldman 1985). She probably also needs medical care and nutritional advice to keep herself healthy enough to work, and she will need an employment-appropriate wardrobe and safe housing. Many argue that only major changes in social policy and a restructuring of the economy at the national level will alleviate the employment, housing, and health crises (Hagen 1989; Vosler 1990; Winnick 1988). Practitioners working with families or individuals cannot wait for societal change. They must address the issues that can be changed through individual effort while remembering that the *cause* is often not within the individual and that a sustained effort at the societal level is still necessary.

Other families encounter a lack of resources as a result of unanticipated events, such as being laid off from work, divorce from or death of a wage earner, accident, or catastrophic illness. The repercussions of such crises can be profound. For example, a husband who sustained a brain injury in an accident may not be able to handle his sales job. The loss of income, the medical costs, and the physical care of the husband may prevent the family from providing financial support and physical care to elderly parents. The young adult daughter may work in a fast-food restaurant and attend community college rather than go to college full-time; later she may drop college altogether as the financial and physical strain becomes too much for her. Such potential repercussions suggest that even sudden and "simple" problems with inadequate resources need immediate, multifaceted intervention.

Problems from lack of resources are further complicated when societal and individual factors combine to maintain the problem. Simply accessing the resources may not be sufficient if the client cannot keep them or solve other problems. For example, finding a job is little help if the individual does not have the skills to keep the job; housing for a homeless family is temporary unless the family's income keeps up with the rent; emergency medical care is insufficient if follow-up care is unavailable or if the client's fears block use of it. Consequently, intervention must take into account the contextual factors that maintain the difficulty.

Assessing Inadequate Resources

Identifying a problem of inadequate resources is often straightforward: the client requests help (for example, finding employment), or the lack of a resource is an obstacle to the resolution of another problem (for example, lack of asthma medication makes it difficult for a child to attend school regularly). However, at times identification of the problem can be more difficult. The client may have health or mental health problems that could be due to stress from a lack of stable basic resources. For example, vitamin deficiencies result from poor diet, which is often caused by inadequate or irregular income (Kruzich 1988). Whether identified as a target problem or an obstacle, the adequacy of basic resources should be reviewed. Vosler (1990) offers a useful rapid assessment instrument, the Family Access to Basic Resources (FABR), that covers current and potential resources in such areas as income from wages, income transfers, housing and utilities, food including food stamps and food pantries, health, education, transportation, clothing, and recreation. It also assesses the stability of access over time as well as availability. Local availability is particularly useful in distinguishing what might be changed at the individual level from what requires macro-level community intervention.

A Framework for Intervention in Problems of Inadequate Resources

Once a problem of inadequate resources is identified, the question is where and how to begin intervention. At one level, the answer is simple: get the resource for the client. Following Maslow's (1970) idea of a hierarchy of needs, the assumption is that a homeless family needs shelter before child care and nutritional practices can be addressed; a mother with no money needs income or income transfer before training in employment skills; a diabetic needs reliable access to medical care before learning dietary management.

At another level, the answer to where and how to intervene is complex, especially when the factors maintaining the problem are complicated. For example, the newly diagnosed diabetic may not use medical care or follow essential regimes because of denial of the disease's impact. Consequently, the following framework is a guide for selecting task strategies that will resolve the immediate resource problem while also addressing its context. The framework takes into account the client's ability to cope with the environment and suggests interventions to increase the client's coping skills. In addition, the better the client copes with environmental factors, the greater is the client's responsibility for problem solving and task completion and the more complex are the task possibilities.

This framework builds on Hashimi's (1981) four-stage continuum of helping procedures for the development of environmental coping skills. At stage 1, for clients least able to deal with the environment, the practitioner intervenes directly and describes the intervention to the client. At stage 4, the practitioner provides information on resources, but the client plans and carries out the tasks. Interim stages involve combinations of practitioner and client responsibility for the tasks, with the practitioner modeling and teaching problem-solving skills. The intervention moves as rapidly as possible from the lower to the higher stages; the teaching of coping skills is an integral part of the strategy in each case and nearly as important as the securing of the resource itself.

Within the environmental coping continuum, intervention strategies address four areas: (1) securing and managing resources, (2) teaching problem-solving skills, (3) resolving internal obstacles to problem alleviation, and (4) establishing supportive social networks, including strategies presented earlier for intervention in the client's social system (see chapter 5). Securing and managing resources is included because a single agency rarely commands all the resources needed, and because the client's skill in accessing resources is an important component of coping with the environment. Teaching problem-solving skills is included because effective problem solving is a critical coping skill that fits well into the task-centered model. Further, a combination of problem-solving training and specific problem resolution is better than either alone in improving the client's problem-solving ability (Fortune 1984). The third area, internal obstacles, is, of course, part of any task-centered strategy; it is important here because such obstacles often sustain problems or make resolution difficult. For example, an individual's shyness may prevent standing up for entitlements, or tensions with members of the extended family may make it difficult to get their assistance. Finally, establishing supportive social networks is included because support systems can buffer stress and because inadequate resources often overburden support systems. For example, in 1986 half the homeless families entering New York City shelters had previously lived "doubled up" with other families until resources become too strained, or until both families were evicted (Kozol 1988).

The stages and the intervention strategies that are appropriate for each stage are outlined in table 11.1. In the process of specifying a target problem, the practitioner should assess the client's current capacity to cope with the environment and make a tentative decision about the

TABLE 11.1

Selecting Interventions for Problems of Inadequate Resources

Strategic Area	Stage 1: Practitioner Action	Stage 2: Joint Decision Making and Task Responsibility	Stage 3: Joint Task Planning, Client Responsibility for Tasks	Stage 4: Client Decision Making and Responsibility for Tasks
Client capacity for environmental coping	Very low—client in crisis, disorganized, few internal or external resources	Low—client has limited skills, information, and resources	Moderate—client has basic skills, needs help planning	Good—client has good skills in decision making and implementation
Client–practitioner responsibility	Practitioner	Collaborative	Collaborative planning, client does tasks	Client
Secure and manage resources	Practitioner plans and gets resources	Practitioner or client gets resources, practitioner "connects" client to resource suppliers	Practitioner offers knowledge, support and guidance; client gets resources	Practitioner is information and referral source; client gets resources
Teach problem solving skills	Practitioner describes steps while doing them Elicits client suggestions	Practitioner models steps, stresses alternatives Detailed planning, small steps	Practitioner prompts for steps Generalize p-s skills through a) use in new situations: i) home tasks, ii) rider tasks, iii) application to different problems b) plan for resolving potential problems	Plan for future Address context

TABLE 11.1 (Continued)

Selecting Interventions for Problems of Inadequate Resources

Strategic Area	Stage 1: Practitioner Action	Stage 2: Joint Decision Making and Task Responsibility	Stage 3: Joint Task Planning, Client Responsibility for Tasks	Stage 4: Client Decision Making and Responsibility for Tasks
Resolve internal obstacles	Stabilize situation by providing: a) basic necessities, b) support, c) reality testing	Limited to addressing beliefs that prevent resource use or network involvement	May spend much time on beliefs and skill deficits that maintain problem	May spend time on contextual problems
Establish supportive social network	If available, involve significant others as resource managers	a) Request help from network members b) Change structural properties through: i) change network norms, ii) emotional or instrumental support to members, iii) specialized training to change content of exchanges, iv) change interaction patterns c) Add members who provide resources by matching with 1) peer or role model, 2) self-help support groups	Same as stage 2 but client has full responsibility	Same as stage 3

stage at which to begin. The suggested interventions are those appropriate for the client's capacity. The practitioner may select interventions at that stage or at a preceding one, but would be ill-advised to expect the client to respond well to higher stage strategies. For example, a homeless man with chronic schizophrenia who is stabilized on medication has some but limited capacity to cope with the environment. He might be expected to collaborate in decision making and task implementation (stage 2) but probably cannot implement all tasks without help in the beginning (stage 3). The practitioner may initially locate temporary housing and have him complete the application (secure resources, stage 2), address his fear of living indoors (internal obstacle preventing resource use, stage 2), encourage the man he shares a park bench with to apply for housing with him (change social network norms, stage 2), and begin teaching problem-solving skills didactically (stage 1). The chosen interventions should help to improve the client's capacity as well as resolve the problem; as this happens, later interventions may be selected from higher stages. For example, as he gains problem-solving skill and confidence, the homeless man may engage in stage 3 interventions: take over all task implementation responsibilities, try out decision-making skills in applying for Supplemental Security Income (SSI), and add new members to his network by joining a Job Club whose consumers are residentially stable.

The remainder of this chapter describes the four stages, their indicators, and the strategies appropriate for each.

Stage 1: Practitioner Action

At the first stage in Hashimi's continuum, "the practitioner intervenes directly in behalf of the client, but describes the intervention to the client, discusses with the client the rationale for the intervention, and elicits suggestions for problem solving from the client" (1981:325). Tasks are conducted by the practitioner, and there are neither client tasks nor session tasks. This stage is appropriate when a client is in an emergency situation, under severe stress, has few resources, or is disorganized in thinking. This applies, for example, to many homeless persons, accident victims, and mentally ill persons.

Securing Resources: Practitioner as Case Manager

At this first stage, the major thrust is to secure the needed resources as rapidly and efficiently as possible. The practitioner consequently plans and implements most tasks, consulting the client for suggestions about possible resources or approaches. For example, the client might list friends or relatives who could provide temporary housing, but the practitioner would negotiate with them, arrange transportation, and secure emergency funding.

Success at this stage requires skill in four areas that correspond to the steps for securing resources from complex agencies. The practitioner must (1) keep up-to-date with the range of possible resources, (2) know the eligibility requirements and internal procedures of resource organizations, (3) possess interpersonal skills to motivate agency representatives to provide the desired resources, and (4) be sufficiently organized and perseverant to monitor and manage the resources.

Knowledge of Potential Resources

The more potential resources the practitioner knows, the better. Practitioners often have "comfortable" referral networks which they are using repetitively and reciprocally (Fizek and Zare 1988; Gottlieb and Olfson 1987). While these networks offer ease, access, and speed in securing the resources, they often result in inappropriate choices and inadequate service for the client. Practitioners who go beyond the familiar service network may make better matches, mobilize informal networks, and help stimulate broader-scale support to correct social problems such as homelessness (Hutchinson, Searight, and Stretch 1986).

According to Murphy (1977), community resources that should be considered include economic organizations; governmental organizations, including housing authorities and schools as well as AFDC or child protective services; educational organizations, such as the PTA; religious organizations; cultural, fraternal, and recreational organizations; civic organizations; volunteer health and welfare organizations, such as the Mental Health Association; and organizations, such as the United Way, that coordinate or plan services. The client-related services available from some of these organizations are well known, for example, income transfer and support services from governmental organizations; shelters and soup kitchens for the homeless run by religious organizations; eyeglasses from civic organizations such as Lions Clubs. Others are often overlooked, for example, local businesses as sources of temporary employment or food donations, church recreational leagues as social involvement for isolated clients, fraternal, ethnic, or cultural clubs as monetary or social support for a member of the same culture.

Knowledge of Bureaucratic Procedures

Second, the practitioner must know the resource organizations' eligibility requirements and procedures. Inappropriate requests are inefficient and will make future cooperation more difficult because of the loss of credibility. For frequently used resource organizations, the practitioner should know the regulations well enough to know where the system can be "pushed."

Knowledge of the resource organization extends to its position in the social service network. In most communities, there is a "domain consensus," or unwritten agreement, about who provides what service to whom (Austin 1981). For example, homeless persons or those who move frequently among urban kin are often ineligible for services that have residency requirements or restrictions on their catchment area (Dore and Dumois 1990), and a shelter for battered women turned away women known to be prostitutes (Greenman 1990). If an otherwise eligible client does not fit into this interorganizational schema, service may not be provided, or the practitioner must be prepared to push the system hard.

Interpersonal Skills

Third, the practitioner needs considerable interpersonal skills to engage agency representatives in serving the client. Automatic cooperation cannot be assumed even with the most legitimate request. Usually, the practitioner starts by describing the situation, focusing on alternative solutions rather than requesting a specific service (Epstein 1988). The client's problem is a challenge that rational, committed people can resolve (Abramson 1983). The other person's goodwill is assumed; as Epstein says, "confront the problem, not the person" (1988:92). If the resource organization's representative is already known, the practitioner may recall past positive experiences or try to evoke pride, compassion, a sense of justice, or other feelings that will increase cooperation (Abramson 1983). Probably most important, the practitioner should identify common concerns, making sure that service to the client is framed in the light of both agencies' interests.

If the initial contact person refuses service, the practitioner should go up the organizational hierarchy to supervisors who have more discretion. If this does not work, a more drastic measure is to come from the top down via one of the heads of the agency or a local politician (Abramson 1983). In moving around an unhelpful contact, however, the practitioner must avoid bad-mouthing or blaming the individual, lest other contacts close organizational ranks in defense of the individual. Until proven otherwise, attempts to identify mutual concerns are more effective than a combative approach.

With a core resource agency, the practitioner tries to establish a key contact to expedite future requests. Abramson (1983) recommends explicitly asking permission to call on the individual for help and solidifying relationships by helping out with problems within one's own organization, giving feedback on common cases, and meeting face-to-face.

Monitoring Services

The fourth critical linkage skill is assessing and monitoring the provision of the service. Too often, the practitioner assumes that the service is being provided when it is not, or the service is provided but at inadequate levels or with unintended consequences. In this respect, the client is an important source of information. In other cases, the resource provider can be contacted directly, a useful tactic when nourishing a relationship with a key contact.

Teaching Problem Solving: Describing the Interventions

Attempts to teach the steps to problem solving are minimal at the first stage, but not ignored. Because clients are often cognitively impaired and rapid provision of the resource is paramount, teaching efforts are limited to clear descriptions of what the practitioner is doing and to reinforcement of the client's efforts to solve the problem. The purpose of the teaching effort is to demonstrate that effective action *can* be taken and to counteract the client's sense of helplessness.

To begin involving the client, the practitioner solicits suggestions and uses them whenever possible. As the situation stabilizes, the client is encouraged to make choices about the overall strategy, again to reinforce the idea that action and choice are possible. For example, with a battered woman chased out of her home, the practitioner would arrange immediate protection, medical care, and housing and describe the choices and procedures. Once the immediate needs are taken care of and once the woman's fear and shock are calmed, perhaps after a meal and sleep, the practitioner may begin exploring the woman's view of her options, such as remaining at a shelter, moving in with relatives, or returning home.

Addressing Internal Obstacles: Stabilizing the Client

Clients in the first stage of environmental coping may be disorganized in their thinking; they may be in shock, severely depressed, or fatalistic about their situation. They may also have other health or mental health problems that make a resolution of the problem difficult. These difficulties will need to be addressed before adequate long-term coping can be expected. However, at the initial stage, the emphasis should be on stabilizing the client's situation rather than on attempting major cognitive changes. Provision of basic necessities (food, sleep, security), the opportunity to ventilate, support, and some reality-testing are normally sufficient cognitive intervention at this point.

There are two exceptions to delaying intervention with internal obstacles. The first is attitudes or misconceptions that prevent the client from resolving the immediate resource problem; for example, a belief that a lack of food is God's punishment and that therefore a free meal cannot be accepted. The second is the perception that nothing can be done; as already mentioned, the emphasis on action, provision of resources, and reinforcement of the client's ideas are all geared to moving the client away from a fatalistic attitude toward active participation in problem solving.

Social Support Networks: Involving Significant Others

The practitioner may expand the intervention system to include the client's family or others as resource managers. For example, in Boston, the families of elderly clients were trained as case managers, working first with the practitioner and then by themselves (Seltzer, Ivry, and Litchfield 1987). Such collaboration requires that the support system is reasonably invested in the client's well-being, able to make a sustained commitment, and free from stress that might disrupt the commitment (Gottlieb 1988). The support persons also need reasonable organizational and interpersonal skills to negotiate with agencies. The problem area should be limited so as to be manageable without professional education; appropriate problem specification is critical to involving others as resource managers.

The areas that the support persons need to be trained in include how to recognize needs and available resources as well as in advocacy or negotiation skills. These are the same areas needed by practitioners; the difference is that the training of the family members is specific to the problem and to the individual for whom resources are needed rather than general. For example, in the Boston project with elderly clients, the family members helped develop a service plan and thus learned the necessary assessment skills (Simmons, Ivry, and Seltzer 1985). They then received written information on local resources for the elderly, including in-home service, day care, respite care, nursing homes, financial entitlements, and legal protective services. The only general training they received was training in advocacy skills. It should be noted that the family members do not replace professional intervention. In the above-mentioned project, the practitioner also secured resources, and the primary outcome was that the elderly clients received more resources in a shorter time (Seltzer et al. 1989).

When appropriate family members are not available, the assessment of the client's situation should include a scan of available support systems. For example, in the case of a homeless family, an important area to consider is the availability of resources for housing—relatives, friends, previous residences, etc. The practitioner may use this knowledge to mobilize the support system on the client's behalf. However, because these interventions are more appropriate at the next stage, they will be described there (see "Social Support Networks: Mobilizing and Creating Support," p. 267).

Stage 2: Joint Decision Making and Task Responsibility

In the second stage of Hashimi's model, "the practitioner works with the client to reach a joint decision on how to solve the problem . . . [and on] which task will be completed by the practitioner and which will be completed by the client" (1981:325). In this stage, both decision making and task implementation are collaborative, and session tasks may be used to teach or practice task-implementation skills. The practitioner is still responsible for managing the efforts to alleviate the problem (including securing of resources), but the client is learning these skills through discussion, collaboration, and action. This stage is an appropriate beginning place for clients who have limited skills, information, and resources but are not in a crisis and do not have a serious disorder. These interventions are also appropriate for clients who started at the first stage but whose situation has stabilized and whose coping skills have improved. In keeping with the hierarchical framework, interventions from stage 1 are also still appropriate. For example, the interventions and skills needed to secure resources are the same; the difference is that the practitioner will make a more systematic effort to teach them to the client.

Teaching Problem Solving: Identifying and Modeling Skills

Task-planning at the second stage follows the usual guidelines of the task-centered model. Alternative approaches to resolving the problem are discussed, and the practitioner takes special care to elicit and credit the client's suggestions. The alternatives are evaluated considering their effects, feasibility, side effects, fit with the client's values, and the person to carry them out. Agreement to an alternative is secured, and a rationale is established. The difference from the typical task-centered approach is the emphasis on describing the problem-solving process to the client. Each activity is clearly labeled ("Now let's look at the consequences of doing that."), and the reasons for doing so explained ("It might lead to something we didn't expect, that would make the next steps more difficult."). For adolescents or others who have difficulty anticipating consequences, stressing the connections between current behavior and future events may be particularly important. Also important is examining several ideas, to reinforce that there are alternatives and choices beyond the ones that have not worked so far. The process of teaching and modeling problem solving should not be time-consuming, nor should it be pursued at the expense of efforts to resolve the problem, but it is an important step in beginning the process of generalizing problem-solving skills.

Securing Resources: Practitioner and Client Both Implement Tasks

The main focus of the effort in stage 2 is securing and managing resources. However, in stage 2, the client is more active than in stage 1, and both the client and the practitioner complete tasks. Determining who should do which task is sometimes difficult, particularly because the client's ability is poor; however, successful effort helps mobilize the client's energy.

At the beginning of service, the practitioner should do the task without hesitation if the client is unlikely to be successful. Practitioner action is especially appropriate if the task involves getting resources, where the practitioner's skill and knowledge can penetrate the system rapidly (Reid 1978; chapter 3). At the beginning, the practitioner may also undertake a task the client can do in order to establish trustworthiness (Dierking, Brown, and Fortune 1980). Later in a case, the practitioner may pick up a task when the client has failed, is engaged in too many tasks at once, or for other reasons is overburdened or despondent about the pace of change. Finally, the practitioner may start at any time to try to strengthen the client's support system, for example, by conferring with family members or neighbors in an effort to draw them in. Otherwise, if the client can do a task with or without the practitioner's help, the client should do it.

When the practitioner undertakes a task, the process should be described to the client with enough detail to increase the client's information about resources and negotiating skills. As a transition to task-completion by the client, the practitioner can model inquiries by calling resource providers during the session. The practitioner might also accompany the client in an application process to "grease the wheels" a bit and to demonstrate skills in dealing with depersonalizing bureaucracies.

When the client carries out a task, sessions may include the usual aids to task implementation, for example, rehearsal of a planned encounter, practice in reading and interpreting forms, or planning how to find someone to look after the children while the mother completes the task. Task planning may be unusually detailed; the tasks may be broken down into very small, specific steps, a schedule determined, the "players" designated, etc.

If a client's task involves steps to secure resources from another agency, the practitioner may implement "connecting" techniques (Weissman 1987). A combination of techniques is appropriate for clients with poor coping skills: (1) providing the name, address, and procedures for the referral source, (2) providing the name of a contact person, (3) writing a note for the client to take that describes the problem and the desired assistance, (4) having the client call for an appointment during the session, (5) finding a member of the support network to accompany the client. When the client successfully completes such tasks and becomes more familiar with the process of dealing with "the system," the more supportive steps can be dropped sequentially (Weissman 1987). For example, a pregnant teen might complete the next visit to a medical clinic alone and then set up appointments by herself. In preparing to apply for AFDC, she might write a statement of the situation and role-play the application interview with the practitioner.

Addressing Internal Obstacles: Changing Irrational Beliefs

In addition to providing practical assistance with completing tasks, the practitioner may work actively on beliefs that act as obstacles to a resolution of the problem. For example, many unemployed persons are despondent rather than showing the optimistic attitude associated with a successful job search (Briar and Knighton 1988). Socially isolated individuals often aggravate their isolation by self-interest or suspicion, which others perceive as demanding, manipulating, or aggressive (Pearson 1990). Those in poor health may not use medical resources because they believe that entering a hospital means death. Many strategies for altering such irrational beliefs are discussed earlier in this volume (chapter 5); other strategies for dealing with internal obstacles to building social support are dealt with later ("Engaging the members of an existing support network," p. 269). However, changing such attitudes should not become an end in itself. At this stage, the resolution of problems and securing the needed resources are paramount; changing beliefs serves primarily to help move the client to the next stage in environmental coping skills while also aiding the client in completing tasks.

Social Support Networks: Mobilizing and Creating Support

Another important strategy added at the second stage is the mobilization of the client's social network. At the first stage, intact, reasonably well-functioning networks were engaged to assist in securing and managing resources. However, in many cases, the support network is exhausted, inadequate, or has never been contacted by the client. For example, men who lose their jobs reduce their interactions with kin and friends who could be an important source of job leads and support (Aldous and Tuttle 1988). Homeless alcoholics' support networks share liquor and sleeping areas (for protection) but are very vulnerable to the loss of a member (Cohen et al. 1988). In such cases, a strategy to bolster social support networks may help resolve immediate problems as well as enhance the client's long-term coping skills.

To date, network interventions by professionals have had mixed results. For example, training partners of smokers to provide support in quitting is of little help (Cohen et al. 1988). However, in projects with poor urban elderly clients, success varied with the type of problem. Network interventions were most successful with problems of sustenance, housing, and information (Cohen and Adler 1986). They were also more successful the fewer the resources available to the individual. Thus, social network interventions appear most appropriate for clients at the lower levels of coping who have fewer resources.

Before network intervention is attempted, a reasonably systematic assessment of the client's network should be conducted. Although this may be difficult because people perceive support in various ways, several reasonably rapid assessment instruments are available. Pearson's (1990) pen-and-paper Personal Support System Inventory focuses primarily on affective support, such as companionship, acceptance, and admiration. Cohen and Sokolovsky's (1979) Network Analysis Profile, developed for Single Room Occupancy hotels (SROs), is appropriate for semiclosed systems such as public housing projects or age-specific housing. More widely applicable is Tracy and Whittaker's (1990) Social Network Map, which can be completed by a client independently or during an interview. In some instances, simply discussing with the client who might be available for what type of help may be sufficient (Gottlieb 1988). Regardless of the procedure used, the assessment should center on the problem and its context as much as on day-to-day interaction; helpers in a crisis often differ from the members of the daily network (Gottlieb 1988). Strengths of the network as well as strains on it should be explored to locate resources and also to emphasize and build on the client's strengths.

The status of the client's social network will guide the selection of an approach to working with the network. First, if a network is available, individual members may be requested to provide instrumental or affective assistance. Second, working with the network at a systems level, the structural properties of an existing but strained network may be changed to make it stronger and more responsive. Third, a limited network may be supplemented by adding members who can provide the needed resource, for example, through a buddy system or peer support groups. The strategy selected can be implemented through combinations of tasks by practitioners, clients, and network members. The task structure for work with external systems, presented in chapter 3, allows specific, well-defined activities to be developed collaboratively by the participants, assigns the responsibility for each activity, and facilitates monitoring the progress.

Engaging the Members of an Existing Support Network

If an existing network is "solid" and not overly strained, members may be asked for assistance when it is likely that they can and would provide the resource. Either the client or the practitioner may approach the individual, depending on the client's wishes. Which person to ask depends on the client's assessment of who is approachable and helpful. Some guidelines, based on typical reactions, suggest that family and close friends are the first to be approached with serious or private difficulties, while friends and neighbors are appropriate choices for routine, daily help with chores (Fisher et al. 1988). If a problem threatens self-esteem, such as financial difficulty, most people avoid their peers. There are also cultural differences in support networks. for example, blacks rely more than whites on family, friends, and church to cope with stress (Ramseur 1989; Taylor and Chatters 1989). Pregnant New York Puerto Rican teenagers are more willing to talk to their families and less willing to talk to their friends about their difficulties than black teens are (Dore and Dumois 1990).

The potential helper should have a similar world view concerning the problem, particularly if that world view differs from that of the dominant culture. For example, American blacks must negotiate two cultures; they use different cultural standards of self-evaluation and emphasize different aspects than whites do (Ramseur 1989). In one refugee resettlement project, Indonesians did better by rebuilding networks among themselves than by being linked to culturally alien agencies and other sources of help (Collins 1983).

In addition, the interpersonal style of the potential helper should be acceptable to the client; otherwise the assistance will be perceived as restrictive, dependency-inducing, or guilt-inducing. Indeed, supporters who become enmeshed, interfere with the client's problem-solving ability, or create counterproductive reactions such as a sense of incompetence or coercion should be avoided (Coyne, Wortman, and Lehman 1988). In general, the client's choice is probably the best guide for avoiding difficulties.

Before approaching a network member for assistance, however, the practitioner should examine why the client went to a professional in the first place. There is usually a reason why the client did not turn to the support network; much of the practitioner's work with support networks may address these obstacles to involvement.

The client may not involve the network because the problem is shameful, stigmatizing, or threatening to the client's self-esteem; for example, self-blame for loss of employment. To overcome the client's reluctance, the problem may be redefined as acceptable to tell the network, for example, as a job loss due to the failure of an industry (Fisher et al. 1988). However, the client should not be pressured to disclose anything so aversive to the worldview of the network that the network would ostracize the client and thus worsen the situation. For example, announcing an unwed pregnancy to fundamentalist Christian peers might well result in expulsion from the church (Denton 1990).

Another obstacle arises when the client believes that the network cannot help with the problem or that a network member is unwilling to help. If such beliefs are incorrect, they may be dealt with like other dysfunctional beliefs, through discussion, tasks to test the beliefs, watching others, simulation, etc. (see chapter 5).

The client's general attitude toward self-efficacy may pose an obstacle to network support (chapter 5). People with an internal locus of control, who are extroverted, or have positive attitudes toward seeking help benefit more from social support (Gottlieb 1988). Similarly, some clients lack the interpersonal skills to secure the cooperation of their social network (Pearson 1990). In both instances, a combination of training in interpersonal skills and cognitive restructuring may help the client engage network members and improve his or her general coping skills. Because the skill deficits are obstacles and not target problems, such efforts should not override other work. Some role-playing, coaching, and discussion as part of task implementation are appropriate.

Network members may present other obstacles. First, the client's problem may threaten network members or the system itself, for example, a diagnosis of AIDS or schizophrenia or accusations of incest. As in the case of the client's perception of a stigma associated with the problem, one recourse is to redefine the problem in less threatening terms; this has been done, for example, in public education campaigns about mental illness, AIDS, and alcoholism (Fisher et al. 1988). Second, the network may not normally offer help in a particular situation; for example, many networks offer food when a family member dies, but some do not. Again, the need can be redefined as one for which assistance is appropriate and welcome. Third, the cause of the difficulty may violate the norms of the network, for example, when food money is lost through gambling. Here, if network support is to be forthcoming, the causes need to be reinterpreted within a cultural context acceptable to the network.

In each of these instances, the practitioner may meet directly with network members to lend professional credibility and authority to the redefinitions. Sometimes, if a key member of the network can be convinced, others will follow without further involvement of the practitioner. Another strategy is to invoke the norms of social responsibility and reciprocity, for example, by highlighting the client's need and his or her previous contributions to members of the network (Fisher et al. 1988). This may be especially effective among black families, where reciprocal obligation is a strong value (Dore and Dumois 1990).

Changing Structural Properties of a Support Network

Challenging network norms is an example of an attempt to change a network's structural properties indirectly. Such structural changes are intended to improve the system's ability to sustain support—a benefit for all members. A network's resources may be low, as happens when the client is a key member or has already used the resources. In such cases, emotional or instrumental support may be extended to network members as well. For example, families of heart attack victims benefit from emotional support and counseling (Blythe 1983); an SRO resident may be given a stipend to provide food to another resident (Cohen and Sokolovsky 1979).

Another way to increase the network's resources is to change the content of exchanges through specialized training (Chapman and Pancoast 1985). For example, spouses of ill elderly clients are trained in nursing chores (Gottlieb 1988), or community "gatekeepers" receive training in crisis intervention and marital counseling (Collins and Pancoast 1976). A drawback of this approach is that network members must invest considerable time and support, which may not be feasible. This approach also risks changing the relationship between the client and the network member to an impersonal and emotionally less supportive one (Hoch and Hemmens 1987).

A fourth systems-level intervention is to alter the pattern of interactions. Ultimately, this is what any network intervention does, even one as simple as suggesting that a client request help from someone. However, the alteration of patterns in a systems intervention is deliberate. For example, one project gave consultation to women who already provided support to trailer court residents; the purpose was to legitimate them and strengthen their support-giving in the network (Collins and Pancoast 1976). Another strategy to change interactions is to drop hints to network members that another person needs something (Cohen and Sokolovsky 1979). A third strategy is to tap "second-order linkages," that is, to introduce a friend of a friend to secure assistance for the client (Cohen and Adler 1986).

Some systems-level interventions require more detailed knowledge of a particular community than can be expected from practitioners with clients from diverse communities. However, many interventions are practicable with only general knowledge of the client's culture. For example, in a child-abuse case, an American Indian mother and child were reintegrated into a large tribal clan support network (Attneave 1979). The practitioner needed knowledge of the Indian social structure, a systems orientation, and patience and skill to work through the various contacts. Two advantages of the network approach were that others besides the client (the child) benefited—the mother, other relatives, and the clan—and that the resolution was potentially durable. Such advantages suggest that network restructuring interventions are especially appropriate when problems may influence many network members.

Even when no interventions for structural change are attempted, the practitioner should be alert to avoid negative structural repercussions of other interventions. For example, providing homemaking services can lead neighbors who previously dropped by to wash up to stop doing so, costing the client their emotional support and weakening the entire network.

Adding Members to the Support Network

A third general approach to working with networks, adding new members who can provide resources, is a specialized form of changing the network's structure. A common approach is to match a client with a peer or volunteer role model who has already dealt successfully with the situation. Examples include the widow-to-widow program, matching teenage mothers with older mothers who model appropriate behavior and advocate for them (Gottlieb 1988); linking homeless families with others to share information about housing, job leads, etc. (Hutchinson, Searight, and Stretch 1986); and church volunteers paired with mentally ill clients (Peterson, Patrick, and Rissmeyer 1990; chapter 8). Ideally, the match "takes," and the client and helper become part of each other's networks, with benefits for both.

Another approach makes larger changes in the network through peer or self-help support groups. The intent here is to supplant rather than supplement and rebuild a network with new members who model and support major behavioral changes. Familiar examples include AA and other Twelve-Step programs, which replace substance-abusing friends with abstinent ones; support groups for battered women, who often lack networks outside the immediate family; clubhouse programs for psychosocial rehabilitation for chronically mentally ill clients; programs, such as Weight Watchers or Mended Hearts, to encourage new health-related behaviors; and a great variety of other self-help groups. In many groups, a "buddy" or "sponsor" provides individual attention and socio-emotional support to enhance the attraction and ease the individual's transition into the new network.

Most support group programs specialize in a specific problem or transition such as illness, death, parenting, geographical relocation, or substance abuse (see chapters 3, 8, and 9). Consequently, such groups may not be readily available. However, they should be included on the practitioner's list of referral resources, and the practitioner should be able to assess when they might benefit the client. In addition, if there are many clients with similar resource difficulties, the practitioner should consider starting a professionally led group to encourage mutual help and networking among members. Another possibility is a large-scale community organization focusing on problems of common concern. For example, a Minneapolis program makes interest-free loans to poor, single, working mothers, who are unlikely to get commercial loans (Jones and Wattenberg 1991); another Minneapolis program provides housing, counseling, and substance abuse treatment for prostitutes as well as advocacy and community education to change the public's attitudes (Greenman 1990); a Kansas City agency created a referral service to locate child care for working parents (Gerland 1990); and in St. Louis, thirteen agencies cooperated in developing a health care plan for the homeless (Hutchinson, Searight, and Stretch 1986).

Stage 3: Joint Task Planning, Client Responsibility for Task Implementation

In the third stage of Hashimi's model, "the practitioner gives the client some direction in analyzing various solutions. . . . The client assumes responsibility for task performance with support and reassurance from the practitioner" (1981:325). At this stage, the practitioner provides information, guides the client in task planning, and provides reassurance for task completion. All or most tasks are carried out by the client, even if the practitioner could do them more quickly. This stage is appropriate for clients who have basic coping skills but are unsure of their analysis of the problems or hesitant to carry out plans, for example, a widow or divorcee not in grief, someone anticipating a job layoff, or the spouse of a victim of Alzheimer's disease preparing for complex medical care. This stage of intervention is also appropriate for clients who started at a lower stage and have learned to analyze problems and whose situations are stable enough so that efficiency is not critical. Interventions may include any of those described for stages 1 or 2, but the coping skills taught will be more sophisticated ones.

Teaching Problem Solving: Generalizing Skills to New Situations

At stage 3, sessions are used to plan tasks to obtain resources (as always, this is the primary focus) and to refine and generalize problem-solving skills. If the client starts at this stage, the steps of problem solving should be labelled as they are used. Once the broad outline is familiar, the practitioner guides the problem solving by prompting or asking questions rather than by taking the lead. The practitioner may give feedback to the client's ideas, explore the repercussions of alternatives, or even suggest other possibilities, but the analysis, choice of action, and planning are clearly the client's. Compared to other stages, more time is spent on ensuring that the client understands and can apply the process of problem solving, but the goal is still the resolution of the problem.

To help generalize problem-solving skills to other problems and situations, the practitioner should encourage the client to use his or her problem-solving skills in many different situations (Stokes and Baer 1977). As a first step, the client may do the planning as a home task, simply to get used to the process in other settings. For example, a job-seeker plans his approach to a potential employer at home, following the guidelines used in previous sessions to plan other job applications. Another strategy is to use "rider" tasks that call for problem solving when the implementation of another task encounters obstacles. For example, if the client is to visit a medical clinic, a rider task might be, "if you can't get the appointment, stop and think through how else to get the checkup." A third strategy is to apply problem-solving skills to a different problem, possibly a minor difficulty that is not part of the task-centered work, for example, how to get the children new outfits for school without spending a lot of money. In all approaches to generalizing, the key is to use the skills in real life situations until they are second nature.

Toward the end of treatment, the client's problem-solving skills are further reinforced by analyzing potential future problems and what could be done if they were encountered (Fishman and Lubetkin 1980). For example, a working mother who has successfully applied for AFDC might review what to do if her benefits are terminated—how to appeal, the documents she would need, etc. If the scenario is realistic, such "fail-safe planning" also helps to maintain the gains from the treatment.

Securing Resources: The Client Implements Tasks

In terms of getting resources, the practitioner offers expert knowledge of formal resources, guidance in the planning process, and support for the client's action. Except for rare instances, the client carries out the tasks independently. The "connecting" techniques used by the practitioner are limited to referral information and perhaps the name of a contact person. The session may include some rehearsal to reassure the client that the plan is feasible or to teach complex negotiation skills, such as confronting the problem rather than the agency representative. The provision of service is monitored through word-of-mouth reports from the client rather than through direct contact with the provider.

Addressing Internal Obstacles: Irrational Beliefs and Skill Deficits

Because the client is coping better at this stage, more session time may be spent working on obstacles that may have aggravated or maintained the problem. These obstacles may include fatalistic attitudes, depression, or poor interpersonal skills, or they may be specific to the target problem. For example, people in economic difficulty may have poor financial management skills or "waste" money by using it in psychological competition with mates (Hogan and Bauer 1988). In such cases, skills training or an insight-oriented discussion would be appropriate. Unemployed individuals may be inefficient in their job search or look in markets where their skills are not needed (Briar and Knighton 1988); job-hunting counseling would be productive for them. An urban black teen might not bother with doctors because he believes that with so much death around him nobody would care about his health (Staggers 1989); in that case, some work on self-esteem and black pride might help.

Such intensive work on obstacles appears to be a diversion from the resolution of the target problem. When is it appropriate? Several conditions should be met before shifting the focus of the sessions. First, the target problem must be well on its way to resolution (i.e., the resource secured), or the obstacle must clearly block its resolution. Second, the obstacle must be clearly related to the occurrence or severity of the target problem; changing the obstacle must be important to help maintain the gains from treatment. Third, the client must agree to the "diversion" and understand its purpose—including that its aim is long-term maintenance, not just the resolution of the immediate problem.

Social Support Networks: Solidifying Support

Despite coping reasonably well, clients may be isolated, or their networks may be strained. Consequently, any of the previously described network interventions may be appropriate. At this stage, however, the client should be able to carry out tasks independently. For example, to engage former coworkers in thinking about job leads, a laid-off husband might drop by the after-church coffee meeting where many gather. To change the network structure, the same client might angle for an introduction to so-and-so's uncle, who, the grapevine says, can put in a good word at the employment office at the nearby electronics plant. Or he might add members to his network and increase his skills by joining a training-and-employment group.

Stage 4: Client Decision Making and Task Implementation

In the final stage, "the practitioner gives information on resources and provides support and reassurance as the client outlines activities and carries out tasks" (Hashimi:325). The practitioner essentially acts as an information and referral source while the client makes decisions, plans, and implements tasks. This stage is appropriate when a client has good decision-making capabilities as well as the skills to implement most plans, for example, a newly relocated family exploring community resources, parents seeking special education for a child with learning disabilities, or clients who have learned problem-solving skills earlier in treatment and are now reasonably confident about their abilities.

Securing Resources and Teaching Problem-solving Skills

Because at this stage the client already possesses good problem-solving skills, generalizing them is rarely a concern. If the only target problem is inadequate resources, the contact between the client and the practitioner may be very brief, even by telephone rather than face-to-face. Sessions may focus on contextual or maintaining factors rather than on the resources and problem-solving skills. If other target problems are the center of attention, inadequate resources may receive only enough attention to impart information and provide reassurance.

The practitioner provides information about available resources, often after the client has narrowed down broad options to one or two strategies. For example, an elderly client needing transportation rules out friends as requiring too much reciprocation; the practitioner describes the local on-call bus service for the handicapped and elderly, how to make appointments for taxicabs, and a church transportation network. The practitioner provides names and phone numbers and perhaps a contact person, but assumes that the client can make a sensible judgment and will contact the appropriate resource without further coaching. However, as always, the practitioner monitors the acquisition of the resource by querying the client during the next contact or by making follow-up calls.

Even though the client is coping well with the environment, the practitioner should review the problem-solving steps toward the end of the contact and engage the client in "fail-safe" planning about potential problems in the future. This is particularly important if access to resources has fluctuated in the past or if the resource will be hard to maintain. For example, if the elderly client has decided to rely on a peer or friend for transportation, she and the practitioner might review her options in case that person becomes ill or moves away.

Addressing Internal Obstacles

At the fourth stage, a common obstacle is the client's lack of confidence. Consequently, support and reassurance should be routine. As in the third stage, however, intervention may also move to the contextual arena of personal or interpersonal factors that maintain a problem, and the strategies and caveats already discussed also apply here. For example, an evicted family was resettled in low-income housing, and the husband secured employment. The practitioner offered assistance to help the husband learn to curb his violent temper, which had contributed to his being fired from a previous job. However, the husband declined to work on it, saying he had "learned his lesson"; thus treatment was terminated.

Social Support Networks

As at stage 3, network intervention may be appropriate if the client is dissatisfied with his or her social support or if problems in the network make a recurrence of the problem likely. Because clients at stage 4 usually have the skills to enjoy and benefit from interpersonal interaction, adding new members through peer support or self-help groups is an appropriate network intervention. It is especially appropriate for persons in transition because new roles mean new social ties and role models. For example, support groups for newly divorced people, such as Parents Without Partners, provide support in the transition as well as new friends and possible mates. Peer support groups are also appropriate for maintaining gain in cases where relapse is frequent, such as problems with substance abuse or gambling; however, they are not a panacea and are not for everyone (see chapter 9). As with other network interventions, linkage with peer support groups should be undertaken only with the full agreement of the client and without undue pressure.

Teaching Environmental Coping in a Time-Limited Contract

The framework just explicated for task-centered practice with inadequate resources includes as a central component improving the client's ability to cope with the environment. Given the complexity of many problems and of environmental coping, how does the framework fit into short-term, time-limited treatment? First, as always in task-centered practice, the target problem is the priority. Time limits are negotiated on the basis of the estimated time needed to acquire the resource and to resolve other target problems, regardless of the client's level of coping with the environment. Treatment ends as contracted. During treatment, the client and the practitioner work to improve the client's coping skills, as outlined in this chapter. However, the level of coping attained is not a criteria for ending the treatment. Treatment should not be extended solely because the client has not reached a more competent stage of functioning.

However, the practitioner may offer another contract to work on obstacles or problems identified during the initial work. For example, if poor impulse control contributed to a family's overspending and financial problems, a new contract might focus on learning to plan and adhere to budgets. If a client's passive-aggressive interactions made getting network support difficult, a new contract might address poor interpersonal skills and social isolation. Specific target problems are identified and agreed upon and time-limited contracts established in accordance with the usual task-centered procedures. The client's poor environmental coping skills may suggest target problems, but that is not an excuse for extending treatment indefinitely with nebulous goals such as "improved coping skills."

Task-centered practice has also been used as a component of a package of interventions to address problems associated with inadequate resources. For example, a New York City project used crisis intervention, task-centered treatment, and life-space interviewing effectively in a shelter for homeless families (Phillips et al. 1988). Broadening task-centered practice to include environmental coping skills, as outlined here, might well increase the efficacy even more.

In task-centered practice with inadequate resources, the priority is to get the lacking resources, while the client assumes as much responsibility as is possible and as is consistent with efficiency. However, a lack of basic resources, such as income, employment, or health care, is often part of complex, enduring problem constellations. Getting the resource does not mean the client can retain it. Consequently, this chapter has outlined a framework for task-centered intervention that takes into account the client's current level of environmental coping and moves him or her toward better coping. The framework calls for simultaneous intervention in four areas: (1) securing the resource, (2) using task-centered procedures to teach problem-solving skills, (3) expanding the treatment context to internal obstacles that accompany and maintain the problem, and (4) expanding the context to the client's social support network.

References

Abramson, J. 1988. "Participation of Elderly Patients in Discharge Planning: Is Self-Determination a Reality?" *Social Work* 33:443–448.
—— 1983. "Six Steps to Effective Referrals." In H. Weissman, I. Epstein, and A. Savage, eds., *Agency Based Social Work: Neglected Aspects of Clinical Practice*. Philadelphia: Temple University Press.
—— 1989. "Making Teams Work." *Social Work with Groups* 12:45–63.
—— 1990. "Enhancing Patient Participation: Clinical Strategies in the Discharge Planning Process." *Social Work in Health Care* 14:53–71.
Abramson, M. 1984. "Collective Responsibility in Inter-Disciplinary Collaboration: An Ethical Perspective for Social Workers." *Social Work in Health Care* 10:35–43.
Abramson, J., and T. Mizrahi. 1986. "Strategies for Enhancing Collaboration Between Social Workers and Physicians." *Social Work in Health Care* 12:1–21.
Abramson, L. Y., M. E. P. Seligman, and J. Teasdale. 1978. "Learned Helplessness in Humans: Critique and Reformulation." *Journal of Abnormal Psychology* 87:49–74.
Ackoff, R. 1979. "The Future of Operational Research Is Past." *Journal of the Operational Research Society* 30:93–104.
Adams-Greenly, M. 1986. "Psychological Staging of Pediatric Cancer Patients and Their Families." *Cancer* 58:449–453.
Akiskal, A. S., and R. C. Simmons. 1985. "Chronic and Refractory Depressions: Evaluation and Management." In E. E. Beckham and W. R. Leber, eds., *Handbook of Depression: Treatment, Assessment and Research*. Homewood, IL: Dorsey Press.
Aldous, J., and R. C. Tuttle. 1988. "Unemployment and the Family." In C. S. Chilman, F. M. Cox, and E. W. Nunnally, eds., *Employment and Economic Problems*. Newbury Park, CA: Sage Publications.

Allen-Meares, P., and B. A. Lane. 1987. "Grounding Social Work Practice in Theory: Ecosystems." *Social Casework* 68:515–521.

American Psychiatric Association. 1987. *Diagnostic and Statistical Manual of Mental Disorders.* 3d ed., revised. Washington, D.C.: The American Psychiatric Association.

Anderson, C. M. 1983. "A Psychoeducational Program for Families of Patients with Schizophrenia." In W. R. McFarlane, ed., *Family Therapy in Schizophrenia.* New York: Guilford Press.

Anderson, C. M., G. Hogarty, and D. J. Reiss. 1980. "Family Treatment of Adult Schizophrenic Patients." *Schizophrenic Bulletin,* 6:490–505.

Anderson, C. M., D. J. Reiss, and G. E. Hogarty. 1986. *Schizophrenia and the Family.* New York: Guilford Press.

Annis, H., and C. S. Davis. 1989. "Relapse Prevention." In R. K. Hester and W. R. Miller, eds., *Handbook of Alcoholism: Treatment, Approaches Effective Alternatives.* New York: Pergamon Press.

Anthony, W. A. 1984. "Psychiatric Rehabilitation." In J. A. Talbott, ed., *The Chronic Mental Patient: Five Years Later.* Orlando, FL: Grune and Stratton.

Anthony, W. A., M. R. Cohen, M. Farkas, and B. F. Cohen. 1989. "Clinical Care Update: The Chronically Mentally Ill." *Community Mental Health Journal* 24:219–228.

Anthony, W. A., M. R. Cohen, and B. F. Cohen. 1983. "Philosophy, Treatment Process, and Principles of the Psychiatric Rehabilitation Approach." *New Directions in Mental Health* 17:67–79.

Anthony, W. A., M. R. Cohen, and B. F. Cohen. 1984. "Psychiatric Rehabilitation." In J. A. Talbott, ed., *The Chronic Mental Patient: Five Years Later.* Orlando, FL: Grune and Stratton.

Aponte, H. J., and J. M. Van Deusen. 1981. "Structural Family Therapy." In A. S. Gurman and D. P. Kniskern, eds., *Handbook of Family Therapy.* New York: The Guilford Press.

Arbogast, R., J. Scratton, and J. Krick. 1978. "The Family as Patient: Preliminary Experience with a Recorded Assessment Schema." *The Journal of Family Practice* 7:1151–1157.

Arnow, B. A., C. B. Taylor, W. S. Agras, and M. J. Telch. 1985. "Enhancing Agoraphobia Treatment Outcome by Changing Couple Communication Patterns." *Behavior Therapy* 16:452–467.

Arrington, A., M. Sullaway, and A. Christensen. 1988. "Behavioral Family Assessment." In I. R. H. Falloon, ed., *Handbook of Behavioral Family Therapy.* New York: Guilford Press.

Ascher, L. M., ed. 1989. *Therapeutic Paradox.* New York: Guilford Press.

Ascher, M. L., and J. S. Efran. 1978. "Use of Paradoxical Intention in a Behavioral Program for Sleep Onset Insomnia." *Journal of Consulting and Clinical Psychology* 46:547–550.

Attneave, C. L. 1979. "Therapy in Tribal Settings and Urban Network Intervention." *Family Process* 8:192–210.

Austin, C. D. 1981. "Client Assessment in Context." *Social Work Research and Abstracts* 17:4–12.

Azar, S. T. 1986. "Cognitive Behavioral Perspectives on the Assessment and Treatment of Child Abuse." In P. C. Kendall, ed., *Advances in Cognitive-Behavioral Research and Therapy*. New York: Academic Press.

—— 1989. "Training Parents of Abused Children." In C. E. Schaefer and J. M. Briesmeister, eds., *Handbook of Parent Training*. New York: John Wiley.

Azar, S. T., and C. A. Rohrbeck. 1986. "Child Abuse and Unrealistic Expectations: Further Validation of the Parent Opinion Questionnaire." *Journal of Consulting and Clinical Psychology* 54:867–868.

Azar, S. T., and C. T. Twentyman. 1984. "An Evaluation of the Effectiveness of Behaviorally Versus Insight-Oriented Group Treatments with Maltreating Mothers." Paper presented at the annual meeting of the Association for the Advancement of Behavior Therapy, Philadelphia.

Azrin, N. H., T. Flores, and S. J. Kaplan. 1975. "Job Finding Club: A Group-Assisted Program for Obtaining Employment. *Behavior Research Therapy* 13:17–27.

Bailey-Dempsey, C. 1991. "Students at Risk of Failure: A Task-Centered Case Management Approach." Ph.D. dissertation proposal, University at Albany, State University of New York.

Bailis, S. 1985. "A Case for Generic Social Work in Health Settings." *Social Work* 30:209–214.

Bandura, A. 1982. "Self-Efficacy Mechanism in Human Agency." *American Psychologist* 37:122–147.

—— 1986. *Social Foundations of Thought and Action: A Social Cognitive Theory.* Englewood Cliffs, NJ: Prentice-Hall.

Barlow, D. H. 1988. *Anxiety and its Disorders.* New York: Guilford Press.

Barlow, D. H., G. T. O'Brien, and C. G. Last. 1984. "Couples Treatment of Agoraphobia." *Behavior Therapy* 15:41–58.

Barlow, D. H., and M. T. Waddell. 1985. "Agoraphobia." In D. H. Barlow, ed., *Clinical Handbook of Psychological Disorders*. New York: Guilford Press.

Barlow, D. H., ed. 1985. *Clinical Handbook of Psychological Disorders: A Step-By-Step Treatment Manual.* New York: Guilford Press.

Barney, J. 1977. "The Prerogative of Choice in Long-Term Care." *The Gerontologist* 17:309–314. .

Barth, R. P. 1985. "Beating the Blues: Cognitive-Behavioral Treatment for Depression in Child-Maltreating Young Mothers." *Clinical Social Work Journal* 13:317–328.

—— 1986. *Social and Cognitive Treatment of Children and Adolescents.* San Francisco: Jossey-Bass.

Barth, R. P., B. J. Blythe, S. P. Schinke, and R. F. Schilling. 1983. "Self-Control Training with Maltreating Parents." *Child Welfare* 55:313–324.

Bass. D. 1990. *Caring Families: Supports and Interventions.* Silver Spring, MD: NASW Press.

Bass, D., M. Tausig, and L. Noelker. 1989. "Elder Impairment, Social Support and Caregiver Strain: A Framework for Understanding Support's Effects." *The Journal of Applied Social Science* 13:80–117.

Bass, M. 1977. "Toward a Model of Treatment for Runaway Girls in Detention." In W. J. Reid and L. Epstein, eds., *Task-Centered Practice*. New York: Columbia University Press.

Baucom, D. H. 1982. "A Comparison of Behavioral Contracting and Problem-Solving/Communications Training in Behavioral Marital Therapy." *Behavior Therapy* 13:162–174.

Beard, J. H., R. N. Propst, and T. J. Malamud. 1982. "The Fountain House Model of Psychiatric Rehabilitation." *Psychosocial Rehabilitation Journal* 5:47–59.

Bech, P., M. Kastrup, and O. J. Rafaelsen. 1986. "Mini-Compendium of Rating Scales for States of Anxiety, Depression Mania, Schizophrenia with Corresponding DSM-III Syndromes." *Acta Psychiatr. Scand.* 73:7–37.

Beck, A. T. 1967. *Depression: Clinical, Experimental, and Theoretical Aspects*. New York: Harper & Row.

—— 1976. *Cognitive Therapy and the Emotional Disorders*. New York: International Universities Press.

—— 1978. *Depression Inventory*. Philadelphia: Center for Cognitive Therapy.

—— 1988. "Cognitive Approaches to Panic Disorder: Theory and Therapy." In S. Rachman and J. D. Maser, eds., *Panic: Psychological Perspectives*. Hillsdale, NJ: Erlbaum.

Beck, A. T., and G. Emery. 1985. *Anxiety Disorders and Phobias: A Cognitive Perspective*. New York: Basic Books.

Beck, A. T., M. Kovacs, and A. Weissman. 1979. "Assessment of Suicidal Intention: The Scale for Suicidal Ideation." *Journal of Consulting and Clinical Psychology* 47:343–352.

Beck, A. T., A. J. Rush, B. F. Shaw, and G. Emery. 1979. *Cognitive Therapy of Depression*. New York: Guilford Press.

Becker, R. E., R. G. Heimberg, and A. S. Bellack. 1987. *Social Skills Training Treatment for Depression*. New York: Pergamon Press.

Becker, W. C. 1971. *Parents Are Teachers*. Champaign, IL: Research Press.

Beckham, E. E., and W. R. Leber, eds. 1985. *Handbook of Depression: Treatment, Assessment and Research*. Homewood, IL.: Dorsey Press.

Bellack, A. S., and K. T. Mueser. 1986. "A Comprehensive Treatment Program for Schizophrenia and Chronic Mental Illness." *Community Mental Health Journal* 22:175–189.

Bellack, A. S., S. M. Turner, M. Hersen, and R. F. Luber. 1984. "An Examination of the Efficacy of Social Skills Training for Chronic Schizophrenic Patients." *Hospital Community Psychiatry* 35:1023–1028.

Benbenishty, R. 1988. "Assessment of Task-Centered Interventions with Families in Israel." *Journal of Social Service Research* 11:19–43.

Bendor, S. 1987. "The Clinical Challenge of Hospital-Based Social Work Practice." *Social Work in Health Care* 13:25–34.

Berkman, B. 1984. "Social Work and the Challenge of DRGs." *Health and Social Work* 9:2–3.

Bernheim, K. F., and A. F. Lehman. 1985. *Working with Families of the Mentally Ill.* New York: W. W. Norton.

Billings, A. 1985. "Psychosocial Stressors, Coping, and Depression." In E. E. Beckham and W. R. Leber, eds., *Handbook of Depression.* Homewood, IL: Dorsey Press.

Billings, A., and R. H. Moos. 1982. "Psychosocial Theory and Research on Depression: An Integrative Framework and Review." *Clinical Psychology Review* 2:213–237.

Birchler, G. R., and S. H. Spinks, 1981. "Behavioral-Systems Marital and Family Therapy: Integration and Clinical Application." *The American Journal of Family Therapy* 8:6–28.

Blechman, E. A., A. S. Tryon, M. H. Ruff, and M. J. McEnroe. 1989. "Family Skills Training and Childhood Depression." In C. E. Schaefer and J. M. Briesmeister, eds., *Handbook of Parent Training.* New York: John Wiley.

Blizinsky, M., and W. J. Reid. 1980. "Problem Focus and Outcome in Brief Treatment." *Social Work* 25:89–98.

Bloom, M., and J. Fischer. 1982. *Evaluating Practice: Guidelines for the Accountable Professional.* Englewood Cliffs, NJ: Prentice-Hall.

Blythe, B. J. 1983. "Social Support Networks in Health Care and Health Promotion." In J. K. Whittaker and J. Garbarino, eds., *Informal Helping in the Human Services.* New York: Aldine de Gruyter.

—— 1990. "Improving the Fit Between Single-Subject Designs and Practice." In L. Videka-Sherman and W. J. Reid, eds., *Advances in Clinical Social Work Research.* Silver Spring, MD: NASW Press.

Blythe, B. J., and T. Tripodi. 1989. *Measurement in Direct Social Work Practice.* Newbury Park, CA: Sage Publications.

Bond, G. R., and J. Dincin. 1986. "Accelerating Entry into Transitional Employment in a Psychosocial Rehabilitation Agency." *Rehabilitation Psychology* 31:143–155.

Bornstein, M., A. Bellack, and M. Hersen. 1980. "Social Skills Training for Highly Aggressive Children." *Behavior Modification* 4:173–186.

Bornstein, P. H., S. B. Hamilton, and M. T. Bornstein. 1986. "Self Monitoring Procedures." In A. R. Ciminero, K. S. Calhoun, and H. E. Adams, eds., *Handbook of Behavioral Assessment.* 2d ed. New York: Wiley.

Bowen, M. 1978. *Family Therapy in Clinical Practice.* New York: Aronson.

Bowman, P. J. 1988. "Postindustrial Displacement and Family Role Strains: Challenges to the Black Family." In P. Voydanoff and L. C. Majka, eds., *Families and Economic Distress: Coping Strategies and Social Policy.* Newbury Park, CA: Sage Publications.

Brehm, J. W. 1972. *Responses to Loss of Freedom: A Theory of Psychological Reactance.* Morristown, NJ: General Learning Press.

Brehm, S. 1976. *The Application of Social Psychology to Clinical Practice.* Washington, D.C.: Hemisphere.

Brehm, S., and J. W. Brehm. 1981. *Psychological Reactance: A Theory of Freedom and Control.* New York: Academic Press.

Brehm, S., and T. Smith. 1986. "Social Psychological Approaches to Psychotherapy and Behavior Change." In S. L. Garfield and A. E. Bergin, eds., *Handbook of Psychotherapy and Behavior Change.* New York: John Wiley.

Breslau, L. 1981. "Problems of Maintaining a Therapeutic Viewpoint." In M. Haug, ed., *Elderly Patients and Their Doctors.* New York: Springer.

Briar, K., and K. Knighton. 1988. "Helping Families with Problems of Unemployment and Underemployment." In C. S. Chilman, F. M. Cox, and E. W. Nunnally, eds., *Employment and Economic Problems.* Newbury Park, CA: Sage Publications.

Briar, S. 1990. "Empiricism in Clinical Practice: Present and Future." In L. Videka-Sherman and W. J. Reid, eds., *Advances in Clinical Social Work Research.* Silver Spring, MD: NASW Press.

Brody, E. 1985. "Parent Care as a Normative Family Stress." *The Gerontologist* 25:19–29.

Brown, L. B. 1977. "Treating Problems of Psychiatric Outpatients." In W. J. Reid and L. Epstein, eds., *Task-Centered Practice.* New York: Columbia University Press.

——— 1980. "Client Problem-Solving Learning in Task-Centered Social Treatment." Ph. D. dissertation, University of Chicago.

Brown-Standridge, M. D. 1989. "A Paradigm for Construction of Family Therapy Tasks." *Family Process* 28:471–489.

Burns, D. D., R. C. Adams, and A. Anastopoulos. 1985. "The Role of Self-Help Assignments in the Treatment of Depression." In E. E. Beckham and W. R. Leber, eds., *Handbook of Depression.* Homewood, IL: Dorsey Press.

Butcher, J. N., and M. P. Koss. 1978. "Research on Brief and Crisis-Oriented Psychotherapies." In S. L. Garfield and A. E. Bergin, eds., *Handbook of Psychotherapy and Behavior Change.* New York: John Wiley.

Butler, G., A. Cullington, G. Hibbert, I. Klimes, and M. Gelder. 1987. "Anxiety Management for Persistent Generalised Anxiety." *British Journal of Psychiatry* 151:535–542.

Cahalan, D. 1982. "Epidemiology: Alcohol Use in American Society." In E. L. Ginsberg, H. R. White, and J. D. Carpenter, eds., *Alcohol: Science and Society Revisited.* Ann Arbor, MI: University of Michigan Press.

Cahalan, D. 1970. *Problem Drinkers.* San Francisco: Jossey-Bass.

Cantor, M. 1983. "Strain Among Caregivers: A Study of Experience in the United States." *The Gerontologist* 23:597–604.

Caputi, M., and W. Heiss. 1984. "The DRG Revolution." *Health and Social Work* 9:5–12.

Caroff, P. 1988. "Clinical Social Work: Present Role and Future Challenge." *Social Work in Health Care* 13:21–33.

Caton, C. 1984. *Management of Chronic Schizophrenia.* New York: Oxford University Press.

Chaney, Edmund F. 1989. "Social Skills Training." In R. K. Hester and W. R. Miller, eds., *Handbook of Alcoholism: Treatment Approaches, Effective Alternatives.* New York: Pergamon Press.

Chapman, N. J., and D. L. Pancoast. 1985. "Working with the Informal Helping Networks of the Elderly: The Experiences of Three Programs." *Journal of Social Issues* 41:47–63.

Chasin, R., S. Roth, and M. Bograd. 1989. "Action Methods in Systemic Therapy: Dramatizing Ideal Futures and Reformed Pasts with Couples." *Family Process* 28:121–136.

Christ, G. 1983. "A Psychosocial Assessment Framework for Cancer Patients and Their Families." *Health and Social Work* 8:57–64.

Christoff, C., and C. Hudson. 1989. "Recent Advances in Alcoholism Diagnosis and Treatment Assessment Research: Implications for Practice." *Social Service Review* 63:533–552.

Christoff, K. A., and J. A. Kelly. 1985. "A Behavioral Approach to Social Skills Training with Psychiatric Patients." In L. L'Abate and M. A. Milan, eds., *Handbook of Social Skills Training and Research.* New York: John Wiley.

Clayton, P. J. 1986. "Prevalence and Course of Affective Disorders." In A. J. Rush and K. Z. Altshuler, eds., *Depression: Basic Mechanisms, Diagnosis and Treatment.* New York: Guilford Press.

Cocozelli, C., and C. G. Hudson. 1989. "Recent Advances in Alcoholism Diagnosis and Treatment Assessment Research: Implications for Practice." *Social Service Review* 63:533–552.

Coe, R. 1986. "Communication and Medical Care Outcomes: Analysis of Conversations Between Doctors and Elderly Patients." In R. Ward and S. Tobin, eds., *Health and Aging.* New York: Springer.

Cohen, B. E., and A. Adler. 1986. "Assessing the Role of Social Network Interventions with an Inner-City Population." *American Journal of Orthopsychiatry* 56:278–288.

Cohen, B. E., and M. R. Burt. 1990. "The Homeless: Chemical Dependency and Mental Health Problems." *Social Work Research and Abstracts* 26:8–17.

Cohen, B. E., and J. Sokolovsky. 1979. "Clinical Use of Network Analysis for Psychiatric and Aged Populations." *Community Mental Health Journal* 15:203–213.

Cohen, B. E., J. Teresi, D. Holmes, and E. Roth. 1988. "Survival Strategies of Older Homeless Men." *Gerontologist* 28:58–65.

Cohen, S., E. Lichtenstein, R. Mermelstein, K. Kingsolver, J. S. Baer, and T. W. Kamarck. 1988. In B. H. Gottlieb, ed., *Marshaling Social Support: Formats, Processes and Effects.* Newbury Park, CA: Sage Publications.

Collins, A. H. 1983. "Rebuilding Refugee Networks." In D. L. Pancoast, P. Parker, and C. Froland, eds., *Rediscovering Self-Help: Its Role in Social Care.* Beverly Hills: Sage Publications.

Collins, A. H., and D. L. Pancoast. 1976. *Natural Helping Networks: A Strategy for Prevention.* Washington, D.C.: National Association of Social Workers.

Cook, T. D., and D. T. Campbell. 1979. *Quasi-Experimentation: Design and Analysis Issues for Field Settings.* Chicago: Rand McNally.

Corcoran, K, ed. 1990. *Structuring Change: Effective Practice for Common Client Problems.* Chicago: Lyceum Press.

Corcoran, K., and J. Fischer. 1987. *Measures for Clinical Practice: A Source Book.* New York: Free Press.

Cormican, E. J. 1977. "Task-Centered Model for Work with the Aged." *Social Casework* 58:490–494.

Costello, R. M. 1975. "Alcoholism Treatment and Evaluation: In Search of Methods II. Collation of Two-Year Follow-up Studies." *International Journal of the Addictions* 10:857–867.

Coulton, C. 1990. "Research in Patient and Family Decision Making Regarding Life-Sustaining and Long-Term Care." *Social Work in Health Care* 15:63–78.

Coulton, C., R. Dunkle, J. Chow, M. Haug, and D. Vielhaber. 1988. "Dimensions of Post-Hospital Care Decision Making: A Factor Analytic Study." *The Gerontologist* 28:218–223.

Coulton, C., R. Dunkle, R. Goode, and J. MacIntosh. 1982. "Discharge Planning and Decision Making." *Health and Social Work* 7:253–261.

Coursey, R. D. 1989. "Psychotherapy with Persons Suffering from Schizophrenia: The Need for a New Agenda." *Schizophrenia Bulletin* 15:349–353.

Coyne, J. C. 1976. "Depression and the Response of Others." *Journal of Abnormal Psychology* 89:186–193.

—— 1986. "Strategic Marital Therapy for Depression." In N. S. Jacobson and A. S. Gurman, eds., *Clinical Handbook of Marital Therapy.* New York: Guilford Press.

Coyne, J. C., C. B. Wortman, and D. R. Lehman, 1988. "The Other Side of Support: Emotional Overinvolvement and Miscarried Helping." In B. H. Gottlieb, ed., *Marshaling Social Support: Formats, Processes and Effects.* Newbury Park, CA: Sage Publications.

Crane, D. R. 1985. "Single-Case Experimental Designs in Family Therapy Research: Limitations and Considerations." *Family Process* 24:69–77.

Criddle, W. D. 1986. "Rational Emotive Psychotherapy in the Treatment of Alcoholism." In N. J. Estes and M. E. Heineman, eds., *Alcoholism Development, Consequences and Interventions,* 3d ed. St. Louis: C. U. Mosby.

Dangel, R. F., and R. A. Polster, eds. 1984. *Parent Training: Foundations of Research and Practice.* New York: Guilford Press.

Davis, I. P., and W. J. Reid. 1988. "Event Analysis in Clinical Practice and Process Research." *Social Casework* 69:298–306.

Davis, K., M. Lillie-Blanton, B. Lyons, F. Mullan, N. Powe, and D. Rowland, 1989. "Health Care for Black Americans." In D. P. Willis, ed., *Health Policies and Black Americans*. New Brunswick, NJ: Transaction Publishers.

Dell, P. F. 1981. "Some Irreverent Thoughts of Paradox." *Family Process* 20:37–51.

Denton, R. T. 1990. "The Religiously Fundamentalist Family: Training for Assessment and Treatment." *Journal of Social Work Education* 26:6–14.

Derogatis, L. 1986. "The Psychosocial Adjustment to Illness Scale (PAIS)." *Journal of Psychosomatic Research* 35:77–91.

Derogatis, L. R., and T. N. Wise. 1989. *Anxiety and Depressive Disorders in the Mental Patient*. Washington, D.C.: American Psychiatric Press.

Deschner, J. P., and J. S. McNeil. 1986. "Results of Anger Control Training for Battering Couples." *Journal of Family Violence* 1:111–120.

deShazer, S. 1982. *Patterns of Brief Family Therapy*. New York: Guilford Press.

DiNardo, P. A., D. H. Barlow, J. Cemy, B. B. Vermilyea, J. A. Vermilyea, W. Himadi, and M. Waddell. 1985. *Anxiety Disorders Interview Schedule-Revised (ADIS-R)*. Albany, N.Y.: Phobia and Anxiety Disorder Clinic, State University of New York at Albany.

Dierking, B., M. Brown, and A. E. Fortune. 1980. "Task-Centered Treatment in a Residential Facility for the Elderly: A Clinical Trial." *Journal of Gerontological Social Work* 2:225–240.

Dobson, K. S., ed. 1988. *Handbook of Cognitive-Behavioral Therapies*. New York: Guilford Press.

Doel, M., and P. Marsh. in press. *Task-Centered Social Work*. U. K.: Wildwood House.

Doerfler, L. A., and C. S. Richards. 1981. Self-Initiated Attempts to Cope with Depression: *Cognitive Therapy and Research*. 5:367–371.

Doherty, W. J. 1981a. "Cognitive Processes in Intimate Conflict, I: Extending Attribution Theory." *American Journal of Family Therapy* 9:3–12.

_____ 1981b. "Cognitive Processes in Intimate Conflict, II: Efficacy and Learned Helplessness. *American Journal of Family Therapy* 9:35–44.

Dore, M. M., and A. O. Dumois 1990. "Cultural Differences in the Meaning of Adolescent Pregnancy." *Families in Society* 71:93–101.

Drew, B. M., J. H. Evans, D. E. Bostow, G. Geiger, and P. W. Drash. 1982. "Increasing Assignment Completion and Accuracy Using a Daily Report Card Procedure." *Psychology in the Schools* 19:540–547.

Duke Older Americans Resource Schedule (OARS). 1978. *Multi-Dimensional Functional Assessment: The OARS Methodology*. 2d ed. Durham, NC: Center for the Study of Aging and Human Development, Duke University.

Dulfano, C. 1985. "Family Therapy of Alcoholism." In S. Zimberg, J. Wallace, and S. Blume, eds., *Practical Approaches to Alcoholism Psychotherapy*, 2d ed. New York: Plenum Press.

Elkin, I. T., Shea, J. T. Watkins, S. D. Imber, S. M. Sotsky, J. F. Collins, D. R.

Glass, P. A. Pilkonis, W. R. Leber, J. P. Docherty, S. J. Fiester, and M. B. Parloff. 1989. "National Institute of Mental Health Treatment of Depression Collaborative Research Program." *Archives of General Psychiatry* 46:971–983.

Ell, K. 1984. "Social Networks, Social Support, and Health Status: A Review." *Social Service Review* 58:133–149.

Ell, K., and L. Haywood. 1984. "Social Support and Recovery From Myocardial Infarction: A Panel Study." *Journal of Social Service Research* 4:1–9.

Ell, K., and H. Northen. 1990. *Families and Health Care: Psycho-Social Practice.* New York: Aldine de Gruyter.

Epstein, L. 1977. "A Project in School Social Work." In W. J. Reid and L. Epstein, eds., *Task-Centered Practice.* New York: Columbia University Press.

—— 1980. *Helping People: The Task-Centered Approach.* St. Louis: C. U. Mosby.

—— 1983. "Short-Term Treatment in Health Settings: Issues, Concepts, Dilemmas." *Social Work in Health Care* 8:77–105.

—— 1988. *Helping People: The Task Centered Approach,* 2d ed. Columbus. OH: Merrill.

Epstein, L., and D. S. Bishop. 1981. "Problem-Centered Systems Therapy of the Family." In A. S. Gurman and D. P. Kniskern, eds., *Handbook of Family Therapy.* New York: Brunner/Mazel.

Epstein, N., L. M. Baldwin, and D. S. Bishop. 1983. "The McMaster Family Assessment Device." *Journal of Marital and Family Therapy* 9:171–180.

Ericson, P. M., and E. L. Rogers. 1973. "New Procedures for Analyzing Relational Communication." *Family Process* 12:245–267.

Estes, N. J., and M. E. Heineman, eds. 1986. *Alcoholism Development, Consequences, and Interventions,* 3d ed. St. Louis: C. U. Mosby.

Ewalt, P. L. 1977. "A Psychoanalytically Oriented Child Guidance Setting. "In W. J. Reid and L. Epstein, eds., *Task-Centered Practice.* New York: Columbia University Press.

Falloon, I. R. H., ed., 1988. *Handbook of Behavioral Family Therapy.* New York: Guilford Press.

Falloon, I. R. H., et al. 1982. "Family Management in the Prevention of Exacerbation of Schizophrenia: A Controlled Study." *New England Journal of Medicine* 306:1437–1440.

Feldman R. 1985. "Employment, Training and Support Services for Female-Headed Families." In H. McAdoo and T. Parham, eds., *Services to Young Families: Program Review and Policy Recommendations.* Washington, D.C.: American Public Welfare Association.

Feldman, L. B., and W. H. Pinsof. 1982. "Problem Maintenance in Family Systems: An Integrative Model." *Journal of Marital and Family Therapy* 7:295–308.

Ferrari, N. 1963. "Freedom of Choice." *Social Work* 8:104–106.

Ferraro, K. 1982. "The Health Consequences of Relocation Among the Aged in the Community." *Journal of Gerontology* 38:90–96.

Fillenbaum, G. 1986. "Multidimensional Functional Assessment." In G. Maddox, ed., *Encyclopedia of Aging*. New York: Springer.

Fisch, R., J. H. Weakland, and L. Segal. 1982. *The Tactics of Change: Doing Therapy Briefly*. San Francisco: Jossey-Bass.

Fischer, J. 1976. *The Effectiveness of Social Casework*. Springfield, IL: Charles Thomas.

———— 1978. *Effective Casework Practice: An Eclectic Approach*. New York: McGraw Hill.

Fisher, J. D., B. A. Goff, A. Nadler, and J. M. Chinsky. 1988. "Social Psychological Influences on Help-Seeking and Support from Peers." In B. H. Gottlieb, ed., *Marshaling Social Support: Formats, Processes and Effects*. Newbury Park, CA: Sage Publications.

Fisher, L., A. Anderson, and J. E. Jones. 1981. "Types of Paradoxical Intervention and Indications/Contraindications for Use in Clinical Practice." *Family Process* 20:25–36.

Fishman, S. T., and B. S. Lubetkin. 1980. "Maintenance and Generalization of Individual Behavior Therapy Programs: Clinical Observations." In P. Karoly and J. J. Steffen, eds., *Improving the Long-Term Effects of Psychotherapy: Models of Durable Outcome*. New York: Gardner Press.

Fizek, L. S., and N. Zare, 1988. "Factors Affecting Referrals from Employee Assistance Programs to Community Agencies." *Employee Assistance Quarterly* 4:31–43.

Fogarty, T. 1976. "Marital Crisis." In P. Guerin, ed., *Family Therapy: Theory and Practice*. New York: Gardner Press.

Follette, W. C., and N. S. Jacobson. 1988. *Handbook of Behavioral Family Therapy*. New York: Guilford Press.

———— 1988. "Behavioral Marital Therapy in the Treatment of Depressive Disorders." In I. R. H. Falloon ed., *Handbook of Behavioral Family Therapy*. New York: Guilford Press.

Fortune, A. E. 1981. "Communication Processes in Social Work Practice." *Social Service Review* 55:93–128.

———— 1984. "Problem-Solving Ability of Social Work Students." *Journal of Education for Social Work* 20:25–33.

———— 1985. "Treatment Groups." In A. E. Fortune, ed., *Task-Centered Practice with Families and Groups*. New York: Springer.

Foster, S. L., R. J. Prinz, and K. D. O'Leary. 1983. "Impact of Problem-Solving Communication Training and Generalization Procedures on Family Conflict." *Child and Family Behavior Therapy* 5:1–23.

Frances, A., B. Hoffman, T. Pass, and S. Andrew. 1987. "A Schizophrenic Woman in a High Expressed Emotion Family." *Hospital and Community Psychiatry* 38:707–717.

Frank, J. 1974. *Persuasion and Healing*. Rev. ed. New York: Schocken Books.

Freeman, A., and K. M. Simon. 1989. "Cognitive Therapy of Anxiety." In A.

Freeman, K. M. Simon, and L. E. Beutler, eds., *Comprehensive Handbook of Cognitive Therapy*. New York: Plenum Press.

Freeman A., K. M. Simon, and L. E. Beutler, eds. 1989. *Comprehensive Handbook of Cognitive Therapy*. New York: Plenum Press.

Friedman, S. 1987. "Technical Considerations in the Behavioral-Marital Treatment of Agoraphobia." *The American Journal of Family Therapy* 15:111–122.

Fuller, R. K., K. K. Lee, and E. Gordis. 1988. "Validity of Self-report in Alcoholism Research: Results of a Veterans Administration Cooperative Study." *Alcoholism* 12:201–205.

Funch, D., and J. Marshall. 1983. "The Role of Stress, Social Support, and Age in Survival From Breast Cancer." *Journal of Psychosomatic Research* 27:77–83.

Gambel, J., M. Heilbronn, and F. Reamer. 1980. "Hospital Social Workers Become Decision Makers in Nursing Home Placement." *Journal of the American Health Care Association* 6:19–23.

Gambrill, E. 1983. *Casework: A Competency-Based Approach*. Englewood Cliffs, NJ: Prentice-Hall.

Gant, B. L., J. D. Barnard, F. E. Kuehn, H. H. Jones, and E. R. Christophersen. 1981. "A Behaviorally Based Approach for Improving Intrafamilial Communication Patterns." *Journal of Clinical Child Psychology* 10:102–106.

Garvin, C. D. 1974. "Task-Centered Group Work." *Social Service Review* 48:494–507.

Garvin, C. D., W. J. Reid, and L. Epstein. 1976. "Task-Centered Group Work." In H. Northen and R. W. Roberts, eds., *Theoretical Approaches to Social Work with Small Groups*. New York: Columbia University Press.

Garvin, C. D., and B. A. Seabury. 1984. *Interpersonal Practice in Social Work—Processes and Procedures*. Englewood Cliffs, NJ: Prentice-Hall.

Gelles, R. J., and C. P. Cornell. 1985. *Intimate Violence in Families*. Beverly Hills, CA: Sage Publications.

Gelso, C. J., and D. H. Johnson. 1983. *Explorations in Time-Limited Counseling and Psychotherapy*. New York: Teachers College Press.

Gerland, O. W. 1990. "Meeting the Needs of Working Families." *Families in Society* 71:372–374.

Germain, C. 1983. "Technological Advances." In A. Rosenblatt and D. Waldfogel, eds., *Handbook of Clinical Social Work*. San Francisco: Jossey-Bass.

—— 1984. *Social Work Practice in Health Care*. New York: Free Press. .

Germain, C., and A. Gitterman. 1979. "The Life Model of Social Work Practice." In F. J. Turner, ed., *Social Work Treatment—Interlocking Theoretical Approaches*, 2d ed., 361–384. New York: Free Press.

Gibbons, J. S., J. Butler, P. Urwin, and J. L. Gibbons. 1978. "Evaluation of a Social Work Service for Self-Poisoning Parents." *British Journal of Psychiatry* 133:111–118.

Gilbert, J. P., R. J. Light, and F. Mosteller. 1975. "Assessing Social Innovations:

An Empirical Base for Policy." In C. J. Benjnett and A. A. Lumsdaine, eds., *Evaluation and Experiment*. New York: Academic Press.

Gingerich, W. J. 1984. "Generalizing Single-Case Evaluation from Classroom to Practice." *Journal of Education for Social Work* 20:74–82.

——— 1990. "Rethinking Single-Case Evaluation." In L. Videka-Sherman and W. J. Reid, eds., *Advances in Clinical Social Work Research*. Silver Spring, MD: NASW Press.

Ginsberg, E. H. 1990. *Effective Interventions: Applying Learning Theory to School Social Work*. New York: Greenwood Press.

Gold, N. 1990. "Motivation: The Crucial but Unexplored Component of Social Work Practice." *Social Work* 35:49–56.

Goldberg, E. M., J. Gibbons, and I. Sinclair. 1984. *Problems, Tasks, and Outcomes*. Winchester, MA: Allen and Unwin.

Goldberg, E. M., and J. Robinson. 1977. "An Area Office of an English Social Service Department." In W. J. Reid and L. Epstein, eds., *Task-Centered Practice*. New York: Columbia University Press.

Goldberg, E. M., and J. S. Stanley. 1978. "A Task-Centered Approach to Probation." In J. King, ed., *Pressures and Changes in the Probation Service*. Cambridge, MA: Institute of Criminology.

Goldman, A. I. 1970. *A Theory of Human Action*. Englewood Cliffs, NJ: Prentice-Hall.

Goldman, H. H. 1984. "Epidemiology." In J. A. Talbott, ed., *The Chronic Mental Patient: Five Years Later*. Orlando, FL: Grune and Stratton.

Goldstein, M. J., and A. M. Strachan. 1987. "The Family and Schizophrenia." In T. Jacob, ed., *Family Interaction and Psychopathology*. New York: Plenum Press.

Goodwin, J., W. Hunt, C. Key, and J. Samet. 1987. "The Effect of Marital Status on Stage, Treatment, and Survival of Cancer Patients." *Journal of the American Medical Society* 258:3125–3130.

Goodyear, B. 1989. "Unsolved Questions About Alcoholism: The Debate (War?) Goes On—Is a Resolution Possible?" *Alcoholism Treatment Quarterly* 6:1–27.

Gordon, S. B., and N. Davidson. 1981. "Behavioral Parent Training." In A. F. Gurman and D. P. Kniskem, eds., *Handbook of Family Therapy*. New York: Brunner-Mazel.

Gordus, J. P., and K. Yamakawa. 1988. "Incomparable Losses: Economic and Labor Market Outcomes for Unemployed Female Versus Male Autoworkers." In P. Voydanoff and L. C. Majka, eds., *Families and Economic Distress: Coping Strategies and Social Policy*. Newbury Park, CA: Sage Publications.

Gottlieb, B. H. 1988. "Marshaling Social Support: The State of the Art in Research and Practice." In B. H. Gottlieb, ed., *Marshaling Social Support: Formats, Processes and Effects*. Newbury Park, CA: Sage Publications.

Gottlieb, J. F., and M. Olfson. 1987. "Current Referral Practices of Mental Health Care Providers." *Hospital and Community Psychiatry* 38:1171–1181.

Gottman, J., et al. 1976. *A Couple's Guide to Communication*. Champaign, IL: Research Press.

Grassi, L., and S. Molinari. 1987. "Family Affective Climate During the Childhood of Adult Cancer Patients." *Journal of Psychosocial Oncology* 4:53–62.

Greenman, M. 1990. "Survivors of Prostitution Find PRIDE." *Families in Society* 71:110–113.

Grinnell, R. M., Jr., N. S. Kyte, and G. J. Bostwick, Jr. 1981. "Environmental Modification." In A. N. Maluccio, ed., *Promoting Competence in Clients: A New/Old Approach to Social Work Practice*. New York: Free Press.

Guerney, B. 1982. "Relationship Enhancement." In E. K. Marshall and P. D. Kurtz, eds., *Interpersonal Helping Skills*. San Francisco: Jossey-Bass.

Gurland, B., and D. Wilder. 1984. "The CARE Interview Revisited: Development of an Efficient, Systematic, Clinical Assessment." *Journal of Gerontology* 39:129–137.

Haas, G., J. F. Clarkin, and I. D. Glick. 1985. "Marital and Family Treatment of Depression." In E. E. Beckham and W. R. Leber, eds., *Handbook of Depression*. Homewood, IL: Dorsey Press.

Hafner, R. J. 1988. "Anxiety Disorders." In I. R. H. Falloon, ed., *Handbook of Behavioral Family Therapy*. New York: Guilford Press.

Hagen, J. L. 1987. "The Heterogeneity of Homelessness." *Social Casework* 67:451–457.

—— 1989. "Homelessness in New York State." *Emerging Issues*. Albany, N. Y.: State University of New York at Albany Press.

Hahlweg, K., D. H. Baucom, and H. Markman. 1988. "Recent Advances in Therapy and Prevention." In I. R. H. Falloon, ed., *Handbook of Behavioral Family Therapy*. New York: Guilford Press.

Hamilton, G. 1951. *Theory and Practice of Social Case Work*. New York: Columbia University Press.

Hari, V. 1977. "Instituting Short-Term Casework in a 'Long-Term' Agency." In W. J. Reid and L. Epstein, eds., *Task-Centered Practice*. New York: Columbia University Press.

Harris, M., and H. C. Bergman. 1987. "Differential Treatment Planning of Young Adult Chronic Patients." *Hospital and Community Psychiatry* 38:638–645.

Hartman, A. 1978. "Diagrammatic Assessment of Family Relationships." *Social Casework* 59:3–18.

Harwood, H. J., D. M. Napcitano, P. L. Kristiansen, and J. L. Collins. 1980. "Economic Costs to Society of Alcohol and Drug Abuse and Mental Illness." Research Triangle Institute. Report submitted to the Alcohol, Drug Abuse and Mental Health Administration, Rockville, MD.

Hasenfeld, Y. 1985. "Citizens' Encounters with Welfare State Bureaucracies." *Social Service Review* 59:622–635.

—— 1987. "Power in Social Work Practice." *Social Service Review* 61:469–483.

Hashimi, J. K. 1981. "Environmental Modification: Teaching Social Coping Skills." *Social Work* 26:323–326.

Heather, N. 1989. "Brief Intervention Strategies." In R. K. Hester and W. R. Miller, eds., *Handbook of Alcoholism: Treatment Approaches: Effective Alternatives*. New York: Pergamon Press.

Heather, N., and I. Robertson. 1983. *Controlled Drinking*. Rev. ed. London: Methuen.

Helzer, J. E., L. N. Robins, J. R. Taylor, K. Carey, R. H. Miller, T. Combs-Orme, and A. Farmer. 1985. "The Extent of Long-Term Moderate Drinking Among Alcoholics Discharged from Medical and Psychiatric Treatment Facilities." *New England Journal of Medicine* 312:1678–1682.

Hepworth, D. H. 1979. "Early Removal of Resistance in Task-Centered Casework." *Social Work* 24:317–322.

Hepworth, D. H., and J. Larsen. 1986. *Direct Social Work Practice: Theory and Skills*. 2d. ed. Homewood, IL: Dorsey Press.

Hester, R. K., and W. R. Miller, eds. 1989. *Handbook of Alcoholism: Treatment Approaches, Effective Alternatives*. New York: Pergamon Press.

—— 1989. "Self-Control Training." In R. K. Hester and W. R. Miller, eds., *Handbook of Alcoholism: Treatment Approaches, Effective Alternatives*. New York: Pergamon Press.

Hoberman, H. M., and P. M. Lewinsohn. 1985. "The Behavioral Treatment of Depression." In E. E. Beckham and W. R. Leber, eds., *Handbook of Depression*. Homewood, IL: Dorsey Press.

Hoch, C., and G. C. Hemmens. 1987. "Linking Informal and Formal Help: Conflict along the Continuum of Care." *Social Service Review* 61:432–446.

Hodgson, R., H. Rankin, and T. Stockwell. 1979. "The Concept of Craving and its Measurement." *Behavior Research and Therapy* 17:379–387.

Hodgson, R., and T. Stockwell. 1985. "The Theoretical and Empirical Basis of the Alcohol Dependence Model: A Social Learning Perspective." In N. Heather, I. Robertson, and P. Davies, eds., *The Misuse of Alcohol: Crucial Issues in Dependence, Treatment and Prevention*. New York: Columbia University Press.

Hofstad, M. O. 1977. "Treatment in a Juvenile Court Setting." In W. J. Reid and L. Epstein, eds., *Task-Centered Practice*. New York: Columbia University Press.

Hogan, M. J., and J. W. Bauer. 1988. "Problems in Family Financial Management." In C. S. Chilman, F. M. Cox, and E. W. Nunnally, eds., *Employment and Economic Problems*. Newbury Park, CA: Sage Publications.

Hogarty, G. E., C. M. Anderson, D. J. Reiss, S. J. Komblith, D. P. Greenwald, C. D. Javna, and M. J. Madonia. 1986. "Family Psychoeducation, Social Skills Training, and Maintenance Chemotherapy in the Aftercare Treatment of Schizophrenia." *Archives of General Psychiatry* 43:633–642.

Hollin, C. R., and P. Trower, eds. 1986. *Handbook of Social Skills Training*, vol. 2. New York: Pergamon Press.

Hollis, F. 1958. "Personality Diagnosis in Casework." In H. J. Parad, ed., *Ego*

Psychology and Dynamic Casework. New York: Family Service Association of America.

—— 1963. "Contemporary Issues for Case Workers." In H. J. Parad and R. R. Miller, eds., *Ego-Oriented Casework*. New York: Family Service Association of America.

Horowitz, A. 1985. "Family Caregiving to the Frail Elderly." In C. Eisendorfer, ed., *Annual Review of Gerontology and Geriatrics* 5:194–246.

Houlihan, D., and R. N. Jones. 1989. "Treatment of a Boy's School Phobia with *in vivo* Systematic Desensitization." *Professional and School Psychology* 6:5–15.

Howard, K. I., S. M. Kopta, M. S. Krause, and D. E. Orlinsky. 1986. "The Dose-Effect Relationship in Psychotherapy." *American Psychologist* 41:159–164.

Hoyer, W., and S. Clancy. 1988. "Factors Affecting Assessment and Treatment Decisions in Long-Term Care." In R. Dunkle and M. Wykle, eds., *Decision Making in Long-Term Care*. New York: Springer.

Hudson, W. W. 1982. *The Clinical Measurement Package: A Field Manual*. Homewood, IL: Dorsey Press.

—— 1990. "Computer-Based Clinical Practice: Present Status and Future Possibilities." In L. Videka-Sherman and W. J. Reid, eds., *Advances in Clinical Social Work Research*. Silver Spring, MD: NASW Press.

Hunt, M., and G. Hunt. 1983. "Simulated Site Visits in the Relocation of Older People." *Health and Social Work* 8:5–14.

Hutchinson, W., P. Searight, and J. Stretch. 1986. "Multi-Dimensional Networking: A Response to the Needs of Homeless Families." *Social Work* 31:427–430.

Iodice, J. D., and J. S. Wodarski, 1987. "Aftercare Treatment for Schizophrenics Living at Home." *Social Work* 32:122–128.

Jackson, A. A. 1983. *Task-Centered Marital Therapy: A Single Case Investigation*. Ph.D. Dissertation, University of Alabama.

Jacob, T., ed. 1987. *Family Interaction and Psychopathology*. New York: Plenum Press.

Jacobs, H. E. 1989. "Vocational Rehabilitation." In R. P. Liberman, ed., *Psychiatric Rehabilitation of Chronic Mental Patients*. Washington, D.C.: American Psychiatric Press.

Jacobs, H. E., et al. 1984. "A Skills-Oriented Model for Facilitating Employment Among Psychiatrically Disabled Persons." *Rehabilitation Counseling Bulletin* 2:887–96.

Jacobson, G. R. 1989a. "A Comprehensive Approach to Pretreatment Evaluation, I: Detection, Assessment, and Diagnosis of Alcoholism." In R. K. Hester and W. R. Miller, eds., *Handbook of Alcoholism: Treatment Approaches, Effective Alternatives*. New York: Pergamon Press.

—— 1989b. "A Comprehensive Approach to Pretreatment Evaluation, II: Other Clinical Considerations." In R. K. Hester and W. R. Miller, eds., *Hand-*

book of Alcoholism: Treatment Approaches, Effective Alternatives. New York: Pergamon Press.

Jacobson, N. S. 1977. "ProblemSolving and Contingency Contracting in the Treatment of Marital Discord." *Journal of Consulting and Clinical Psychology* 48:92–100.

Jacobson, N. S., and A. S. Gurman, eds. 1986. *Clinical Handbook of Marital Therapy.* New York: Guilford Press.

Jacobson, N. S., and G. Margolin. 1979. *Marital Therapy: Strategies Based on Social Learning and Behavior Exchange Principles.* New York: Brunner-Mazel.

Janis, I., and L. Mann. 1977. *Decision Making: A Psychological Analysis of Conflict, Choice and Commitment.* New York: Free Press.

Jannoun, L., C. Oppenheimer, and M. Gelder. 1982. "A Self-Help Treatment Program for Anxiety State Patients." *Behavior Therapy* 13:103–111.

Jansson, L., and L. G. Ost. 1982. "Behavioral Treatments for Agoraphobia: An Evaluative Review." *Clinical Psychology Review* 2:311–336.

Jayaratne, S. 1982. "Characteristics and Theoretical Orientations of Clinical Social Workers: A National Survey." *Journal of Social Service Research* 4:17–29.

——— 1990. "Clinical Significance: Problems and New Developments." In L. Videka-Sherman and W. J. Reid, eds., *Advances in Clinical Social Work Research.* Silver Spring, MD: NASW Press.

Jesse, E. H., and L. L'Abate. 1985. "Paradoxical Treatment of Depression in Married Couples." In L. L'Abate, ed., *The Handbook of Family Psychology and Therapy,* vol. 2. Homewood, IL: Dorsey Press.

Johnson, D. A. W. 1984. "Observation on the Use of Long-Acting Depot Neuroleptic in the Maintenance Therapy of Schizophrenia." *Journal of Clinical Psychiatry* 45:13–21.

Johnson, D. H., and C. G. Gelso. 1980. "The Effectiveness of Time Limits in Counseling and Psychotherapy: A Critical Review." *The Counseling Psychologist* 9:70–85.

Johnson, H. D. 1986. "Emerging Concerns in Family Therapy." *Social Work* 31:299–306.

Johnson, J. H., and I. G. Sarason. 1978. "Life Stress, Depression, and Anxiety: Internal-External Control as a Moderator Variable." *Journal of Psychosomatic Research* 22:205–208.

Jones, E. 1987. "Brief Systemic Work in Psychiatric Settings Where a Family Member has been Diagnosed as Schizophrenic." *Journal of Family Therapy* 9:3–25.

Jones, L. E. 1990. "Unemployment and Child Abuse." *Families in Society* 71:579–586.

Jones, L. E., and E. Wattenberg. 1991. "Working, Still Poor: A Loan Program's Role in the Lives of Low-Income Single Parents." *Social Work* 36:146–153.

Kahney, H. 1986. *Problem Solving: A Cognitive Approach.* Philadelphia: Open University Press.

Kane, R. 1975. "The Interprofessional Team as a Small Group." *Social Work in Health Care* 1:19–32.

Kanter, J. 1989. "Clinical Case Management: Definition, Principles, Components." *Hospital and Community Psychiatry* 40:361–368.

Katschnig, H., and T. Konieczna, 1989. "What Works in Work with Relatives?—A Hypothesis." *British Journal of Psychiatry* 155:44–150.

Kaufflan, E., and E. M. Pattison. 1981. "Differential Methods of Family Therapy in the Treatment of Alcoholism." *Journal of Studies of Alcohol* 42:951–971.

Kazdin, A. E. 1981. "Drawing Valid Inferences from Single Case Designs." *Journal of Consulting and Clinical Psychology* 49:183–192.

Kendall, P. C., and J. D. Norton-Ford. 1982. "Therapy Outcome Research Methods." In P. C. Kendall and J. N. Butcher, eds., *Handbook of Research Methods in Clinical Psychology*. New York: John Wiley.

Kennedy, W. A. 1965. "School Phobia: Rapid Treatment of Fifty Cases." *Journal of Abnormal Psychology* 70:285–289.

Kerr, M. E. 1981. "Family Systems Theory and Therapy." In A. S. Gurman and D. P. Kniskern, eds., *Handbook of Family Therapy*. New York: Brunner/Mazel.

Kerson, T., and L. Kerson. 1985. *Understanding Chronic Illness: The Medical and Psychosocial Dimensions of Nine Diseases*. New York: Free Press.

Kifer, R. E., M. A. Lewis, D. R. Green, and E. L. Phillips. 1979. "Training Pre-Delinquent Youths and Their Parents to Negotiate Conflict Situations." *Journal of Applied Behavioral Analysis* 7:357–364.

Kolko, D. J., and M. Milan. 1983. "Reframing and Paradoxical Instruction to Overcome 'Resistance' in the Treatment of Delinquent Youths: A Multiple Baseline Analysis." *Journal of Consulting and Clinical Psychology* 51:655–661.

Kopp, J. 1988. "Self-Monitoring: A Literature Review of Research and Practice." *Social Work Research and Abstracts* 24:8–20.

Koss, M., and J. N. Butcher. 1986. "Research on Brief Psychotherapy." In S. L. Garfield and A. E. Bergin, eds., *Handbook of Psychotherapy and Behavior Change*. New York: John Wiley.

Kozol, J. 1988. *Rachel and Her Children: Homeless Families in America*. New York: Fawcett Columbine.

Kruzich, J. M. 1988. "Helping Families with Income Problems." In C. S. Chilman, F. M. Cox, and E. W. Nunnally, eds., *Employment and Economic Problems*. Newbury Park, CA: Sage Publications.

Kuehnel, T. G., and R. P. Liberman. 1988. "Functional Assessment." In R. P. Liberman, ed., *Psychiatric Rehabilitation of Chronic Mental Patients*. Washington, D.C.: American Psychiatric Press.

L'Abate, L., and M. A. Milan. 1985. *Handbook of Social Skills Training and Research*. New York: John Wiley.

Lamb, H. R. 1982. *Treating the Long-Term Mentally Ill*. San Francisco: Jossey-Bass.

Lamb, H. R., and V. Goertzel. 1977. "The Long-Term Patient in the Era of Community Treatment." *Archives of General Psychiatry* 34:679–682.

Langer, J., and J. Rodin. 1976. "The Effects of Choice and Enhanced Personal Responsibility for the Aged." *Journal of Personality and Social Psychology* 34:191–198.

Langer, J., I. Janis, and J. Wolfer. 1975. "Reduction of Psychological Stress in Surgical Patients." *Journal of Experimental Psychology* 11:155–165.

Larrance, D. L., and C. T. Twentyman. 1983. "Maternal Attributions in Child Abuse." *Journal of Abnormal Psychology* 92:449–157.

Larsen, J., and C. Mitchell. 1980. "Task-Centered Strength-Oriented Group Work with Delinquents." *Social Casework* 61:154–163.

Last, C. G. 1985. "School Phobia." M. Hersen and C. G. Last, eds. In *Behavior Therapy Case Book*. New York: Springer.

Lawton, M. P., P. Windley, and T. Byerts. 1982. *Aging and the Environment: Theoretical Approaches*. New York: Springer.

Lazarus, R. S. 1989. "Constructs of the Mind in Mental Health and Psychotherapy." In A. Freeman, K. M. Simon, and L. E. Beutler, eds., *Comprehensive Handbook of Cognitive Therapy*. New York: Plenum Press.

Lazarus, R. S., and S. Folkman. 1984. *Stress, Appraisal, and Coping*. New York: Springer.

LeCroy, C. W., and C. C. Goodwin. 1988. "New Directions in Teaching Social Work Methods: A Content Analysis of Course Outlines." *Journal of Social Work Education* 24:43–49.

Leff, J. 1989. "Family Factors in Schizophrenia." *Psychiatric Annals* 19:542–547.

Leff, J., L. Kuipers, R. Berkowitz, R. Eberlein-Vries, and D. Sturgeon. 1982. "A Controlled Trial of Social Intervention in the Families of Schizophrenic Patients." *British Journal of Psychiatry* 141:121–134.

Leff, J., et al. 1985. "A Controlled Study of Social Intervention in Families of Schizophrenic Patients: Two Year Follow-up." *British Journal of Psychiatry* 146:594–600.

Lester, G. W. 1985. "Alternate Psychotherapies for Depression: Transactional Analysis, Gestalt Therapy, and Reality Therapy." In E. E. Beckham and W. R. Leber, eds., *Handbook of Depression*. Homewood, IL: Dorsey Press.

Lettieri, D. J., J. E. Nelson, and M. S. Sayers. 1985. NIAA Treatment Handbook Series 2. *Alcoholism: Treatment Assessment Research Instruments*. Rockville, MD: U. S. Department of Health and Human Services.

Levine, K. G., and A. Lightburn. 1989. "Belief Systems and Social Work Practice." *Social Casework* 70:139–145.

Levitt, J. L., and W. J. Reid. 1981. "Rapid Assessment Instruments for Social Work Practice. "*Social Work Research and* Abstracts 17:13–19.

Levy, R. L., and R. D. Carter. 1976. "Compliance with Practitioner Instigations." *Social Work* 21:188–193.

Levy, R. L., and J. L. Shelton. 1990. "Tasks in Brief Therapy." In R. A. Wells and V. J. Giannetti, eds., *Handbook of Brief Psychotherapies*. New York: Plenum Press.

Lewinsohn, P. M., H. M. Hoberman, L. Terri, and M. Hautzinger. 1985. "An

Integrative Theory of Depression." In S. Reiss and R. Bootzin, eds., *Theoretical Issues in Behavior Therapy*. New York: Academic Press.

Lewis, J. M. 1986. "Family Structure and Stress." *Family Process* 25:235–247.

Lewis, J. M., W. R. Beavers, J. T. Gossett, and V. Austin Phillips. 1976. *No Single Thread: Psychological Health in Family Systems*. New York: Brunner-Mazel.

Liberman R. P., ed. 1988. *Psychiatric Rehabilitation of Chronic Mental Patients*. Washington, D.C.: American Psychiatric Press.

—— 1988. "Social Skills Training." In R. P. Liberman, ed., *Psychiatric Rehabilitation of Chronic Mental Patients*. Washington, D.C.: American Psychiatric Press.

—— 1988. "Behavioral Family Management." In R. P. Liberman, ed., *Psychiatric Rehabilitation of Chronic Mental Patients*. Washington, D.C.: American Psychiatric Press.

Liberman, R. P., W. J. DeRisi, and K. Mueser. 1989. *Social Skills Training for Psychiatric Patients*. New York: Pergamon Press.

Liberman, R. P., K. Mueser, and S. Glynn. 1988. "Modular Behavioral Strategies." In I. R. H. Falloon, ed., *Handbook of Behavioral Family Therapy*. New York: Guilford Press.

Liberman, R. P., K. T. Mueser, and C. J. Wallace. 1986. "Social Skills Training for Schizophrenic Individuals at Risk for Relapse." *American Journal of Psychiatry* 143:523–526.

Liberman, R. P., E. G. Wheeler, L. A. J. M. DeVisser, J. Kuehnel, and T. Kuehnel. 1980. *Handbook of Marital Therapy: A Positive Approach to Helping Troubled Relationships*. New York: Plenum Press.

Lieberman, M., and S. Tobin. 1983. *The Experience of Old Age*. New York: Basic Books.

Long, S. H. 1989. "Public Versus Employment-Related Health Insurance: Experience and Implications for Black and Nonblack Americans." In D. P. Willis, ed., *Health Policies and Black Americans*. New Brunswick, NJ: Transaction Publishers.

Love, R. E. 1984. "The Community Support Program: Strategy for Reform?" In J. A. Talbott, ed., *The Chronic Mental Patient: Five Years Later*. New York: Grune and Stratton.

Lutzker, J. R. 1984. "Project 12-Ways: Treating Child Abuse and Neglect from an Ecobehavioral Perspective." In R. F. Dangel and R. A. Polster, eds., *Parent Training: Foundations of Research and Practice*. New York: Guilford Press.

Lutzker, J. R., and J. M. Rice. 1984. "Project 12-Ways. Measuring Outcome of a Large In-Home Service for Treatment and Prevention of Child Abuse and Neglect." *Child Abuse and Neglect*, 8:519–524.

Madden, D. J., and H. T. Harbin. 1983. "Family Structures of Assaultive Adolescents." *Journal of Marital and Family Therapy* 9:311–316.

Maddus, J. E., and M. A. Stanley. 1986. "Self-Efficacy Theory in Contemporary Psychology: An Overview." *Journal of Social and Clinical Psychology* 4:249–255.

Mahoney, M. J. 1974. *Cognition and Behavior Modification.* Cambridge, MA: Ballinger.

Mailick, M. 1979. "The Impact of Severe Illness on the Individual and Family: An Overview." *Social Work in Health Care* 5:117–128.

Mailick, M., and A. Ashley. 1981. "Politics of Interprofessional Collaboration: Challenge to Advocacy." *Social Casework* 62:131–137.

Manton, K. G., C. H. Patrick, and K. W. Johnson. 1989. "Health Differentials Between Blacks and Whites: Recent Trends in Mortality and Morbidity." In D. P. Willis, ed., *Health Policies and Black Americans.* New Brunswick, NJ: Transaction Publishers.

Marlatt, G. A. 1985. "Cognitive Factors in the Relapse Process." In G. A. Marlatt and J. R. Gordon, eds., *Relapse Prevention: Maintenance Strategies in Addictive Behavior Change.* New York: Guilford Press.

Marshall, V. 1981. "Physician Characteristics and Relationships with Older Patients." In M. Haug, ed., *Elderly Patients and Their Doctors.* New York: Springer.

Martin, P. Y., and G. G. O'Connor. 1989. *The Social Environment: Open Systems Applications.* White Plains, N.Y.: Longman.

Maslow, A. H. 1970. *Motivation and Personality.* New York: Harper and Row.

Massey, R. 1988. "Adlerian Theory and Therapy." In R. A. Dorfman, ed., *Paradigms of Clinical Social Work.* New York: Brunner-Mazel.

McCrady, B. S. 1989. "Outcomes of Family-Involved Alcoholism Treatment." In M. Galanter, ed., *Alcoholism* vol. 7: *Treatment Research.* New York: Plenum Press.

McCrady, B. S., and S. Irvine. 1989. "Self-Help Groups." In R. K. Hester and W. R. Miller, eds., *Handbook of Alcoholism: Treatment Approaches, Effective Alternatives.* New York: Pergamon Press.

McCubbin, H., and J. Comeau. 1987. "FIRM: Family Inventory of Resources for Management." In H. McCubbin and A. Thompson, eds., *Family Assessment Inventories for Research and Practice.* Madison: University of Wisconsin Press.

McGoldrick, M., J. K. Pearce, and J. Giordano, eds. 1982. *Ethnicity and Family Therapy.* New York: Guilford Press.

McMahon, R. J., and R. Forehand. 1984. "Parent Training for the Noncompliant Child: Treatment Outcome, Generalization, and Adjunctive Therapy Procedures." In R. F. Dangel and R. A. Polster, eds., *Parent Training: Foundations of Research and Practice.* New York: Guilford Press.

McQueen A., M. Monkman, and J. Kagle. 1982. "The Transactions Between People and Environment Framework: Focusing Social Work Intervention in Health Care." *Social Work in Health Care* 8:105–116.

Meichenbaum, D. 1985. *Stress Innoculation Training.* New York: Pergamon Press.

Meichenbaum, D., and D. C. Turk. 1987. *Facilitating Treatment Adherence: A Practitioner's Guidebook.* New York: Plenum Press.

Mercer, S., and R. Kane. 1979. "Helplessness and Hopelessness Among the

Institutionalized Aged: An Experiment." *Health and Social Work* 4:91–115.

Merck Manual. 1984. 3d. ed. Rahway, NJ: Merck.

Meyer, C. H. 1983. "Selecting Appropriate Practice Models." In A. Rosenblatt and D. Waldfogel, eds., *Handbook of Clinical Social Work*. San Francisco: Jossey-Bass.

Miklowitz, D. J., M. J. Goldstein, I. R. H. Falloon, and J. A. Doane. 1984. "Interactional Correlates of Expressed Emotion in the Families of Schizophrenics." *British Journal of Psychiatry* 144:482–487.

Miller, I. W., N. B. Epstein, D. S. Bishop, and G. I. Keitner. 1985. "The McMaster Family Assessment Device: Reliability and Validity." *Journal of Marital and Family Therapy* 11:345–356.

Miller, W. R. 1987. "Motivation and Treatment Goals." In M. B. Sobell and L. C. Sobell, eds., *Moderation as a Goal of the Outcome of Treatment for Alcohol Problems: A Dialogue*. New York: Haworth Press.

——— 1989. "Follow-up Assessment." In R. K. Hester and W. R. Miller, eds., *Handbook of Alcoholism: Treatment Approaches, Effective Alternatives*. New York: Pergamon Press.

——— 1989. "Increasing Motivation for Change." In R. K. Hester and W. R. Miller, eds., *Handbook of Alcoholism: Treatment Approaches, Effective Alternatives*. New York: Pergamon Press.

——— 1989. "Matching Individuals with Interventions." In R. K. Hester and W. R. Miller, eds., *Handbook of Alcoholism: Treatment Approaches, Effective Alternatives*. New York: Pergamon Press.

Miller, W. R., and L. M. Baca. 1983. "Two-year Follow-up of Bibliotherapy and Therapist-Directed Controlled Drinking Training for Problem Drinkers." *Behavior Therapy* 14:441–448.

Miller, W. R., and M. A. Joyce. 1979. "Prediction of Abstinence, Controlled Drinking, and Heavy Drinking Outcome Following Behavioral Self-Control Training." *Journal of Consulting and Clinical Psychology* 47:773–775.

Minuchin, S. 1967. *Families of the Slums*. New York: Basic Books.

——— 1974. *Families and Family Therapy*. Cambridge, MA: Harvard University Press.

Minuchin, S., and C. H. Fishman. 1981. *Family Therapy Techniques*. Cambridge, MA: Harvard University Press.

Minuchin, S., B. L. Rosman, and L. Baker. 1978. *Psychosomatic Families: Anorexia Nervosa in Context*. Cambridge, MA: Harvard University Press.

Mizrahi, T., and J. Abramson. 1985. "Sources of Strain Between Physicians and Social Workers: Implications for Social Workers in Health Care Settings." *Social Work in Health Care* 10:33–51.

Monti, P. M., D. B. Abrams, R. M. Kadden, and N. L. Cooney. 1989. *Treating Alcohol Dependence: A Coping Skills Training Guide*. New York: Guilford Press.

Moore, S. T. 1990. "A Social Work Practice Model of Case Management: The Case Management Grid." *Social Work* 35:444–448.

Moos, R. 1984. *Coping with Physical Illness 2: New Perspectives*. New York: Plenum Press.

Morgan, R. R. 1975. "An Exploratory Study of Three Procedures to Encourage School Attendance." *Psychology in the Schools* 12:209–215.

Moxley, D. P. 1989. *The Practice of Case Management*. Newbury Park, CA: Sage Publications.

Murphy, M. J. 1977. "Utilizing Existing Community Resources." In F. M. Cox, J. L. Erlich, J. Rothman, and J. E. Tropman, eds., *Tactics and Techniques of Community Practice*. Itasca, IL: F. E. Peacock.

Myers, H. F. 1989. "Urban Stress and Mental Health in Black Youth: An Epidemiologic and Conceptual Update." In R. J. Jones, ed., *Black Adolescents*. Berkeley, CA: Cobb and Henry.

Nace, E. P. 1987. *The Treatment of Alcoholism*. New York: Brunner/Mazel.

Nason, F. 1990. "Beyond Relationship: The Current Challenge in Clinical Practice." *Social Work in Health Care* 14:9–24.

Nathan, P. E., and B. S. McCrady. 1987. "Bases for the Use of Abstinence in the Behavioral Treatment of Alcohol Abusers." In M. B. Sobell and L. C. Sobell, eds., *Moderation as a Goal of the Outcome of Treatment for Alcohol Problems: A Dialogue*. New York: Haworth Press.

Nathan, P. E., and A. H. Skinstad. 1987. "Outcomes of Treatment for Alcohol Problems: Current Methods, Problems and Results." *Journal of Consulting and Clinical Psychology* 55:332–340.

Newcome, K. 1985. "Task-Centered Group Work with the Chronically Mentally Ill in Day Treatment." In A. E. Fortune ed., *Task-Centered Practice with Families and Groups*. New York: Springer.

Nezu, A. M., C. M. Nezu, and M. G. Perri. 1989. *Problem-Solving Therapy for Depression: Theory, Research, and Clinical Guidelines*. New York: John Wiley.

Nichols, M. P. 1987. *The Self in the System: Expanding the Limits of Family Therapy*. New York: Brunner-Mazel.

Nietzel, M. T., R. L. Russell, K. A. Hemmings, and M. L. Gretter. 1987. "Clinical Significance of Psychotherapy for Unipolar Depression: A Meta-Analytic Approach to Social Comparison." *Journal of Consulting and Clinical Psychology* 55:156–161.

Nishiura, E., C. Whitten, and D. Jenkins. 1980. "Screening for Psychological Problems in Health Settings." *Health and Social Work* 5:22–28.

Nofz, M. P. 1988. "Alcohol Abuse and Culturally Marginal American Indians." *Social Casework* 69:67–73.

Norris, V., M. A. Parris Stephens, and J. Kinney. 1990. "The Impact of Family Interactions on Recovery from Stroke: Help or Hindrance." *The Gerontologist* 30:535–542.

Novaco, R. W. 1975. *Anger Control: The Development and Evaluation of an Experimental Treatment*. Lexington, MA: Heath.

—— 1979. "Cognitive Regulation of Anger and Stress." In P. Kendall and S. Hollon, eds., *Cognitive-Behavioral Interventions*. New York: Academic Press.

——— 1979. "Anger and Coping with Stress: Cognitive Behavioral Interventions." In J. Foreyt and D. Rathjen, eds., *Cognitive Behavior Therapy: Research and Application*. New York: Plenum Press.

O'Farrell, T. J., and K. S. Cowles. 1989. "Marital and Family Therapy." In R. K. Hester and W. R.Miller, eds., *Handbook of Alcoholism: Treatment Approaches Effective Alternatives*. New York: Pergamon Press.

O'Leary, D. K., and H. Turkowitz. 1981. "A Comparative Outcome Study of Behavioral Marital Therapy and Communication Therapy." *Journal of Marital and Family Therapy* 7:159–169.

Olson, D. H., H. I. McCubbin, and Associates. 1983. *Families: What Makes Them Work*. Newbury Park, CA: Sage Publications.

Orcutt, B. A. 1990. *Science and Inquiry in Social Work Practice*. New York: Columbia University Press.

Osborn, A. F. 1963. *Applied Imagination*. New York: Scribners.

Oxford, J., and A. Hawker. 1974. "An Investigation of an Alcoholism Halfway House, II: The Complex Question of Client Motivation." *British Journal of Addiction* 69:315–323.

Papp, P. 1976. "Family Choreography." In P., Jr., ed., *Family Therapy: Theory and Practice*. New York: Gardner Press.

Parad, H. J., and L. G. Parad. 1968. "A Study of Crisis-Oriented Planned Short-Term Treatment, Part 1." *Social Casework* 46:346–355.

Paredes, A. 1989. "Clinical Pharmacology in the Treatment of Alcohol Dependence: Manipulation of Neurobehavioral Mechanisms of Drinking." In M. Galanter, ed., *Alcoholism vol. 7: Treatment Research*. New York: Plenum Press.

Parihar, B. 1983. *Task-Centered Management in Human Services*. Springfield, IL: Charles C. Thomas.

Parsons, R. J., S. H. Hernandez, and J. D. Jorgensen. 1988. "Integrated Practice: A Framework for Problem Solving." *Social Work* 33:417–421.

Patterson, G. R. 1976. "The Aggressive Child: Victim and Architect of a Coercive System." In E. J. Marsh, L. A. Hamerlynck, and L. C. Handy, eds., *Behavior Modification and Families*. New York: Brunner-Mazel.

Pearlin, L. I., and C. Schooler. 1978. "The Structure of Coping." *Journal of Health and Social Behavior* 1:2–21.

Pearson, R. E. 1990. *Counseling and Social Support: Perspectives and Practice*. Newbury Park, CA: Sage Publications.

Perlman, H. H. 1957. *Social Casework: A Problem-Solving Process*. Chicago: University of Chicago Press.

Perris, C. 1989. "Cognitive Therapy with the Adult Depressed Patient." In A. Freeman, K. M. Simon, and L. E. Beutler, eds., *Comprehensive Handbook of Cognitive Therapy*. New York: Plenum Press.

Peterson, C. L., S. L. Patrick, and D. J. Rissmeyer. 1990. "Social Work's Contribution to Psychosocial Rehabilitation." *Social Work* 35:468–472.

Petronko, M. 1989. "Agoraphobia." In A. M. Nezu and C. M. Nezu, eds., *Clinical*

Decision Making in Behavior Therapy. Champaign, IL: Research Press Company.

Phillips, M. H., N. Dechillo, D. Kronenfeld, and V. Middleton. 1988. "Homeless Families: Services Make a Difference." *Social Casework* 69:48–53.

Phipps, C., and R. P. Liberman. 1988. "Community Support." In R. P. Liberman ed., *Psychiatric Rehabilitation of Chronic Mental Patients.* Washington, D.C.: American Psychiatric Press.

Pinkston, E. M. 1984. "Individualized Behavioral Intervention for Home and School." In R. F. Dangel and R. A. Polster, eds., *Parent Training.* New York: Guilford Press.

Pinsof, W. 1983. "Integrative Problem-Centered Therapy: Toward the Synthesis of Family and Individual Psychotherapies." *Journal of Marital and Family Therapy* 9:19–35.

Pohl, J., and S. Fuller. 1980. "Perceived Choice, Social Interaction, and Dimensions of Morale of Residents in a Home for the Aged." *Research in Nursing and Health* 3:147–157.

Pokorny, A. D., B. A. Miller, and H. B. Kaplan. 1972. "The Brief MAST: A Shortened Version of the Michigan Alcoholism Screening Test." *American Journal of Psychiatry* 129:342–345.

Polich, J. M., D. Armor, and H. B. Braiker. 1981. *The Course of Alcoholism: Four Years After Treatment.* New York: John Wiley.

Polster, R. A., and R. F. Dangel. 1984. "Behavioral Parent Training: Where It Came From and Where It's At." In R. F. Dangel and R. A. Polster, eds., *Parent Training.* New York: Guilford Press.

Polster, R. A., R. F. Dangel, and R. Rapp. 1987. "Research in Behavioral Parent Training in Social Work: A Review." *Journal of Social Service Research* 10:37–51.

Polster, R. P., and E. M. Pinkston. 1979. "A Delivery System for the Treatment of Underachievement." *Social Service Review* 53:35–55.

Poulshock, S., and G. Deimling. 1984. "Families Caring for Elders in Residence: Issues in the Measurement of Burden." *Journal of Gerontology* 39:230–239.

Prohaska, T., and W. McCauley. 1983. "Role of Family Care and Living Arrangements in Acute Care Discharge Recommendations." *Journal of Gerontological Social Work* 5:67–80.

Quinn, M., A. Fontana, and M. Reznikoff. 1985. "Psychological Distress in Reaction to Lung Cancer as a Function of Spousal Support and Coping Strategy." *Journal of Psychosocial Oncology* 4:79–90.

Rachman, S. J., M. Craske, K. Tallman, and C. Solyman. 1986. "Does Escape Behavior Strengthen Agoraphobic Avoidance? A Replication." *Behavior Therapy* 17:366–384.

Rachman, S. J., and J. D. Massey, eds. 1988. *Panic: Psychological Perspectives.* Hillsdale, NJ: Erlbaum.

Ramseur, H. P. 1989. "Psychologically Healthy Black Adults: A Review of Theory and Research." In R. L. Jones, ed., *Black Adult Development and Aging*. Berkeley, CA: Cobb and Henry.

Rapp, C. A., and R. Chamberlain. 1985. "Case Management Services For the Chronically Mentally Ill." *Social Work* 30:417–422.

Raskin, D. E., and Z. E. Klein. 1976. "Losing a Symptom Through Keeping It." *Archives of General Psychiatry* 33:548–555.

Rathbone-McCuan, E. 1985. "Intergenerational Family Practice with Older Families." In A. E. Fortune, ed., *Task-Centered Practice with Families and Groups*. New York: Springer.

Raveis, V., K. Siegel, and M. Sudit. 1989. "Psychological Impact of Caregiving on the Careprovider: A Critical Review of Extant Research." *The Journal of Applied Social Sciences* 13:40–79.

Rayman, P. 1988. "Unemployment and Family Life: The Meaning for Children." In P. Voydanoff and L. C. Majka, eds., *Families and Economic Distress: Coping Strategies and Social Policy*. Newbury Park, CA: Sage Publications.

Redd, M. L. 1989. "Alcoholism and Drug Addiction Among Black Adults." In R. L. Jones, ed., *Black Adult Development and Aging*. Berkeley, CA: Cobb and Henry.

Rehr, H. 1986. "Discharge Planning: An Ongoing Function of Quality Care." *Quality Review Bulletin* 12:47–50.

Reid, W. J. 1975. "A Test of the Task-Centered Approach." *Social Work* 20:3–9.

—— 1977. "Process and Outcome in the Treatment of Family Problems." In W. J. Reid and L. Epstein, eds., *Task-Centered Practice*. New York: Columbia University Press.

—— 1978. *The Task-Centered System*. New York: Columbia University Press.

—— 1981. "Family Treatment within a Task-Centered Framework." In E. R. Tolson and W. J. Reid, eds., *Models of Family Treatment*. New York: Columbia University Press.

—— 1985. *Family Problem-Solving*. New York: Columbia University Press.

—— 1986. "Task Centered Social Work." In F. J. Turner, ed., *Social Treatment*, 3d ed. New York Free Press.

—— 1987. "Research in Social Work." In A. Minahan, ed., *Encyclopedia of Social Work*, 18th Edition. New York: NASW Press.

—— 1987a. "Evaluating an Intervention in Developmental Research." *Journal of Social Service Research* 11:17–39.

—— 1987b. "The Family Problem-Solving Sequence." *American Journal of Family Therapy* 14:135–146.

—— 1988. "Brief Task-Centered Treatment." In R. Dorfman, ed., *Paradigms of Clinical Social Work*. New York: Brunner/Mazel.

—— 1990a. "Change-Process Research: A New Paradigm?" In L. Videka-Sherman and W. J. Reid, eds., *Advances in Clinical Social Work Research*. Silver Spring, MD: NASW Press.

—— 1990b. "An Integrative Model for Short-Term Treatment. " In R. A. Wells and V. J. Giannetti, eds., *Handbook of the Brief Psychotherapies*. New York: Plenum Press.

Reid, W. J. and I. Davis. 1987. "Qualitative Methods in Single Case Research." In N. Gottlieb, ed., *Perspectives on Practitioners as Evaluators of Direct Practice*. Seattle: School of Social Work, University of Washington.

Reid, W. J., and T. Donovan. 1990. "Treating Sibling Violence." *Family Therapy* 71:49–59.

Reid, W. J., and L. Epstein. 1972. *Task-Centered Casework*. New York: Columbia University Press.

Reid, W. J., and L. Epstein, eds. 1977. *Task-Centered Practice*. New York: Columbia University Press.

Reid, W. J., and P. Hanrahan. 1988. "Measuring Implementation of Social Treatment." In K. J. Conrad and C. Roberts-Gray, eds., *Evaluating Program Environments*. San Francisco: Jossey-Bass.

Reid, W. J., L. Epstein, L. B., Brown, E. R. Tolson, and R. H. Rooney. 1980. "Task-Centered School Social Work." *Social Work in Education* 2:7–24.

Reid, W. J., and K. Helmer. 1987. "Session Tasks in Family Treatment." *Family Therapy* 13:177–185.

Reid, W. J., and A. W. Shyne, 1969. *Brief and Extended Casework*. New York: Columbia University Press.

Reid, W. J., and A. D. Smith. 1989. *Research in Social Work*, 2d ed. New York: Columbia University Press.

Reid, W. J., and P. Strother. 1988. "Super Problem Solvers: A Systematic Case Study." *Social Service Review* 62:430–445.

Reis, E., R. Linhart, and J. Lazerson. 1982. "Using a Standard Form to Collect Psychosocial Data About Hemophilia Patients." *Health and Social Work* 7:206–214.

Reiss, D. J. 1988. "Pschoeducational Family Treatment of Schizophrenia: Dealing with the Slowness of Change." *International Journal of Mental Health* 17:65–74.

Richey, C. A., B. J. Blythe, and S. B. Berlin. 1987, "Do Social Workers Evaluate Their Practice? " *Social Work Research and Abstracts* 232:14–20.

Richmond, M. 1917. *Social Diagnosis*. New York: Russell Sage Foundation.

Riley, D. M., L. C. Sobell, G. I. Leo, M. B. Sobell, and F. Klajner. 1987. "Behavioral Treatment of Alcohol Problems: A Review and Comparison of Behavioral and Nonbehavioral Studies." In W. M. Cox, ed., *Treatment and Prevention of Alcohol Problems: A Resource Manual*. Orlando, FL: Academic Press.

Robin, A. 1981. "A Controlled Evaluation of Problem-Solving Communication Training with Parent-Adolescent Conflict." *Behavior Therapy* 12:593–609.

Robin, A. L., and S. L. Foster. 1989. *Negotiating Adolescence: A Behavioral Family Systems Approach to Parent-Adolescent Conflict*. New York: Guilford Press.

Rodin, J. 1986. "Aging and Health: Effects of the Sense of Control." *Science* 223:1271–1276.

Rogers, E. M., and F. F. Shoemaker. 1971. *Communication of Innovations: A Cross-Cultural Approach.* New York: Free Press.

Rohrbaugh, M., H. Tennen, S. Press, and L. White. 1981. "Compliance, Defiance, and Therapeutic Paradox: Guidelines for Strategic Use of Paradoxical Interventions." *American Journal of Orthopsychiatry* 51:454–467.

Rolland, J. 1987. "Chronic Illness and the Life Cycle: A Conceptual Framework." *Family Process* 26:203–221.

—— 1988a. "A Conceptual Model of Chronic and Life-Threatening Illness and its Impact on Families." In C. Chilman, E. Nunnally, and F. Cox, eds., *Chronic Illness and Disability* 2. Newbury Park, CA: Sage Publications.

—— 1988b. "Chronic Illness and the Family Life Cycle." In B. Carter and M. McGoldrick, eds., *The Changing Family Life Cycle: A Framework for Family Therapy.* New York: Gardner Press.

Rooney, R. H. 1978. "Separation Through Foster Care: Toward a Problem-Oriented Practice Model Based on Task-Centered Casework." Ph. D. dissertation, University of Chicago.

—— 1981. "A Task-Centered Reunification Model for Foster Care." In A. A. Malluccio and P. Sinanoglu, eds., *Working with Biological Parents of Children in Foster Care.* New York: Child Welfare League of America.

—— 1988a. "Socialization Strategies for Involuntary Clients." *Social Casework* 69:131–139.

—— 1988b. "Measuring Task-Centered Training Effects on Practice: Results of an Audiotape Study in a Public Agency." *Journal of Continuing Social Work Education* 4:2–7.

—— in press. *Strategies for Work with Involuntary Clients.* New York: Columbia University Press.

Rooney, R. H., and M. Wanless. 1985. "A Model for Caseload Management Based on Task-Centered Casework." In A. E. Fortune, ed., *Task-Centered Practice with Families and Groups.* New York: Springer.

Rosenberg, S. E. 1985. "Brief Dynamic Psychotherapy for Depression." In E. E. Beckham and W. R. Leber, eds., *Handbook of Depression.* Homewood, IL: Dorsey press.

Rosow, I. 1981. "Coalitions in Geriatric Medicine." In M. Haug, ed., *Elderly Patients and Their Doctors.* New York: Springer.

Rounsaville, B. J., G. L. Klerman, M. M. Weissman, and E. S. Chevron. 1985. "Short-Term Interpersonal Psychotherapy (IPT) for Depression." In E. E. Beckham and W. R. Leber, eds., *Handbook of Depression.* Homewood, IL: Dorsey Press.

Roy-Byrne, P. P., and W. Katon. 1987. "An Update on Treatment of the Anxiety Disorder." *Hospital and Community Psychiatry* 38:835–843.

Rubin, A. 1990. "Is Case Management Effective for Persons with Serious Mental Illness? A Research Review." Paper presented at NASW annual meeting, November 16.

Rush, A. J., and K. Z. Altshuler, eds. 1986. *Depression: Basic Mechanisms, Diagnosis, and Treatment.* New York: Guilford Press.

Russell, C. S., D. A. Bagarozzi, R. B. Atilano, and J. E. Morris. 1984. "A Comparison of Two Approaches to Marital Enrichment and Conjugal Skills Training: Minnesota Couples Communication Program and Structured Behavioral Exchange Contracting." *The American Journal of Family Therapy* 12:13–25.

Rzepnicki, T. L. 1985. "Task-Centered Intervention in Foster Care Services: Working With Families who Have Children in Placement." In A. E. Fortune, ed., *Task-Centered Practice with Families and Groups.* New York: Springer.

Saari, C. 1986. *Clinical Social Work Treatment: Does it Work?* New York: Gardner Press.

Sacco, W. P., and A. T. Beck. 1985. "Cognitive Therapy of Depression." In E. E. Beckham and W. R. Leber, eds., *Handbook of Depression.* Homewood, IL: Dorsey Press.

Sackett, D. L., and R. B. Haynes, eds. 1976. *Compliance with Therapeutic Regimens.* Baltimore: Johns Hopkins University Press.

Salmon, W. 1977. "Service Program in a State Public Welfare Agency." In W. J. Reid and L. Epstein, eds., *Task-Centered Practice.* New York: Columbia University Press.

Sanchez-Craig, M., H. M. Annis, A. R. Bornet, and K. R. MacDonald. 1984. "Random Assignment to Abstinence and Controlled Drinking: Evaluation of a Cognitive-Behavioral Program for Problem Drinkers." *Journal of Consulting and Clinical Psychology* 52:390–403.

Sanchez-Craig, M. and H. Lei. 1986. "Disadvantages to Imposing the Goal of Abstinence on Problem Drinkers: An Empirical Study." *British Journal of Addiction* 81:505–512.

Sanchez-Craig, M., and D. A. Wilkinson. 1987. "Treating Problem Drinkers Who are not Severely Dependent on Alcohol." In M. B. Sobell and L. C. Sobell, eds., *Moderation as a Goal of the Outcome of Treatment for Alcohol Problems: A Dialogue.* New York: Haworth Press.

Sands, R. 1989. "The Social Worker Joins the Team: A Look at the Socialization Process." *Social Work in Health Care* 14:1–15.

Sands, R., J. Stafford, and M. McClelland. 1990. "I Beg to Differ: Conflict in the Interdisciplinary Team." *Social Work in Health Care* 14.

Schaefer, C. E., and J. M. Briesmeister, eds. 1989. *Handbook of Parent Training: Parents as Co-Therapists for Children's Behavior Problems.* New York: John Wiley.

Schön, D. 1983. *The Reflective Practitioner.* New York: Basic Books.

Schuchter, S. R., and S. Zisook. 1987. "The Therapeutic Tasks of Grief." In S. Zisook, ed., *Biopsychosocial Aspects of Bereavement.* Washington, D.C.: American Psychiatric Press.

Schulz, R. 1976. "Effects of Control and Predictability on the Psychological

Well-Being of the Institutionalized Aged." *Journal of Personality and Social Psychology* 33:563–573.

Segal, B. 1989. "Forward." In M. B. Sobell and L. C. Sobell, eds., *Moderation as a Goal of the Outcome of Treatment for Alcohol Problems: A Dialogue*. New York: Haworth Press.

Segraves, R. 1982. *Marital Therapy: A Combined Psychodynamic-Behavioral Approach*. New York: Plenum Press.

Seligman, M. E. 1988. "Competing Theories of Panic." In S. J. Rachman and J. D. Massey, eds., *Panic: Psychological Perspectives*. Hillsdale, NJ: Erlbaum.

Seltzer, M. M., J. Ivry, and L. C. Litchfield. 1987. "Family Members as Case Managers: Partnership between the Formal and Informal Support Networks." *Gerontologist* 27:722–728.

Seltzer, M. M., L. C. Litchfield, L. Lowry, and R. J. Levin. 1989. "Families as Case Managers: A Longitudinal Study." *Family Relations* 38:332–336.

Selzer, M. L. 1971. "The Michigan Alcoholism Screening Test: The Quest for a New Diagnostic Instrument." *American Journal of Psychiatry* 127:89–94.

Shanas, E., and V. Nostrand. 1988. "The Family, the Elderly, and Long-Term Care." In R. Dunkle and M. Wykle, eds., *Decision Making in Long-Term Care*. New York: Springer.

Sheehan, N., and P. Nuttal. 1988. "Conflict, Emotion, and Personal Strain Among Family Caregivers." *Family Relations* 37:92–98.

Shelton, J. L., and J. M. Ackerman. 1974. *Homework in Counseling and Psychotherapy*. Springfield, IL: Charles C. Thomas.

Shelton, J. L, and R. L. Levy. 1981. *Behavioral Assignments and Treatment Compliance: A Handbook of Clinical Strategies*. Champaign, IL: Research Press.

Shepard, G. 1986. "Social Skills Training and Schizophrenia." In C. R. Hollin and P. Trower, eds., *Handbook of Social Skills Training*, vol. 2. New York: Pergamon Press.

Silliman, R., J. Earp, and E. Wagner. 1988. "Stroke: The Perspective of Family Caregivers." *The Journal of Applied Gerontology* 6:363–371.

Simmons, K. H., J. Ivry, and M. M. Seltzer. 1985. "Agency-Family Collaboration." *Gerontologist* 25:343–346.

Siporin, M. 1975. *Introduction to Social Work Practice*. New York: MacMillan.

Skinner, H. A. 1984. "Assessing Alcohol Use by Patients in Treatment." In R. G. Smart, et al., eds., *Research Advances in Alcohol and Drug Problems*, vol. 8. New York: Plenum Press.

Skinner, H. A., and B. Allen. 1982. "Alcohol Dependence Syndrome: Measurement and Validation." *Journal of Abnormal Psychology* 91:199–209.

Skinner, H. A., and J. L. Horn. 1984. *Alcohol Dependence Scale (ADS) User's Guide*. Toronto: Addiction Research Foundation of Ontario.

Slivinske, L., and V. Fitch. 1987. "The Effect of Control Enhancing Interventions on the Well-Being of Elderly Individuals Living in Retirement Communities." *The Gerontologist* 27:176–181.

Small, R., and S. Schinke. 1983. "Teaching Competence in Residential Group Care." *Journal of Social Science Research* 7:1–16.

Smilkstein, G. 1978. "The Family APGAR Index: A Proposal for a Family Function Test and its Use by Physicians." *Journal of Family Practice* 6:1231–1239.

Sobell, M. B., and L. C. Sobell. 1987. "Conceptual Issues Regarding Goals in the Treatment of Alcohol Problems." In M. B. Sobell and L. C. Sobell, eds., *Moderation as a Goal of the Outcome of Treatment for Alcohol Problems: A Dialogue*. New York: Haworth Press.

Sobell, M. B., and L. C. Sobell., eds. 1987. *Moderation as a Goal of the Outcome of Treatment for Alcohol Problems: A Dialogue*. New York: Haworth Press.

Solomon, R. 1983. "Serving Families of the Institutionalized Aged: The Four Crises." In G. Getzel and M. Mellor, eds., *Gerontological Social Work Practice in Long Term Care*. New York: Haworth Press.

Spanier, G. B. 1976. "Measuring Dyadic Adjustment: New Scales for Assessing the Quality of Marriage and Similar Dyads." *Journal of Marriage and the Family*. 38:15–28.

Spielberger, C. D., R. L. Gorsuch, and R. E. Lushene. 1970. *State-Trait Anxiety Inventory*. Palo Alto: Consulting Psychologists Press.

Staggers, B. 1989. "Health Care Issues of Black Adolescents." In R. J. Jones, ed., *Black Adolescents*. Berkeley, CA: Cobb and Henry.

Staudemire, A., and D. F. Blazer. 1985. "Depression in the Elderly." In E. E. Beckham and W. R. Leber, eds., *Handbook of Depression*. Homewood, IL: Dorsey Press.

Steffen, J. J., V. B. Steffen, and P. E. Nathan. 1986. "Behavioral Approaches to Alcohol Abuse." In N. J. Estes and M. E. Heineman, eds., *Alcoholism Development Consequences and Interventions*, 3d ed. St Louis: C. U. Mosby.

Steinglass, P. 1981. "The Alcoholic Family at Home: Pattern of Interaction in Drug, Wet, and Transitional Stages of Alcoholism." *Archives of General Psychiatry* 38:578–584.

—— 1987. "Psychoeducational Family Therapy for Schizophrenia: A Review Essay." *Psychiatry* 50 14–23.

Steinglass, P., S. Weiner, and J. Mendelson. 1971. "Interactional Issues as Determinants of Alcoholism." *American Journal of Psychiatry* 128:275–280.

Stern, J. B., and I. G. Fodor. 1989. "Anger Control in Children: A Review of Social Skills and Cognitive Behavioral Approaches to Dealing with Aggressive Children." *Child and Family Behavior Therapy* 111–120.

Stern, S. B. 1989. "Behavioral Family Therapy for Families of Adolescents." In B. A. Thyer, ed., *Behavioral Family Therapy*. Springfield, IL: Charles C. Thomas.

—— in press. "Anger Management in Parent-Adolescent Conflict." *The American Journal of Family Therapy*.

Stierlin, H. 1972. *Separating Parents and Adolescents*. New York: Quadrangle.

Stockwell, T. R., R. J. Hodgson, G. Edwards, C. Taylor, and H. Rankin. 1979.

"The Development of a Questionnaire to Measure Severity of Alcohol Dependence." *British Journal of Addiction* 74:131–139.

Stockwell, T., D. Murphy, and R. Hodgson. 1983. "The Severity of Alcohol Dependence Questionnaire: Its Use, Reliability and Validity." *British Journal of Addiction* 78:145–155.

Stockwell, T., and C. Town. 1989. "Anxiety and Stress Management." In R. K. Hester and W. R. Miller, eds., *Handbook of Alcoholism: Treatment Approaches, Effective Alternatives*. New York: Pergamon Press.

Stokes, T. F., and D. M. Baer. 1977. "An Implicit Technology of Generalization." *Journal of Applied Behavior Analysis* 10:349–367.

Stone, R., G. Cafferta, and J. Stangl. 1987. "Caregivers of the Frail Elderly: A National Profile." *The Gerontologist* 27:616–626.

Storms, M. D., and K. D. McCaul 1976. "Attribution Process and Emotional Exacerbation of Dysfunctional Behavior." In J. H. Harvey, W. J. Ickers, and R. F. Kidd, eds., *New Directions in Attribution Research*. Hillsdale, NJ: Erlbaum.

Stoudmire, A., and D. G. Blazer. 1985. "Depression in the Elderly." In E. E. Beckham and W. R. Leber, eds., *Handbook of Depression*. Homewood, IL: Dorsey Press.

Strauss, J. S., and W. T. Carpenter. 1977. "Prediction of Outcome in Schizophrenia III: Five-Year Outcome and its Predictors." *Archives of General Psychiatry* 34:159–163.

Strauss, R. 1972. "Hospital Organization from the Viewpoint of Patient-Centered Goals." In B. Georgopoulos, ed., *Organizational Research on Health Institutions*. Ann Arbor: University of Michigan Institute for Social Research.

Strupp, H. H., 1989. "Can the Practitioner Learn from the Researcher?" *American Psychologist* 44:717–724.

Stuart, R. B. 1980. *Helping Couples Change: A Social Learning Approach to Marital Therapy*. New York: Guilford Press.

Studt, E. 1968. "Social Work Theory and Implications for the Practice of Methods." *Social Work Education Reporter* 16:22–46.

Syme, S. L., and L. F. Berkman. 1981. "Social Class, Susceptibility, and Sickness." In P. Conrad and R. Kern, eds., *The Sociology of Health and Illness: Critical Perspectives*. New York: St. Martin's Press.

Szykula, S. A., and M. J. Fleischman. 1985. "Reducing Out-of-home Placements of Abused Children: Two Controlled Studies. *Child Abuse and Neglect* 9:277–284.

Tagliacozzo, D., and H. Mauksch. 1979. "The Patient's View of the Patient's Role." In E. Gartly Jaco, ed., *Patients, Physicians and Illness*. 3d. ed. New York: Free Press.

Talbott, J. A. 1981. *The Chronic Mentally Ill*. New York: Human Sciences Press.
—— ed. 1984. *The Chronic Mental Patient: Five Years Later*. Orlando, FL: Grune and Stratton.

Tarrier, N., C. Barrowclough, C. Vaughn, J. S. Bamrah, K. Porceddu, S. Watt, and H. Freeman. 1989. "Community Management of Schizophrenia: A Two-year Follow-up of a Behavioral Intervention with Families." *British Journal of Psychiatry* 154:625–628.

Taylor, C. 1977. "Counseling in a Service Industry." In W. J. Reid and L. Epstein, eds., *Task-Centered Practice*. New York: Columbia University Press.

Taylor, R. J., and L. M. Chatters. 1989. "Family, Friend, and Church Support Networks of Black Americans." In R. L. Jones, ed., *Black Adult Development and Aging*. Berkeley, CA: Cobb and Henry.

Taylor, S. 1979. "Hospital Patient Behavior: Reactance, Helplessness, or Control?" *The Journal of Social Issues* 35:156–184.

Thibault, Jane, M. 1984. "The Analysis and Treatment of Indirect Self-Destructive Behaviors of Elderly Patients." Ph. D. dissertation, University of Chicago.

Thomas, E. J. 1977. *Marital Communication and Decision-Making-Analysis, Assessment, and Change*. New York: Free Press.

—— 1984. *Designing Interventions for the Helping Professions*. Newbury Park, CA: Sage Publications.

Thomas, E. J., C. Santa, D. Bronson, and D. Oyserman. 1987. "Unilateral Family Therapy with the Spouses of Alcoholics." *Journal of Social Service Research* 10:145–162.

Thyer, B. A. 1987. *Treating Anxiety Disorders*. Newbury Park, CA: Sage Publications.

Thyer, B. A., and K. M. Sowers-Hoag. 1986. "The Etiology of School Phobia: A Behavioral Approach." *School Social Work Journal* 10:86–98.

Todd, T. C. 1988. "Behavioral and Systemic Family Therapy: A Comparison." In I. R. H. Falloon, ed., *Handbook of Behavioral Family Therapy*. New York: Guilford Press.

Tolson, E. 1977. "Alleviating Marital Communication Problems." In W. J. Reid and L. Epstein, eds., *Task-Centered Practice*. New York: Columbia University Press.

—— 1988. *The Metamodel and Clinical Social Work*. New York: Columbia University Press.

Tolson, E. R., W. J. Reid, and C. D. Garvin. in press. *Task-Centered Practice within the Generalist Perspective*. New York: Columbia University Press.

Tomm, K. 1982. "Towards a Cybernetic Systems Approach to Family Therapy." In F. W. Kaslow, ed., *The International Book of Family Therapy*. New York: Brunner/Mazel.

Townsend, A. 1986. *Family Caregivers' Perspectives on Institutionalization Decisions*. Memphis: The University of Tennessee, Center for Health Sciences and Department of Medicine. (ERIC Document Reproduction Service No. CG 020 923).

Tracy, E. M., and J. K. Whittaker. 1990. "The Social Network Map: Assessing Social Support." *Families in Society* 71:461–470.

Trull, T. J., M. T. Nietzel, and A. Main. 1988. "The Use of Meta-Analysis to Assess the Clinical Significance of Behavior Therapy for Agoraphobia." *Behavior Therapy* 19:527–538.

Tunnell, G., M. Alpert, J. Jacobs, and J. Osiason. 1988. "Designing a Family Psychoeducation Program to Meet Community Needs: The NYU-Bellevue Project." *International Journal of Mental Health* 17:75–88.

Turk, D., and R. Kerns. 1985. "The Family in Health and Illness." In D. Turk and R. Kerns, eds., *Health, Illness and Families*. New York: John Wiley.

Turk, D. C., T. E. Rudy, and P. Salovey. 1986. "Implicit Models of Illness." *Journal of Behavioral Medicine* 9:453–474.

Turner, F. J., ed. 1986. *Social Treatment*, 3d ed. New York: Free Press.

U. S. Department of Health and Human Services, Public Health Service. 1986. *Health, United States, 1986*. Washington, D.C.: United States Government Printing Office.

Vaillant, G. E. 1983. *The Natural History of Alcoholism*. Cambridge: Harvard University Press.

Vaillant, G. E., and E. S. Milofsky. 1982. "Natural History of Male Alcoholism: IV. Paths to Recovery." *Archives of General Psychiatry* 39:127–133.

Vandiver, V., and S. A. Kirk. in press. "Case Management for Persons with Schizophrenia." In K. Corcoran, ed., *Structured Change*. Chicago: Lyceum Press.

Vaughn, C. D., and J. Leff. 1976. "The Measurement of Expressed Emotion in the Families of Psychiatric Patients." *British Journal of Social and Clinical Psychology* 15:157–165.

Videka-Sherman, L., and W. J. Reid, eds. 1990. *Advances in Clinical Social Work Research*. Silver Spring, MD: NASW Press.

Vigilante, F., and M. Mailick. 1988. "Needs-Resource Evaluation in the Assessment Process." *Social Work* 33:101–104.

Vosler, N. R. 1990. "Assessing Family Access to Basic Resources: An Essential Component of Social Work Practice." *Social Work* 35:434–441.

Wahler, R. G., and A. D. Afton. 1980. "Attentional Process in Insular and Noninsular Mothers: Some Differences in their Summary Reports about Child Problem Behaviors." *Child Behavior Therapy*, 2:34–31.

Wahler, R. G., and J. E. Dumas. 1984. "Changing the Observational Coding Styles of Insular and Noninsular Mothers." In R. F. Dangel and R. A. Polster, eds., *Parent Training*. New York: Guilford Press.

Wallace, C. J., and R. P. Liberman. 1985. "Social Skills Training of Patients with Schizophrenia: A Controlled Clinical Trial." *Psychiatry Research* 15: 239–247.

Wallace, J. 1985. "Behavior Modification Methods as Adjuncts to Therapy." In S. Zimberg, J. Wallace, and S. Blume, eds., *Practical Approaches to Alcoholism Psychotherapy*, 2d ed. New York: Plenum Press.

—— 1985. "Critical Issues in Alcoholism Therapy." In S. Zimberg, J. Wallace, and S. Blume, eds., *Practical Approaches to Alcoholism Psychotherapy*, 2d ed. New York: Plenum Press.

Waring, E. M., R. Manchanda, and C. Carver. 1989. "Family Therapy for Schizophrenia." *British Journal of Psychiatry* 155:122–133.

Watzlawick, P., J. H. Beavin, and D. D. Jackson. 1967. *Pragmatics of Human Communication*. New York: W. W. Norton.

Weiss, R. L. 1975. "Contracts, Cognition, and Change: A Behavioral Approach to Marriage Therapy." *The Counseling Psychologist* 5:15–25.

Weissman, A. 1977. "In the Steel Industry." In W. J. Reid and L. Epstein, eds., *Task-Centered Practice*. New York: Columbia University Press.

—— 1987. "Linkage in Direct Practice. In A. Minahan, ed., *Encyclopedia of Social Work*, 18th ed. Silver Spring, MD: NASW Press.

Wells, R. A. 1982. *Planned Short-Term Treatment*. New York: Free Press.

Wells, R. A., and J. Figurel. 1979. "Techniques of Structured Communication Training." *The Family Coordinator* 28:273–281.

Wexler, P. 1977. "A Case From a Medical Setting." In W. J. Reid and L. Epstein, eds., *Task-Centered Practice*. New York: Columbia University Press.

White, A. R., ed. 1973. *The Philosophy of Action*. London: Oxford University Press.

Whiteman, M., D. Fanshel, and J. F. Grundy. 1987. "Cognitive-Behavioral Interventions Aimed at Anger of Parents at Risk of Child Abuse." *Social Work* 32:469–474.

Winnick, A. J. 1988. "The Changing Distribution of Income and Wealth in the United States, 1960–1985: An Examination of the Movement Toward Two Societies, 'Separate and Unequal'." In P. Voydanoff and L. C. Majka, eds., *Families and Economic Distress: Coping Strategies and Social Policy*. Newbury Park, CA: Sage Publications.

Winokur, G. 1978. "Mania, Depression: Family Studies, Genetics, and Relation to Treatment." In M. A. Lipton, A. DiMascio, and K. Killam, eds., *Psychopharmacology: A Generation of Progress*. New York: Raven Press.

Wise, F. 1977. "Conjoint Marital Treatment." In W. J. Reid and L. Epstein eds., *Task-Centered Practice*. New York: Columbia University Press.

Wittlin, B. J. 1988. "Practical Psycho-Pharmacology." In R. P. Liberman ed., *Psychiatric Rehabilitation of Chronic Mental Patients*. Washington, D.C.: American Psychiatric Press.

Wodarski, J. S., M. Saffir, and M. Frazier. 1982. "Using Research to Evaluate the Effectiveness of Task-Centered Casework." *The Journal of Applied Social Sciences* 7:70–82.

Wolfe, D. A., J. Sandler, and K. Kaufmnan. 1981. "A Competency-Based Parent Training Program for Abused Parents." *Journal of Consulting and Clinical Psychology* 49:633–640.

Wolock, I., E. Schlesinger, M. Dinerman, and R. Seaton. 1987. "The Posthospital Needs and Care of Patients: Implications for Discharge Planning." *Social Work in Health Care* 12:61–76.

Wood, G. G., and R. R. Middleman. 1989. *The Structural Approach to Direct Practice in Social Work*. New York: Columbia University Press.

Wood, K. M. 1990. "Epistemological Issues in the Development of Social Work Practice Knowledge." In L. Videka-Sherman and W. J. Reid, eds., *Advances in Clinical Social Work Research*. Silver Spring, MD: NASW Press.

Wood, K. M., and L. L. Geismar. 1989. *Families at Risk*. New York: Human Sciences Press.

Wool, M. 1990a. "Understanding Depression in Medical Patients, Part I: Diagnostic Considerations." *Social Work in Health Care* 14:25–38.

—— 1990b. "Understanding Depression in Medical Patients, Part II: Clinical Intervention." *Social Work in Health Care* 14:39–52.

World Health Organization. 1982. "Diagnosis and Classification of Mental Disorders and Alcohol and Drug Related Problems." (Summary Working Papers) Copenhagen, April.

Wynne, L. C., ed., 1988a. *The State of the Art in Family Therapy Research: Controversies and Recommendations*. New York: Family Process Press.

—— 1988b. "The 'Presenting Problem' and Theory-Based Family Variables: Keystones for Family Therapy Research." In L. C. Wynne, ed., *The State of the Art in Family Therapy Research: Controversies and Recommendations*. New York: Family Process Press.

York, J., and R. Caslyn. 1977. "Family Involvement in Nursing Homes." *The Gerontologist* 17:500–505.

Zane, M. D., and D. Powell. 1985. "The Management of Patients in a Phobia Clinic." *American Journal of Psychotherapy* 39:331–345.

Zarit, S., and J. Zarit. 1983. "Cognitive Impairment." In P. Lewinsohn and L. Teri, eds., *Clinical Geropsychology*. New York: Pergamon Press.

Zimberg, S. 1985. "Principles of Alcoholism Psychotherapy." In S. Zimberg, J. Wallace, and S. Blume, eds., *Practical Approaches to Alcoholism Psychotherapy*, 2d ed. New York: Plenum Press.

Zimberg, S., J. Wallace, and S. Blume, eds. 1985. *Practical Approaches to Alcoholism Psychotherapy*, 2d ed. New York: Plenum Press.

Zimmerman, S., and C. S. Chilman. 1988. "Poverty and Families." In C. S. Chilman, F. M. Cox, and E. W. Nunnally, eds., *Employment and Economic Problems*. Newbury Park, CA: Sage Publications.

Zung, W. K. W. 1971. "A Rating Instrument for Anxiety Disorders." *Psychosomatics* 12:371–379.

Author Index

Subject Index